Richard Holt Hutton, Walter Bagehot, Forrest Morgan

The Works of Walter Bagehot

Vol. 2

Richard Holt Hutton, Walter Bagehot, Forrest Morgan

The Works of Walter Bagehot
Vol. 2

ISBN/EAN: 9783337215972

Printed in Europe, USA, Canada, Australia, Japan

Cover: Foto ©Thomas Meinert / pixelio.de

More available books at **www.hansebooks.com**

THE WORKS OF ·

WALTER BAGEHOT

M. A., AND FELLOW OF UNIVERSITY COLLEGE, LONDON

WITH MEMOIRS BY R. H. HUTTON

NOW FIRST PUBLISHED IN FULL

BY

The Travelers Insurance Company

OF HARTFORD, CONNECTICUT

EDITED BY FORREST MORGAN

IN FIVE VOLUMES

VOL. II

Hartford

1889

CONTENTS OF VOL. II.

LITERARY STUDIES.

EDWARD GIBBON.*

(1856.)

A WIT † said of Gibbon's autobiography that he did not know the difference between himself and the Roman empire. He has narrated his "progressions from London to Buriton and from Buriton to London" in the same monotonous majestic periods that record the fall of states and empires; the consequence is, that a fascinating book gives but a vague idea of its subject. It may not be without its use to attempt a description of him in plainer though less splendid English.

The diligence of their descendant accumulated many particulars of the remote annals of the Gibbon family; but its real founder was the grandfather of the historian, who lived in the times of the "South Sea." He was a capital man of business according to the custom of that age, — a dealer in many kinds of merchandise; like perhaps the "complete tradesman" of Defoe, who was to understand the price and quality of *all* articles made within the kingdom. The preference, however, of Edward Gibbon the grandfather was for the article "shares"; his genius, like that of Mr. Hudson, had a natural tendency towards a commerce in the metaphysical and non-existent : and he was fortunate in the age on which his lot was thrown, — it afforded many opportunities of gratifying that taste.

---

* The History of the Decline and Fall of the Roman Empire. By Edward Gibbon, Esq. With Notes by Dean Milman and M. Guizot. Edited, with additional Notes, by William Smith, LL.D. In Eight Volumes. London, 1855. Murray.

† Bagehot himself. — ED.

Much has been written on panics and manias,—much more than with the most outstretched intellect we are able to follow or conceive; but one thing is certain,— that at particular times a great many stupid people have a great deal of stupid money. Saving people have often only the faculty of saving : they accumulate ably and contemplate their accumulations with approbation, but what to do with them they do not know. Aristotle, who was not in trade, imagined that money is barren ; and barren it is to quiet ladies, rural clergymen, and country misers. Several economists have plans for preventing improvident speculation,— one would abolish Peel's Act and substitute one-pound notes, another would retain Peel's Act and make the calling for one-pound notes a capital crime; but our scheme is, not to allow any man to have a hundred pounds who cannot prove to the satisfaction of the Lord Chancellor that he knows what to do with a hundred pounds. The want of this easy precaution allows the accumulation of wealth in the hands of rectors, authors, grandmothers, who have no knowledge of business, and no idea except that their money now produces nothing, and ought and must be forced immediately to produce something. "I wish," said one of this class, "for the largest immediate income, and I am therefore naturally disposed to purchase an *advowson.*" At intervals, from causes which are not to the present purpose, the money of these people— the blind capital (as we call it) of the country—is particularly large and craving: it seeks for some one to devour it, and there is "plethora"; it finds some one, and there is "speculation"; it is devoured, and there is "panic." The age of Mr. Gibbon was one of these. The interest of money was very low, perhaps under three per cent. : the usual consequence followed, —able men started wonderful undertakings; the ablest of all, a company for carrying on an undertaking of great importance, but no one to know what it was.*

---

* See Chap. vi. of "Lombard Street," Vol. v. of this series.—Ed.

Mr. Gibbon was not idle. According to the narrative of his grandson, he already filled a considerable position, was worth £60,000, and had great influence both in Parliament and in the City. He applied himself to the greatest bubble of all,—one so great that it is spoken of in many books as the cause and parent of all contemporary bubbles,—the South Sea Company; the design of which was to reduce the interest on the national debt, which oddly enough it did reduce, and to trade exclusively to the South Sea or Spanish America, where of course it hardly did trade. Mr. Gibbon became a director, sold and bought, traded and prospered; and was considered, perhaps with truth, to have obtained much money. The bubble was essentially a fashionable one. Public' intelligence and the quickness of communication did not then, as now, at once spread pecuniary information and misinformation to secluded districts; but fine ladies, men of fashion —the London world, ever anxious to make as much of its money as it can, and then wholly unwise (it is not now very wise) in discovering how the most *was* to be made of it—"went in" and speculated largely. As usual, all was favorable so long as the shares were rising. The price was at one time very high and the agitation very general; it was, in a word, the railway mania in the "South Sea." After a time, the shares "hesitated," declined, and fell; and there was an outcry against everybody concerned in the matter, very like the outcry against the οἱ περὶ Hudson in our own time. The results, however, were very different. Whatever may be said—and judging from the * late experience, a good deal is likely to be said — as to the advantages of civilization and education, it seems certain that they tend to diminish a simple-minded energy. The Parliament of 1720 did not, like the Parliament of 1847,† allow itself to be bored and

---

* Added (to the distortion of the sense) in the reprint. —ED.

† Summoned very early to inquire into the causes of the commercial distress precipitated by the collapse of the railway mania started by Hudson. —ED.

incommoded by legal minutiæ, nor did it forego the use
of plain words. A committee reported the discovery
of "a train of the deepest villany and fraud hell ever
contrived to ruin a nation"; the directors of the
company were arrested, and Mr. Gibbon among the
rest. He was compelled to give in a list of his effects ;
the general wish was that a retrospective act should
be immediately passed, which would impose on him
penalties something like, or even more severe than,
those now enforced on Paul and Strahan.* In the end,
however, Mr. Gibbon escaped with a parliamentary
conversation upon his affairs. His estate amounted to
£140,000 ; and as this was a great sum, there was an
obvious suspicion that he was a great criminal. The
scene must have been very curious. "Allowances of
twenty pounds or one shilling were facetiously moved.
A vague report that a director had formerly been concerned in *another* project by which some unknown
persons had lost their money was admitted as a proof
of his actual guilt. One man was ruined because he
had dropped a foolish speech that his horses should
feed upon gold ; another because he was grown so
proud that one day, at the Treasury, he had refused
a civil answer to persons much above him."† The
vanity of his descendant is evidently a little tried by
the peculiar severity with which his grandfather was
treated. Out of his £140,000 it was only proposed
that he should retain £15,000 ; and on an amendment
even this was reduced to £10,000. Yet there is some
ground for believing that the acute energy and practiced pecuniary power which had been successful

* William Strahan, Sir John Dean Paul, and Robert Makin Bates, forming
the banking house of "Strahan & Co.," which had lasted for two centuries
and was a great depository of trust funds, and also the naval-agency firm of
"Holford & Co." much trusted by officers and their widows, failed in June,
1855, with liabilities of some £500,000; and in October were convicted of
fraudulent conversion of trust funds to their own use, and sentenced to transportation for fourteen years. — ED.

† Gibbon's "Memoirs." I have credited in this way only passages whose
origin is left in doubt by the text. — ED.

in obtaining so large a fortune were likewise applied with science to the inferior task of retaining some of it. The historian indeed says, "On these ruins" (the £10,000 aforesaid), "with the skill and credit of which Parliament had not been able to despoil him, my grandfather at a mature age erected the edifice of a new fortune: the labors of sixteen years were amply rewarded; and I have reason to believe that the second structure was not much inferior to the first." But this only shows how far a family feeling may bias a skeptical judgment. The credit of a man in Mr. Gibbon's position could not be very lucrative; and his skill must have been enormous to have obtained so much at the end of his life, in such circumstances, in so few years. Had he been an early Christian, the narrative of his descendant would have contained an insidious hint that "pecuniary property *may* be so secreted as to defy the awkward approaches of political investigation." That he died rich is certain, for two generations lived solely on the property he bequeathed.

The son of this great speculator, the historian's father, was a man to spend a fortune quietly. He is not related to have indulged in any particular expense,* and nothing is more difficult to follow than the pecuniary fortunes of deceased families: but one thing is certain, that the property which descended to the historian — making every allowance for all minor and subsidiary modes of diminution, such as daughters, settlements, legacies, and so forth — was enormously less than £140,000; and therefore if those figures are correct, the second generation must have made itself very happy out of the savings of the past generation, and without caring for the poverty of the next. Nothing that is related of the historian's father indicates a strong judgment or an acute discrimination; and there are some scarcely dubious signs of a rather weak character.

---

* Gibbon says the Buriton farm did not pay, which explains everything.— ED.

Edward Gibbon, the great, was born on the 27th of April, 1737. Of his mother we hear scarcely anything; and what we do hear is not remarkably favorable. It seems that she was a faint, inoffensive woman, of ordinary capacity, who left a very slight trace of her influence on the character of her son, did little, and died early. The real mother—as he is careful to explain—of his understanding and education was her sister and his aunt, *Mrs.* Catherine Porten, according to the speech of that age;* a maiden lady of much vigor and capacity, and for whom her pupil really seems to have felt as much affection as was consistent with a rather easy and cool nature. There is a panegyric on her in the "Memoirs"; and in a long letter upon the occasion of her death, he deposes:—"To her care I am indebted in earliest infancy for the preservation of my life and health. . . . To her instructions I owe the first rudiments of knowledge, the first exercise of reason, and a taste for books which is still the pleasure and glory of my life; and though she taught me neither language nor science, she was certainly the most useful preceptor I ever had. As I grew up, an intercourse of thirty years endeared her to me as the faithful friend and the agreeable companion. You have seen with what freedom and confidence we lived—"† etc., etc. To a less sentimental mind, which takes a more tranquil view of aunts and relatives, it is satisfactory to find that somehow he could not write to her. "I wish," he continues, "I had as much to applaud, and as little to reproach, in my own behavior towards Mrs. Porten since I left England; and when I reflect that my letters would have soothed and comforted her decline, I feel—" what an ardent nephew would naturally feel at so unprecedented an event. Leaving his maturer years out of the question,—a possible rhapsody of affectionate eloquence,—she seems to have been of

* See note to page 359, Vol. 1. of this series.—ED.
† To Lord Sheffield, May 10, 1786.

the greatest use to him in infancy. His health was very imperfect. We hear much of rheumatism and lameness and weakness; and he was unable to join in work and play with ordinary boys. He was moved from one school to another, never staying anywhere very long, and owing what knowledge he obtained rather to a strong retentive understanding than to any external stimulants or instruction. At one place he gained an acquaintance with the Latin elements at the price of "many tears and some blood." At last he was consigned to the instruction of an elegant clergyman, the Rev. Philip Francis, who had obtained notoriety by a metrical translation of Horace the laxity of which is even yet complained of by construing schoolboys, and who, with a somewhat Horatian taste, went to London as often as he could, and translated *invisa negotia** as "boys to beat."

In school work, therefore, Gibbon had uncommon difficulties and unusual deficiencies; but these were much more than counterbalanced by a habit which often accompanies a sickly childhood and is the commencement of a studious life,—the habit of desultory . reading. The instructiveness of this is sometimes not comprehended. S. T. Coleridge used to say that he felt a great superiority over those who had not read —and fondly read—fairy tales in their childhood: he thought they wanted a sense which he possessed, the perception, or apperception—we do not know which he used to say it was—of the unity and wholeness of the universe. As to fairy tales, this is a hard saying; but as to desultory reading, it is certainly true. Some people have known a time in life when there was no book they could not read. The fact of its being a book went immensely in its favor. In early life there is an opinion that the obvious thing to do with a horse is to ride it; with a cake, to eat it; with sixpence, to spend it. A few boys carry this further, and think the natural thing to do with a

* "Hateful business." (Book i., Epistle xiv.)

book is to read it. There is an argument from design in the subject: if the book was not meant for that purpose, for what purpose was it meant? Of course, of any understanding of the works so perused there is no question or idea. There is a legend of Bentham, in his earliest childhood, climbing to the height of a huge stool and sitting there evening after evening, with two candles, engaged in the perusal of Rapin's history; it might as well have been any other book. The doctrine of utility had not then dawned on its immortal teacher; *cui bono* was an idea unknown to him. He would have been ready to read about Egypt, about Spain, about coals in Borneo, the teak-wood in India, the current in the river Mississippi, on natural history or human history, on theology or morals, on the state of the Dark Ages or the state of the light ages, on Augustulus or Lord Chatham, on the first century or the seventeenth, on the moon, the millennium, or the whole duty of man. Just then, reading is an end in itself. At that time of life you no more think of a future consequence, — of the remote, the very remote possibility of deriving knowledge from the perusal of a book, than you expect so great a result from spinning a peg-top. You spin the top, and you read the book; and these scenes of life are exhausted. In such studies, of all prose perhaps the best is history: one page is so like another, battle No. 1 is so much on a par with battle No. 2. Truth may be, as they say, stranger than fiction, abstractedly; but in actual books, novels are certainly odder and more astounding than correct history. It will be said, What is the use of this? why not leave the reading of great books till a great age? why plague and perplex childhood with complex facts remote from its experience and inapprehensible by its imagination? The reply is, that though in all great and combined facts there is much which childhood cannot thoroughly imagine, there is also in very many a great deal which can only be truly apprehended for the

first time at that age. Catch an American of thirty;
tell him about the battle of Marathon: what will he
be able to comprehend of all that you mean by it,
of all that halo which early impression and years of
remembrance have cast around it? He may add up
the killed and wounded, estimate the missing, and
take the dimensions of Greece and Athens; but he
will not seem to care much. He may say, "Well,
sir, perhaps it was a smart thing in that small territory; but it is a long time ago, and in my country
James K. Burnup—" did that which he will at length
explain to you. Or try an experiment on yourself:
read the account of a Circassian victory, equal in
numbers, in daring, in romance, to the old battle.
Will you be able to feel about it at all in the same
way? It is impossible. You cannot form a new set
of associations; your mind is involved in pressing
facts, your memory choked by a thousand details;
the liveliness of fancy is gone with the childhood by
which it was enlivened. Schamyl will never seem as
great as Leonidas or Miltiades; Cnokemof, or whoever
the Russian is, cannot be so imposing as Xerxes; the
unpronounceable place cannot strike on your heart
like Marathon or Platæa. Moreover, there is the further advantage which Coleridge shadowed forth in
the remark we cited: youth has a principle of consolidation; we begin with the whole. Small sciences
are the labors of our manhood; but the round universe is the plaything of the boy. His fresh mind
shoots out vaguely and crudely into the infinite and
eternal. Nothing is hid from the depth of it; there
are no boundaries to its vague and wandering vision.
Early science, it has been said, begins in utter nonsense; it would be truer to say that it starts with
boyish fancies. How absurd seem the notions of the
first Greeks! Who could believe now that air or water
was the principle, the pervading substance, the eternal
material of all things? Such affairs will never explain
a thick rock. And what a white original for a green

and sky-blue world! Yet people disputed in those ages not whether it was either of those substances, but which of them it was. And doubtless there was a great deal, at least in quantity, to be said on both sides. Boys are improved; but some in our own day have asked, "Mamma, I say, what did God make the world of?" and several, who did not venture on speech, have had an idea of some one gray primitive thing, felt a difficulty as to how the red came, and wondered that marble could *ever* have been the same as moonshine. This is in truth the picture of life: we begin with the infinite and eternal, which we shall never apprehend; and these form a framework, a schedule, a set of co-ordinates to which we refer all which we learn later. At first, like the old Greek, "we look up to the whole sky, and are lost in the one and the all"; in the end we classify and enumerate, learn each star, calculate distances, draw cramped diagrams on the unbounded sky, write a paper on α Cygni and a treatise on ε Draconis, map special facts upon the indefinite void, and engrave precise details on the infinite and everlasting. So in history: somehow the whole comes in boyhood; the details later and in manhood. The wonderful series going far back to the times of old patriarchs with their flocks and herds, the keen-eyed Greek, the stately Roman, the watching Jew, the uncouth Goth, the horrid Hun, the settled picture of the unchanging East, the restless shifting of the rapid West, the rise of the cold and classical civilization, its fall, the rough impetuous Middle Ages, the vague warm picture of ourselves and home,—when did we learn these? Not yesterday nor to-day; but long ago, in the first dawn of reason, in the original flow of fancy. What we learn afterwards are but the accurate littlenesses of the great topic, the dates and tedious facts. Those who begin late learn only these; but the happy first feel the mystic associations and the progress of the whole.

There is no better illustration of all this than Gibbon. Few have begun early with a more desultory reading, and fewer still have described it so skillfully.

"From the ancient I leaped to the modern world: many crude lumps of Speed, Rapin, Mezeray, Davila, Machiavel, Father Paul, Bower, etc., I devoured like so many novels; and I swallowed with the same voracious appetite the descriptions of India and China, of Mexico and Peru. My first introduction to the historic scenes which have since engaged so many years of my life must be ascribed to an accident. In the summer of 1751 I accompanied my father on a visit to Mr. Hoare's, in Wiltshire; but I was less delighted with the beauties of Stourhead than with discovering in the library a common book, the 'Continuation of Echard's Roman History,' which is indeed executed with more skill and taste than the previous work. To me the reigns of the successors of Constantine were absolutely new; and I was immersed in the passage of the Goths over the Danube when the summons of the dinner-bell reluctantly dragged me from my intellectual feast. This transient glance served rather to irritate than to appease my curiosity; and as soon as I returned to Bath I procured the second and third volumes of Howell's 'History of the World,' which exhibit the Byzantine period on a larger scale. Mahomet and his Saracens soon fixed my attention; and some instinct of criticism directed me to the genuine sources. Simon Ockley, an original in every sense, first opened my eyes; and I was led from one book to another till I had ranged round the circle of Oriental history. Before I was sixteen I had exhausted all that could be learned in English of the Arabs and Persians, the Tartars and Turks; and the same ardor urged me to guess at the French of D'Herbelot, and to construe the barbarous Latin of Pocock's 'Abulfaragius.'"

To this day the schoolboy student of the "Decline and Fall" feels the traces of that schoolboy reading. Once, he is conscious, the author like him felt, and solely felt, the magnificent progress of the great story and the scenic aspect of marvelous events.

A more sudden effect was at hand. However exalted may seem the praises which we have given to loose and unplanned reading, we are not saying that it is the sole ingredient of a good education. Besides this sort of education, which some boys will voluntarily and naturally give themselves, there needs, of course, another and more rigorous kind, which must be impressed upon them from without. The terrible difficulty of early life — the *use* of pastors and masters really is, that they compel boys to a distinct mastery of that which they do not wish to learn. There is nothing to be said for a preceptor who is not dry. Mr. Carlyle describes with bitter satire the fate of one of his heroes who was obliged to acquire whole systems of information in which he, the hero, saw no use, and which he kept as far as might be in a vacant corner of his mind. And this is the very point: dry language, tedious mathematics, a thumbed grammar, a detested slate form gradually an interior separate intellect, exact in its information, rigid in its requirements, disciplined in its exercises. The two grow together: the early natural fancy touching the far extremities of the universe, lightly playing with the scheme of all things; the precise, compacted memory slowly accumulating special facts, exact habits, clear and painful conceptions. At last, as it were in a moment, the cloud breaks up, the division sweeps away: we find that in fact these exercises which puzzled us, these languages which we hated, these details which we despised, are the instruments of true thought; are the very keys and openings, the exclusive access to the knowledge which we loved.

In this second education the childhood of Gibbon had been very defective. He had never been placed under any rigid training. In his first boyhood he disputed with his aunt, "that were I master of Greek and Latin, I must interpret to myself in English the thoughts of the original, and that such extemporary versions must be inferior to the elaborate translations of professed scholars: a silly sophism," as he remarks, "which could not easily be confuted by a person ignorant of any other language than her own." Ill health, a not very wise father, an ill-chosen succession of schools and pedagogues, prevented his acquiring exact knowledge in the regular subjects of study. His own description is the best: "erudition that might have puzzled a doctor, and a degree of ignorance of which a schoolboy would have been ashamed." The amiable Mr. Francis, who was to have repaired the deficiency, went to London and forgot him. With an impulse of discontent his father took a resolution, and sent him to Oxford at sixteen.

It is probable that a worse place could not have been found. The University of Oxford was at the nadir of her history and efficiency. The public professorial training of the Middle Ages had died away, and the intramural collegiate system of the present time had not begun. The University had ceased to be a teaching body, and had not yet become an examining body. "The professors," says Adam Smith, who had studied there, "have given up almost the pretense of lecturing."* "The examination," said a great judge some years later,†"was a farce in my time. I was asked who founded University College; and I said, though the fact is now doubted, that King Alfred founded it: and *that* was the examination." The colleges, deprived of the superintendence and watchfulness of their natural sovereign, fell, as Gibbon remarks, into "port and prejudice." The fellows were a close corporation; they were chosen from every conceivable motive,—because they were respectable men, because they were "good fellows," because they were brothers of other fellows, because their fathers had patronage in the Church. Men so appointed could not be expected to be very diligent in the instruction of youth: many colleges did not even profess it; that of All Souls has continued down to our own time to deny that it has anything to do with it. Undoubtedly, a person who came thither accurately

---

* Tho exact words are, "The greater part of the public professors have for these many years given up altogether even the pretense of teaching." ("Wealth of Nations," Book v., Chap. i.)—ED.

† Eldon, in Twiss, Vol. i., Chap. ii.; much "boiled down." — ED.

and rigidly drilled in technical scholarship found many means and a few motives to pursue it: some tutorial system probably existed at most colleges; learning was not wholly useless in the Church; the English gentleman has ever loved a nice and classical scholarship. But these advantages were open only to persons who had received a very strict training, and who were voluntarily disposed to discipline themselves still more: to the mass of mankind the University was a "graduating machine"; the colleges, monopolist residences, — hotels without bells.

Taking the place as it stood, the lot of Gibbon may be thought rather fortunate. He was placed at Magdalen, whose fascinating walks, so beautiful in the later autumn, still recall the name of Addison, — the example of the merits, as Gibbon is of the deficiencies, of Oxford. His first tutor was, in his own opinion,

"one of the best of the tribe: Dr. Waldegrave was a learned and pious man, of a mild disposition, strict morals, and abstemious life, who seldom mingled in the politics or the jollity of the college. But his knowledge of the world was confined to the University; his learning was of the last rather than the present age; his temper was indolent; his faculties, which were not of the first rate, had been relaxed by the climate: and he was satisfied, like his fellows, with the slight and superficial discharge of an important trust. As soon as my tutor had sounded the insufficiency of his pupil in school learning, he proposed that we should read every morning, from ten to eleven, the comedies of Terence. The sum of my improvement in the University of Oxford is confined to three or four Latin plays; and even the study of an elegant classic, which might have been illustrated by a comparison of ancient and modern theaters, was reduced to a dry and literal interpretation of the author's text. During the first weeks I constantly attended these lessons in my tutor's room; but as they appeared equally devoid of profit and pleasure, I was once tempted to try the experiment of a formal apology. The apology was accepted with a smile. I repeated the offense with less ceremony; the excuse was admitted with the same indulgence: the slightest motive of laziness or indisposition, the most trifling avocation at home or abroad, was allowed as a worthy impediment; nor did my tutor appear conscious of my absence or neglect. Had the hour of lecture been constantly filled, a single hour was a small portion of my academic leisure. No plan of study was recommended for my use; no exercises were prescribed for his inspection: and at the most precious season of youth, whole days and weeks were suffered to elapse without labor or amusement, without advice or account."

The name of his second tutor is concealed in asterisks, and the sensitive conscience of Dean Milman will not allow him to insert a name "which Gibbon thought proper to suppress." The account, however, of the anonymous person is sufficiently graphic:—

"Dr. * * * well remembered that he had a salary to receive, and only forgot that he had a duty to perform. Instead of guiding the studies and watching over the behavior of his disciple, I was never summoned to attend even the ceremony of a lecture; and excepting one voluntary visit to his rooms, during the eight months of his titular office the tutor and pupil lived in the same college as strangers to each other."

It added to the evils of this neglect, that Gibbon was much younger than most of the students; and that his temper, which was through life reserved, was then very shy. His appearance, too, was odd: "a thin little figure, with a large head, disputing and" arguing "with the greatest ability."* Of course he was a joke among undergraduates; he consulted his tutor as to studying Arabic, and was seen buying "La Bibliothèque Orientale D'Herbelot," and immediately a legend was diffused that he had turned Mohammedan. The random cast was not so far from the mark: cut off by peculiarities from the society of young people, deprived of regular tuition and systematic employment, tumbling about among crude masses of heterogeneous knowledge, alone with the heated brain of youth, he did what an experienced man would expect,—he framed a theory of all things. No doubt it seemed to him the most natural thing in the world. Was he to be the butt of ungenial wine parties, or

---

* Lord Sheffield, in note to the "Memoirs," quoting Pavilliard.

spend his lonely hours on shreds of languages? Was he not to know the *truth?* There were the old problems, the everlasting difficulties, the *mœnia mundi*, the Hercules's Pillars of the human imagination,—"fate, free-will, foreknowledge absolute."* Surely these should come first: when we had learned the great landmarks, understood the guiding stars, we might amuse ourselves with small points and make a plaything of curious information. What particular theory the mind frames when in this state is a good deal matter of special accident: the data for considering these difficulties are not within its reach. Whether man be or be not born to solve the "mystery of the knowable," he certainly is not born to solve it at seventeen, with the first hot rush of the untrained mind. The selection of Gibbon was remarkable: he became a Roman Catholic.

It seems now so natural that an Oxford man should take this step, that one can hardly understand the astonishment it created. Lord Sheffield tells us that the Privy Council interfered; and with good administrative judgment examined a London bookseller †— some Mr. Lewis — who had no concern in it. In the manor-house of Buriton it would have probably created less sensation if "dear Edward" had announced his intention of becoming a monkey. The English have ever believed that the Papist is a kind of *creature;* and every sound mind would prefer a beloved child to produce a tail, a hide of hair, and a taste for nuts, in comparison with transubstantiation, wax candles, and a belief in the glories of Mary.

What exact motives impelled Gibbon to this step cannot now be certainly known,—the autobiography casts a mist over them; but from what appears, his conversion partly much resembled, and partly altogether differed from, the Oxford conversions of our own time. We hear nothing of the "notes of a church," or the "sin of the Reformation"; and Gibbon

---

* "Paradise Lost," Book ii.   † Of Roman Catholic books. — ED.

had not an opportunity of even rejecting Mr. Sewell's*
theory that it is "a holy obligation to acquiesce in
the opinions of your grandmother." His memoirs
have a halo of great names, — Bossuet, the " History
of Protestant Variations," etc., etc., — and he speaks
with becoming dignity of "falling by a noble hand."
He mentioned also to Lord. Sheffield, as having had
a preponderating influence over him, the works of
Father Parsons, who lived in Queen Elizabeth's time.
But in all probability these were secondary persuasions,
justifications after the event. No young man — or
scarcely any young man — of seventeen was ever con-
verted by a systematic treatise, especially if written
in another age, wearing an obsolete look, speaking
a language which scarcely seems that of this world.
There is an unconscious reasoning, — "The world has
had this book before it so long, and has withstood it :
there must be something wrong; it seems all right on
the surface, but a flaw there must be." The mass of
the volumes, too, is unfavorable. "All the paper arguments in the world," says the young convert in
"Loss and Gain,"† "are unequal to giving one a
view in a moment." What the youthful mind requires is this short decisive argument, this view in a
moment, this flash as it were of the understanding,
which settles all, and diffuses a conclusive light at
once and forever over the whole. It is so much the
pleasanter if the young mind can strike this view out
for itself, from materials which are forced upon it
from the controversies of the day; if it can find a
certain solution of pending questions, and show itself
wiser even than the wisest of its own, the very last
age. So far as appears, this was the fortune of Gibbon.
"It was not long," he says, "since Dr. Middleton's
'Free Inquiry' had sounded an alarm in the theological world; much ink and much gall had been spilt in
defense of the primitive miracles, and the two dullest of

* Professor of Moral Philosophy at Oxford; prolific theological writer. — ED.
† J. H. Newman's, Chap. xvii. There are two novels with this title.— ED.

their champions were crowned with academic honors by the University of Oxford. The name of Middleton was unpopular; and his proscription very naturally led me to peruse his writings and those of his antagonists." It is not difficult to discover in this work easy and striking arguments which might lead an untaught mind to the communion of Rome. As to the peculiar belief of its author, there has been much controversy, with which we have not here the least concern; but the natural conclusion to which it would lead a simple intellect is, that all miracles are equally certain or equally uncertain.

"It being agreed, then," says the acute controversialist, "that in the original promise of these miraculous gifts there is no intimation of any particular period to which their continuance was limited, the next question is, by what sort of evidence the precise time of their duration is to be determined? But to this point one of the writers just referred to excuses himself, as we have seen, from giving any answer; and thinks it sufficient to declare in general that *the earliest fathers unanimously affirm them to have continued down to their times.* Yet he has not told us, as he ought to have done, to what age he limits the character of *the earliest fathers:* whether to the second or to the third century, or, with the generality of our writers, means also to include the fourth. But to whatever age he may restrain it, the difficulty at last will be, to assign a reason why we must needs stop there. In the mean while, by his appealing thus to the *earliest fathers* only, as unanimous on this article, a common reader would be apt to infer that the later fathers are more cold or diffident or divided upon it; whereas the reverse of this is true, and the more we descend from those earliest fathers, the more strong and explicit we find their successors in attesting the perpetual succession and daily exertion of the same miraculous powers in their several ages: so that if the cause must be determined by *the unanimous consent of fathers*, we shall find as much reason to believe that those powers were continued even to the latest ages as to any other, how early and primitive soever, after the days of the apostles.

"But the same writer gives us two reasons why he does not choose to say anything upon the subject of their duration: first, because *there is not light enough in history to settle it;* secondly, because *the thing itself is of no concern to us.*

"As to his first reason, I am at a loss to conceive what further light a professed advocate of the primitive ages and fathers can possibly require in this case: for as far as the church historians can illustrate or throw light upon anything, there is not a single point in all history so constantly, explicitly, and unanimously affirmed by them all, as the continual succession of these powers through all ages, from the earliest father who first mentions them down to the time of the Reformation; which same succession is still further deduced, by persons of the most eminent character for their probity, learning, and dignity, in the Romish Church, to this very day. So that the only doubt which can remain with us is, whether the church historians are to be trusted or not: for if any credit be due to them in the present case, it must reach either to all or to none; because the reason of believing them in any one age will be found to be of equal force in all, as far as it depends on the characters of the persons attesting or the nature of the things attested."*

In *terms* this and the whole of Middleton's argument is so shaped as to avoid including in its scope the miracles of Scripture, which are mentioned throughout with eulogiums and acquiescence, and so as to make you doubt whether the author believed them or not. This is exactly one of the pretenses which the young strong mind delights to tear down. It would argue, "This writer evidently *means* that the apostolic miracles have just as much evidence [as], and no more than, the popish or the patristic; and how strong"—for Middleton is a master of telling statement—"he shows that evidence to be! I won't give up the apostolic miracles, I cannot; yet I must believe what has as much of historical testimony in its favor. It is no *reductio ad absurdum* that we must go over to the Church of Rome; it is the most diffused of Christian creeds, the oldest of Christian churches." And so the logic of the skeptic becomes, as often since, the most efficient instrument of the all-believing and all-determining Church.

The consternation of Gibbon's relatives seems to have been enormous; they cast about what to do. From the experience of Oxford, they perhaps thought

* Preface to the "Free Inquiry."

that it would be useless to have recourse to the Anglican clergy: this resource had failed. So they took him to Mr. Mallet, a deist, to see if he could do anything; but he did nothing. Their next step was nearly as extraordinary: they placed him at Lausanne, in the house of M. Pavilliard, a French Protestant minister. After the easy income, complete independence, and unlimited credit of an English undergraduate, he was thrown into a foreign country, deprived, as he says, by ignorance of the language, both "of speech and of hearing,"—in the position "of a schoolboy," with a small allowance of pocket-money, and without the Epicurean comforts on which he already set some value. He laments the "indispensable comfort of a servant," and the "sordid and uncleanly* table of Madame Pavilliard." In our own day the watchful sagacity of Cardinal Wiseman would hardly allow a promising convert of expectations and talents to remain unsolaced in so pitiful a situation; we should hear [of †] soothing offers of flight or succor, [of †] some insinuation of a popish domestic and interesting repasts: but a hundred years ago the attention of the Holy See was very little directed to our English youth, and Gibbon was left to endure his position.

It is curious that he made himself comfortable. Though destitute of external comforts which he did not despise, he found what was the greatest luxury to his disposition, steady study and regular tuition. His tutor was of course to convert him if he could: but as they had no language in common, there was the preliminary occupation of teaching French. During five years both tutor and pupil steadily exerted themselves to repair the defects of a neglected and ill-grounded education: we hear of the perusal of Terence, Virgil, Horace, and Tacitus; Cicero was translated into French, and translated back again into

---

*Gibbon's words are "coarse and homely"; but as he speaks elsewhere of her "uncleanly avarice," the text fairly expresses his meaning. — ED.
† *Review*, properly. — ED.

Latin. In both languages the pupil's progress was
sound and good : from letters of his which still exist,
it is clear that he then acquired the exact and steady
knowledge of Latin of which he afterwards made so
much use ; his circumstances compelled him to master
French. If his own letters are to be trusted, he would
be an example of his own doctrine, that no one is
thoroughly master of more than one language at a
time ; they read like the letters of a Frenchman trying
and failing to write English: but perhaps there was
a desire to magnify his Continental progress, and
towards the end of the time some wish to make his
friends fear he was forgetting his own language.

Meantime the work of conversion was not forgotten. In some letters which are extant, M. Pavilliard
celebrates the triumph of his logic. "J'ai renversé,"
says the pastor, "l'infaillibilité de l'Église. J'ai prouvé
que jamais Saint Pierre n'a été chef des apôtres, que
quand il l'auroit été, le pape n'est point son succes-
seur ; qu'il est douteux que Saint Pierre ait jamais
été à Rome, mais supposé qu'il y ait été, il n'a pas
été évêque de cette ville ; que la transubstantiation
est une invention humaine, et peu ancienne dans
l'Église,"* etc.: and so on through the usual list of
Protestant arguments. He magnifies a little Gibbon's
strength of conviction, as it makes the success of his
own logic seem more splendid ; but states two curious
things: first, that Gibbon at least *pretended* to believe
in the Pretender; and what is more amazing still, —
all but incredible, — that he fasted. Such was the
youth of the Epicurean historian !

It is probable, however, that the skill of the Swiss
pastor was not the really operating cause of the event.

* "I have overthrown the infallibility of the Church ; I have proved that
St. Peter was never the head of the apostles, and that even if he was, the pope
is not his successor ; that it is doubtful whether St. Peter ever was at Rome,
but supposing that he was, he was not the bishop of that city ; that transubstantiation is a human invention, and quite modern in the Church." (June 26,
1754. See full text in note to the "Memoirs" ; the original French in some
editions, a translation in others. — ED.)

Perhaps experience shows that the converts which
Rome has made with the threat of unbelief and the
weapons of the skeptic have rarely been permanent or
advantageous to her. It is at best but a dangerous
logic to drive men to the edge and precipice of skepticism, in the hope that they will recoil in horror to the
very interior of credulity. Possibly men may show
their courage: they may vanquish the *argumentum
ad terrorem;* they may not find skepticism so terrible. This last was Gibbon's case. A more insidious
adversary than the Swiss theology was at hand to
sap his Roman Catholic belief. Pavilliard had a fair
French library, not ill stored in the recent publications of that age, of which he allowed his pupil the
continual use: it was as impossible to open any of
them and not come in contact with infidelity as to
come to England and not to see a green field. Skepticism is not so much a part of the French literature
of that day as its animating spirit, — its essence, its
vitality: you can no more cut it out and separate it
than you can extract from Wordsworth his conception of nature, or from Swift his common-sense. And
it is of the subtlest kind. It has little in common
with the rough disputation of the English deist or
the perplexing learning of the German theologian,
but works with a tool more insinuating than either.
It is in truth but the spirit of the world, which does
not argue, but assumes; which does not so much
elaborate as hints; which does not examine, but suggests. With the traditions of the Church it contrasts
traditions of its own; its technicalities are *bon sens,
l'usage du monde, le fanatisme, l'enthousiasme;* to
high hopes, noble sacrifices, awful lives, it opposes
quiet ease, skillful comfort, placid sense, polished
indifference. Old as transubstantiation may be, it is
not older than Horace and Lucian. Lord Byron, in
the well-known lines, has coupled the names of the
two literary exiles on the Leman Lake: the page
of Voltaire could not but remind Gibbon that the

skepticism from which he had revolted was compatible
with literary eminence and European fame, gave a
piquancy to ordinary writing, was the very expression
of caustic caution and gentlemanly calm.
The grave and erudite habits of Gibbon soon developed themselves. Independently of these abstruse
theological disputations, he spent many hours daily—
rising early and reading carefully—on classical and
secular learning. He was not, however, wholly thus
engrossed: there was in the neighborhood of Lausanne
a certain Mademoiselle Curchod, to whom he devoted
some of his time. She seems to have been a morbidly,
rational lady; at least she had a grave taste.* Gibbon
could not have been a very enlivening lover: he was
decidedly plain, and his predominating taste was for
solid learning. But this was not all: she formed an
attachment to M. Necker, afterwards the most slow
of premiers, whose financial treatises can hardly have
been agreeable even to a Genevese beauty. This was,
however, at a later time; so far as appears, Gibbon
was her first love. How extreme her feelings were,
one does not know; those of Gibbon can scarcely
be supposed to have done him any harm. However,
there was an intimacy, a flirtation, an engagement—
when, as usual, it appeared that neither had any
money. That the young lady should procure any
seems to have been out of the question; and Gibbon,
supposing that he might, wrote to his father.† The
reply was unfavorable. Gibbon's mother was dead;
Mr. Gibbon senior was married again, and even in
other circumstances would have been scarcely ready
to encourage a romantic engagement to a lady with
nothing. She spoke no English, too, and marriage
with a person speaking only French is still regarded

* This deduction is drawn from false premises. Her letters show that Gibbon had a rather attractive delicacy of person (including fine hair and a pretty
hand), and engaging manners, and his conversation was always witty and stimulating; and she does not appear to have formed any strong attachment to
Necker till she gave it as a husband's due. See note on next page. — ED.

† Incorrect: he asked it in person, on his return to England. — ED.

as a most unnatural event; forbidden not indeed by
the literal law of the Church, but by those higher instinctive principles of our nature to which the blunt-
est own obedience. No father could be expected to
violate at once pecuniary duties and patriotic principles : Mr. Gibbon senior forbade the match. The
young lady does.not seem to have been quite ready to
relinquish all hope; but she had shown a grave taste,
and fixed her affections on a sound and cold mind.
"I sighed," narrates the historian, "as a lover; but
I obeyed as a son." "The letter in which Gibbon
communicated to Mademoiselle Curchod the opposition
of his father to their marriage," says M. Suard, "still
exists in manuscript. The first pages are tender and
melancholy, as might be expected from an unhappy
lover; the latter became by degrees calm and reasonable; and the letter concludes with these words :—
'C'est pourquoi, mademoiselle, j'ai l'honneur d'être
votre très-humble et très-obéissant serviteur, Edouard
Gibbon.'"* Her father died soon afterwards, and she
"retired to Geneva, where, by teaching young ladies,
she earned a hard subsistence for herself and her
mother"; but the tranquil disposition of her admirer
preserved him from any romantic display of sympathy and fidelity.† He continued to study various

---

* "I have therefore, mademoiselle, the honor to be your very humble and
very obedient servant, Edward Gibbon." (Suard's "Memoir.")

† Gibbon's account of this affair, till very lately the only source of knowledge concerning it, is highly disingenuous: his part in it seems to have been
very mean, and her affection a marvel of constancy and generosity. Her
letters show that instead of notifying at once of his father's refusal, and
his own indisposition to make love a substitute for material comforts and
scholarship, he was four years in England before writing at all,—probably
with the cowardly hope that she would spare him the disagreeable task by
marrying some one else. He returned to Lausanne shortly after, and she
wrote him a letter pleading only for definite knowledge of his feelings, and
tried to get Rousseau to intercede for her,—which he sensibly refused to do,
though much disgusted with Gibbon; the latter answered her appeal coldly,
and she closed the correspondence with a scathing denunciation of his unworthiness of love like hers. It was only after this that, first provisionally
accepting a Swiss country advocate, she laid siege to and captured Necker,
a rich Paris banker and man of affairs, apparently from motives of elevated
ambition rather than affection. See *Atlantic Monthly* for February, 1888.—ED.

readings in Cicero, as well as the passage of Hannibal over the Alps; and with those affectionate resources set sentiment at defiance. Yet thirty years later the lady, then the wife of the most conspicuous man in Europe, was able to suggest useful reflections to an aged bachelor, slightly dreaming of a superannuated marriage :—

"Gardez-vous, monsieur, de former un de ces liens tardifs: le mariage qui rend heureux dans l'âge mûr c'est celui qui fut contracté dans la jeunesse. Alors seulement la réunion est parfaite, les goûts se communiquent, les sentimens se répondent, les idées deviennent communes, les facultés intellectuelles se modèlent mutuellement. Toute la vie est double, et toute la vie est une prolongation de la jeunesse; car les impressions de l'âme commandent aux yeux, et la beauté qui n'est plus conserve encore son empire. Mais pour vous, monsieur, dans toute la vigueur de la pensée, lorsque toute l'existence est décidée, l'on ne pourroit sans un miracle trouver une femme digne de vous; et une association d'un genre imparfait rappelle toujours la statue d'Horace, qui joint à une belle tête le corps d'un stupide poisson. Vous êtes marié avec la gloire."*

She was then a cultivated French lady, giving an account of the reception of the "Decline and Fall" at Paris, and expressing rather peculiar ideas on the style of Tacitus. The world had come round to her side, and she explains to her old lover rather well her happiness with M. Necker.

---

* "Beware, sir, of forming one of these late unions: the marriage which makes one happy in mature age is that which was contracted in youth. Only then is the union perfect, the tastes blend, the feelings correspond, the ideas are held in common, the intellectual faculties model themselves on each other. All life is double, and all life is a prolongation of youth ; but the impressions of the soul rule over the eyes, and the beauty which is no more preserves its empire still. But for you, sir, in all the vigor of thought, when your whole life is settled, one could not except by miracle chance on a woman worthy of you ; and a union of an unequal sort always recalls the statue of Horace, which joins to a beautiful head the body of a stupid fish. You have married Glory." (June 15, 1792. The French text is that given in Gibbon's "Correspondence" edited by Lord Sheffield ; but that in the "Mélanges de Mme. Necker" varies materially, and was probably printed from a careless duplicate kept by the lady. For "mutuellement" it has "l'une sur l'autre"; for "et une association d'un," "un lien de ce"; and the sentence beginning "qui joint" is omitted altogether. — ED.)

After living nearly five years at Lausanne, Gibbon returned to England. Continental residence has made a great alteration in many Englishmen; but few have undergone so complete a metamorphosis as Edward Gibbon. He left his own country a hot-brained and ill-taught youth, willing to sacrifice friends and expectations for a superstitious and half-known creed: he returned a cold and accomplished man, master of many accurate ideas, little likely to hazard any coin for any faith; already, it is probable, inclined in secret to a cautious skepticism,—placing thereby, as it were, upon a system the frigid prudence and unventuring incredulity congenial to his character. His change of character changed his position among his relatives. His father, he says, met him as a friend; and they continued thenceforth on a footing of "easy intimacy." Especially after the little affair of Mademoiselle Curchod, and the "very sensible view he took in that instance of the matrimonial relation," there can be but little question that Gibbon was justly regarded as a most safe young man; singularly prone to large books, and a little too fond of French phrases and French ideas, but yet with a great feeling of common-sense, and a wise preference of permanent money to transitory sentiment. His father allowed him a moderate and but a moderate income, which he husbanded with great care, and only voluntarily expended in the purchase and acquisition of serious volumes. He lived an externally idle but really studious life, varied by tours in France and Italy; the toils of which, though not in description very formidable, a trifle tried a sedentary habit and somewhat corpulent body. The only English avocation which he engaged in was, oddly enough, war. It does not appear the most likely in this pacific country, nor does he seem exactly the man for *la grande guerre;* but so it was: and the fact is an example of a really Anglican invention. The English have discovered pacific war. We may not be able to

kill people as well as the French, or fit out and feed
distant armaments as neatly as they do; but we are
unrivaled at a quiet armament here at home, which
never kills anybody and never wants to be sent
anywhere. A "constitutional militia" is a beautiful
example of the mild efficacy of civilization, which
can convert even "the great man-slaying profession"
(as Carlyle calls it) into a quiet and dining association. Into this force Gibbon was admitted; and immediately, contrary to his anticipations and very
much against his will, was called out for permanent
duty. The hero of the *corps* was a certain dining
Sir Thomas, who used at the end of each new bottle
to announce with increasing joy how much soberer
he had become. What his fellow-officers thought of
Gibbon's French predilections and large volumes it is
not difficult to conjecture; and he complains bitterly
of the interruption to his studies. However, his easy
composed nature soon made itself at home; his polished tact partially concealed from the "mess" his
recondite pursuits, and he contrived to make the
Hampshire armament of classical utility.

"I read," he says, "the 'Analysis of Cæsar's Campaign in
Africa.' Every motion of that great general is laid open with a
critical sagacity; a complete military history of his campaigns
would do almost as much honor to M. Guichardt as to Cæsar.
This finished the 'Mémoires,' which gave me a much clearer notion
of ancient tactics than I ever had before. Indeed, my own military knowledge was of some service to me, as I am well acquainted
with the modern discipline and exercise of a battalion; so that
though much inferior to M. Folard and M. Guichardt, who had
seen service, I am a much better judge than Salmasius, Casaubon,
or Lipsius, — mere scholars, who perhaps had never seen a battalion
under arms."*

The real occupation of Gibbon, as this quotation
might suggest, was his reading; and this was of a
peculiar sort. There are many kinds of readers, and
each has a sort of perusal suitable to his kind. There

* "Journal," May 23, 1762.

is the voracious reader, like Dr. Johnson, who extracts with grasping appetite the large features, the
mere essence of a trembling publication, and rejects
the rest with contempt and disregard. There is the
subtle reader, who pursues with fine attention the
most imperceptible and delicate ramifications of an
interesting topic, marks slight traits, notes changing
manners, has a keen eye for the character of his
author, is minutely attentive to every prejudice and
awake to every passion, watches syllables and waits
on words, is alive to the light air of nice associations
which float about every subject,—the motes in the
bright sunbeam, the delicate gradations of the passing shadows. There is the stupid reader, who prefers
dull books; is generally to be known by his disregard
of small books and English books, but likes masses
in modern Latin,—"Grævius de torpore mirabili,"
"Horrificus de gravitate sapientiæ." But Gibbon was
not of any of these classes. He was what common
people would call a matter-of-fact, and philosophers
nowadays a *positive* reader. No disciple of M. Comte
could attend more strictly · to precise and provable
phenomena; his favorite points are those which can
be weighed and measured. Like the dull reader, he
had perhaps a preference for huge books in unknown
tongues; but on the other hand, he wished those
books to contain real and accurate information. He
liked the firm earth of positive knowledge. His fancy
was not flexible enough for exquisite refinement, his
imagination too slow for light and wandering literature; but. he felt no love of dullness in itself, and
had a prompt acumen for serious eloquence. This
was his kind of reflection:—

"The author of the *Adventurer*, No. 127 (Mr. Joseph Warton,
concealed under the signature of 'Z.'), concludes his ingenious
parallel of the ancients and moderns by the following remark:—
'The age will never again return, when a Pericles, after walking
with Plato in a portico built by Phidias and painted by Apelles,
might repair to hear a pleading of Demosthenes or a tragedy of

Sophocles.' It will never return, because it never existed. Pericles (who died in the fourth year of the LXXXIXth Olympiad, ant. Ch. 429: Dio. Sic. 1. xii. 46) was confessedly the patron of Phidias and the contemporary of Sophocles; but he could enjoy no very great pleasure in the conversation of Plato, who was born the same year that he himself died ('Diogenes Laertius in Platone;' v. Stanley's 'History of Philosophy,' p. 154). The error is still more extraordinary with regard to Apelles and Demosthenes, since both the painter and the orator survived Alexander the Great, whose death is above a century posterior to that of Pericles (in 323). And indeed, though Athens was the seat of every liberal art from the days of Themistocles to those of Demetrius Phalereus, yet no particular era will afford Mr. Warton the complete synchronism he seems to wish for; as tragedy was deprived of her famous triumvirate before the arts of philosophy and eloquence had attained the perfection which they soon after received from the hands of Plato, Aristotle, and Demosthenes."*

And wonderful is it for what Mr. Hallam calls "the languid students of our present age" to turn over the journal of his daily studies. It is true, it seems to have been revised by himself, and so great a narrator would group effectively facts with which he was so familiar; but allowing any discount (if we may use so mean a word) for the skillful art of the impressive historian, there will yet remain in the "Extraits de mon Journal" a wonderful monument of learned industry. You may open them anywhere:— "'Dissertation on the Medal of Smyrna,' by M. de Boze: replete with erudition and taste; containing curious researches on the pre-eminence of the cities of Asia. — 'Researches on the Polypus,' by Mr. Trembley. A new world! throwing light on physics, but darkening metaphysics. — Vegetius's 'Institutions.' This writer on tactics has good general notions; but his particular account of the Roman discipline is deformed by confusion and anachronisms."† Or, "I this

---

* This passage is to be found only in Lord Sheffield's five-volume edition of the Miscellanies (1814), being No. 30 of the "Index Expurgatorius" (Vol. v.); the so-called "reprint" of 1837 omits this and other matter. — ED.

† Dec. 5, 1762.

day began a very considerable task, which was, to read Cluverius's 'Italia Antiqua,' in two volumes in folio, Leyden 1624, Elzevirs;"* and it appears he did read it as well as begin it, which is the point where most enterprising men would have failed. From the time of his residence at Lausanne his Latin scholarship had been sound and good, and his studies were directed to the illustration of the best Roman authors; but it is curious to find on Aug. 16, 1762, after his return to England, and when he was twenty-four years old, the following extract:—

"I have at last finished the 'Iliad.' As I undertook it to improve myself in the Greek language, which I had totally neglected for some years past, and to which I never applied myself with a proper attention, I must give a reason why I began with Homer, and that contrary to Le Clerc's advice. I had two. First, as Homer is the most ancient Greek author (excepting perhaps Hesiod) who is now extant; and as he was not only the poet, but the lawgiver, the theologian, the historian, and the philosopher of the ancients,—every succeeding writer is full of quotations from or allusions to his writings, which it would be difficult to understand without a previous knowledge of them. In this situation, was it not natural to follow the ancients themselves, who always began their studies by the perusal of Homer? Secondly, no writer ever treated such a variety of subjects. As every part of civil, military, or economical life is introduced into his poems, and as the simplicity of his age allowed him to call everything by its proper name, almost the whole compass of the Greek tongue is comprised in Homer. I have so far met with the success I hoped for, that I have acquired a great facility in reading the language, and treasured up a very great stock of words. What I have rather neglected is, the grammatical construction of them, and especially the many various inflexions of the verbs. In order to acquire that dry but necessary branch of knowledge, I propose bestowing some time every morning on the perusal of the 'Greek Grammar of Port Royal,' as one of the best extant. I believe that I read nearly one-half of Homer like a mere schoolboy, not enough master of the words to elevate myself to the poetry. The remainder I read with a good deal of care and criticism, and made many observations on them. Some I have inserted here; for the rest I shall find a proper place.

* Oct. 13, 1762.

Upon the whole, I think that Homer's few faults (for some he certainly has) are lost in the variety of his beauties. I expected to have finished him long before. The delay was owing partly to the circumstances of my way of life and avocations, and partly to my own fault; for while every one looks on me as a prodigy of application, I know myself how strong a propensity I have to indolence."

Posterity will confirm the contemporary theory that he was a "prodigy" of steady study. Those who know what the Greek language is, how much of the "Decline and Fall" depends on Greek authorities, how few errors the keen criticism of divines and scholars has been able to detect in his employment of them, will best appreciate the patient every-day labor which could alone repair the early neglect of so difficult an attainment.

It is odd how little Gibbon wrote, at least for the public, in early life. More than twenty-two years elapsed from his first return from Lausanne to the appearance of the first volume of his great work: and in that long interval his only important publication— if it can indeed be so called—was a French essay, "Sur l'Étude de la Littérature," which contains some sensible remarks and shows much regular reading; but which is on the whole a "conceivable treatise," and would be wholly forgotten if it had been written by any one else. It was little read in England, and must have been a serious difficulty to his friends in the militia; but the Parisians read it (or said they had read it, which is more in their way), and the fame of being a French author was a great aid to him in foreign society. It flattered, indeed, the French *literati* more than any one can now fancy. The French had then the idea that it was uncivilized to speak any other language, and the notion of *writing* any other seemed quite a *bêtise*. By a miserable misfortune you might not know French, but at least you could conceal it assiduously; white paper anyhow might go unsoiled; posterity at least should not hear of such ignorance. The Parisian was to be the universal tongue.

And it did not seem absurd, especially to those only slightly acquainted with foreign countries, that this might in part be so. Political eminence had given their language a diplomatic supremacy. No German literature existed as yet; Italy had ceased to produce important books. There was only England left to dispute the literary omnipotence; and such an attempt as Gibbon's was a peculiarly acceptable flattery, for it implied that her most cultivated men were beginning to abandon their own tongue, and to write like other nations in the cosmopolitan *lingua franca*. A few far-seeing observers, however, already contemplated the train of events which at the present day give such a preponderating influence to our own writers, and make it an arduous matter even to explain the conceivableness of the French ambition. Of all men living then or since, David Hume was the most likely from prejudice and habit to take an unfavorable view of English literary influence: he had more literary fame than he deserved in France, and less in England; he had much of the French neatness, he had but little of the English nature: yet his cold and discriminating intellect at once emancipated him from the sophistries which imposed on those less watchful. He wrote to Gibbon:—

"I have only one objection, derived from the language in which it is written. Why do you compose in French, and carry fagots into the wood, as Horace says with regard to the Romans who wrote in Greek? I grant that you have a like motive to those Romans, and adopt a language much more generally diffused than your native tongue; but have you not remarked the fate of those two ancient languages in following ages? The Latin, though then less celebrated and confined to more narrow limits, has in some measure outlived the Greek, and is now more generally understood by men of letters. Let the French, therefore, triumph in the present diffusion of their tongue: our solid and increasing establishments in America, where we need less dread the inundation of barbarians, promise a superior stability and duration to the English language." *

* Oct. 24, 1767. Given in note to the "Memoirs."

The cool skeptic was correct. The great breeding people have gone out and multiplied; colonies in every
clime attest our success. French is the *patois* of Europe; English is the language of the world.

Gibbon took the advice of his sagacious friend, and
prepared himself for the composition of his great work
in English. His studies were destined, however, to
undergo an interruption. "Yesterday morning," he
wrote to a friend, "about half an hour after seven, as
I was destroying an army of barbarians, I heard a
double rap at the door, and my friend Mr. Eliot was
soon introduced. After some idle conversation, he told
me that if I was desirous of being in Parliament, he
had an *independent* seat very much at my service." *
The borough was Liskeard; and the epithet "independent" is of course ironical, Mr. Eliot being himself the constituency of that place. The offer was
accepted, and one of the most learned of members of
Parliament took his seat.

The political life of Gibbon is briefly described:
he was a supporter of Lord North. That well-known
statesman was in the most exact sense a representative
man, although representative of the class of persons
most out of favor with the transcendental thinkers
who invented this name. Germans deny it, but in
every country common opinions are very common.
Everywhere there exists the comfortable mass: quiet,
sagacious, short-sighted, — such as the Jews whom
Rabshakeh tempted by their vine and their fig-tree,
such as the English with their snug dining-room and
after-dinner nap, domestic happiness and Bullo coal;
sensible, solid men, without stretching irritable reason,
but with a placid, supine instinct, without originality
and without folly; judicious in their dealings, respected
in the world; wanting little, sacrificing nothing:
"good-tempered people," in a word, "caring for nothing until they are themselves hurt." † Lord North was

* To Mr. Holroyd, Sept. 10, 1774.
† The substance of Hazlitt's first paragraph on Lord Eldon. — ED.

one of this class : you could hardly make him angry. "No doubt," he said, tapping his fat sides, "I am that odious thing, a minister; and I believe other people wish they were so too."* Profound people look deeply for the maxims of his policy; and it being on the surface, of course they fail to find it. He did not what the mind, but what the *body* of the community wanted to have done; he appealed to the real people, the large English commonplace herd. His abilities were great, and with them he did what people with no abilities wished to do and could not do. Lord Brougham has published his letters to the King,† showing that which partial extracts had made known before, that Lord North was quite opposed to the war he was carrying on : was convinced it could not succeed; hardly, in fact, wished it might. Why did he carry it on ? *Vox populi*, the voice of well-dressed men, commanded it to be done; and he cheerfully sacrificed American people, who were nothing to him, to English, who were something, and a king, who was much. Gibbon was the very man to support such a ruler. His historical writings have given him a posthumous eminence; but in his own time he was doubtless thought a sensible safe man, of ordinary thoughts and intelligible actions. To do him justice, he did not pretend to be a hero. "Vous n'avez pas oublié," he wrote to his friend Deyverdun, "que je suis entré au Parlement sans patriotisme, sans ambition; et que toutes mes vues se bornoient à la place commode et honnête d'un *Lord of Trade.*" ‡ "Wise in his generation" was written on his brow; he quietly and gently supported the policy of his time.

Even, however, amid the fatigue of parliamentary attendance, — the fatigue, in fact, of attending a

---

* Condensed from Charles Butler's "Reminiscences," xii. 2.
† The King's letters to him. — Ed.
‡ "You have not forgotten that I have entered Parliament without patriotism and without ambition ; and that all my views are bounded by the comfortable and modest position of a Lord of Trade."

nocturnal and oratorical club, where you met the best people, who could not speak, as well as a few of the worst, who *would*, — Gibbon's history made much progress. The first volume, a quarto, one-sixth of the whole, was published in the spring of 1776, and at once raised his fame to a high point. Ladies actually read it, — read about Bætica and Tarraconensis, the Roman legions and the tribunitian powers. Grave scholars wrote dreary commendations. "The first impression," he writes, "was exhausted in a few days; a second and third edition were scarcely adequate to the demand; and the bookseller's property was twice invaded by the pirates of Dublin. My book was on every table" — tables must have been rather few in that age — "and almost on every toilette; the historian was crowned by the taste or fashion of the day; nor was the general voice disturbed by the barking of any *profane* critic." The noise penetrated deep into the unlearned classes. Mr. Sheridan, who never read anything, "on principle," said that the crimes of Warren Hastings surpassed anything to be found "in the correct sentences of Tacitus" or "on the *luminous* page of Gibbon."† Some one seems to have been struck with the jet of learning, and questioned the great wit: "I said," he replied, "*voluminous*."‡

History, it is said, is of no use: at least a great critic, who is understood to have in the press a very elaborate work in that kind,* not long since seemed to allege that writings of this sort did not establish a theory of the universe, and were therefore of no avail. But whatever may be the use of this sort of composition in itself and abstractedly, it is certainly of great use relatively and to literary men. Consider the position of a man of that species. He sits beside a library fire, with nice white paper, a good pen, a capital style, — every means of saying everything, but nothing to say. Of course he is an able man; of course he has an active intellect, beside wonderful culture: but still,

---

* Probably Carlyle and his " Frederick the Great " are meant. — ED.
† Speech on the trial.   ‡ *Vide* Byron, Moore, Milman, etc.

one cannot always have original ideas. Every day cannot be an era; a train of new speculation very often will not be found: and how dull it is to make it your business to write, to stay by yourself in a room to write, and then to have nothing to say! It is dreary work mending seven pens, and waiting for a theory to "turn up." What a gain if something would happen! then one could describe it. Something has happened, and that something is history. On this account, since a sedate Greek discovered this plan for a grave immortality, a series of accomplished men have seldom been found wanting to derive a literary capital from their active and barbarous kindred. Perhaps when a Visigoth broke a head, he thought that that was all: not so, — he was making history; Gibbon has written it down.

The manner of writing history is as characteristic of the narrator as the actions are of the persons who are related to have performed them; often much more so. It may be generally defined as a view of one age taken by another; a picture of a series of men and women painted by one of another series. Of course this definition seems to exclude contemporary history; but if we look into the matter carefully, is there such a thing? What are all the best and most noted works that claim the title? Memoirs, scraps, materials: composed by men of like passions with the people they speak of, involved it may be in the same events, describing them with the partiality and narrowness of eager actors; or even worse, by men far apart in a monkish solitude, familiar with the lettuces of the convent garden, but hearing only faint dim murmurs of the great transactions which they slowly jot down in the barren chronicle. These are not to be named in the same short breath or included in the same narrow word with the equable, poised, philosophic narrative of the retrospective historian. In the great histories there are two topics of interest, — the man as a type of the age in which he lives, the events and manners of the age he is describing; very often almost all the interest is the contrast of the two.

You should do everything, said Lord Chesterfield, in minuet time. It was in that time that Gibbon wrote his history, and such was the manner of the age. You fancy him in a suit of flowered velvet, with a bag and sword, wisely smiling, composedly rounding his periods. You seem to see the grave bows, the formal politeness, the finished deference. You perceive the minuetic action accompanying the words: "Give," it would say, "Augustus a chair; Zenobia, the humblest of your slaves; Odoacer, permit me to correct the defect in your attire." As the slap-dash sentences of a rushing critic express the hasty impatience of modern manners; so the deliberate emphasis, the slow acumen, the steady argument, the impressive narration bring before us — what is now a tradition — the picture of the correct eighteenth-century gentleman, who never failed in a measured politeness, partly because it was due in propriety towards others, and partly because from his own dignity it was due most obviously to himself.

And not only is this true of style, but it may be extended to other things also. There is no one of the many literary works produced in the eighteenth century more thoroughly characteristic of it than Gibbon's history. The special characteristic of that age is its clinging to the definite and palpable; it had a taste beyond everything for what is called "solid information." In literature, the period may be defined as that in which authors had ceased to write for students and had not begun to write for women. In the present day, no one can take up any book intended for general circulation without clearly seeing that the writer supposes most of his readers will be ladies or young men; and that in proportion to his judgment he is attending to their taste. Two or three hundred years ago, books were written for professed and systematic students, — the class the fellows of colleges were designed to be,—who used to go on studying them all their lives. Between these there was a time in which the more marked class of literary consumers were strong-headed, practical men. Education had not become so general or so feminine as to make the present style—what is called the "brilliant style"—at all necessary; but there was enough culture to make the demand of common diffused persons more effectual than that of special and secluded scholars. A book-buying public had arisen of sensible men, who would not endure the awful folio style in which the schoolmen wrote. From peculiar causes, too, the business of that age was perhaps more free from the hurry and distraction which disable so many of our practical men now from reading. You accordingly see in the books of the last century what is called a "masculine tone": a firm, strong, perspicuous narration of matter of fact, a plain argument, a contempt for everything which distinct definite people cannot entirely and thoroughly comprehend. There is no more solid book in the world than Gibbon's history. Only consider the chronology: it begins before the year ONE and goes down to the year 1453, and is a schedule or series of schedules of important events during that time. Scarcely any fact deeply affecting European civilization is wholly passed over, and the great majority of facts are elaborately recounted. Laws, dynasties, churches, barbarians appear and disappear. Everything changes: the old world — the classical civilization of form and definition — passes away, a new world of free spirit and inward growth emerges; between the two lies a mixed weltering interval of trouble and confusion, when everybody hates everybody, and the historical student leads a life of skirmishes, is oppressed with broils and feuds. All through this long period Gibbon's history goes with steady consistent pace; like a Roman legion through a troubled country, *hæret pede pes:* * up-hill and

* "Foot clings on foot."

down-hill, through marsh and thicket, through Goth or
Parthian, the firm defined array passes forward, a
type of order and an emblem of civilization. Whatever may be the defects of Gibbon's history, none can
deny him a proud precision and a style in marching
order.

Another characteristic of the eighteenth century is
its taste for dignified pageantry. What an existence
was that of Versailles! How gravely admirable to
see the *grand monarque* shaved and dressed and pow-
dered, to look on and watch a great man carefully
amusing himself with dreary trifles! Or do we not
even now possess an invention of that age, — the great
eighteenth-century footman, still in the costume of
his era, with dignity and powder, vast calves and
noble mien? What a world it must have been when
all men looked like that! Go and gaze with rapture
at the foot-board of a carriage, and say, Who would
not obey a premier with such an air? Grave, tranquil, decorous pageantry is a part, as it were, of the
essence of the last age. There is nothing more characteristic of Gibbon : a kind of pomp pervades him ;
he is never out of livery. He ever selects for narration those themes which look most like a levee : grave
chamberlains seem to stand throughout : life is a vast
ceremony, the historian at once the dignitary and the
scribe.

The very language of Gibbon shows these qualities.
Its majestic march has been the admiration, its rather
pompous cadence the sport, of all perusers. It has
the greatest merit of a historical style, — it is always
going on; you feel no doubt of its continuing in
motion. Many narrators of the reflective class — Sir
Archibald Alison, for example — fail in this : your constant feeling is, "Ah! he has pulled up; he is going
to be profound : he never will go on again." Gibbon's
reflections connect the events, they are not sermons
between them. But notwithstanding, the manner of
the "Decline and Fall" is the last which should be

recommended for strict imitation: it is not a style in which you can tell the truth. A monotonous writer is suited only to monotonous matter. Truth is of various kinds: grave, solemn, dignified, —petty, low, ordinary; and a historian who has to tell the truth must be able to tell what is vulgar as well as what is great, what is little as well as what is amazing. Gibbon is at fault here: he *cannot* mention Asia *Minor.* The petty order of sublunary matters, the common gross existence of ordinary people, the neces-· sary littlenesses of necessary life, are little suited to his sublime narrative. Men on the *Times* feel this acutely: it is most difficult at first to say many things in the huge imperial manner; and after all you cannot tell everything. "How, sir," asked a reviewer of Sydney Smith's life, "do you say a 'good fellow' in print?" "Mr. ——," replied the editor, "you should not say it at all." Gibbon was aware of this rule: he omits what does not suit him; and the consequence is, that though he has selected the most various of historical topics, he scarcely gives you an idea of variety. The ages change, but the varnish of the narration is the same.

It is not unconnected with this fault that Gibbon gives us but an indifferent description of individual character: people seem a good deal alike. The cautious skepticism of his cold intellect, which disinclined him to every extreme, depreciates great virtues and extenuates great vices; and we are left with a tame neutral character, capable of nothing extraordinary,— hateful, as the saying is, "both to God and to the enemies of God."

A great point in favor of Gibbon is the existence of his history. Some great historians seem likely to fail here. A good judge was asked which he preferred, Macaulay's "History of England" or Lord Mahon's: "Why," he replied, "you observe Lord Mahon has written his history; and by what I see, Macaulay's will be written not only for but *among* posterity."

Practical people have little idea of the practical ability required to write a large book, and especially a large history. Long before you get to the pen, there is an immensity of pure business; heaps of material are strewn everywhere, but they lie in disorder, unread, uncatalogued, unknown. It seems a dreary waste of life to be analyzing, indexing, extracting works and passages in which one per cent. of the contents are interesting and not half of that percentage will after all appear in the flowing narrative. As an accountant takes up a bankrupt's books filled with confused statements of ephemeral events, the disorderly record of unprofitable speculations, and charges this to that head and that to this,—estimates earnings, specifies expenses, demonstrates failures; so the great narrator, going over the scattered annalists of extinct ages, groups and divides, notes and combines, until from a crude mass of darkened fragments there emerges a clear narrative, a concise account of the result and upshot of the whole. In this art Gibbon was a master. The laborious research of German scholarship, the keen eye of theological zeal, a steady criticism of eighty years, have found few faults of detail: the account has been worked right, the proper authorities consulted, an accurate judgment formed, the most telling incidents selected. Perhaps experience shows that there is something English in this talent. The Germans are more elaborate in single monographs; but they seem to want the business ability to work out a complicated narrative, to combine a long whole. The French are neat enough, and their style is very quick: but then it is difficult to believe their facts; the account on its face seems too plain, and no true Parisian ever was an antiquary. The great classical histories published in this country in our own time show that the talent is by no means extinct; and they likewise show, what is also evident, that this kind of composition is easier with respect to ancient than with respect to modern times.

The barbarians burned the books; and though all
the historians abuse them for it, it is quite evident
that in their hearts they are greatly rejoiced, — if the
books had existed they would have had to read them.
Macaulay has to peruse every book printed with long
fs, and it is no use after all: somebody will find some
stupid MS., an old account-book of an "ingenious
gentleman," and with five entries therein destroy a
whole hypothesis. But Gibbon was exempt from this:
he could count the books the efficient Goths bequeathed,
and when he had mastered them he might pause.
Still, it was no light matter, as any one who looks at
the books — awful folios in the grave Bodleian — will
most certainly credit and believe. And he did it all
himself: he never showed his book to any friend, or
asked any one to help him in the accumulating work,
not even in the correction of the press. "Not a sheet,"
he says, "has been seen by any human eyes, excepting those of the author and the printer; the faults
and the merits are exclusively my own." And he
wrote most of it with one pen, which must certainly
have grown erudite towards the end.

The nature of his authorities clearly shows what
the nature of Gibbon's work is. History may be
roughly divided into "universal" and "particular":
the first being the narrative of events affecting the
whole human race — at least the main historical nations,
the narrative of whose fortunes is the story of civilization; and the latter being the relation of events
relating to one or a few particular nations only. Universal history, it is evident, comprises great areas of
space and long periods of time; you cannot have a
series of events visibly operating on all great nations
without time for their gradual operation, and without tracking them in succession through the various
regions of their power. There is no instantaneous
transmission in historical causation; a long interval is
required for universal effects. It follows that universal history necessarily partakes of the character of a

summary. You cannot recount the cumbrous annals
of long epochs without condensation, selection, and
omission : the narrative, when shortened within the
needful limits, becomes concise and general; what
it gains in time, according to the mechanical phrase,
it loses in power. The particular history, confined
within narrow limits, can show us the whole contents of these limits, explain its features of human
interest, recount in graphic detail all its interesting
transactions, touch the human heart with the power
of passion, instruct the mind with patient instances
of accurate wisdom. The universal is confined to a
dry enumeration of superficial transactions; no action
can have all its details; the canvas is so crowded
that no figure has room to display itself effectively.
From the nature of the subject, Gibbon's history is
of the latter class, the sweep of the narrative is so
wide; the decline and fall of the Roman empire being in some sense the most universal event which has
ever happened, — being, that is, the historical incident
which has most affected all civilized men and the
very existence and form of civilization itself, — it is
evident that we must look rather for a comprehensive
generality than a telling minuteness of delineation.
The history of a thousand years does not admit the
pictorial detail which a Scott or a Macaulay can accumulate on the history of a hundred. Gibbon has
done his best to avoid the dryness natural to such
an attempt : he inserts as much detail as his limits
will permit; selects for more full description, striking people and striking transactions; brings together
at a single view all that relates to single topics;
above all, by a regular advance of narration, never
ceases to imply the regular progress of events and
the steady course of time. None can deny the magnitude of such an effort. After all, however, these are
merits of what is technically termed "composition,"
and are analogous to those excellences in painting
or sculpture that are more respected by artists than

appreciated by the public at large. The fame of Gibbon is highest among writers: those especially who have studied for years particular periods included in his theme (and how many those are! for in the East and West he has set his mark on all that is great for ten centuries) acutely feel and admiringly observe how difficult it would be to say so much and leave so little untouched; to compress so many telling points; to present in so few words so apt and embracing a narrative of the whole. But the mere unsophisticated reader scarcely appreciates this, — he is rather awed than delighted: or rather, perhaps, he appreciates it for a little while, then is tired by the roll and glare; then, on any chance, — the creaking of an organ or the stirring of a mouse, — in time of temptation he falls away. It has been said, The way to answer all objections to Milton is, to take down the book and read him: the way to reverence Gibbon is, not to read him at all, but look at him, from outside, in the bookcase, and think how much there is within; what a course of events, what a muster-roll of names, what a steady solemn sound! You will not like to take the book down; but you will think how much you could be delighted if you would.

It may be well, though it can be only in the most cursory manner, to examine the respective treatment of the various elements in this vast whole. The history of the "Decline and Fall" may be roughly and imperfectly divided into the picture of the Roman empire, the narrative of barbarian incursions, the story of Constantinople; and some few words may be hastily said on each.

The picture — for so, from its apparent stability when contrasted with the fluctuating character of the later period, we may call it — which Gibbon has drawn of the united empire has immense merit. The organization of the imperial system is admirably dwelt on; the manner in which the old republican institutions were apparently retained but really altered is

compendiously explained; the mode in which the
imperial will was transmitted to and carried out in
remote provinces is distinctly displayed: but though
the mechanism is admirably delineated, the dynamical
principle—the original impulse—is not made clear.
You never feel you are reading about the Romans;
yet no one denies their character to be most marked,—
poets and orators have striven for the expression of it.
Macaulay has been similarly criticized; it has been
said that notwithstanding his great dramatic power,
and wonderful felicity in the selection of events on
which to exert it, he yet never makes us feel that we
are reading about Englishmen,—the coarse clay of
our English nature *cannot* be represented in so fine
a style. In the same way, and to a much greater
extent (for this is perhaps an unthankful criticism, if
we compare Macaulay's description of anybody with
that of any other historian), Gibbon is chargeable
with neither expressing nor feeling the essence of the
people concerning whom he is writing. There was,
in truth, in the Roman people a warlike fanaticism,
a puritanical essence, an interior, latent, restrained,
enthusiastic religion, which was utterly alien to the
cold skepticism of the narrator. Of course he was
conscious of it,—he indistinctly felt that at least
there was something he did not like; but he could
not realize or sympathize with it without a change
of heart and nature. The old pagan has a sympathy
with the religion of enthusiasm far above the reach
of the modern Epicurean.

It may indeed be said, on behalf of Gibbon, that
the old Roman character was in its decay, and that
only such slight traces of it were remaining in the
age of Augustus and the Antonines that it is no
particular defect in him to leave it unnoticed; yet
though the intensity of its nobler peculiarities was on
the wane, many a vestige would perhaps have been
apparent to so learned an eye, if his temperament and
disposition had been prone to seize upon and search

for them. Nor is there any adequate appreciation of the compensating element, of the force which really held society together; of the fresh air of the Illyrian hills; of that army which, evermore recruited from northern and rugged populations, doubtless brought into the very center of a degraded society the healthy simplicity of a vital if barbarous religion.

It is no wonder that such a mind should have looked with displeasure on primitive Christianity. The whole of his treatment of that topic has been discussed by many pens, and three generations of ecclesiastical scholars have illustrated it with their emendations; yet if we turn over this, the latest and most elaborate edition, containing all the important criticisms of Milman and of Guizot, we shall be surprised to find how few instances of definite exact error such a scrutiny has been able to find out. As Paley, with his strong sagacity, at once remarked, the subtle error rather lies hid in the sinuous folds than is directly apparent on the surface of the polished style. "Who," said the shrewd archdeacon, "can refute a sneer?" And yet even this is scarcely the exact truth. The objection of Gibbon is in fact an objection rather to religion than to Christianity: as has been said, he did not appreciate and could not describe the most inward form of pagan piety; he objected to Christianity because it was the intensest of religions. We do not mean by this to charge Gibbon with any denial [of], any overt distinct disbelief in, the existence of a supernatural Being: this would be very unjust; his cold composed mind had nothing in common with the Jacobinical outbreak of the next generation. He was no doubt a theist after the fashion of natural theology; nor was he devoid of more than scientific feeling. All constituted authorities struck him with emotion, all ancient ones with awe. If the Roman empire had descended to his time, how much he would have reverenced it! He had doubtless a great respect for the "First Cause": it had many

titles to approbation; "it was not conspicuous," he
would have said, "but it was potent." A sensitive
decorum revolted from the jar of atheistic disputation.
We have already described him more than enough: a
sensible middle-aged man in political life; a bachelor,
not himself gay, but living with gay men; equable
and secular; cautious in his habits, tolerant in his
creed; as Porson said, "never failing in natural feeling, except when women were to be ravished and
Christians to be martyred."* His writings are in
character. The essence of the far-famed fifteenth and
sixteenth chapters is in truth but a description of un-
worldly- events in the tone of this world, of awful
facts in unmoved voice, of truths of the heart in the
language of the eyes. The wary skeptic has not even
committed himself to definite doubts. These celebrated chapters were in the first manuscript much
longer, and were gradually reduced to their present
size by excision and compression. Who can doubt
that in their first form they were a clear or compara-
tively clear expression of exact opinions on the Christian history, and that it was by a subsequent and
elaborate process that they were reduced to their
present and insidious obscurity? The toil has been
effectual: "Divest," says Dean Milman of the introduction to the fifteenth chapter, "this whole passage
of the latent sarcasm betrayed by the subsequent tone
of the whole disquisition, and it might commence a
Christian history, written in the most Christian spirit
of candor." †

It is not for us here to go into any disquisition as
to the comparative influence of the five earthly causes
to whose secondary operation the specious historian
ascribes the progress of Christianity; weariness and
disinclination forbid. There can be no question that

---

* Porson's actual words are, "Nor does his humanity ever slumber, unless when women are ravished and the Christians persecuted." (Letters to
Travis.) — ED.

† Preface to his edition of the "Decline and Fall."

the polity of the Church and the zeal of the converts
and other such things did most materially conduce to
the progress of the Gospel; but few will now attribute to these much of the effect.   The real cause is
the heaving of the mind after the truth: troubled
with the perplexities of time, weary with the vexation
of ages, the spiritual faculty of man turns to the
truth as the child turns to its mother.   The thirst of
the soul was to be satisfied, the deep torture of the
spirit to have rest.   There was an appeal to those

"High instincts before which our mortal nature
Did tremble like a guilty thing surprised."*

The mind of man has an appetite for the truth.

"Hence, in a season of calm weather,
Though inland far we be,
Our souls have sight of that immortal sea
Which brought us hither, —
Can in a moment travel thither,
And see the children sport upon the shore,
And hear the mighty waters rolling evermore."†

All this was not exactly in Gibbon's way, and he
does not seem to have been able to conceive that it
was in any one else's.   Why his chapters had given
offense he could hardly make out; it actually seems
that he hardly thought that other people believed
more than he did.   "We may be well assured," says
he of a skeptic of antiquity, "that a writer conversant
with the world would never have ventured to expose
the gods of his country to public ridicule, had they
not been already the objects of secret contempt among
the polished and enlightened orders of society."‡
"Had I," he says of himself, "believed that the majority of English readers were so fondly attached even
to the name and shadow of Christianity; had I fore-

* Wordsworth, "Intimations of Immortality," ix.
† Ibid.
‡ "Decline and Fall," Chap. ii., in re Lucian.

seen that the pious, the timid, and the prudent would feel or affect to feel with such exquisite sensibility,— I might perhaps have softened the two invidious chapters, which would create many enemies and conciliate few friends."* The state of belief at that time is a very large subject; but it is probable that in the cultivated cosmopolitan classes the Continental skepticism was very rife, that among the hard-headed classes the rough spirit of English deism had made progress. Though the mass of the people doubtless believed much as they now believe, yet the entire upper class was lazy and corrupt, and there is truth in the picture of the modern divine:—

"The thermometer of the Church of England sank to its lowest point in the first thirty years of the reign of George III. . . . In their preaching, nineteen clergymen out of twenty carefully abstained from dwelling upon Christian doctrines: such topics exposed the preacher to the charge of fanaticism. Even the calm and sober Crabbe, who certainly never erred from excess of zeal, was stigmatized in those days by his brethren as a 'Methodist,' because he introduced into his sermons the motives of future reward and punishment: an orthodox clergyman (they said) should be content to show his people the worldly advantage of good conduct, and to leave heaven and hell to the ranters. Nor can we wonder that such should have been the notions of country parsons, when, even by those who passed for the supreme arbiters of orthodoxy and taste, the vapid rhetoric of Blair was thought the highest standard of Christian exhortation."†

It is among the excuses for Gibbon, that he lived in such a world.

There are slight palliations also in the notions then prevalent of the primitive Church. There was the Anglican theory, that it was a *via media*, the most correct of periods; that its belief is to be the standard, its institutions the model, its practice the test of subsequent ages. There was the notion, not formally drawn out, but diffused through and implied in a hundred books of "evidence[s‡],"—a notion in opposition

---

* "Memoirs."

† "Church Parties," in *Edinburgh Review* for October, 1853; by W. J. Conybeare.   ‡ *Review*, better.— ED.

to every probability, and utterly at variance with the
New Testament,—that the first converts were sober,
hard-headed, cultivated inquirers; Watsons, Paleys,
Priestleys, on a small scale; weighing evidence, analyzing facts, suggesting doubts, dwelling on distinctions; cold in their dispositions, moderate in their
morals, cautious in their creed. We now know that
these were not they "of whom the world was not
worthy."* It is ascertained that the times of the first
Church were times of excitement; that great ideas
falling on a mingled world were distorted by an untrained intellect, even in the moment in which they
were received by a yearning heart; that strange
confused beliefs—Millennarianism, Gnosticism, Ebion-
itism—were accepted not merely by outlying obscure
heretics, but in a measure, half-and-half, one notion
more by one man, another more by his neighbor,
confusedly and mixedly, by the mass of Christians;
that the appeal was not to the questioning thinking
understanding, but to unheeding all-venturing emotion,—to that lower class "from whom faiths ascend"
and not to the cultivated and exquisite class by whom
they are criticized; that fervid men never embraced
a more exclusive creed. You can say nothing favorable of the first Christians except that they *were*
Christians. We find "no form nor comeliness"† in
them; no intellectual accomplishments, no caution in
action, no discretion in understanding. There is no
admirable quality except that, with whatever distortion or confusion or singularity, they at once accepted
the great clear outline of belief in which to this day
we live, move, and have our being. The offense of
Gibbon is his disinclination to this simple essence;
his excuse, the historical errors then prevalent as to
the primitive Christians, the real defects so natural in
their position, the false merits ascribed to them by
writers who from one reason or another desired to
treat them as "an authority."

---

*Hebrews xi. 38.   † Isaiah liii. 2.

On the whole, therefore, it may be said of the first and in some sense the most important part of Gibbon's work, that though he has given an elaborate outline of the framework of society, and described its detail with pomp and accuracy, yet that he has not comprehended or delineated its nobler essence, pagan or Christian. Nor perhaps was it to be expected that he should, for he inadequately comprehended the dangers of the time: he thought it the happiest period the world has ever known; he would not have comprehended the remark—

"To see the old world in its worst estate, we turn to the age of the satirists and of Tacitus, when all the different streams of evil coming from east, west, north, south, the vices of barbarism and the vices of civilization, remnants of ancient cults and the latest refinements of luxury and impurity, met and mingled on the banks of the Tiber. What could have been the state of society when Tiberius, Caligula, Nero, Domitian, Heliogabalus were the rulers of the world? To a good man, we should imagine that death itself would be more tolerable than the sight of such things coming upon the earth."*

So deep an ethical sensibility was not to be expected in the first century; nor is it strange when, after seventeen hundred years, we do not find it in their historian.

Space has failed us, and we must be unmeaningly brief. The second head of Gibbon's history—the narrative of the barbarian invasions—has been recently criticized, on the ground that he scarcely enough explains the gradual but unceasing and inevitable manner in which the outer barbarians were affected by and assimilated to the civilization of Rome. Mr. Congreve† has well observed that the impression which Gibbon's narrative is insensibly calculated to convey is, that there was little or no change in the state of the Germanic tribes between the time of Tacitus and the final invasion of the empire,—a conclusion which is obviously incredible. To the general reader there

---

* Jowett's "Epistles of St. Paul," Chap. 1. of Romans, "State of the Ancient World."

† "Lectures on the Roman Empire of the West."

will perhaps seem some indistinctness in this part of
the work; nor is a free confused barbarism a congenial subject for an imposing and orderly pencil.
He succeeds better in the delineation of the riding
monarchies, if we may so term them, — of the eques-
trian courts of Attila or Timour, in which the great
scale, the concentrated power, the very enormity of
the barbarism give, so to speak, a shape to unshape-
liness; impart, that is, a horrid dignity to horse-flesh
and mare's milk, an imposing oneness to the vast
materials of a crude barbarity.   It is needless to say
that no one would search Gibbon for an explanation
of the reasons or feelings by which the Northern tribes
were induced to accept Christianity.

It is on the story of Constantinople that the popularity of Gibbon rests.   The vast extent of the topic;
the many splendid episodes it contains; its epic unity
from the moment of the far-seeing selection of the
city by Constantine to its last fall; its position as a
link between Europe and Asia; its continuous history;
the knowledge that through all that time it was, as
now, a diadem by the water-side, a lure to be snatched
by the wistful barbarian, a marvel to the West, a
prize for the North and for the East, — these and such
as these ideas are congenial topics to a style of pomp
and grandeur.   The East seems to require to be treated
with a magnificence unsuitable to a colder soil.   The
nature of the events, too, is suitable to Gibbon's cursory, imposing manner.   It is the history of a form
of civilization, but without the power thereof; a show
of splendor and vigor, but without bold life or interior reality.   What an opportunity for a historian
who loved the imposing pageantry and disliked the
purer essence of existence!   There were here neither
bluff barbarians nor simple saints; there was nothing admitting of particular accumulated detail.   We
do not wish to know the interior of the stage; the
imposing movements are all which should be seized.
Some of the features, too, are curious in relation to

those of the historian's life: the clear accounts of the theological controversies, followed out with an appreciative minuteness so rare in a skeptic, are not disconnected with his early conversion to the scholastic Church; the brilliancy of the narrative reminds us of his enthusiasm for Arabic and the East; the minute description of a licentious epoch evinces the habit of a mind which, not being bold enough for the practice of license, took a pleasure in following its theory. There is no subject which combines so much of unity with so much of variety.

It is evident, therefore, where Gibbon's rank as a historian must finally stand. He cannot be numbered among the great painters of human nature, for he has no sympathy with the heart and passions of our race; he has no place among the felicitous describers of detailed life, for his subject was too vast for minute painting, and his style too uniform for a shifting scene. But he is entitled to a high — perhaps to a first — place among the orderly narrators of great events, the composed expositors of universal history, the tranquil artists who have endeavored to diffuse a cold polish over the warm passions and desultory fortunes of mankind.

The life of Gibbon after the publication of his great work was not very complicated. During its composition he had withdrawn from Parliament and London to the studious retirement of Lausanne. Much eloquence has been expended on this voluntary exile, and it has been ascribed to the best and most profound motives. It is indeed certain that he liked a lettered solitude, preferred easy Continental society, was not quite insensible to the charm of scenery, had a pleasure in returning to the haunts of his youth; prosaic and pure history, however, must explain that he went abroad to *save*.* Lord North had gone out of power;

---

* This was no abstruse discovery: Gibbon plainly states it in his letters, and Macaulay rather absurdly castigates the younger Pitt for not pensioning him. — ED.

Mr. Burke, the Cobden of that era, had procured the abolition of the Lords of Trade: the private income of Gibbon was not equal to his notion of a bachelor London life. The same sum was, however, a fortune at Lausanne. Most things, he acknowledged, were as dear; but then he had not to buy so many things. Eight hundred a year placed him high in the social scale of the place. The inhabitants were gratified that a man of European reputation had selected their out-of-the-way town for the shrine of his fame; he lived pleasantly and easily among easy, pleasant people; a gentle hum of local admiration gradually arose, which yet lingers on the lips of erudite *laquais de place*.* He still retains a fame unaccorded to any other historian, —they speak of the "Hôtel Gibbon": there never was even an *estaminet* Tacitus, or a *café* Thucydides.

This agreeable scene, like many other agreeable scenes, was broken by a great thunder-clap. The French revolution has disgusted many people; but perhaps it has never disgusted any one more than Gibbon. He had swept and garnished everything about him. Externally he had made a neat little hermitage in a gentle, social place; internally he had polished up a still theory of life, sufficient for the guidance of a cold and polished man. Everything seemed to be tranquil with him: the rigid must admit his decorum, the lax would not accuse him of rigor; he was of the world, and an elegant society naturally loved its own. On a sudden the hermitage was disturbed. No place was too calm for that excitement, scarcely any too distant for that uproar. The French war was a war of opinion, entering households, disturbing villages, dividing quiet friends. The Swiss took some of the infection; there was a not unnatural discord between the people of the Pays de Vaud and their masters the people of Berne. The letters of Gibbon are filled with invectives on the "Gallic barbarians" and panegyrics

* Servants who show strangers "the sights."

on Mr. Burke; military details, too, begin to abound,—
the peace of his retirement was at an end. It was
an additional aggravation that the Parisians should
do such things. It would not have seemed unnatural
that Northern barbarians—English, or other uncivilized nations—should break forth in rough riot or cruel
license; but that the people of the most civilized of
all capitals, speaking the sole dialect of polished life,
enlightened with all the enlightenment then known,
should be guilty of excesses unparalleled, unwitnessed,
unheard-of, was a vexing trial to one who had admired
them for many years. The internal creed and belief
of Gibbon was as much attacked by all this as were
his external circumstances. He had spent his time, his
life, his energy, in putting a polished gloss on human
tumult, a sneering gloss on human piety: on a sudden,
human passion broke forth,—the cold and polished
world seemed to meet its end; the thin superficies of
civilization was torn asunder; the fountains of the
great deep seemed opened, impiety to meet its end;*
the foundations of the earth were out of course. We
now, after long familiarity and in much ignorance, can
hardly read the history of those years without horror:
what an effect must they have produced on those whose
minds were fresh, and who knew the people killed!

"Never," Gibbon wrote to an English nobleman, "did a revolution affect to such a degree the private existence of such numbers
of the first people of a great country. Your examples of misery I
could easily match with similar examples in this country and the
neighborhood; and our sympathy is the deeper, as we do not possess like you the means of alleviating in some degree the misfortunes of the fugitives."†

It violently affected his views of English politics. He
before had a tendency, in consideration of his cosmopolitan cultivation, to treat them as local littlenesses,

---

*I dare not disturb these three words, but they are palpably absurd;
probably caught from two lines before, either by Bagehot or the compositor, in
place of the intended expression.—ED.
† To Lord Sheffield, Nov. 10, 1792.

parish squabbles; but now his interest was keen and eager.

"But," he says, "in this rage against slavery, in the numerous petitions against the slave trade, was there no leaven of new democratical principles? no wild ideas of the rights and natural equality of man? It is these I fear. Some articles in newspapers, some pamphlets of the year, the "Jockey Club," have fallen into my hands. I do not infer much from such publications; yet I have never known them of so black and malignant a cast. I shuddered at Grey's motion; disliked the half-support of Fox, admired the firmness of Pitt's declaration, and excused the usual intemperance of Burke. Surely such men as ——, ——, ——, have talents for mischief. I see a club of reform which contains some respectable names. Inform me of the professions, the principles, the plans, the resources of these reformers. Will they heat the minds of the people? Does the French democracy gain no ground? Will the bulk of your party stand firm to their own interest and that of their country? Will you not take some active measures to declare your sound opinions, and separate yourselves from your rotten members? If you allow them to perplex Government, if you trifle with this solemn business, if you do not resist the spirit of innovation in the first attempt, if you admit the smallest and most specious change in our parliamentary system, you are lost. You will be driven from one step to another; from principles just in theory to consequences most pernicious in practice: and your first concessions will be productive of every subsequent mischief, for which you will be answerable to your country and to posterity. Do not suffer yourselves to be lulled into a false security: remember the proud fabric of the French monarchy. Not four years ago it stood founded, as it might seem, on the rock of time, force, and opinion; supported by the triple aristocracy of the Church, the nobility, and the Parliaments. They are crumbled into dust; they are vanished from the earth. If this tremendous warning has no effect on the men of property in England; if it does not open every eye and raise every arm, — you will deserve your fate. If I am too precipitate, enlighten; if I am too desponding, encourage me. My pen has run into this argument; for, as much a foreigner as you think me, on this momentous subject I feel myself an Englishman."*

The truth clearly is, that he had arrived at the conclusion that he was the sort of person a populace

* To Lord Sheffield, May 30, 1792.

kill. People wonder a great deal why very many of the victims of the French revolution were particularly selected; the Marquis de Custine, especially, cannot divine why they executed *his* father. The historians cannot show that they committed any particular crimes; the marquises and marchionesses seem very inoffensive. The fact evidently is, that they were killed for being polite; the world felt itself unworthy of them. There were so many bows, such· regular smiles, such calm superior condescension, — could a mob be asked to endure it? Have we not all known a precise, formal, patronizing old gentleman, —bland, imposing, something like Gibbon? Have we not suffered from his dignified attentions? If *we* had been on the Committee of Public Safety, can we doubt what would have been the fate of that man? Just so, wrath and envy destroyed in France an upperclass world.

After his return to England, Gibbon did not do much or live long. He completed his "Memoirs," the most imposing of domestic narratives, the model of dignified detail. As we said before, if the Roman empire *had* written about itself, this was how it would have done so. He planned some other works, but executed none; judiciously observing that building castles in the air was more agreeable than building them on the ground. His career was, however, drawing to an end; earthly dignity had its limits, even the dignity of a historian. He had long been stout; and now symptoms of dropsy began to appear. After a short interval, he died on the 16th of January, 1794. We have sketched his character, and have no more to say. After all, what is our criticism worth? It only fulfills his aspiration, "that a hundred years hence I may still continue to be abused."*

---

* "Memoirs."

THOMAS BABINGTON MACAULAY.*

(1856.)

THIS is a marvelous book. Everybody has read it, and every one has read it with pleasure. It has little advantage of subject: when the volumes came out, an honest man said, "I suppose something happened between the years 1689 and 1697; but what happened I do not know." Every one knows now; no period with so little obvious interest will henceforth be so familiarly known. Only a most felicitous and rather curious genius could and would shed such a light on such an age. If in the following pages we seem to cavil and find fault, let it be remembered that the business of a critic is criticism; that it is *not* his business to be thankful; that he must attempt an estimate rather than a eulogy.

Macaulay seems to have in a high degree the temperament most likely to be that of a historian. This may be summarily defined as the temperament which inclines men to take an interest in actions as contrasted with objects, and in past actions in preference to present actions. We should expand our meaning. Some people are unfortunately born scientific. They take much interest in the objects of nature; they feel a curiosity about shells, snails, horses, butterflies; they are delighted at an ichthyosaurus and excited at a polyp; they are learned in minerals, vegetables, animals; they have skill in fishes and attain renown in pebbles; in the highest cases they know the great

---

* The History of England from the Accession of James II. By Thomas Babington Macaulay. Longmans.

(58)

causes of grand phenomena, can indicate the courses
of the stars or the current of the waves: but in every
case their minds are directed not to the actions of
man, but to the scenery amidst which he lives; not to
the inhabitants of this world, but to the world itself;
not to what most resembles themselves, but to that
which is most unlike. What compels men to take an
interest in what they do take an interest in, is commonly a difficult question, — for the most part, indeed,
it is an insoluble one; but in this case it would
seem to have a negative cause, — to result from the
absence of an intense and vivid nature. The inclination of mind which abstracts the attention from that
in which it can feel sympathy to that in which it
cannot, seems to arise from a want of sympathy. A
tendency to devote the mind to trees and stones as
much as, or in preference to, men and women, appears
to imply that the intellectual qualities, the abstract
reason, and the inductive scrutiny which can be applied equally to trees and to men, to stones and to
women, predominate over the more special qualities
solely applicable to our own race, — the keen love, the
eager admiration, the lasting hatred, the lust of rule
which fastens men's interests on people and to people.
As a confirmation of this, we see that even in the
greatest cases, scientific men have been calm men.
Their actions are unexceptionable; scarcely a spot
stains their excellence; if a doubt is to be thrown
on their character, it would be rather that they were
insensible to the temptations than that they were involved in the offenses of ordinary men. An aloofness
and abstractedness cleave to their greatness; there is
a coldness in their fame. We think of Euclid as of
fine ice; we admire Newton as we admire the peak
of Teneriffe. Even the intensest labors, the most
remote triumphs of the abstract intellect seem to carry
us into a region different from our own, to be in a
terra incognita of pure reasoning, to cast a chill on
human glory.

We know that the taste of most persons· is quite opposite: the tendency of man is to take an interest in man, and almost in man only. The world has a vested interest in itself. Analyze the minds of the crowd of men, and what will you find? Something of the outer earth, no doubt: odd geography, odd astronomy,—doubts whether Scutari is in the Crimea', investigations whether the moon is less or greater than Jupiter; some idea of herbs, more of horses; ideas, too, more or less vague, of the remote and supernatural,—notions which the tongue cannot speak, which it would seem the world would hardly bear if thoroughly spoken. Yet, setting aside these which fill the remote corners and lesser outworks of the brain, the whole stress and vigor of the ordinary faculties is expended on their possessor and his associates, on the man and on his fellows. In almost all men, indeed, this is not simply an intellectual contemplation; we not only look on, but act. The impulse to busy ourselves with the affairs of men goes further than the simple attempt to know and comprehend them: it warms us with a further life; it incites us to stir and influence those affairs; its animated energy will not rest till it has hurried us into toil and conflict. At this stage the mind of the historian, as we abstractedly fancy it, naturally breaks off: it has more interest in human affairs than the naturalist, it instinctively selects the actions of man for occupation and scrutiny in preference to the habits of fishes or the structure of stones, but it has not so much vivid interest in them as the warm and active man. To know is sufficient for it; it can bear not to take a part. A want of impulse seems born with the disposition. To be constantly occupied about the actions of others; to have constantly presented to your contemplation and attention, events and occurrences memorable only as evincing certain qualities of mind and will, which very qualities in a measure you feel within yourself, and yet to be without an impulse to

exhibit them in the real world, "which is the world
of all of us;"* to contemplate, yet never act; to "have
the House before you," and yet to be content with
the reporters' gallery,—shows a chill impassiveness
of temperament, a sluggish insensibility to ardent
impulse, a heavy immobility under ordinary emotion.
.The image of the stout Gibbon placidly contemplating
the animated conflicts, the stirring pleadings of Fox
and Burke, watching a revolution and heavily taking
no part in it, gives an idea of the historian as he is
likely to be. "Why," it is often asked, "is history
dull? it is a narrative of life, and life is of all things
the most interesting." The answer is, that it is written by men too dull to take the common interest in
life, in whom languor predominates over zeal and
sluggishness over passion.

Macaulay is not dull, and it may seem hard to
attempt to bring him within the scope of a theory
which is so successful in explaining dullness; yet, in
a modified and peculiar form, we can perhaps find in
his remarkable character unusually distinct traces of
the insensibility which we ascribe to the historian.
The means of scrutiny are ample,—Macaulay has not
spent his life in a corner; if posterity should refuse—
of course they will not refuse—to read a line of his
writings, they would yet be sought out by studious
inquirers as those of a man of high political position,
great notoriety, and greater oratorical power. We are
not therefore obliged, as in so many cases even among
contemporaries, to search for the author's character
in his books alone; we are able from other sources
to find out his character, and then apply it to explain
the peculiarities of his works. Macaulay has exhibited
many high attainments, many dazzling talents, much
singular and well-trained power; but the quality which
would most strike the observers of the interior man
is what may be called his *in*experiencing nature. Men
of genius are in general distinguished by their extreme susceptibility to external experience. Finer and

* Wordsworth, "Prelude," Book xi.

softer than other men, every exertion of their will,
every incident of their lives influences them more
deeply than it would others. Their essence is at once
finer and more impressible; it receives a distincter
mark and receives it more easily than the souls of
the herd. From a peculiar sensibility, the man of
genius bears the stamp of life commonly more clearly,
than his fellows; even casual associations make a
deep impression on him: examine his mind, and you
may discern his fortunes. Macaulay has nothing of
this: you could not tell what he has been; his mind
shows no trace of change. What he is, he was; and
what he was, he is. He early attained a high development, but he has not increased it since; years have
come, but they have whispered little; as was said of
the second Pitt, "He never grew, he was cast." The
volume of "Speeches" which he has published place
the proof of this in every man's hand: his first
speeches are as good as his last, his last scarcely
richer than his first. He came into public life at an
exciting season, he shared of course in that excitement, and the same excitement still quivers in his
mind. He delivered marvelous rhetorical exercises on
the Reform Bill when it passed; he speaks of it with
rhetorical interest even now. He is still the man of
'32: from that era he looks on the past; he sees "Old
Sarum" in the seventeenth century and Gatton in the
civil wars. You may fancy an undertone:—The Norman barons commenced the series of reforms which
"we consummated"; Hampden was preparing for
"the occasion in which I had a part," William for
"the debate in which I took occasion to observe—"
With a view to that era everything begins; up to
that moment everything ascends. That was the
"fifth act" of the human race; the remainder of history is only an afterpiece. All this was very natural
at the moment: nothing could be more probable than
that a young man of the greatest talents, entering at
once into important life at a conspicuous opportunity,

should exaggerate its importance; he would fancy it
was the "crowning achievement," the greatest "in
the tide of time." But the singularity is, that he
should retain the idea now; that years have brought
no influence, experience no change. The events of
twenty years have been full of rich instruction on
the events of twenty years ago; but they have not
instructed him,—his creed is a fixture. It is the
same on his peculiar topic,—on India. Before he
went there he made a speech on the subject: Lord
Canterbury, who must have heard a million speeches,
said it was the best he had ever heard. It is difficult to fancy that so much vivid knowledge could be
gained from books—from horrible Indian treatises;
that such imaginative mastery should be possible without actual experience. Not forgetting or excepting
the orations of Burke, it was perhaps as remarkable a
speech as was ever made on India by an Englishman
who had not been in India. Now he has been there he
speaks no better,—rather worse; he spoke excellently
without experience, he speaks no better with it,—if
anything, it rather puts him out. His speech on the
Indian charter a year or two ago was not finer than
that on the charter of 1833. Before he went to India
he recommended that writers should be examined in
the classics; after being in India he recommended
that they should be examined in the same way. He
did not say he had seen the place in the mean time:
he did not think that had anything to do with it.
You could never tell from any difference in his style
what he had seen or what he had not seen. He is so
insensible to passing objects that they leave no distinctive mark, no intimate peculiar trace.

Such a man would naturally think literature more
instructive than life. Hazlitt said of Mackintosh,
"He might like to read an *account* of India; but
India itself, with its burning, shining face, would be
a mere blank, an endless waste to him. . . . Persons of
this class . . . have no more to say to a matter of

fact staring them in the face without a label in its mouth than they would to a hippopotamus."* This was a keen criticism on Sir James, savoring of the splenetic mind from which it came. As a complete estimate, it would be a most unjust one of Macaulay; but we know that there is a whole class of minds which prefers the literary delineation of objects to the actual eyesight of them. To some, life is difficult. An insensible nature, like a rough hide, resists the breath of passing things; an unobserving retina in vain depicts whatever a quicker eye does not explain. But any one can understand a book: the work is done, the facts observed, the formulæ suggested, the subjects classified. Of course it needs labor and a following fancy to peruse the long lucubrations and descriptions of others: but a fine detective sensibility is unnecessary; type is plain, an earnest attention will follow it and know it. To this class Macaulay belongs; and he has characteristically maintained that dead authors are more fascinating than living people.

"These friendships," he tells us, "are exposed to no danger from the occurrences by which other attachments are weakened or dissolved. Time glides on: fortune is inconstant; tempers are soured; bonds which seemed indissoluble are daily sundered by interest, by emulation, or by caprice. But no such cause can affect the silent converse which we hold with the highest of human intellects. That placid intercourse is disturbed by no jealousies or resentments. These are the old friends who are never seen with new faces; who are the same in wealth and in poverty, in glory and in obscurity. With the dead there is no rivalry; in the dead there is no change. Plato is never sullen; Cervantes is never petulant; Demosthenes never comes unseasonably; Dante never stays too long. No difference of political opinion can alienate Cicero; no heresy can excite the horror of Bossuet."†

But Bossuet is dead, and Cicero was a Roman, and Plato wrote in Greek; years and manners separate us from the great. After dinner, Demosthenes *may* come unseasonably, Dante *might* stay too long. *We*

---

*Essay in the "Spirit of the Age."   † Essay on Bacon.

are alienated from the politician and have a horror of the theologian. Dreadful idea, having Demosthenes for an intimate friend! he had pebbles in his mouth; he was always urging action; he spoke such good Greek, — we cannot dwell on it, it is too much. Only a mind impassive to our daily life, unalive to bores and evils, to joys and sorrows, incapable of the deepest sympathies, a prey to print, could imagine it. The mass of men have stronger ties and warmer hopes; the exclusive devotion to books tires: we require to love and hate, to act and live.

It is not unnatural that a person of this temperament should preserve a certain aloofness even in the busiest life; Macaulay has ever done so. He has been in the thick of political warfare, in the van of party conflict; whatever a keen excitability would select for food and opportunity, has been his: but he has not been excited. He has never thrown himself upon action, he has never followed trivial details with an anxious passion. He has ever been a man for a great occasion. He was by nature a *deus ex machina:* somebody has had to fetch him. His heart was in Queen Anne's time; when he came, he spoke as Lord Halifax might have spoken. Of course it may be contended that this is the *eximia ars,** that this solitary removed excellence is particularly and essentially sublime; but, simply and really, greater men have been more deeply "immersed in matter."† The highest eloquence quivers with excitement; there is life-blood in the deepest action; a man like Strafford seems flung upon the world. An orator should never talk like an observatory; no coldness should strike upon the hearer.

It is characteristic also that Macaulay should be continually thinking of posterity. In general that expected authority is most ungrateful: those who think of it most, it thinks of least. The way to secure its

---

* "Choice character."
† "Locke on the Human Understanding," Book iv., Chap. iii., l. 2.

favor is, to give vivid essential pictures of the life before you; to leave a fresh glowing delineation of the scene to which you were born, of the society to which you have peculiar access. This is gained not by thinking of your posterity, but by living in society; not by poring on what is to be, but by enjoying what is. That spirit of thorough enjoyment which pervades the great delineators of human life and human manners was not caused by being "made after supper of a cheese-paring"*; it drew its sustenance from a relishing, enjoying, sensitive life, and the flavor of the description is the reality of that enjoyment. Of course this is not so in science: you may leave a name by an abstract discovery without having led a vigorous existence; yet what a name is this! Taylor's theorem will go down to posterity, — possibly its discoverer was forever dreaming and expecting it would; but what does posterity know of the deceased Taylor? *Nominis umbra*† is rather a compliment; for it is not substantial enough to have a shadow. But in other walks — say in political oratory, which is the part of Macaulay's composition in which his value for posterity's opinion is most apparent — the way to interest posterity is to think but little of it. What gives to the speeches of Demosthenes the interest they have? The intense, vivid, glowing interest of the speaker in all that he is speaking about. Philip is not a person "whom posterity will censure," but the man "whom I hate"; the matter in hand not one whose interest depends on the memory of men, but in which an eager intense nature would have been absorbed if there had been no posterity at all, on which he wished to deliver his own soul. A *casual* character, so to speak, is natural to the most intense words: externally even, they will interest the "after world" more for having interested the present world; they must have a life of *some* place and *some* time before they

---

* "2 King Henry IV.," iii. 2.

† *Stat nominis umbra* ("the shadow of a name endures"), the famous motto of "Junius." — ED.

can have one of all space and all time. Macaulay's
oratory is the very opposite of this. Schoolboyish it
is not, for it is the oratory of a very sensible man;
but the theme of a schoolboy is not more devoid of
the salt of circumstance. The speeches on the Reform
Bill have been headed, ".Now, a man came up from
college and spoke thus;" and like a college man, he
spoke rather to the abstract world than to the present. He knew no more of the people who actually
did live in London than of people who would live in
London, and there was therefore no reason for speaking to one more than to the other. After years of
politics, he speaks so still: he looks on a question
(he says) as posterity will look on it; he appeals from
this to future generations; he regards existing men
as painful prerequisites of great-grandchildren. This
seems to proceed, as has been said, from a distant
and unimpressible nature; but it is impossible to deny
that it has one great advantage, — it has made him
take pains. A man who speaks to people a thousand
years off will naturally speak carefully; he tries to
be heard over the clang of ages, over the rumors of
myriads. Writing for posterity is like writing on foreign post paper; you cannot say to a man at Calcutta
what you would say to a man at Hackney. You
think, "The yellow man is a very long way off; this
is fine paper, it will go by a ship:" so you try to say
something worthy of the ship, something noble which
will keep and travel. Writers like Macaulay, who
think of future people, have a respect for future people: each syllable is solemn, each word distinct. No
author trained to periodical writing has so little of
its slovenliness and its imperfection.

This singularly constant contemplation of posterity
has colored his estimate of social characters. He has
no toleration for those great men in whom a lively
sensibility to momentary honors has prevailed over a
consistent reference to the posthumous tribunal. He
is justly severe on Lord Bacon : —

"In his library all his rare powers were under the guidance of an honest ambition, of an enlarged philanthropy, of a sincere love of truth. There no temptation drew him away from the right course. Thomas Aquinas could pay no fees, Duns Scotus could confer no peerages, the 'Master of the Sentences'* had no rich reversions in his gift. Far different was the situation of the great philosopher when he came forth from his study and his laboratory to mingle with the crowd which filled the galleries of Whitehall. In all that crowd there was no man equally qualified to render great and lasting services to mankind. But in all that crowd there was not a heart more set on things which no man ought to suffer to be necessary to his happiness, — on things which can often be obtained only by the sacrifice of integrity and honor. To be the leader of the human race in the career of improvement, to found on the ruins of ancient intellectual dynasties a more prosperous and a more enduring empire, to be revered by the latest generations as the most illustrious among the benefactors of mankind, — all this was within his reach. But all this availed him nothing, while some quibbling special pleader was promoted before him to the bench; while some heavy country gentleman took precedence of him by virtue of a purchased coronet; while some pandar, happy in a fair wife, could obtain a more cordial salute from Buckingham; while some buffoon, versed in all the latest scandal of the court, could draw a louder laugh from James."

Yet a less experience or a less opportunity of experience would have warned a mind more observant that the bare desire for long posthumous renown is but a feeble principle in common human nature; Bacon had as much of it as most men. The keen excitability to this world's temptations must be opposed by more exciting impulses, by more retarding discouragements, — by conscience, by religion, by fear; if you would vanquish earth, you must "invent heaven." It is the fiction of a cold abstractedness that the possible respect of unseen people can commonly be more desired than the certain homage of existing people.

In a more conspicuous manner, the chill nature of the most brilliant among English historians is shown in his defective dealing with the passionate eras of our history. He has never been attracted, or not

---

* Peter the Lombard, author of a famous collection of "Sentences" from the Church fathers. — ED.

proportionally attracted, by the singular mixture of
heroism and slavishness, of high passion and base
passion, which mark the Tudor period. The defect is
apparent in his treatment of a period on which he has
written powerfully, — the time of the civil wars: he
has never in the highest manner appreciated either of
the two great characters — the Puritan and the Cavalier — which are the form and life of those years. What
historian, indeed, has ever estimated the Cavalier
character? There is Clarendon, the grave, rhetorical,
decorous lawyer, piling words, congealing arguments;
very stately, a little grim. There is Hume, the Scotch
metaphysician, who has made out the best case for
such people as never were, for a Charles who never
died, for a Strafford who would never have been
attainted; a saving, calculating North-countryman,
fat, impassive, who lived on eightpence a day. What
have these people to do with an enjoying English
gentleman? It is easy for a *doctrinaire* to bear a
post-mortem examination, — it is much the same
whether he be alive or dead; but not so with those
who live during their life, whose essence is existence,
whose being is in animation. There seem to be some
characters who are not made for history, as there are
some who are not made for old age. A Cavalier is
always young. The buoyant life arises before us, rich
in hope, strong in vigor, irregular in action: men
young and ardent, "framed in the prodigality of nature;"* open to every enjoyment, alive to every passion, eager, impulsive; brave without discipline, noble
without principle; prizing luxury, despising danger;
capable of high sentiment, but in each of whom the

> "Addiction was to courses.vain;
> His companies unlettered, rude and shallow,
> His hours filled up with riots, banquets, sports,
> And never noted in him any study,
> Any retirement, any sequestration
> From open haunts and popularity."†

---

* "King Richard III.," 1. 2.   † "Henry V.," 1. 1.

We see these men setting forth or assembling to
defend their king and church, and we see it without
surprise: a rich daring loves danger, a deep excitability likes excitement. If we look around us, we
may see what is analogous: some say that the battle
of the Alma was won by the "uneducated gentry";
the "uneducated gentry" would be Cavaliers now.
The political sentiment is part of the character; the
essence of Toryism is enjoyment. Talk of the ways
of spreading a wholesome Conservatism throughout
this country! Give painful lectures, distribute weary
tracts (and perhaps this is as well,—you may be able
to give an argumentative answer to a few objections,
you may diffuse a distinct notion of the dignified
dullness of politics); but as far as communicating
and establishing your creed are concerned, try a little pleasure. The way to keep up old customs is, to
enjoy old customs; the way to be satisfied with the
present state of things is, to enjoy that state of
things. Over the "Cavalier" mind this world passes
with a thrill of delight; there is an exultation in a
daily event, zest in the "regular thing," joy at an
old feast. Sir Walter Scott is an example of this:
every habit and practice of old Scotland was inseparably in his mind associated with genial enjoyment;
to propose to touch one of her institutions, to abolish
one of those practices, was to touch a personal pleasure,—a point on which his mind reposed, a thing
of memory and hope. So long as this world is this
world, will a buoyant life be the proper source of
an animated Conservatism. The "church-and-king"
enthusiasm has even a deeper connection with the
Cavaliers. Carlyle has said, in his vivid way, "Two
or three young gentlemen have said, 'Go to, I will
make a religion.'"* This is the exact opposite of
what the irregular enjoying man can think or conceive. What! is he, with his untrained mind and his
changeful heart and his ruleless practice, to create a

_____

* "Essay on Characteristics," Book iii.: "In France, among the younger
nobler minds, . . . this and the other earnest man has not been wanting,
who could whisper audibly," etc.

creed ? is the gushing life to be asked to construct a
cistern ? is the varying heart to be its own master, the
evil practice its own guide ? Sooner will a ship invent
its own rudder, devise its own pilot, than the eager
being will find out the doctrine which is to restrain
him. The very intellect is a type of the confusion
of the soul : it has little arguments on a thousand
subjects ; hearsay sayings ; original flashes, small and
bright, struck from the heedless mind by the strong
impact of the world, — and it has nothing else. It
has no systematic knowledge ; it has a hatred of regular attention. What can an understanding of this
sort do with refined questioning or subtle investigation ?
It is obliged in a sense, by its very nature, to take
what comes ; it is overshadowed in a manner by the
religion to which it is born. Its conscience tells it
that it owes obedience to something ; it craves to
worship something : that something, in both cases, it
takes from the past. " Thou hast not chosen me, but
I have chosen thee," * might his faith say to a believer
of this kind : a certain bigotry is altogether natural
to him ; his creed seems to him a primitive fact,
as certain and evident as the stars. The political
faith (for it is a faith) of these persons is of a kind
analogous : the virtue of loyalty assumes in them a
passionate aspect, and overflows, as it were, all the
intellect which belongs to the topic. This virtue,
this need of our nature, arises, as political philosophers tell us, from the conscious necessity which man
is under of obeying an external moral rule. We feel
that we are by nature and by the constitution of all
things under an obligation to conform to a certain
standard ; and we seek to find or to establish, in the
sphere without, an authority which shall enforce it,
shall aid us in compelling others and also in mastering ourselves. When a man impressed with this
principle comes in contact with the institution of civil
government, as it now exists and as it has always

* " Ye have not chosen me, but I have chosen you." — John xv. 16.

existed, he finds what he wants,—he discovers an authority; and he feels bound to submit to it. We do not, of course, mean that all this takes place distinctly and consciously in the mind of the person; on the contrary, the class of minds most subject to its influence are precisely those which have in general the least defined and accurate consciousness of their own operations or of what befalls them. In matter of fact, they find themselves under the control of laws and of a polity from the earliest moment that they can remember, and they obey it from habit and custom years before they know why. Only in later life, when distinct thought is from an outward occurrence forced upon them, do they feel the necessity of some such power; and in proportion to their passionate and impulsive disposition they feel it the more. The law has in a less degree on them the same effect which military discipline has in a greater: it braces them to defined duties and subjects them to a known authority. Quieter minds find this authority in an internal conscience: but in riotous natures its still small voice is lost if it be not echoed in loud harsh tones from the firm and outer world;

> "Their breath is agitation, and their life
> A storm whereon they ride;"*

from without they crave a bridle and a curb. The doctrine of non-resistance is no *accident* of the Cavalier character, though it seems at first sight singular in an eager tumultuous disposition: so inconsistent is human nature, that it proceeds from the very extremity of that tumult. They know that they cannot allow themselves to question the authority which is upon them,—they feel its necessity too acutely; their intellect is untrained in subtle disquisitions, their conscience fluctuating, their passions rising. They are sure that if they once depart from that authority, their whole soul will be in anarchy. As a riotous

* "Childe Harold," Canto iii., verse 44.

state tends to fall under a martial tyranny, a passionate mind tends to subject itself to an extrinsic law, to enslave itself to an outward discipline. "That is what the king says, boy, and that was ever enough for Sir Henry Lee."* A hereditary monarch is indeed the very embodiment of this principle,—the authority is so defined, so clearly vested, so evidently intelligible; it descends so distinctly from the past, it is imposed so conspicuously from without. Anything free refers to the people ; anything elected seems self-chosen. The "divinity" that "doth hedge a king"† consists in his evidently representing an unmade, unchosen, hereditary duty.

The greatness of this character is not in Macaulay's way, and its faults are. Its license affronts him, its riot alienates him. He is forever contrasting the dissoluteness of Prince Rupert's horse with the restraint of Cromwell's pikemen ; a deep enjoying nature finds no sympathy. The brilliant style passes forward ; we dwell on its brilliancy, but it is cold : Macaulay has no tears for that warm life, no tenderness for that extinct joy. The ignorance of the Cavalier, too, moves his wrath : they were "ignorant of what every schoolgirl knows." Their loyalty to their sovereign is the devotion of the Egyptians to the god Apis, who‡ selected a "calf to adore."‖ Their non-resistance offends the philosopher, their license is commented on with the tone of a precisian, their indecorum does not suit the dignity of the narrator. Their rich, free nature is unappreciated, the tingling intensity of their joy is unnoticed. In a word, there is something of the schoolboy about the Cavalier, there is somewhat of a schoolmaster about the historian.

It might be thought, at first sight, that the insensibility and coldness which are unfavorable to the

---

*Non-existent : probably a misty memory of this from Chap. xxxvii. of "Woodstock":—"The King, had he no other subject in England, should dispose at will of those of the house of Lee."—ED.

†"Hamlet," iv. 5.   ‡A characteristic misplacement.—ED.

‖Second Essay on Lord Chatham.

appreciation of the Cavalier would be particularly favorable to that of the Puritan; some may say that a
natural aloofness from things earthly would dispose
a man to the doctrines of a sect which enjoins above
all other commandments, abstinence and aloofness
from those things. In Macaulay's case it certainly
has had no such consequence. He was bred up in the
circle which more than any other has resembled that
of the greatest and best Puritans, in the circle which
has presented the evangelical doctrine in its most influential and celebrated and not its least genial form;
yet he has revolted against it. "The bray of Exeter
Hall"* is a phrase which has become celebrated; it
is an odd one for his father's son. The whole course
of his personal fortunes, the entire scope of his historical narrative, show an utter want of sympathy with
the Puritan disposition. It would be idle to quote
passages: it will be enough to recollect the contrast
between the estimate, say of Cromwell, by Carlyle
and that by Macaulay, to be aware of the enormous
discrepancy; the one's manner evinces an instinctive
sympathy, the other's an instinctive aversion.

We believe that this is but a consequence of the
same impassibility of nature which we have said so
much of. M. de Montalembert, in a striking *éloge* on
a French historian, †—a man of the Southey type,—
after speaking of his life in Paris during youth (a
youth cast in the early and exciting years of the first
Revolution, and of the prelude to it), and graphically
portraying a man subject to skepticism but not given
to vice, staid in habits but unbelieving in opinion,
without faith and without irregularity, winds up the
whole by the sentence that "*he was hardened at once
against good and evil.*" ‡ In his view, the insensibility

* "Exeter Hall sets up its bray." — Speech on the Maynooth College Bill.
† Droz (author of the "History of Louis XVI.," etc.), whom Montalembert succeeded in the Académie Française, and whose *éloge* he pronounced
according to custom on Dec. 5, 1852. — ED.
‡ Canceled in the collected edition of Montalembert's Works.—ED.

which was a guard against exterior temptation was
also a hindrance to inward belief; and there is a philosophy in this. The nature of man is not two things,
but one thing; we have not one set of affections,
hopes, sensibilities to be affected by the present world,
and another and a different to be affected by the invisible world. We are moved by grandeur or we are
not, we are stirred by sublimity or we are not, we
hunger after righteousness or we do not, we hate
vice or we do not; we are passionate or not passionate, loving or not loving, cold or not cold; our heart
is dull or it is wakeful; our soul is alive or it is
dead. Deep under the surface of the intellect lies
the stratum of the passions, of the intense, peculiar,
simple impulses which constitute the heart of man;
there is the eager essence, the primitive desiring being.
What stirs this latent being we know: in general it is
stirred by everything. Sluggish natures are stirred
little, wild natures are stirred much; but all are
stirred somewhat. It is not important whether the
object be in the visible or invisible world: whoso loves
what he has seen, will love what he has not seen;
whoso hates what he has seen, will hate what he has
not seen. Creation is, as it were, but the garment of
the Creator: whoever is blind to the beauty on its surface will be insensible to the beauty beneath; whoso is
dead to the sublimity before his senses will be dull to
that which he imagines; whoso is untouched by the
visible man will be unmoved by the invisible God.
These are no new ideas, and the conspicuous evidence
of history confirms them: everywhere the deep religious organization has been deeply sensitive to this
world. If we compare what are called sacred and
profane literatures, the depth of human affection is
deepest in the sacred; a warmth as of life is on the
Hebrew, a chill as of marble is on the Greek. In
Jewish history the most tenderly religious character
is the most sensitive to earth. Along every lyric of
the Psalmist thrills a deep spirit of human enjoyment:

he was alive as a child to the simple aspects of the world; the very errors of his mingled career are but those to which the open, enjoying character is most prone; its principle, so to speak, was a tremulous passion for that which he had seen as well as that which he had not seen. There is no paradox, therefore, in saying that the same character which least appreciates the impulsive and ardent Cavalier is also the most likely not to appreciate the warm zeal of an overpowering devotion.

Some years ago it would have been necessary to show at length that the Puritans had such a devotion: the notion had been that they were fanatics who simulated zeal, and hypocrites who misquoted the Old Testament. A new era has arrived; one of the great discoveries which the competition of authors has introduced into historical researches has attained a singular popularity. Times are changed; we are rather now, in general, in danger of holding too high an estimate of the Puritanical character than a too low or contemptuous one. Among the disciples of Carlyle it is considered that having been a Puritan is the next best thing to having been in Germany. But though we cannot sympathize with everything that the expounders of the new theory allege, and though we should not select for praise the exact peculiarities most agreeable to the slightly grim "gospel of earnestness," we acknowledge the great service which they have rendered to English history. No one will now ever overlook that in the greater, in the original Puritans, — in Cromwell, for example, — the whole basis of the character was a passionate, deep, rich religious organization.

This is not in Macaulay's way. It is not that he is skeptical; far from it. "Divines of all persuasions," he tells us, "are agreed that there is a religion,"*

---

* The nearest approach to this amazing "quotation" I find in Macaulay is this from the review of "Gladstone on Church and State":—"In all ages and nations, men of all orders of intellect . . . have believed in the existence of some superior mind."—ED.

and he acquiesces in their teaching. But he has no passionate self-questionings, no indomitable fears, no asking perplexities. He is probably pleased at the exemption : he has praised Bacon for a similar want of interest.

"Nor did he ever meddle with those enigmas which have puzzled hundreds of generations, and will puzzle hundreds more. He said nothing about the grounds of moral obligation, or the freedom of the human will. He had no inclination to employ himself in labors resembling those of the damned in the Grecian Tartarus, — to spin forever on the same wheel round the same pivot. . . . He lived in an age in which disputes on the most subtle points of divinity excited an intense interest throughout Europe, and nowhere more than in England. He was placed in the very thick of the conflict. He was in power at the time of the Synod of Dort, and must for months have been daily deafened with talk about election, reprobation, and final perseverance. Yet we do not remember a line in his works from which it can be inferred that he was either a Calvinist or an Arminian. While the world was resounding with the noise of a disputatious philosophy and a disputatious theology, the Baconian school, like *Allworthy* seated between *Square* and *Thwackum*,* preserved a calm neutrality, — half scornful, half benevolent, — and content with adding to the sum of practical good, left the war of words to those who liked it."

This may be the writing of good sense, but it is not the expression of an anxious or passionate religious nature.

Such is the explanation of Macaulay's not prizing so highly as he should prize the essential excellences of the Puritan character. He is defective in the one point in which they were very great; he is eminent in the very point in which they were most defective. A spirit of easy cheerfulness pervades his writings, a pleasant geniality overflows his history; the rigid asceticism, the pain for pain's sake of the Puritan is altogether alien to him. Retribution he would deny; sin is hardly a part of his creed. His religion is one of thanksgiving; his notion of philosophy — it would

---

* In Fielding's "Tom Jones."

be a better notion of his own writing — is, *illustrans commoda vitæ.**

The English Revolution is the very topic for a person of this character: it is evidently an unimpassioned movement. It requires no appreciation of the Cavalier or of the zealot; no sympathy with the romance of this world, no inclination to pass beyond and absorb the mind's energies in another. It had neither the rough enthusiasm of barbarism nor the delicate grace of high civilization; the men who conducted it had neither the deep spirit of Cromwell's Puritans nor the chivalric loyalty of the enjoying English gentleman. They were hard-headed sensible men, who knew that politics were a kind of business; that the essence of business is compromise, of practicality concession. They drove no theory to excess; for they had no theory. Their passions did not hurry them away; for their temperament was still, their reason calculating and calm. Locke is the type of the best character of his era: there is nothing in him which a historian such as we have described could fail to comprehend, or could not sympathize with when he did comprehend. He was the very reverse of a Cavalier: he came of a Puritan stock; he retained through life a kind of chilled Puritanism; he had nothing of its excessive, overpowering interior zeal, but he retained the formal decorum which it had given to the manners, the solid earnestness of its intellect, the heavy respectability of its character. In all the nations across which Puritanism has passed, you may notice something of its indifference to this world's lighter enjoyments; no one of them has been quite able to retain its singular interest in what is beyond the veil of time and sense. The generation to which we owe our Revolution was in the first stage of the descent: Locke thought a zealot a dangerous person, and a poet little better than a rascal. It has been said, with perhaps an allusion to Macaulay, that

---

* " Explaining the comforts of life."

our historians have held that "all the people who
lived before 1688 were either knaves or fools." This
is of course an exaggeration; but those who have
considered what sort of person a historian is likely
to be, will not be surprised at his preference for the
people of that era. They had the equable sense which
he appreciates; they had not the deep animated passions to which his nature is insensible.

Yet though Macaulay shares in the common temperament of historians, and in the sympathy with and
appreciation of the characters most congenial to that
temperament, he is singularly contrasted with them
in one respect: he has a vivid fancy, they have a
dull one. History is generally written on the principle
that human life is a transaction; that people come
to it with defined intentions and a calm self-possessed
air, as stock-jobbers would buy "omnium," as tim-
ber merchants buy "best middling": people are alike
and things are alike; everything is a little dull, every
one a little slow; manners are not depicted, traits are
not noticed; the narrative is confined to those great
transactions which can be understood without any imaginative delineation of their accompaniments. There
are two kinds of things, — those which you need only
to *understand,* and those which you need also to
imagine. That a man bought nine hundredweight of
hops is an intelligible idea, — you do not want the hops
delineated or the man described; that he went into
society suggests an inquiry, — you want to know what
the society was like and how far he was fitted to be
there. The great business transactions of the political
world are of the intelligible description. Macaulay
has himself said, —

"A history in which every particular incident may be true, may
on the whole be false. The circumstances which have most influence
on the happiness of mankind, — the changes of manners and morals,
the transition of communities from poverty to wealth, from knowledge
to ignorance, from ferocity to humanity, — these are for the most
part noiseless revolutions. Their progress is rarely indicated by

what historians are pleased to call 'important events.' They are not achieved by armies or enacted by senates. They are sanctioned by no treaties and recorded in no archives. They are carried on in every school, in every church, behind ten thousand counters, at ten thousand firesides. The upper current of society presents no certain criterion by which we can judge of the direction in which the under current flows. We read of defeats and victories; but we know that nations may be miserable amidst victories and prosperous amidst defeats. We read of the fall of wise ministers and of the rise of profligate favorites; but we must remember how small a proportion the good or evil effected by a single statesman can bear to the good or evil of a great social system."*

But of this sluggishness of imagination he has certainly no trace himself. He is willing to be "behind ten thousand counters," to be a guest "at ten thousand firesides"; he is willing to "see ordinary men as they appear in their ordinary business and in their ordinary pleasures"; he has no objection to "mingle in the crowds of the exchange and the coffee-house"; he would "obtain admittance to the convivial table and the domestic hearth"; so far as his dignity will permit, he will "bear with vulgar expressions": and a singular efficacy of fancy gives him the power to do so. Some portion of the essence of human nature is concealed from him, but all its accessories are at his command. He delineates any trait; he can paint and justly paint any manners he chooses.

"The perfect historian," he tells us, "is he in whose work the character and spirit of an age is exhibited in miniature. He relates no fact, he attributes no expression to his characters which is not authenticated by sufficient testimony; but by judicious selection, rejection, and arrangement, he gives to truth those attractions which have been usurped by fiction. In his narrative a due subordination is observed, — some transactions are prominent, others retire; but the scale on which he represents them is increased or diminished, not according to the dignity of the persons concerned in them, but according to the degree in which they elucidate the condition of society and the nature of man. He shows us the court, the camp,

---

* Essay on "History." All the remaining quotations on the page are from the same source.

and the senate; but he shows us also the nation. He considers no anecdote, no peculiarity of manner, no familiar saying, as too insignificant for his notice, which is not too insignificant to illustrate the operation of laws, of religion, and of education, and to mark the progress of the human mind. Men will not merely be described, but will be made intimately known to us. The changes of manners will be indicated not merely by a few general phrases or a few extracts from statistical documents, but by appropriate images presented in every line.

"If a man such as we are supposing should write the history of England, he would assuredly not omit the battles, the sieges, the negotiations, the seditions, the ministerial changes; but with these he would intersperse the details which are the charm of historical romances. At Lincoln Cathedral there is a beautiful painted window, which was made by an apprentice out of the pieces of glass which had been rejected by his master; it is so far superior to every other in the church that according to the tradition, the vanquished artist killed himself from mortification. Sir Walter Scott, in the same manner, has used those fragments of truth which historians have scornfully thrown behind them, in a manner which may well excite their envy; he has constructed out of their gleanings, works which, even considered as histories, are scarcely less valuable than theirs. But a truly great historian would reclaim those materials which the novelist has appropriated. The history of the government and the history of the people would be exhibited in that mode in which alone they can be exhibited justly, in inseparable conjunction and intermixture. We should not then have to look for the wars and votes of the Puritans in Clarendon, and for their phraseology in 'Old Mortality'; for one half of King James in Hume, and for the other half in the 'Fortunes of Nigel.'"*

So far as the graphic description of exterior life goes, he has completely realized his idea.

This union of a flowing fancy with an insensible organization is very rare; in general, a delicate fancy is joined with a poetic organization, — exactly why, it would be difficult to explain. It is for metaphysicians in large volumes to explain the genesis of the human faculties; but as a fact, it seems to be clear that for the most part, imaginative men are the most sensitive to the poetic side of human life and natural scenery.

* Essay on "History."

They are drawn by a strong instinct to what is sublime, grand, and beautiful. They do not care for the coarse business of life; they dislike to be cursed with its ordinary cares. Their nature is vivid: it is interested by all which naturally interests; it dwells on the great, the graceful, and the grand. On this account it naturally runs away from history, — the very name of it is too oppressive: are not all such works written in the *Index Expurgatorius* of the genial satirist as works which it was impossible to read?* The coarse and cumbrous matter revolts the soul of the fine and fanciful voluptuary. Take it as you will, human life is like the earth on which man dwells. There are exquisite beauties, grand imposing objects, scattered here and there: but the spaces between these are wide; the mass of common clay is huge; the dead level of vacant life, of commonplace geography, is immense. The poetic nature cannot bear the preponderance; it seeks relief in selected scenes, in special topics, in favorite beauties. History, which is the record of human existence, is a faithful representative of it at least in this: the poetic mind cannot bear the weight of its narrations and the commonplaceness of its events.

This peculiarity of character gives to Macaulay's writing one of its most curious characteristics. He throws over matters which are in their nature dry and dull, — transactions, budgets, bills, — the charm of fancy which a poetical mind employs to enhance and set forth the charm of what is beautiful. An attractive style is generally devoted to what is in itself specially attractive; here it is devoted to subjects which are often unattractive, are sometimes even repelling, — at the best are commonly neutral, not inviting attention if they do not excite dislike. In these new volumes there is a currency reform, pages on Scotch Presbyterianism, a heap of parliamentary debates: who could be expected to make anything interesting of such topics? It is not cheerful to read in the morning papers the debates of yesterday, though

---

* Lamb, "Detached Thoughts on Books and Reading."

they happened last night; one cannot like a Calvin-
istic divine when we see him in the pulpit; it is awful
to read on the currency, even when it concerns the
bank-notes which we use: how then can we care for
a narrative when the divine is dead, the shillings
extinct, the whole topic of the debate forgotten and
passed away? Yet such is the power of style, so
great is the charm of very skillful words, of narration which is always passing forward, of illustration
which always hits the mark, that such subjects as
these not only become interesting, but very interesting. The proof is evident: no book is so sought after.
The Chancellor of the Exchequer said "all members
of Parliament had read it": what other books could
ever be fancied to have been read by them? A county
member — a real county member — hardly reads two
volumes *per* existence. Years ago Macaulay said a
History of England might become more in demand
at the circulating libraries than the last novel: he
has actually made his words true, — it is no longer a
phrase of rhetoric, it is a simple fact.

The explanation of this remarkable notoriety is,
the contrast of the topic and the treatment. Those
who read for the sake of entertainment are attracted
by the one; those who read for the sake of instruction
are attracted by the other. Macaulay has something
that suits the readers of Mr. Hallam; he has something which will please the readers of Mr. Thackeray.
The first wonder to find themselves reading such a
style; the last are astonished at reading on such
topics, — at finding themselves studying by casualty.
This marks the author: only a buoyant fancy and
an impassive temperament could produce a book so
combining weight with levity.

Something similar may be remarked of the writings of a still greater man, — of Edmund Burke. The
contrast between the manner of his characteristic
writings and their matter is very remarkable. He
too threw over the detail of business and of politics

those graces and attractions of manner which seem in some sort inconsistent with them; which are adapted for topics more intrinsically sublime and beautiful. It was for this reason that Hazlitt asserted that no woman ever cared for Burke's writings:* the matter, he said, was "hard and dry," † and no superficial glitter or eloquence could make it agreeable to those who liked what is in its very nature fine and delicate. The charm of exquisite narration has in a great degree, in Macaulay's case, supplied the deficiency; but it may be *perhaps* remarked that some trace of the same phenomenon has again occurred, from similar causes, and that his popularity, though great among both sexes, is in some sense more masculine than feminine. The absence of this charm of narration — to which accomplished women are, it would seem, peculiarly sensitive — is very characteristic of Burke. His mind was the reverse of historical: although he had rather a coarse, incondite temperament, not finely susceptible to the best influences, to the most exquisite beauties of the world in which he lived, he yet lived in that world thoroughly and completely. He did not take an interest, as a poet does, in the sublime because it is sublime, in the beautiful because it is beautiful; but he had the passions of more ordinary men in a degree, and of an intensity, which ordinary men may be most thankful that they have not. In no one has the intense faculty of intellectual hatred — the hatred which the absolute dogmatist has for those in whom he incarnates and personifies the opposing dogma — been fiercer or stronger; in no one has the intense ambition to rule and govern — in scarcely any one has the daily ambition of the daily politician — been fiercer and stronger: he, if any man, cast himself upon his time. After one of his speeches, peruse one of Macaulay's: you seem transported to another sphere. The

---

* "No woman ever liked Burke or disliked Goldsmith." — "On Egotism," in the "Table Talk."

† This "quotation" is purely imaginary, a vague memory of other matter in the essay. — ED.

fierce living interest of the one contrasts with the cold rhetorical interest of the other; you are in a different part of the animal kingdom: you have left the viviparous intellect, you have left products warm and struggling with hasty life; you have reached the oviparous, and products smooth and polished, cold and stately.

In addition to this impassive nature inclining him to write on past transactions, to this fancy enabling him to adorn and describe them, Macaulay has a marvelous memory to recall them, and what we may call the Scotch intellect enabling him to conceive them. The memory is his most obvious power; an enormous reading seems always present to him. No effort seems wanted, no mental excogitation. According to his own description of a like faculty, "It would have been strange indeed if you had asked for anything that was not to be found in that immense storehouse. The article you required was not only there, it was ready. It was in its own compartment. In a moment it was brought down, unpacked, and explained."* He has a literary illustration for everything, and his fancy enables him to make a skillful use of his wealth; he always selects the exact likeness of the idea which he wishes to explain. And though it be less obvious, yet his writing would have been deficient in one of its most essential characteristics if it had not been for what we have called his Scotch intellect, which is a curious matter to explain. It may be thought that Adam Smith had little in common with Sir Walter Scott: Sir Walter was always making fun of him; telling odd tales of his abstraction and singularity; not obscurely hinting that a man who could hardly put on his own coat, and certainly could not buy his own dinner, was scarcely fit to decide on the proper course of industry and the mercantile dealings of nations: yet when Sir Walter's own works come to be closely examined, they will be found to contain a good

* Essay on Sir James Mackintosh.

deal of political economy of a certain sort—and not
a very bad sort. Any one who will study his description of the Highland clans in "Waverley," his
observations on the industrial side (if so it is to be
called) of the Border life, his plans for dealing with
the poor of his own time, will be struck not only with
a plain sagacity, which we could equal in England, but
with the digested accuracy and theoretical completeness which they show. You might cut paragraphs
even from his lighter writings which would be thought
acute in the "Wealth of Nations." There appears to
be in the genius of the Scotch people—fostered, no
doubt, by the abstract metaphysical education of their
universities, but also, by way of natural taste, supporting that education and rendering it possible and
popular—a power of reducing human actions to formulæ or principles. An instance is now in a high
place. People who are not lawyers—rural people,
who have sense of their own, but have no access to
the general repute and opinion which expresses the
collective sense of the great world—never can be
brought to believe that Lord Campbell is a great man:
they read his speeches in the House of Lords, his occasional flights of eloquence on the bench, his attempts
at pathos, his stupendous *gaucheries*, and they cannot
be persuaded that a person guilty of such things can
have really first-rate talent; if you ask them how he
came to be Chief Justice of England, they mutter
something angry, and say, "Well, Scotchmen *do* get
on somehow." This is really the true explanation: in
spite of a hundred defects, Lord Campbell has the
Scotch faculties in perfection. He reduces legal matters to a sound broad principle better than any man
who is now a judge; he has a steady, comprehensive,
abstract, distinct consistency, which elaborates a formula and adheres to a formula: and it is this which
has raised him from a plain—a very plain—Scotch
lawyer to be Lord Chief Justice of England. Macaulay has this too. Among his more brilliant qualities,

it has escaped the attention of critics; the more so, because his powers of exposition and expression make it impossible to conceive for a moment that the amusing matter we are reading is really Scotch economy.

"During the interval," he tells us, "between the Restoration and the Revolution, the riches of the nation had been rapidly increasing. Thousands of busy men found every Christmas that after the expenses of the year's housekeeping had been defrayed out of the year's income, a surplus remained; and how that surplus was to be employed was a question of some difficulty. In our time, to invest such a surplus, at something more than three per cent., on the best security that has ever been known in the world, is the work of a few minutes. But in the seventeenth century, a lawyer, a physician, a retired merchant, who had saved some thousands and who wished to place them safely and profitably, was often greatly embarrassed. Three generations earlier, a man who had accumulated wealth in a profession generally purchased real property, or lent his savings on mortgage. But the number of acres in the kingdom had remained the same; and the value of those acres, though it had greatly increased, had by no means increased so fast as the quantity of capital which was seeking for employment. Many, too, wished to put their money where they could find it at an hour's notice, and looked about for some species of property which could be more readily transferred than a house or a field. A capitalist might lend on bottomry or on personal security; but if he did so, he ran a great risk of losing interest and principal. There were a few joint-stock companies, among which the East India Company held the foremost place; but the demand for the stock of such companies was far greater than the supply. Indeed, the cry for a new East India Company was chiefly raised by persons who had found difficulty in placing their savings at interest on good security. So great was that difficulty, that the practice of hoarding was common. We are told that the father of Pope the poet, who retired from business in the City about the time of the Revolution, carried to a retreat in the country a strong box containing nearly twenty thousand pounds, and took out from time to time what was required for household expenses;* and it is highly probable that this was not a solitary case. At present the quantity of coin which is hoarded by private persons is so small that it would, if brought forth, make no perceptible addition to the circulation. But in the earlier part of the

* This tradition is now disproved; the money was invested in the French funds. — ED.

reign of William III., all the greatest writers on currency were of
opinion that a very considerable mass of gold and silver was hidden
in secret drawers and behind wainscots.

"The natural effect of this state of things was, that a crowd
of projectors, ingenious and absurd, honest and knavish, employed
themselves in devising new schemes for the employment of redund-
ant capital. It was about the year 1688 that the word 'stockjobber'
was first heard in London. In the short space of four years a
crowd of companies, every one of which confidently held out to
subscribers the hope of immense gains, sprang into existence: the
Insurance Company, the Paper Company, the Lutestring Company,
the Pearl-Fishery Company, the Glass-Bottle Company, the Alum
Company, the Blythe Coal Company, the Swordblade Company.
There was a Tapestry Company, which would soon furnish pretty
hangings for all the parlors of the middle class and for all the
bedchambers of the higher. There was a Copper Company, which
proposed to explore the mines of England, and held out a hope
that they would prove not less valuable than those of Potosi. There
was a Diving Company, which undertook to bring up precious effects
from shipwrecked vessels, and which announced that it had laid in
a stock of wonderful machines, resembling complete suits of armor.
In front of the helmet was a huge glass eye, like that of a Cyclop;
and out of the crest went a pipe, through which the air was to be
admitted. The whole process was exhibited on the Thames. Fine
gentlemen and fine ladies were invited to the show, were hospitably
regaled, and were delighted by seeing the divers in their panoply
descend into the river, and return laden with old iron and ship's
tackle. There was a Greenland Fishing Company, which could not
fail to drive the Dutch whalers and herring-busses out of the
Northern Ocean. There was a Tanning Company, which promised
to furnish leather superior to the best that was brought from
Turkey or Russia. There was a society which undertook the office
of giving gentlemen a liberal education on low terms, and which
assumed the sounding name of the Royal Academies Company. In
a pompous advertisement it was announced that the directors of
the Royal Academies Company had engaged the best masters in
every branch of knowledge, and were about to issue twenty thousand tickets at twenty shillings each. There was to be a lottery:
two thousand prizes were to be drawn; and the fortunate holders
of the prizes were to be taught, at the charge of the company,
Latin, Greek, Hebrew, French, Spanish, conic sections, trigonometry,
heraldry, japanning, fortification, book-keeping, and the art of playing the theorbo. Some of these companies took large mansions,

and printed their advertisements in gilded letters. Others, less ostentatious, were content with ink, and met at coffee-houses in the
neighborhood of the Royal Exchange. Jonathan's and Garraway's
were in a constant ferment with brokers, buyers, sellers, meetings
of directors, meetings of proprietors. Time bargains soon came
into fashion. Extensive combinations were formed, and monstrous
fables were circulated, for the purpose of raising or depressing the
price of shares. Our country witnessed for the first time those
phenomena with which a long experience has made us familiar. A
mania, of which the symptoms were essentially the same with those
of the mania of 1720, of the mania of 1825, of the mania of
1845, seized the public mind. An impatience to be rich, a contempt for those slow but sure gains which are the proper reward of
industry, patience, and thrift, spread through society. The spirit
of the cogging dicers of Whitefriars took possession of the grave
senators of the City, wardens of trades, deputies, aldermen. It
was much easier and much more lucrative to put forth a lying pro-
spectus announcing a new stock, to persuade ignorant people that
the dividends could not fall short of twenty per cent., and to
part with five thousand pounds of this imaginary wealth for ten
thousand solid guineas, than to load a ship with a well-chosen cargo
for Virginia or the Levant. Every day some new bubble was
puffed into existence, rose buoyant, shone bright, burst, and was
forgotten." *

You will not find the cause of panics so accurately
explained in the dryest of political economists, — in
the Scotch MacCulloch.

These peculiarities of character and mind may be
very conspicuously traced through the "History of
England" and in the "Essays." Their first and most
striking quality is the *intellectual entertainment* which
they afford. This, as practical readers know, is a kind
of sensation which is not very common, and which is
very productive of great and healthy enjoyment. It
is quite distinct from the amusement which is derived
from common light works. The latter is very great;
but it is passive. The mind of the reader is not
awakened to any independent action: you see the
farce, but you see it without effort; not simply without painful effort, but without any perceptible mental

* "History of England," Chap. xix.

activity whatever. Again, entertainment of intellect is contrasted with the high enjoyment of consciously following pure and difficult reasoning: such a sensation is a sort of sublimated pain. The highest and most intense action of the intellectual powers is like the most intense action of the bodily on a high mountain: we climb and climb; we have a thrill of pleasure, but we have also a sense of effort and anguish. Nor is the sensation to be confounded with that which we experience from the best and purest works of art. The pleasure of high tragedy is also painful: the whole soul is stretched, the spirit pants, the passions scarcely breathe; it is a rapt and eager moment, too intense for continuance, — so overpowering that we scarcely know whether it be joy or pain. The sensation of intellectual entertainment is altogether distinguished from these by not being accompanied by any pain, and yet being consequent on or being contemporaneous with a high and constant exercise of mind. While we read works which so delight us, we are conscious that we are delighted and are conscious that we are not idle; the opposite pleasures of indolence and exertion seem for a moment combined. A sort of elasticity pervades us; thoughts come easily and quickly; we seem capable of many ideas; we follow cleverness till we fancy that we are clever. This feeling is only given by writers who stimulate the mind just to the degree which is pleasant, and who do not stimulate it more; who exact a moderate exercise of mind, and who seduce us to it insensibly. This can only be, of course, by a charm of style; by the inexplicable *je ne sais quoi* which attracts our attention; by constantly raising and constantly satisfying our curiosity. And there seems to be a further condition: a writer who wishes to produce this constant effect must not appeal to any single separate faculty of mind, but to the whole mind at once. The fancy tires if you appeal only to the fancy; the understanding is aware of its dullness if you appeal

only to the understanding; the curiosity is soon sa-
tiated unless you pique it with variety. This is the
very opportunity for Macaulay: he has fancy, sense,
abundance; he appeals to both fancy and understanding. There is no sense of effort; his books read like
an elastic dream. There is a continual sense of instruction; for who had an idea of the transactions
before? The emotions, too, which he appeals to are
the easy admiration, the cool disapprobation, the gentle worldly curiosity which quietly excite us, never
fatigue us, which we could bear forever. To read
Macaulay for a day would be to pass a day of easy
thought, of pleasant placid emotion.

Nor is this a small matter: in a state of high civilization it is no simple matter to give multitudes a
large and healthy enjoyment. The old bodily enjoyments are dying out,—there is no room for them
any more; the complex apparatus of civilization cum-
bers the ground. We are thrown back upon the
mind, and the mind is a barren thing,—it can spin
little from itself; few that describe what they see are
in the way to discern much. Exaggerated emotions,
violent incidents, monstrous characters crowd our
canvas; they are the resource of a weakness which
would obtain the fame of strength. Reading is about
to become a series of collisions against aggravated
breakers, of beatings with imaginary surf. In such
times a book of sensible attraction is a public benefit;
it diffuses a sensation of vigor through the multitude.
Perhaps there is a danger that the extreme popularity
of the manner may make many persons fancy they
understand the matter more perfectly than they do:
some readers may become conceited; several boys believe that they too are Macaulays. Yet, duly allowing
for this defect, it is a great good that so many people
should learn so much on such topics so agreeably;
that they should feel that they *can* understand them;
that their minds should be stimulated by a consciousness of health and power.

The same peculiarities influence the style of the narrative. The art of narration is the art of writing in hooks and eyes: the principle consists in making the appropriate thought follow the appropriate thought, the proper fact the proper fact; in first preparing the mind for what is to come, and then letting it come. This can only be achieved by keeping continually and insensibly before the mind of the reader some one object, character, or image, whose variations are the events of the story, whose unity is the unity of it. Scott, for example, keeps before you the mind of some one person, — that of Morton in "Old Mortality," of Rebecca in "Ivanhoe," of Lovel in "The Antiquary," —whose fortunes and mental changes are the central incidents, whose personality is the string of unity. It is the defect of the great Scotch novels that their central figure is frequently not their most interesting topic; that their interest is often rather in the accessories than in the essential principle, — rather in that which surrounds the center of narration than in the center itself. Scott tries to meet this objection by varying the mind which he selects for his unit: in one of his chapters it is one character, in the next a different; he shifts the scene from the hero to the heroine, from the "protector of the settlement" of the story to the evil being who mars it perpetually: but when narrowly examined, the principle of his narration will be found nearly always the same, — the changes in the position, external or mental, of some one human being. The most curiously opposite sort of narration is that of Hume: he seems to carry a *view*, as the moderns call it, through everything. He forms to himself a metaphysical — that perhaps is a harsh word — an intellectual conception of the time and character before him, and the gradual working out or development of that view is the principle of his narration; he tells the story of the conception. You rise from his pages without much remembrance of or regard for the mere people, but with a clear notion of an elaborated view, skillfully abstracted and perpetually impressed upon you. A critic of detail should scarcely require a better task than to show how insensibly and artfully the subtle historian infuses his doctrine among the facts; indicates somehow—you can scarcely say how—their relation to it; strings them, as it were, upon it, concealing it in seeming beneath them, while in fact it altogether determines their form, their grouping, and their consistency. The style of Macaulay is very different from either of these: it is a diorama of political pictures. You seem to begin with a brilliant picture,—its colors are distinct, its lines are firm; on a sudden it changes, at first gradually, you can scarcely tell how or in what, but truly and unmistakably,—a slightly different picture is before you; then the second vision seems to change,—it too is another and yet the same; then the third shines forth and fades: and so without end. The unity of this delineation is the identity—the apparent identity—of the picture; in no two moments does it seem quite different, in no two is it identically the same. It grows and alters as our bodies would appear to alter and grow, if you could fancy any one watching them and being conscious of their daily little changes. The events are picturesque variations; the unity is a unity of political painting, of represented external form. It is evident how suitable this is to a writer whose understanding is solid, whose sense is political, whose fancy is fine and delineative.

To this merit of Macaulay is to be added another: no one describes so well what we may call the *spectacle* of a character. The art of delineating character by protracted description is one which grows in spite of the critics. In vain is it alleged that the character should be shown dramatically; that it should be illustrated by events; that it should be exhibited in its actions. The truth is, that these homilies are excellent, but incomplete; true, but out of season. There is a utility in verbal portrait, as Lord Stanhope says there is in painted. Goethe used to observe that in society—in a *tête-à-tête*, rather—you often thought of your companion as if he was his portrait: you were silent; you did not care what he said, but you considered him as a picture, as a whole, especially as regards yourself and your relations towards him. * You require something of the same kind in literature: *some* description of a man is clearly necessary as an introduction to the story of his life and actions. But more than this is wanted: you require to have the object placed before you as a whole; to have the characteristic traits mentioned, the delicate qualities drawn out, the firm features gently depicted. As the practice which Goethe hints at is of all others the most favorable to a just and calm judgment of character, so the literary substitute is essential as a steadying element, as a summary to bring together and give a unity to our views. We must see the man's face: without it we seem to have heard a great deal about the person, but not to have known him; to be aware that he had done a good deal, but to have no settled, ineradicable notion what manner of man he was. This is the reason why critics like Macaulay, who sneer at the practice when estimating the works of others, yet make use of it at great length and (in his case) with great skill when they come to be historians themselves. The kind of characters whom Macaulay can describe is limited—at least we think so—by the bounds which we indicated just now: there are some men whom he is too impassive to comprehend; but he can always tell us of such as he does comprehend, what they looked like and what they were.

A great deal of this vividness Macaulay of course owes to his style. Of its effectiveness there can be no doubt; its agreeableness no one who has just been reading it is likely to deny: yet it has a defect. It is not, as Bishop Butler would have expressed it, such a style as "is suitable to such a being as man, in

---

* "Elective Affinities," Part II., Chap. II.

such a world as the present one,"*—it is too omniscient. Everything is too plain; all is clear, nothing
is doubtful. Instead of probability being, as the great
thinker expressed it, "the very guide of life,"† it has
become a rare exception, an uncommon phenomenon.
You rarely come across anything which is not decided;
and when you do come across it, you seem to wonder
that the positiveness which has accomplished so much
should have been unwilling to decide everything.
This is hardly the style for history. The data of historical narratives, especially of modern histories, are
a heap of confusion: no one can tell where they lie
or where they do not lie, what is in them or what is
not in them. Literature is called the "fragment of
fragments": little has been written, and but little of
that little has been preserved. So history is a vestige
of vestiges: few facts leave any trace of themselves,
any witness of their occurrence; of fewer still is that
witness preserved: a slight track is all anything
leaves, and the confusion of life, the tumult of change
sweeps even that away in a moment. It is not possible that these data can be very fertile in certainties.
Few people would make anything of them: a memoir
here, a MS. there, two letters in a magazine, an assertion by a person whose veracity is denied,—these are
the sort of evidence out of which a flowing narrative
is to be educed; and of course it ought not to be too
flowing. If you please, sir, tell me what you do *not*
know," was the inquiry of a humble pupil addressed
to a great man of science: it would have been a relief
to the readers of Macaulay if he had shown a little
the outside of uncertainties which there must be, the
gradations of doubt which there ought to be, the
singular accumulation of difficulties which must beset
the extraction of a very easy narrative from very
confused materials.

This defect in style is indeed indicative of a defect in understanding: Macaulay's mind is eminently

---

*See note to page 109.   † Introduction to Butler's "Analogy."

gifted, but there is a want of graduation in it. He
has a fine eye for probabilities, a clear perception of
evidence, a shrewd guess at missing links of fact;
but each probability seems to him a certainty, each
piece of evidence conclusive, each analogy exact. The
heavy Scotch intellect is a little prone to this: one
figures it as a heap of formulæ, and if fact *b* is re-
ducible to formula B, that is all which it regards; the
mathematical mill grinds with equal energy at flour
perfect and imperfect, at matter which is quite certain and at matter which is only a little probable. .
But the great cause of this error is, an abstinence .
from practical action. Life is a school of probability.
In the writings of every man of patient practicality,
in the midst of whatever other defects, you will find
a careful appreciation of the degrees of likelihood, a
steady balancing of them one against another; a disinclination to make things too clear, to overlook the
debit side of the account in mere contemplation of
the enormousness of the credit. The reason is obvious: action is a business of risk; the real question is
the magnitude of that risk. Failure is ever impending, success is ever uncertain; there is always, in the
very best of affairs, a slight probability of the former,
a contingent possibility of the non-occurrence of the
latter. For practical men, the problem ever is to test
the amount of these inevitable probabilities; to make
sure that no one increases too far; that by a well-
varied choice the number of risks may in itself be a
protection,—be an insurance to you, as it were, against
the capricious result of any one. A man like Macaulay, who stands aloof from life, is not so instructed;
he sits secure; nothing happens in his study: he does
not care to test probabilities; he loses the detective
sensation.

Macaulay's so-called inaccuracy is likewise a phase
of this defect. Considering the enormous advantages
which a picturesque style gives to ill-disposed critics, the number of points of investigation which it

suggests, the number of assertions it makes sentence by sentence, the number of ill-disposed critics that there are in the world; remembering Macaulay's position, set on a hill to be spied at by them, — he can scarcely be thought an inaccurate historian. Considering all things, they have found few certain blunders, hardly any direct mistakes. Every sentence of his style requires minute knowledge. The vivid picture has a hundred details; each of those details must have an evidence, an authority, a proof. A historian like .Hume passes easily over a period: his chart is large; .if he gets the conspicuous headlands, the large harbors duly marked, he does not care. Macaulay puts in the depth of each wave, every remarkable rock, every tree on the shore. Nothing gives a critic so great an advantage: it is difficult to do this for a volume, simple for a page. It is easy to select a particular event and learn all which any one can know about it; examine Macaulay's descriptions, say he is wrong, that X is not buried where he asserts, that a little boy was one year older than he states: but how would the critic manage if he had to work out all this for a million facts, for a whole period? Few men, we suspect, would be able to make so few errors of simple and provable fact. On the other hand, few men would arouse a sleepy critic by such startling assertion. If Macaulay finds a new theory, he states it as a fact. Very likely it really is the most probable theory; at any rate, we know of no case in which his theory is not one among the most plausible: if it had only been so stated, it would have been well received. His view of Marlborough's character, for instance, is a specious one: it has a good deal of evidence, a large amount of real probability, but it has scarcely more; Marlborough *may* have been as bad as is said, but we can hardly be *sure* of it at this time.

Macaulay's "party spirit" is another consequence of his positiveness: when he inclines to a side, he inclines to it too much. His opinions are a shade too

strong; his predilections some degrees at least too
warm. William is too perfect, James too imperfect.
The Whigs are a trifle like angels; the Tories like
(let us say) "our inferiors." Yet this is evidently an
honest party spirit; it does not lurk in the corners of
sentences, it is not insinuated without being alleged;
it does not, like the unfairness of Hume, secrete itself
so subtly in the turns of the words that when you
look to prove it, it is gone: on the contrary, it rushes
into broad day. William is loaded with panegyric;
James is always spoken evil of. Hume's is the artful
pleading of a hired advocate, Macaulay's the bold
eulogy of a sincere friend. As far as effect goes,
this is an error, — the very earnestness of the affection
leads to a reaction: we are "tired of having" William
"called 'the just'"; we cannot believe so many pages;
"all that" can scarcely be correct. As we said, if
the historian's preference for persons and parties had
been duly tempered and mitigated, if the probably
good were only said to be probably good, if the rather
bad were only alleged to be rather bad, the reader
would have been convinced, and the historian would
have escaped the savage censure of envious critics.

The one thing which detracts from the pleasure
of reading these volumes is the doubt whether they
should have been written. Should not these great
powers be reserved for great periods? Is this abounding, picturesque style suited for continuous history?
Are small men to be so largely described? Should
not admirable delineation be kept for admirable people? we think so, — you do not want Raphael to paint
sign-posts, or Palladio to build dirt pies. Much of history is necessarily of little value, — the superficies of
circumstance, the scum of events. It is very well
to have it described, — indeed, you must have it described: the chain must be kept complete; the narrative of a country's fortunes will not allow of breaks
or gaps: yet all things need not be done equally well.
The life of a great painter is short; even the industry

of Macaulay will not complete this history. It is a pity to spend such powers on such events; it would have been better to have some new volumes of essays solely on great men and great things. The diffuseness of the style would have been then in place; we could have borne to hear the smallest *minutiæ* of magnificent epochs. If an inferior hand had executed the connecting links, our notions would have acquired an insensible perspective: the works of the great artist, the best themes would have stood out from the canvas; they are now confused by the equal brilliancy of the adjacent inferiorities.

Much more might be said on this narrative: as it will be read for very many years, it will employ the critics for very many years. It would be unkind to make all the best observations; something—as Mr. Disraeli said in a Budget speech—something should be left for "future statements of this nature." There will be an opportunity: whatever those who come after may say against this book, it will be and remain the "Pictorial History of England."

BISHOP BUTLER.*

(1854.)

ABOUT the close of the last century, some one discovered the wife of a country rector in the act of
destroying, for culinary purposes, the last remnants of
a box of sermons which seemed to have been written by Joseph Butler. The lady was reproved, but the
exculpatory rejoinder was, "Why, the box was full
once, and I thought they were my husband's." Nevertheless, when we first saw the above announcement
of unpublished remains, we hoped her exemplary diligence had not been wholly successful, and that some
important writings of Butler had been discovered. In
this we have been disappointed: the remains in question are slight and rather trivial. The longest is an
additional letter addressed to Dr. Clarke; and in all
the rest there is scarcely anything very characteristic,
except the remark, "What a wonderful incongruity
it is for a man to see the doubtfulness in which
things are involved, and yet be impatient out of action
or vehement in it! Say a man is a skeptic, and add
what was said of Brutus, *quicquid vult valde vult,*†
and you say there is the greatest contrariety between
his understanding and his temper that can be expressed
in words,"‡—an observation which might be borne
in mind by some English writers who panegyrize
Julius Cæsar, and the many French ones who panegyrize Napoleon.

(100)

The life of Butler is one of those in which the events are few, the transitions simple, and the final result strange. He was the son of a Dissenting shop-keeper in Berkshire; was always of a meditative disposition and reading habit; grew to manhood, was destined to the Dissenting ministry, began to question the principles of Dissent; entered at Oriel College, made valuable acquaintances there, rose in the Church by means of them; obtained first the chaplaincy of the Rolls, then a decent living, then the rectory of Stanhope, — the "golden" rectory, one of the best in the English Church; was recommended by his old friends to Queen Caroline, talked philosophy to her, pleased her (this being her favorite topic), was made Bishop of Bristol, and thence translated to the richest of Anglican dignities, the prince-bishopric of Durham, and there died.

These are the single steps, and there is none of them which is remote from our ordinary observation; we should not be surprised to see any of them every day. But when we look on the life as a whole ; when we see its nature : when we observe the son of a Dissenting tradesman, a person of simple and pious disposition, of retiring habits, and [of] scrupulous and investigating mind, — in a word, the least worldly of ecclesiastics, — attain to the most secular of ecclesiastical dignities, be a prince as well as a bishop, become the great magnate of the North of England, and dispense revenues to be envied by many a foreign potentate, — we perceive the peculiarity of such a man with such beginnings attaining such a fortune. No man would guess from Butler's writings that he ever had the disposal of five pounds : it is odd to think what he did with the mining property and landed property, the royalties and rectories, coal dues and curacies, that he must have heard of from morning till evening.

It is certainly most strange that such a man should ever have been made a bishop : in general we observe that those become most eminent in the sheepfold who partake most eminently of the qualities of the wolf. Nor is this surprising. The church is (as the Article defines it) a "congregation of men," "faithful" indeed, but faithful in various degrees. In every corporation or combination of men, no matter for what purpose collected, there are certain secular qualities which attain eminence as surely as oil rises above water; attorneys are for the world, and the world is for attorneys. Activity, vigor, sharp-sightedness, tact, boldness, watchfulness, and such qualities as these, raise a man in the church as certainly as in the state; so long as there is wealth and preferment in the one, they will be attained a good deal as wealth and office are in the other. The *prowling* faculties will have their way; those who hunger and thirst after riches will have riches, and those who hunger not will not. Still, to this there are exceptions, and Butler's case is one of them; we might really fancy the world had determined to give for once an encouraging instance of its sensibility to rectitude, of the real and great influence of real and great virtue.

The period at which Butler's elevation occurred certainly does not diminish the oddness of the phenomenon. We are not indeed of those, mostly disciples of Carlyle or Newman, who speak with untempered contempt of the eighteenth century; rather, if we might trust our own feelings, we view it with appreciating regard. It was the age of substantial comfort: the grave and placid historian (we speak of Mr. Hallam), going learnedly over the generations of men, is disposed to think that there never was so much happiness before or since.* Employment was plentiful, industry remunerative; the advantages of material civilization were enjoyed and its penalties scarcely foreseen. The troubles of the seventeenth century had died out, those of the nineteenth had not begun; cares were few; the stir and conflict in which we live had barely commenced. It was not an age to trouble itself

---

* "Constitutional History of England," Chap. xvi., last paragraph.

with prospective tasks; it had no feverish excitement nor over-intellectual introspection; it lived on the fat of the land; *quieta non movere* was its motto. Like most comfortable people, those of that time possessed a sleepy, supine sagacity; they had no fine imaginings, no exquisite fancies, but a coarse sense of what was common, a "large roundabout common-sense" (these are Locke's words*) which was their guide in what concerned them. Some may not think this romantic enough to be attractive; and yet it has a beauty of its own. They did not "look before or after," nor "pine for what was not"†: they enjoyed what was; a solid homeliness was their mark. Exactly as we like to see a large lazy animal lying in the placid shade, without anxiety for the future and chewing the cud of the past, we like to look back at the age of our great-grandfathers, so solid in its habits and placid in the lapse of years. Nevertheless—and this is what is to our purpose—we must own at once that the very merits of that age are "of the earth, earthy"‡: there was no talk then of "obstinate questionings" or "incommunicable dream"§; heroism, enthusiasm, the sense of the supernatural, deep feeling seem in a manner foreign to the very idea of it. This is the point of view in which the Tractarian movement was described as tending towards the realization of "something deeper and truer than satisfied the last century."‖ For the clergy, the time was indeed evil: the popular view of the profession seems accurately expressed in a well-known book of memoirs :—

"'But if this was your opinion,' . . . 'how came you not to let your friend Sherlock [the well-known bishop] into the secret?

---

* Not quite: "large, sound, roundabout sense" ("Conduct of the Understanding," 3, 3). — ED.

† Shelley, "To a Skylark."

‡ 1 Cor. xv. 47.

§ Shelley, "Alastor;" the first of the two also in Wordsworth, "Intimations of Immortality," ix.

‖ John Henry Newman, letter to Dr. Jelf on Tract No. 90.

Why did not you tell him that half the pack, and those hounds on whom you most depended, were drawn off, and the game escaped and safe, instead of leaving his Lordship there to bark and yelp by himself, and make the silly figure he has done?' 'Oh,' said Lord Carteret, 'he talks like a parson; and consequently is so used to talk to people that don't mind him that I left him to find it out at his leisure, and shall have him again for all this whenever I want him.' " *

The fact of Butler's success is to be accounted for, as we have said, by his personal excellence. Mr. Talbot liked him, *Bishop* Talbot liked him, the Queen liked him, the King liked him. He says himself in these Remains, " Good men surely are not treated in this world as they deserve; yet 'tis seldom, very seldom their goodness which makes them disliked, even in cases where it may seem to be so: but 'tis some behavior or other which, however excusable, perhaps infinitely overbalanced by their virtues, yet is offensive, possibly wrong; however such, it may be, as would pass off very well in a man of the world." † And he must have been alive to the fact in practice. He had every excuse for making virtue detestable: he was educated a Baptist, and brought up at a Dissenting academy; he was born in the vulgarest years of English Puritanism, when it had fallen from its first estate, when it had least influence with the higher classes, when the revival which dates from John Wesley had not begun, and the very memory of gentlemen such as Hutchinson or Hampden had passed away. A certain instinctive refinement, a "niceness" and gentleness of nature, preserved him not only from the coarser consequences of his position, but even from that angularity of mind which is not often escaped by those early trained to object to what is established.

Of his character the principal point may be described in the words which [Dr.] Arnold so often uses to denote the end and aim of his education,

* Lord Hervey's "Memoirs of the Reign of George II.," Chap. xxxi., *in re* Carteret's attack on the Scotch for the Porteous affair.
† " Fragments," No. 2.

"moral thoughtfulness " *; a certain considerateness is as it were, diffused over all his sentences. To most men, conscience is an occasional — almost an external — voice; to Butler it was a daily companion, a close anxiety. In a recent novel this disposition is skillfully delineated and delicately contrasted with its opposite; we may quote the passage, though it is incumbered with some detail.

"But what was a real trouble to Charles" (this is the person whose character is in question), "it got clearer and clearer to his apprehension that his intimacy with Sheffield was not quite what it had been. They had indeed passed the vacation together, and saw of each other more than ever: but their sympathies in each other were not as strong, they had not the same likings and dislikings, — in short, they had not such congenial minds as they fancied when they were Freshmen; there was not so much heart in their conversations, and they more easily endured to miss each other's company. They were both reading for honors, reading hard; but Sheffield's whole heart was in his work, and religion was but a secondary matter to him. He had no doubts, difficulties, anxieties, sorrows, which much affected him. It was not the certainty of faith which made a sunshine in his soul and dried up the mists of human weakness; rather, he had no perceptible need within him of that vision of the Unseen which is the Christian's life. He was unblemished in his character, exemplary in his conduct, but he was content with what the perishable world gave him. Charles's characteristic, perhaps above anything else, was a habitual sense of the Divine Presence; a sense which of course did not insure uninterrupted conformity of thought and deed to itself, but still there it was, — the pillar of the cloud before him and guiding him. He felt himself to be God's creature, and responsible to him; God's possession, not his own." †

Again, the same character is brought home to us in a part of Walton's delineation of Hooker, — which indeed, except perhaps for the great quickness attributed to his intellect, might as a whole stand well enough for a description of Butler: —

"His complexion (if we may guess by him at the age of forty) was sanguine, with a mixture of choler; and yet his motion was slow, even in his youth, and so was his speech, never expressing an

---

* Stanley's Arnold, near the close of Chap. viii.
† John Henry Newman's "Loss and Gain," Vol. ii., Chap. ix.

earnestness in either of them, but a gravity suited to the aged. And it is observed (so far as inquiry is able to look back at this distance of time) that at his being a schoolboy he was an early questionist; quietly inquisitive, Why this was, and that was not, to be remembered? why this was granted, and that denied? This being mixed with a remarkable modesty and a sweet serene quietness of nature. . . . It is observable that he was never known to be . . . extreme in any of his desires; never heard to repine or dispute with Providence, but by a quiet gentle submission and resignation of his will to the wisdom of the Creator, bore the burden of the day with patience: . . . and by this, and a grave behavior, which is a divine charm, he begot an early reverence unto his person even from those that at other times, and in other companies, took a liberty to cast off that strictness of behavior and discourse that is required in a collegiate life."

Something of this is a result of disposition; yet on the whole it seems mainly the effect of the "moral thoughtfulness" which has been mentioned.

The very name of this quality reminds us of a difficulty. We cannot but doubt, with the experience of this age, how far this can be made or ought to be made the abiding sentiment of all men; how far such teaching as that of Arnold's tends to introduce a too stiff and anxious habit of mind; how far the perpetual presence of a purpose will interfere with the simple happiness of life, and how far also it _can_ be forced on the "lilies of the field"*; how far the care of anxious minds and active thoughts is to be obtruded on the young, on the cheerful, on the natural. Other questions, too, might be asked: if the inculcation of this temper and habit as a daily universal obligation, a perpetual and general necessity for all characters, would not or might not impair the sanguine energy and masculine activity which are necessary for social action; whether it does not, in matter of fact, even now "burn and brand"† into excitable fancies a few stern truths more deeply than a feeble reason will bear or the equilibrium of the world demands? But

* Matt. vi. 28.
† "Borne and branded on my soul." — "Lady of the Lake," Canto iv.

whatever be the issue of such questions, on which
there is perhaps now no decided or established opinion, there can be no question of the charm of such a
character in those to whom it is natural. We may
admire what we cannot share, reverence what we do
not imitate. As those who cannot comprehend a
strain of soothing music look with interest on those
who can; as those who cannot feel the gentle glow
of a quiet landscape, yet stand aside and seem inferior
to those who do, — so in character the buoyant and
the bold, the harsh and the practical may, at least for
the moment, moralize and look upwards, reverence and
do homage, when they come to a close experience of
what is gentler and simpler, more anxious and more
thoughtful, kinder and more religious than themselves.
At any rate, so thought the contemporaries of Butler.
They did, as a Frenchman would say, "their possible"
for a good man; at least they made him a bishop.

We gather, however, that their kindness was
scarcely successful: Butler was very prosperous, but
it does not appear that he was at all happy. In the
midst of the princely establishment of his rich epis-
copate, so anxious a nature found time to be rather
melancholy. The responsibilities of so cumbrous a
position were but little pleasant to an apprehensive
disposition; wealth and honor were finery and fool-
ishness to a quiet and shrinking man. A small room
in a tranquil college, daily walks and thoughtful talk,
a little income and a few friends, — these and these
only suit a still and meditative mind; such, however,
were denied him. He is said to have taken much
pleasure in discussion and interchange of mind; but
his life was passed in courts and country parsonages,
— the one too noisy, the last too still, to think or
reason. Nor were there many people whom we know
of that were congenial to him in that age; scarcely
any name of a friend of his has come down to us.
One indeed there is, — that of Bishop Secker, afterwards Archbishop of Canterbury; the author of a

treatise on the Catechism, a serious work still used for
the purposes of tuition, with which indeed the name
of the writer is now with some so associated by early
habit that it is difficult to fancy even Butler on equal
social terms with him,—the notion of talking to him
seems like being asked to converse familiarly with
the Catechism itself.

A not unremarkable circumstance, however, shows
that Secker, though he was educated at the same academy, could not have been on any terms of extreme
intimacy with Butler. Some time after Butler's death
there was a rumor that he had died a Papist. There
is no doubt, in fact, that Butler's opinions, being
formed on principles of evidence and reasoning too
strict to be extremely popular, were not likely to be
agreeable to those about him; and when an Englishman sees anything in religion which he does not
like, he always *prima facie* imputes it to the pope.
Besides this general and strong argument, there were
two particular ones : first, that he had erected a cross
in the episcopal chapel at Bristol; secondly, that he
was of a melancholy and somewhat of an ascetic turn,
—reasons which, though doubtless of force in their
day and generation, are not likely to be of avail with
us, who know so much more about crosses and fasting
than they did then. We might have expected that
Secker, as Butler's old friend and schoolfellow, would
have been able from his personal knowledge to throw
a good deal of light upon the question; he was only,
however, able to advance "*presumptive* arguments
that Bishop Butler did not die a Papist,"* which
were no doubt valuable, but yet give no great idea of
the intimacy between the writer and the person about
whom he was writing. Such arguments may easily
be found, and have always convinced every one that
there was no truth in this rumor; the only reason
for which we wish that Secker had been able to say
he had heard Butler talk on the subject, and that he

---

*See Bishop Halifax's Preface to the "Analogy."—ED.

was no Papist, is, that we should then have known
to whom Butler talked. There is nothing in Butler's
writings at all showing any leaning to the peculiar tenets of Roman-Catholicism, and there is much
which shows a strong opinion against them; and it
was far too extreme a doctrine to be at all agreeable
to his very English, moderate, and shrinking mind.

Calumny, however, is commonly instructive. It
must be granted that though there is no trace or
tendency in the writings of Butler [of or] to the
peculiar superstitions advocated by the pope, there
is a strong and prevailing tinge of what may be
called the "principle of superstition,"—that is, the
religion of fear. Some may doubt, especially at the
present day, whether there be any true religion of
that kind at all; yet it seems, as Butler would have
said, but a proper feeling in "such creatures as we
are, in such a world as the present one." *

We may reflect that there are two kinds of religion; which may for some purposes be called, the
one the "natural" and the other the "supernatural."
The former seems to take its rise from mere contemplation of external beauty: we look on the world,
and we see that it is good. The Greek of former
time, reclining softly in his own bright land, "looked
up to the whole sky, and declared that the One was
God." From the blue air and the fair cloud, the
green earth and the white sea, a Presence streams
upon us. It "modulates"

"With murmurs of the air,
And motions of the forests and the sea,
And voice of living beings, and woven hymns
Of night and day, and the deep heart of man."†

But the true home of the idea is in the starlight
sky; we instinctively mingle it with an admiration

---

* " Such a creature as man, placed in the circumstances [in] which we
are in this world."—Preface to Sermons.
† Shelley, " Alastor. "

of infinite space, a cold purity is around us, and the
clear and steel-like words of the poet justly reflect
the doctrine of the clear and steel-like heaven :—

> " The magic car moved on.
> Earth's distant orb appeared
> The smallest light that twinkles in the heaven ;
> Whilst round the chariot's way
> Innumerable systems rolled,
> And countless spheres diffused
> An ever-varying glory.
> It was a sight of wonder : some
> Were hornèd like the crescent moon ;
> Some shed a mild and silver beam
> Like Hesperus across the western sea ;
> Some dashed athwart with trains of flame,
> Like worlds to death and ruin driven ;
> Some shone like suns, and as the chariot passed,
> Eclipsed all other light.

> "Spirit of nature! here,
> In this interminable wilderness
> Of worlds, at whose immensity
> Even soaring fancy staggers,
> Here is thy fitting temple !
> Yet not the lightest leaf
> That quivers to the passing breeze
> Is less instinct with thee :
> Yet not—"*

And so on ; and so it will be as long as there are
poets to look upon the sky, or a sky to be looked
at by them. The truth is, that there is a certain expressiveness (if we may so speak) in nature which
persons of imagination naturally feel more acutely
than others, and which cannot easily be in its full
degree brought home to others except in quotations of
their writings ; from which " smiling of the world,"
as it has been called, more than from any other outward appearance, we infer the existence of an im-
material and animating spirit. This expressiveness
perhaps produces its effect on the mind by a principle

---

* Shelley, " Queen Mab."

analogous to—perhaps in a severe analysis identical
with—the interpretative faculty by which we acquire
a cognizance of the existence of other human minds.
There appear to be certain natural signs and tokens
from which we (like other animals) instinctively infer—
or rather (for there is no conscious reasoning) in which
we silently *see*—life and thought and mind. In this
way we interpret the detail of natural expression,—
the smile, the glance of the eye, the common interjec-
tions, the universal tokens of our simplest emotions;
those signs and marks and expressions which we make
in our earliest infancy, without teaching and by instinct, we appear also, by instinct and without learning,
to read off, interpret, and comprehend, when used to
us by others. The comprehension of this language is
perhaps as much an instinct as the using of it. There
is no occasion, however, for acute metaphysics : whatever was the origin of this faculty, such a power of
interpreting material phenomena, such a faculty of *seeing* life, undoubtedly there is; however we come by
the power, we *can* distinguish living from dead creatures. At any rate, if, like other living creatures, we
take a natural cognizance of the simple expressions
of life and mind, and without tuition comprehend
the language and meaning of natural signs, in like
manner—though less clearly and forcibly, because our
attention is so much less forcibly directed to them—
do we interpret the significance of the beauty and the
sublimity of outward nature. "In the mountains"
do we "feel our faith."* We seem to know there is
something behind. There is a perception

> "Of something far more deeply interfused,
> Whose dwelling is the light of setting suns,
> And the round ocean and the living air,
> And the blue sky, and in the mind of man ,
> A motion and a spirit that impels
> All thinking things, all objects of all thought,
> And rolls through all things."†

* Wordsworth, "Excursion," Book I.   † Wordsworth, "Tintern Abbey."

The Greek mythology is one entire and unmixed embodiment of this "religion of nature," as we may term it, — this poetic interpretation of the spirit that speaks to us in the signs and symbols within us; nor can any sensitive or imaginative mind scrutinize itself without being distinctly conscious of its teaching.

Now, of the poetic religion there is nothing in Butler; no one could tell from his writings that the universe was beautiful. If the world were a Durham mine or an exact square, if no part of it were more expressive than a gravel pit or a chalk quarry, the teaching of Butler would be as true as it is now. A young poet — not a very wise one — once said he "did not like the Bible: there was nothing about flowers in it." * He might have said so of Butler with great truth : a most ugly and stupid world one would fancy *his* books were written in. But in return and by way of compensation for this, there is a religion of another sort, — a religion the source of which is within the mind, as the other's was found to be in the world without : the religion to which we just now alluded as the religion (by an odd yet expressive way of speaking) of *superstition.* The source of this, as most persons are practically aware, is in the conscience. The moral principle (whatever may be said to the contrary by complacent thinkers) is really and to most men a principle of fear. The delights of a good conscience may be reserved for better things, but few men who know themselves will say that they have often felt them by vivid and actual experience; a sensation of shame, of reproach, of remorse, of sin (to use the word we instinctively shrink from because it expresses the meaning), is what the moral principle really and practically thrusts on most men. Conscience is the condemnation of ourselves; we expect a penalty. As the Greek proverb teaches, "where there is shame there is fear;" where there is the deep and intimate anxiety of guilt, — the feeling which has driven murderers and other than murderers

* Hazlitt, "Northcote's Conversations," x.

forth to wastes and rocks and stones and tempests, — we see, as it were, in a single complex and indivisible sensation, the pain and sense of guilt and the painful anticipation of its punishment. How to be free from this is the question; how to get loose from this: how to be rid of the secret tie which binds the strong man and cramps his pride, and makes him angry at the beauty of the universe, — which will not let him go forth like a great animal, like the king of the forest, in the glory of his might, but restrains him with an inner fear and a secret foreboding that if he do but exalt himself he shall be abased, if he do but set forth his own dignity he will offend ONE who will deprive him of it. This, as has often been pointed out, is the source of the bloody rites of heathendom. You are going to battle, you are going out in the bright sun with dancing plumes and glittering spear; your shield shines, and your feathers wave, and your limbs are glad with the consciousness of strength, and your mind is warm with glory and renown — with coming glory and unobtained renown: for who are you to hope for these; who are *you* to go forth proudly against the pride of the sun, with your secret sin and your haunting shame and your real fear? First lie down and abase yourself; strike your back with hard stripes; cut deep with a sharp knife, as if you would eradicate the consciousness; cry aloud; put ashes on your head; bruise yourself with stones, — then perhaps God may pardon you. Or, better still (so runs the incoherent feeling), give him something — your ox, your ass, whole hecatombs if you are rich enough; anything, it is but a chance, — you do not know what will please him; at any rate, what you love best yourself, — that is, most likely, your firstborn son. Then, after such gifts and such humiliation, he may be appeased, he may let you off; he may without anger let you go forth, Achilles-like, in the glory of your shield; he may *not* send you home as he would else, the victim of rout and treachery, with broken arms and foul limbs, in weariness and humiliation.

Of course it is not this kind of fanaticism that we impute to a prelate of the English Church; human sacrifices are not respectable, and Achilles was not rector of Stanhope. But though the costume and circumstances of life change, the human heart does not; its feelings remain. The same anxiety, the same consciousness of personal sin which led in barbarous times to what has been described, show themselves in civilized life as well. In this quieter period, their great manifestation is scrupulosity: a care about the ritual of life; an attention to meats and drinks, and "cups and washings."* Being so unworthy as we are, feeling what we feel, abased as we are abased, who shall say that these are beneath us? In ardent imaginative youth they may seem so: but let a few years come, let them dull the will or contract the heart or stain the mind; then the consequent feeling will be, as all experience shows, not that a ritual is too mean, too low, too degrading for human nature, but that it is a mercy we have to do no more, — that we have only to wash in Jordan, that we have not even to go out into the unknown distance to seek for Abana and Pharpar, rivers of Damascus.† We have no right to judge; we cannot decide; we must do what is laid down for us, — we fail daily even in this; we must never cease for a moment in our scrupulous anxiety to omit by no tittle and to exceed by no iota. An accomplished divine of the present day has written a dissertation to show that this sort of piety is that expressed by the Greek word εὐλάβεια, "piety contemplated on the side in which it is *a fear* of God," and which he derives from "εὐ λαμβάνεσθαι, the image underlying the word being that of the careful taking hold, the cautious handling of some precious yet delicate vessel, which with ruder or less anxious handling might easily be broken;" and he subsequently adds:—

* "Washings of cups."— Mark vii. 4.   † 2 Kings v. 12.

"The only three places in the New Testament in which εὐλαβής occurs are these: Luke ii. 25; Acts ii. 5, viii. 2. We have uniformly translated it 'devout,' nor could any better equivalent be offered for it. It will be observed that on all these occasions it is used to express Jewish—and as one might say, Old Testament—piety. On the first it is applied to Simeon (δίκαιος καὶ εὐλαβής); on the second to those Jews who came from distant parts to keep the commanded feasts at Jerusalem; and on the third there can scarcely be a doubt that the ἄνδρες εὐλαβεῖς who carry Stephen to his burial are not, as might at first sight appear, *Christian* brethren, but devout Jews, who showed by this courageous act of theirs, as by their great lamentation over the slaughtered saint, that they abhorred this deed of blood,—that they separated themselves in spirit from it, and thus, if it might be, from all the judgments which it would bring down on the city of those murderers. Whether it was also further given them to believe on the Crucified, who had such witnesses as Stephen, we are not told; we may well presume that it was.

"If we keep in mind that in that mingled fear and love which together constitute the piety of man toward God, the Old Testament placed its emphasis on the fear, the New places it on the love (though there was love in the fear of God's saints then, and there must be fear in their love now), it will at once be evident how fitly εὐλαβής was chosen to set forth their piety under the Old Covenant who, like Zacharias and Elizabeth, 'were righteous before God, walking in all the commandments and ordinances of the Lord blameless,'* and leaving nothing willingly undone which pertained to the circle of their prescribed duties. For this sense of accurately and scrupulously performing that which is prescribed, with the consciousness of the danger of slipping into a careless negligent performance of God's service, and of the need therefore of anxiously watching against the adding to or diminishing from or in any other way altering that which is commanded, lies over in the words εὐλαβής, εὐλάβεια, when used in their religious significance.

"Plutarch, in more than one very instructive passage, exalts the εὐλάβεια of the old Romans in divine matters, as contrasted with the comparative carelessness of the Greeks. Thus, in his 'Coriolanus' (c. 25), after other instances in proof, he goes on to say, 'Of late time also they did renew and begin a sacrifice thirty times one after another, because they thought still there fell out one fault or other in the same, so holy and devout were they to the gods' (τοιαύτη μὲν εὐλάβεια πρὸς τὸ θεῖον Ῥωμαίων). Elsewhere he portrays

---

* Luke i. 6.

Æmilius Paulus (c. 3) as eminent for his εὐλάβεια. The passage is long, and I will only quote a portion of it, availing myself again of old Sir Thomas North's translation, which, though somewhat loose, is in essentials correct:—'When he did anything belonging to his office of priesthood, he did it with great experience, judgment, and diligence; leaving all other thoughts, and without omitting any ancient ceremony or adding to any new; contending oftentimes with his companions in things which seemed light and of small moment; declaring unto them that though we do presume the gods are easy to be pacified, and that they readily pardon all faults and scapes committed by negligence, yet if it were no more but for respect of commonwealth's sake, they should not slightly or carelessly dissemble or pass over faults committed in those matters."*

This is the view suggested by what Butler has happily called the "presages of conscience" †; by the "natural fear and apprehension" of punishment, "which restrains from . . . crimes" and "is a declaration of nature against them." ‡ The great difficulty of religious philosophy is, to explain how we know that these two Beings are the same; from what course and principle of reasoning it is that we acquire our knowledge that the *curiosus Deus*, the watchful Deity, who is ever in our secret hearts, who seeks us out in the fairest scenes, who is apt to terrify our hearts, whose very eyes seem to shine through nature, is the same Being that animates the universe with its beauty and its light; smooths the heaviness from our brow and the weight from our hearts; pervades the floating cloud and buoyant air;

"And from the breezes, whether low or loud,
And from the rain of every passing cloud,
And from the singing of the summer birds,
And from all sounds, all silence," §

gives hints of joy and hope. This seems the natural dualism: the singular contrast of the God of imagination and the God of conscience, the God of

* Trench, "On the Synonyms of the New Testament," §§ x., xlviii.
† "Analogy," Part I., Chap. III., 4.
‡ Ibid., Part I., Chap. iii., 3.
§ Shelley, "Epipsychidion."

beauty and the God of fear. How do we know that the Being who refreshes is the same as He who imposes the toil; that the God of anxiety is the same as the God of help; that the intensely personal Deity of the inward heart is the same as the almost neutral spirit of external nature, which seems a thing more than a person, a light and impalpable vapor just beautifying the universe and no more?

If we are to offer a suggestion, as we have stated a difficulty, we should hold that the only way of obviating or explaining the contrast, which is so perplexing to susceptible minds, is by recurring to the same primary assumption which is required to satisfy our belief in God's infinity, omnipotence, or veracity. We cannot *prove* in any way that God is infinite, any more than that space is infinite; nor that God is omnipotent, since we do not know what powers there are in nature; that he is perfectly true, for we have had no experience or communication with him in which his veracity could be tested. We assume these propositions; and treat them, moreover, not as hypothetical assumptions or provisional theories, to be discarded if new facts should be discovered and to be rejected if more elaborate research should require it, but as positive and clear certainties, on which we must ever act, and to which we must reduce and square all new information that may be brought home to us. In these respects we assume that God is perfect, and it is only necessary for the solution of our difficulty to assume that he is perfect in all. We have in both cases the same amount and description of evidence, the same inward consciousness, the same speaking and urging voice requiring us to believe. In every step of religious argument we require the assumption, the belief—the faith, if the word is better—in an absolutely *perfect* Being, in and by whom we are, who is omnipotent as well as most holy, who "moves on the face"* of the whole world and ruleth

---

* Gen. i. 2.

"all things by the word of his power."* If we grant
this, the difficulty of the opposition between what
we have called the "natural" and the "supernatural"
religion is removed; and without granting it, that
difficulty is perhaps insuperable. It follows from the
very idea and definition of an infinitely perfect Being,
that he is without us as well as within us; ruling
the clouds of the air and the fishes of the sea as well
as the fears and thoughts of man; smiling through
the smile of nature as well as warning with the pain
of conscience; "sine qualitate bonum, sine quantitate
magnum, sine indigentia creatorem, sine situ præsiden-
tem, sine habitu omnia continentem, sine loco ubique
totum, sine tempore sempiternum, sine ulla sui muta-
tione mutabilia facientem, nihilque patientem."† If
we assume this, life is simple; without this all is dark.

The religion of the imagination is, in its consequences upon the character, free and poetical. No
one need trouble himself to set about its defense:
its agreeability sufficiently defends it, and its congeniality to a refined and literary age. The religion of
the conscience will seem to many of the present day
selfish and morbid; and doubtless it may become so
if it be allowed to eat into the fiber of the character
and to supersede the manliness by which it should be
supported. The whole of religion, of course, is not
of this sort, and it is one which only very imperfect beings can have a share in: but so long as men
are very imperfect, the sense of great imperfection
should cleave to them; and while the consciousness
of sin is on the mind, the consequent apprehension
of deserved punishment seems in its proper degree to
be a reasonable service. However, any more of this
discussion is scarcely to our purpose. No attentive
reader of Butler's writings will hesitate to say that

---

* Heb. i. 3.

† "Good without quality, great without quantity, creator without need,
presiding without location, containing everything without condition, everywhere without place, eternal without time, making changeable things with
no change of his own, suffering nothing."—St. Augustine, "De Trinitate,"
Book v., Chap. I., § 2.

he, at all events, was an example of the "anxious
and scrupulous worshiper, who makes a conscience
of changing anything, of omitting anything, being in
all things fearful to offend"*; and most likely it was
from this habit and characteristic of his mind that
he obtained the unenviable reputation of living and
dying a Papist.

Of Butler's personal habits nothing in the way of
detail has descended to us. He was never married,
and there is no evidence of his ever having spoken to
any lady save Queen Caroline. We hear, however,
for certain that he was commonly present at her
Majesty's philosophical parties, at which all questions,
religious and moral, speculative and practical, were
discussed with a freedom that would astonish the
present generation. Less intellectual unbelief existed
probably at that time than there is now, but there
was an infinitely freer expression of what did exist.
The French revolution frightened the English people;
the awful calamities and horrors of that period were
thought to be (as in part they were) the results and
consequences of the irreligious opinions which just
before prevailed. Skepticism became—what in the
days of Lord Hervey it was not—an ungentlemanly
state of mind. At no meeting of the higher classes,
certainly at none where ladies are present, is there
a tenth part of the plain questioning and *bona fide*
discussion of primary Christian topics that there was
at the select suppers of Queen Caroline. The effect
of these may be seen in many passages, and even in
the whole tendency, of Butler's writings: no great
Christian writer, perhaps, is so exclusively occupied
with elementary topics and philosophical reasonings.
His mind is ever directed towards the first principles of belief; and doubtless this was because, more
than any other, he lived with men who plainly and
clearly denied them. His frequent allusion to the
difficulties of such discussions are likewise suggestive

* Trench, *ubi supra*.

of a familiar personal experience. The whole list of
directions which he gives the clergy of Durham on
religious argument shows a daily familiarity with
skeptical men.

"It is come," he says, "I know not how, to be taken for granted
by many persons that Christianity is not so much as a subject
of inquiry, but that it is now at length discovered to be fictitious.
And accordingly they treat it as if in the present age this were an
agreed point among all people of discernment, and nothing remained
but to set it up as a principal subject of mirth and ridicule, as it
were by way of reprisals for its having so long interrupted the
pleasures of the world."*

No one would so describe the tone of talk now, nor
would there be an equal reason for remembering Butler's general caution against rashly entering the lists
with the questioners: among gentlemen a clergyman
has scarcely the chance.

"Then again, the general evidence of religion is complex and
various. It consists of a long series of things, one preparatory to
and confirming another, from the very beginning of the world to the
present time, and it is easy to see how impossible it must be in a
cursory conversation to unite all this into one argument, and represent it as it ought; and could it be done, how utterly indisposed
people would be to attend to it, say in a cursory conversation:
whereas unconnected objections are thrown out in few words, and
are easily apprehended without more attention than is usual in
common talk. So that notwithstanding we have the best cause in
the world, and though a man were very capable of defending it,
yet I know not why he should be forward to undertake it upon so
great a disadvantage, and to so little good effect, as it must be done
amid the gayety and carelessness of common conversation."†

It is not likely, from these remarks, that Butler had
much pleasure at the Queen's talking parties.

What his pleasures were, indeed, does not very
distinctly appear. In reading we doubt if he took
any keen interest. A voracious reader is apt, when

---

* This passage is not from the "Charge to the Clergy," as the text implies, but from the "Advertisement" to the "Analogy."—ED.

† "Charge to the Clergy of Durham."

he comes to write, to exhibit his reading in casual references and careless innuendoes, which run out insensibly from the fullness of his literary memory; but of this in Butler there is nothing. His writings contain little save a bare (and often not a very plain) statement of the necessary argument; you cannot perhaps find a purely literary allusion in his writings,—none, at all events, which shows he had any favorite books, whose topics were ever present to his mind, and whose well-known words might be a constant resource in moments of weariness and melancholy. There is, too, a philippic in the well-known "Preface" against vague and thoughtless reading, which seems as if he felt the evil consequences more than the agreeableness of that sin. Some men find a compensation in the excitement of writing for all other evils and exclusions; but it is probable that if Butler hated anything, he hated his pen. Composition is pleasant work for men of ready words, fine ears, and thick-coming illustrations: wit and eloquence please the writer as much as the reader; there is even some pleasantness in feeling that you have given a precise statement of a strong argument. But Butler, so far from having the pleasures of eloquence, had not even the comfort of perspicuity. He never could feel that he had made an argument tell by his way of wording it; it tells in his writings, if it tells at all, by its own native and inherent force. In some places the mode of statement is even stupid; it seems selected to occasion a difficulty. You often see that writers—Gibbon, for instance—believe that their words are good to eat as well as to read; they had plainly a pleasure in rolling them about in the mouth like sugar-plums, and gradually smoothing off any knots or excrescences: but there is nothing of this in Butler.

The circumstance of so great a thinker being such a poor writer is not only curious in itself, but indicates the class of thinkers to which Butler belongs.

Philosophers may be divided into seers on the one hand, and into gropers on the other. Plato, to use a contrast which is often used for other purposes, is the type of the first: on all subjects he seems to have before him a landscape of thought, with clear outline and pure air, keen rocks and shining leaves, an Attic sky and crystal-flowing river, each detail of which was as present, as distinct, as familiar to his mind as the view from the Acropolis or the road to Decelea. As were his conceptions, so is his style: what Protagoras said and Socrates replied, what Thrasymachus and Polemo, what Gorgias and Callicles, all comes out in distinct sequence and accurate expression; each feature is engraved on the paper, an exact beauty is in every line. What a contrast is the style of Aristotle! He sees nothing; he is like a man groping in the dark about a room which he knows. He hesitates and suggests; proposes first one formula and then another; rejects both, gives a multitude of reasons, and ends at last with an expression which he admits to be incorrect, and an apologetic "Let it make no difference." There are whole passages in his writings — the discussion about Solon and happiness in the "Ethics" is an instance — in which he appears like a schoolboy who knows the answer to a sum, but cannot get the figures to come to it.

This awkward and hesitating manner is likewise that of Butler. He seems to have an obscure feeling, an undefined perception of what the truth is; but his manipulation of words and images is not apt enough to bring it out. Like the miser in the story, he has a shilling *about* him somewhere, if people will only give him time and solitude to make research for it. As a person hunting for a word or name he has forgotten, he knows what it is, *only* he cannot say it. The fault is one characteristic of a strong and sound mind wanting in imagination; the visual faculty is deficient. The soundness of such men's understandings insures a correct report of what comes before them, and their strength is shown in vigorous observations upon it, but they are unable to bring those remarks out,—the delineative power is wanting : they have no picture of the particulars in their minds; no instance or illustration occurs to them. Popular, in the large sense of the term, such writers can never be ; influential they may often become. The learned have time for difficulties ; the critical mind is pleased with crooked constructions ; the detective intellect likes the research for lurking and half-hidden truth. In this way, portions of Aristotle have been noted these thousand years as Chinese puzzles ; and without detracting for a moment from Butler's real merit, it may be allowed that some of his influence, especially that which he enjoys in the English universities, is partially due to that obscurity of style which renders his writings such apt exercises for the critical intellect, which makes the truth when found seem more valuable from the difficulty of finding it, and [which] gives scope for an able lecturer to elucidate, annotate, and expound.

The fame of Butler rests mainly on two remarkable courses of reasoning, one of which is contained in the well-known Sermons, the second in the "Analogy." Both seem to be in a great measure suggested by the circumstances and topics of the time : there was a certain naturalness in Butler's mind which took him straight to the questions on which men differed around him. Generally, it is safer to prove what no one denies, and easier to explain difficulties which no one has ever felt; a quiet reputation is best obtained in the literary *quæstiunculæ* of important subjects. But a simple and straightforward man studies great topics because he feels a want of the knowledge which they contain; and if he has ascertained an apparent solution of any difficulty, he is anxious to impart it to others. He goes straight to the real doubts and fundamental discrepancies,—to those on which it is easy to excite odium and difficult to give satisfaction; he leaves to others the amusing skirmishing and superficial literature accessory to such studies. Thus there is nothing light in Butler; all is grave, serious, and essential,—nothing else would be characteristic of him.

The Sermons of Butler are primarily intended as an answer to that recurring topic of ethical discussion, the Utilitarian Philosophy. He is occasionally spoken of by enthusiastic disciples as having uprooted this forever; but this is hardly so,—the selfish system still lives and flourishes. Nor must any writer on the fundamental differences of human opinion propose to himself such an aim. The source of the great heresies of belief lies in their congeniality to certain types of character frequent in the world, and liable to be reproduced by inevitable and recurring circumstances. We do not mean that the variations of creeds are the native and essential variances of the minds which believe them; for this would render truth a matter of personal character, and make general discussion impossible. We believe that all minds are originally so constituted as to be able to acquire right opinions on all subjects of the first importance to them : but nevertheless, that the native bent of their character instinctively inclines them to particular views; that one man is naturally prone to one error and another to its opposite; that this is increased by circumstances, and becomes for practical purposes invincible, unless it be met on the part of every man by early and vigorous resistance. The Epicurean philosophy is an example of these recurring and primary errors, inasmuch as it is congenial to clear, vigorous, and hasty minds, which have no great depth of feeling and no searching introspection of thought; which prefer a ready solution to an accurate, an easy to an elaborate, a simple to a profound. Draw a slight worldliness—and the events of life will draw it—over such a mind, and you have the best

Epicurean. There is a use, however, in discussing
topics like these. Nothing would be more perverse
than to abstain from proving certain truths because
some men were naturally prone to the opposite errors :
rather, on the contrary, should we din them into the
ears and thrust them upon the attention of mankind ;
go out into the highways and hedges, and leave as
few as possible for invincible ignorance to mislead
or to excuse. It is much in every generation to state
the ancient truth in the manner which that generation
requires ; to state the old answer to the old difficulty ;
to transmit if not discover, convince if not invent :
to translate into the language of the living the truths
first discovered by the dead. This defense, though
suggested by the subject, is not, however, required
by Butler : he may claim the higher praise of having
explained his subject in a manner essentially more
satisfactory than his predecessors.

We are not concerned to follow Butler into the
entire range of this ancient and well-discussed topic ;
we are only called on to make, and we shall only
make, two or three remarks on the position which
he occupies with respect to it. His grand merit is
the simple but important one of having given a less
complex and more graphic description of the facts of
human consciousness than any one had done before.
Before his time the Utilitarians had the advantage of
appearing to be the only people who talked about real
life and human transactions ; the doctrines avowed
by their opponents were cloudy, lofty, and impalpable. Platonic philosophy in its simple form is utterly
inexplicable to the English mind : a plain man will
not soon succeed in making anything of an archety-
pal idea. If an ordinary sensible Englishman takes
up even such a book as Cudworth's "Immutable
Morality," it is nearly inevitable that he should put
it down as mystical fancy. True as a considerable
portion of the conclusions of that treatise are or may
be, nevertheless the truth is commonly so put as to

puzzle an Englishman, and the error so as particularly to offend him. We may open at random.

"Wherefore," says Cudworth, "the result of all that we have
hitherto said is this, that the intelligible natures and essences of
things are neither arbitrary nor fantastical, — that is, neither alterable by any will whatsoever, nor changeable by opinion ; and
therefore everything is necessarily and immutably to science and
knowledge what it is, — whether absolutely, or relatively to all
minds and intellects in the world. So that if moral good and evil,
just and unjust, signify any reality, either absolute or relative, in
the things so denominated, as they must have some certain natures,
which are the actions or souls of men, they are neither alterable
by mere will nor opinion.

"Upon which ground that wise philosopher, Plato, in his
'Minos,' determines that νόμος, a law, is not δόγμα πόλεως, any arbitrary decree of a city or supreme governors, — because there may
be unjust decrees, which therefore are no laws, — but τοῦ ὄντος
ἐξεύρεσις, the invention of that which is, or which is absolutely or
immutably just in its own nature ; though it be very true also
that the arbitrary constitutions of those that have lawful authority
of commanding, when they are not materially unjust, are laws also
in a secondary sense, by virtue of that natural and immutable
justice or law that requires political order to be observed.

"But I have not taken all this pains only to confute skepticism
or fantasticism, or merely to defend or corroborate our argument
for the immutable natures of just and unjust ; but also for some
other weighty purposes that are very much conducing to the business that we have in hand. And first of all, that the soul is not
a mere *rasa tabula*, a naked and passive thing, which has no
innate furniture or activity of its own, nor anything at all in it
but what was impressed on it without ; for if it were so, then
there could not possibly be any such thing as moral good and evil,
just and unjust, forasmuch as these differences do not arise merely
from the outward objects, or from the impresses which they make
upon us by sense, there being no such thing in them. In which
sense it is truly affirmed by the author of the 'Leviathan' (page
24*) that there is no 'common rule of good and evil to be taken
from the nature of the objects themselves,'—that is, either considered absolutely in themselves, or relatively to external sense only,
—but according to some other interior analogy which things have
to a certain inward determination in the soul itself, from whence

* Part 1., Chap. vi.

the foundation of all this difference must needs arise, as I shall
show afterwards; not that the anticipations of morality spring
merely from intellectual forms and notional ideas of the mind, or
from certain rules or propositions arbitrarily printed upon the soul
as upon a book, but from some other more inward and vital
principle in intellectual beings as such, whereby they have a natural determination in them to do some things and to avoid others,
which could not be if they were mere naked passive things."*

It is instructive to compare Butler's way of stating
a doctrine substantially similar.

"Mankind has various instincts and principles of action, as
brute creatures have ; some leading most directly and immediately
to the good of the community, and some most directly to private
good.

"Man has several which brutes have not ; particularly reflection
or conscience, an approbation of some principles or actions and disapprobation of others.

"Brutes obey their instincts or principles of action, according
to certain rules ; suppose the constitution of their body, and the
objects around them.

"The generality of mankind also obey their instincts and principles, all of them, — those propensions we call good, as well as the
bad, — according to the same rules ; namely, the constitution of their
body and the external circumstances which they are in.

"Brutes, in acting according to the rules before mentioned,
their bodily constitution and circumstances, act suitably to their
whole nature.

"Mankind also, in acting thus, would act suitably to their whole
nature, if no more were to be said of man's nature than what has
been now said ; if that, as it is a true, were also a complete, adequate account of our nature.

"But that is not a complete account of man's nature. Somewhat further must be brought in to give us an adequate notion of
it ; namely, that one of those principles of action, conscience or
reflection, compared with the rest as they all stand together in the
nature of man, plainly bears upon it marks of authority over all
the rest, and claims the absolute direction of them all, to allow or
forbid their gratifications ; a disapprobation of reflection being in
itself a principle manifestly superior to a mere propension. And
the conclusion is, that to allow no more to this superior principle
or part of our nature, than to other parts ; to let it govern and

* Chap. vi.

guido only occasionally in common with the rest, as its turn happens to come from the temper and circumstances one happens to
be in, — this is not to act conformably to the constitution of man.
Neither can any human creature be said to act conformably to his
constitution of nature, unless he allows to that superior principle
the absolute authority which is due to it. And this conclusion is
abundantly confirmed from hence: that one may determine what
course of action the economy of man's nature requires, without so
much as knowing in what degrees of *strength* the several principles
prevail, or which of them have actually the greatest influence.

"The practical reason of insisting so much upon this natural
authority of the principle of reflection or conscience is, that it
seems in a great measure overlooked by many, who are by no
means the worst sort of men. It is thought sufficient to abstain
from gross wickedness, and to be humane and kind to such as
happen to come in their way: whereas, in reality, the very constitution of our nature requires that we bring our whole conduct
before this superior faculty; wait its determination; enforce upon
ourselves its authority; and make it the business of our lives, as
it is absolutely the whole business of a moral agent, to conform
ourselves to it. This is the true meaning of that ancient precept,
Reverence thyself."*

We do not mean that Cudworth's style is not as
good [as] or better than the style of Butler: but that
the language and illustrations of the latter belong to
the same world as that we live in, have a relation to
practice, and recall sentiments we remember to have
felt and sensations which are familiar to us; while
those of Cudworth, on the contrary, seem difficult, and
are strange in the ears of the common people.

We do not need to go more deeply into the discussion of Butler's doctrine, for it is familiar to our
readers. If there is any incorrectness in the delineation which he has given of conscience, it is in the
passages in which he speaks or seems to speak of
it more as an animating or suggesting than as a
criticizing or regulative faculty. The error of this
representation has been repeatedly pointed out and
illustrated in these pages. † It is probable, indeed,
that Butler's attention had scarcely been directed

---

* Preface to Sermons.   † Of the *Prospective Review.*

with sufficient precision to this portion of the subject. It follows easily, from his favorite principles, that when two impulses — say benevolence and self-love — contend for mastery in the mind, and conscience pronounces that one is a higher and better motive of action than the other, the office of conscience is judicial and not impulsive. Conscience gives its opinion, and the will obeys or disobeys at its pleasure; the impelling spring of action is the selected impulse on which the will finally decides to act. At the same time, it must be admitted that there are cases when, for practical purposes, conscience is an impelling and goading faculty; we mean when it is opposed by indolence. There is a heavy lassitude of the will which is certainly spurred, sometimes effectually and sometimes in vain, by our conscience. Possibly the correct language may be, that in such cases the desire of ease is opposed by the desire of doing our duty; and that in this case also the office of conscience is simply to say that the latter is higher than the former. To us it seems, however, if we may trust our consciousness on points of such exact nicety, that it is more graphically true to speak of the sluggishness of the will being goaded and stimulated by the activity of conscience; there is a native inertness in the voluntary faculty which will not come forth unless great occasion is shown it. At any rate, something like this was perhaps the meaning of Butler; and he, no doubt, would have included in the term "conscience" the desire to do our duty as such, and because it is such.

Butler has been claimed by Mr. Austin, in his "Province of Jurisprudence" (and sometimes since by other writers), as a supporter of the "Compound Utilitarian" scheme, as it has been called, which regards the promotion of general happiness as the single inherent characteristic of virtuous actions, and considers the conscience as a special instinct for directing men in determining what actions are for the

general interest and what are not. This theory is of
course distinct from the common Epicurean scheme,
which either denies like Bentham the fact of a conscience *in limine,* * or like Mill professes to explain it
away as an effect of illusion and association. The
"Composite" theory, on the other hand, distinctly
admits the existence and obligatory authority of conscience, but regards it as a ready, expeditious, and so
to say telegraphic mode of arriving at results which
could otherwise be reached only by toilsome and
dubious discussions of general utility. In our judgment, however, the writings of Butler hardly warrant
an authoritative ascription to him of this philosophy.
He doubtless held that the promotion of general happiness, taking all time and all the world into a complete account, is *one* characteristic and ascertainable
property of virtue; but there is nothing to show that
he thought it was the only one. On the contrary, we
think we could show with some plausibility, from
several passages, that in his judgment, virtuous actions had besides several essential and appropriate
qualities. He was at all events the last man to deny
that they might have; and his whole reasoning on
the subject of moral probation seems to imply that
inasmuch as such a state is, according to every appearance, not at all the readiest or surest means of
promoting satisfaction and enjoyment, it cannot have
been selected for the cultivation of either satisfaction or enjoyment. It is one thing to hold that, the
nature of man being what it is, a virtuous life is the
happiest as well as best; and another, that such a
life is the best because it is the happiest, and that
the nature of man was created in the manner it is
in order to produce such happiness. The first is of
course the doctrine of Butler; the second there does
not seem any certain ground for imputing to him.

The religious side of morals is rather indicated and
implied than elaborated or worked out by Butler;

---

* "At the outset."

yet as we formerly said, a constant reference to the "presages of conscience" pervades his writings. Although he has nowhere drawn out the course of reasoning fully, or step by step, it is certain that he relied on the moral evidence for a moral Providence; not indeed with foolhardy assurance, but with the cautious confidence which was habitual to him. The ideas which are implied in the term "justice"—the connection between virtue and reward, sin and punishment, a sacred law and holy Ruler—were plainly the trains of reflection most commonly present to his mind.

Persons who give credence to an intuitive conscience are so often taunted with the variations and mutability of human nature that it is worth noticing how complete is the coincidence, in essential points of feeling, between minds so different as Butler, Kant, and Plato. We can scarcely imagine among thoughtful men a greater diversity of times and characters: the great Athenian in his flowing robes daily conversing in captious Athens, the quiet rector wandering in Durham coal fields, the smoking professor in ungainly Königsberg, would, if the contrast were not too great for art, form a trio worthy of a picture. The whole series of truths and reasonings which we have called the supernatural religion, or that of conscience, is, however, as familiar to one as to the other, and is the most important if not the most conspicuous feature in the doctrinal teaching of all three. The very great differences of nomenclature and statement, the entire contrast in the style of expression, do but heighten the wonder of the essential and interior correspondence. The doctrine has certainly shown its capability of coexisting with several forms of civilization; and at least the simplest explanation of its diffusion is by supposing that it has a real warrant in the nature and consciousness of man.

Such is the doctrine of the Sermons. The argument of the "Analogy" is of a different and more

complicated kind; and from its refinement, requires
to be stated with care and precaution. As the Sermons are in a great measure a reply to the caricá-
turists of Locke, the "Analogy" is in reality designed
as a confutation of Shaftesbury and Bolingbroke. It
was the object of those writers, as of others since, to
disprove the authority of the Christian and Jewish
revelation[s], by showing that they enjoined on man
conduct forbidden by the law of nature, and likewise
imputed to the Deity actions of an evil tendency and
degrading character. These writers are commonly,
and perhaps best, met by a clear denial of the fact, —
by showing in detail that Christianity is really open
to no such objections, contains no such precepts, and
imputes no such actions; the reply of Butler is much
more refined and peculiar.

The argument has been thus expounded and its
supposed bearing explained by Professor Rogers, in
the notice of Butler the title of which we have ventured to affix to this article : —

"Further, we cannot but think that the conclusiveness of
Butler's work as against its true object, *the deist*, has often been
underrated by many even of its genuine admirers. Thus, Dr.
Chalmers, for instance, who gives such glowing proofs of his admiration of the work, and expatiates in a congenial spirit on its merits,
affirms that 'they overrate the power of analogy who look to it
for any very distinct or positive contribution to the Christian argument. To repel objections, in fact, is the great service which this
'Analogy' has rendered to the cause of revelation, and it is the
only service which we seek for at its hands.'* This, abstractedly,
is true; but *in fact,* considering the *position* of the bulk of the
objectors, that they have been invincibly persuaded of the truth of
theism, and that their objections to Christianity have been exclusively or chiefly of the kind dealt with in the 'Analogy,' the work
is much more than an *argumentum ad hominem,* — it is not simply
of negative value. To such *objectors* it logically establishes the
truth of Christianity, or it forces them to recede from theism, which
the bulk will not do. If a man says, 'I am invincibly persuaded
of the truth of proposition A, but I cannot receive proposition B,

---

* "Prelections on Butler's 'Analogy.'" (The two sentences are in-
verted from the original.—ED.)

because objections a, β, γ are opposed to it; if these were removed, my objections would cease:' then, if you can show that a, β, γ equally apply to the proposition A (his reception of which, he says, is based on invincible evidence), you do really compel such a man to believe that not only B *may* be true, but that it *is* true, unless he be willing (which few in the parallel case are) to abandon proposition A as well as B. This is precisely the condition in which the majority of deists have ever been, if we may judge from their writings. It is usually the *a priori* assumption that certain facts in the history of the Bible, or some portions of its doctrine, are unworthy of the Deity and incompatible with his character or administration, that has chiefly excited the incredulity of the deist, far more than any dissatisfaction with the positive evidence which substantiates the divine origin of Christianity. Neutralize these objections by showing that they are *equally* applicable to what he declares he cannot relinquish, the doctrines of theism, and you show him, if he has a particle of logical sagacity, not only that Christianity may be true, but that it is so: and his only escape is by relapsing into atheism, or resting his opposition on other objections of a very feeble character in comparison, and which probably few would ever have been contented with alone; for, *apart* from those objections which Butler repels, the historical evidence for Christianity — the evidence on behalf of the integrity of its records and the honesty and sincerity of its founders, showing that they *could* not have constructed such a system if they *would*, and *would* not, supposing them impostors, if they *could* — is stronger than that for any [other] fact in history.

"In consequence of this position of the argument, Butler's book, to large classes of objectors, though practically an *argumentum ad hominem*, not only proves Christianity *may* be true, but in all logical fairness proves it *is* so. This he himself, with his usual judgment, points out. He says, 'And objections which are equally applicable to both natural and revealed religion are, properly speaking, answered by its being shown that they are so, *provided the former be admitted to be true.*'"

No one can deny the ingenuity of this line of reasoning; but we can only account for the great assent which it has received by supposing that the goodness of the cause for which it is commonly brought forward has not unnaturally led to an undue approbation of the argument itself. From the amount of authority in its favor, we feel some diffidence; but otherwise we should have said without hesitation that it was open to several objections.

In the first place, so far from its being probable that revelation would have contained the same difficulties as nature, we should have expected that it would explain those difficulties. The very term "supernatural revelation" implies that, previously and by nature, man is to a great extent in ignorance; that particularly he is unaware of some fact or series of facts which God deems it fit that he should know. The instinctive presumption certainly is, that those facts would be most important to us. No doubt it is possible that for incomprehensible reasons a special revelation should be made of facts purely indifferent, — of the date when London was founded, or the precise circumstances of the invasion by William the Conqueror; but this is in the highest degree improbable. What seems likely (and the whole argument is essentially one of likelihood), according to our mind, is, that the revelation which God would vouchsafe to us would be one affecting our daily life and welfare; would communicate truths either on the one hand conducing to our temporal happiness in the present world, or removing the many doubts and difficulties which surround the general plan of Providence, the entire universe, and our particular destiny. These are the two classes of truths on which we seem to require help, and it is in the first instance more probable that assistance would be given us on those points on which it is most required.

The argument of Butler, of course, relates to our religious difficulties; and it seems impossible to deny that this is the exact class of difficulty which it is most likely a revelation, if given, would explain. No one who reasons on this subject is likely to doubt that the natural faculties of man are more clearly adequate to our daily and temporal happiness than to the explanation of the perplexities which have confounded men since the beginning of speculation; of

which the mere statement is so vast; which relate to
the scheme of the universe and the plan of God. This
is the one principle on which the most extreme skeptics and the most thorough advocates of revelation
meet and agree. The skeptic says, "Man is not born
to resolve the mystery of the universe; but he must
nevertheless attempt it, that he may keep within the
limits of the knowable:" which really means that he
is to fold* his hands and be quiet; to abstain from all
religious inquiry; to confine himself to this life, and
be industrious and practical within its limits. The
advocate of revelation is forever denying the competency of man's faculties to explain or puzzle out what
in the large sense most concerns him. There are difficulties celestial and difficulties terrestrial; but it is
certainly more likely that God would interfere mirac-
ulously to explain the first than to remove the second.

Let us look at the argument more at length. The
supposition and idea of a "miraculous revelation"
rest on the ignorance of man. The scene of nature
is stretched out before him: it has rich imagery and
varied colors and infinite extent; its powers move
with a vast sweep; its results are executed with exact precision; it gladdens the eyes and enriches the
imagination; it tells us something of God,—something important, yet not enough. For example, difficulties abound; poverty and sin, pain and sorrow,
fear and anger press on us with a heavy weight.
On every side our knowledge is confined and our
means of enlarging it small. Of this the outer world
takes no heed; nature is "unfeeling"†; her laws roll
on; "beautiful and dumb," she passes forward and
vouchsafes no sign. Indeed, she seems to hide, as
one might fancy, the dark mysteries of life which
seem to lie beneath; our feeble eyes strain to look
forward, but her "painted veil"‡ hangs over all, like

---

* *Review,* "use," more consonantly with the sense.—ED.
† Goethe, "The Godlike" (short poem).
‡ "Lift not the painted veil which those who live
  Call life."—Shelley, Sonnet (1818).

an October mist upon the morning hills. Here, as
it seems, revelation intervenes: God will break the
spell that is upon us, will meet our need, will break
as it were through the veil of nature; he will show
us of himself. It is not likely, surely, that he will
break the everlasting silence to no end; that having
begun to speak, he will tell us nothing; that he will
leave the difficulties of life where he found them, that
he will repeat them in his speech, that he will revive
them in his word. It seems rather as if his faintest
disclosure, his least word, would shed abundant light
on all doubts, would take the weight from our minds,
would remove the gnawing anguish from our hearts.
Surely, surely, if he speaks he will make an end of
speaking, he will show us some good, he will destroy
"the veil that is spread over all nations"* and the
"covering that is cast over all peoples"†; he will not
"darken counsel by words without knowledge." ‡

To this line of argument we know of but one
objection: it may be said that from the immensity
of the universe in which man is, reasons may exist
for communicating to him facts of which he cannot
appreciate the importance, but a belief in which
may nevertheless be most important to his ultimate
welfare. Of this kind, according to some divines, is
the doctrine of the Atonement: as they think, it is
impossible to explain the mode in which the death
of Christ conduces to the forgiveness of sin, or why
a belief in it should be made, as they think it is, a
necessary preliminary to such forgiveness. They consider that this is a revealed matter of fact; part of
a system of things which is not known now, which
would very likely be above our understanding if it
were explained, which at all events is not explained.
We reply that the revelation of an inexplicable fact
is possible, and that if adequate evidence could be
adduced in its favor we might be bound to acquiesce

* Isaiah xxv. 7.   † Ibid.
‡ Job xxxviii. 2.

in it: but that on the other hand, such a revelation is extremely improbable; so far as we can see, there was no occasion for it; it helps in nothing, explains to us nothing; it enlarges our knowledge only thus far, — that for some unknown reason we are bound to believe something from which certain effects follow in a manner which we cannot understand. Such a revelation is, as has been said, possible; but it is much more likely, *a priori*, that a revelation, if given, would be a revelation of facts suited to our comprehension and throwing a light on the world in which we are.

The same remark is applicable to a revelation commanding rites and ceremonies which do not come home to the conscience as duties, and of which the reasons are not explained to us by the revelation itself. The Pharisaic code of "cups and washings" is an obvious instance: it is obviously most improbable that we should be ordered to do these things. The fact may be so; but the evidence of it should be overwhelming, and should be examined with almost suspicious and skeptical care. A revelation of a rule of life which approves itself to the heart, which awakens conscience, which seems to come from God, is the greatest conceivable aid to man, the greatest explanation of our most practical perplexities; a revelation of rites and ordinances is a revelation of new difficulties, telling us nothing of God, imposing an additional task-work on ourselves.

We are to remember that the "Analogy" is, as the Germans would speak, a *kritik* of every possible revelation. The first principle of it rests on the inquiry, "What would it be likely that a revelation, if vouchsafed, would contain?" The whole argument is one of preconception, presumption, and probability. It claims to establish a principle which may be used in defense of any revelation, the Mohammedan as well as the Christian; according to it, as soon as you can show that a difficulty exists in nature, you may immediately expect to find it in revelation. If carried out to its extreme logical development, it would come to this : that if a catalogue were constructed of all the inexplicable arrangements and difficulties of nature, you might confidently anticipate that these very same difficulties, in the same degree and in the same points, would be found in revelation ; both being from the same Author, it is presumed that each would resemble the other. The principle even to this length is enunciated by Mr. Rogers : the difficulties of nature are the a, β, γ of the extract; and he asserts that if you can show that all of them exist in one system, you have every reason to expect *all* of them in the other. Yet surely, what can be more monstrous than that a supernatural communication from God should simply enumerate all the difficulties of his natural government and not enlighten us as to any of them ; should revive our perplexities without removing them ; should not satisfy one doubt or one anxiety, but repeat and proclaim every fact which can give a basis to them both ?

The case does not rest here : there is a second ground of objection to the argument of the "Analogy" on which we are inclined to lay nearly equal stress. As has been said, it is most likely that a revelation from God would explain at least a part of the religious difficulties of man ; and in matter of fact, all systems purporting to be revelations have in their respective degrees professed to do so. They all deal with what may be called the "system" of the universe, — its moral plan and scheme : the destiny of man therein, the motives from which God created it, and the manner in which he directs it. Throughout the whole range of doctrines, from Mormonism up to Christianity, no one has ever gained any acceptance, has ever perhaps been sincerely put forward, which did not deal with this whole range of facts ; which did not tell man, according to his* view, whence he

* *Review*, "its."

is and whither he goes. Revelations, as such, are communications concerning eternity. Now, it seems to us that so far from its being likely, *a priori*, that a revelation of this sort would contain the same perplexing difficulties which cause so much evil in this world, in the same degree in which they exist here, it would be scarcely possible by any evidence, *a posteriori*, to establish the communication of such a system from the Divine Being. It seems clear on the surface of the subject that, the extent of the unknown world being so enormous in comparison with that which is known, this scene being so petty and the plan of Providence so vast,—earth being little and space infinite, Time short and Eternity long,—a difficulty which is of no moment in so contracted a sphere as this becomes of infinite moment when extended to the sphere of the Almighty. From the smallness of the region which we see, the short time which we live, from the few things which we know, it may well be that there are points which perplex the feebleness of our understanding and puzzle the best feelings of our hearts. We see, as some one expresses it, the universe "not in plan but in section"; and we cannot expect to understand very much of it. But when our knowledge increases, when by a revelation that plan is unfolded to us, when God vouchsafes to communicate to us the 'system on which he acts,—then it is rational to expect those difficulties would diminish, would gradually disappear as the light dawned upon us, would vanish finally when the dayspring arose on our hearts. If a difficulty of nature be repeated in revelation, it would seem to show that it was not, as we had before supposed, a consequence of our shortsighted views and contracted knowledge, but a real inherent element in the scheme of the universe; not a petty shade on a petty globe, but a pervading inherent stain, extending over all things, destroying the beauty of the universe, impairing the perfectness of all creation. Take as an instance, the extreme doctrine of Antinomian Calvinism: suppose that the eternal condition of man depended in no degree on his acts or works, or upon himself in any form, but on an arbitrary act of selection by God, which chose some, independently of any antecedent fitness on their part, for eternal happiness, and consigned all others, irrespective of their guilt or innocence, to eternal ruin. Nothing, of course, can be more shocking than such a doctrine when stated in simple language; and if it really were contained in any document that professes to be a revelation, we should be plainly justified in passing it by as a document which no evidence would prove to have been inspired by God. Yet the doctrine certainly does not want partial analogies in this world. The condition of men here does seem to be in a considerable measure the result not of what they do or of what their characters are, but of the mere circumstances in which they are placed, over which they have no control, choice, or power. One man is born in a ditch, another in a palace; one with a gloomy and painful, another with a cheerful and happy mind; one to honor, another to dishonor. We invent words — "fortune," "luck," "chance" — to express in a subtle way the notion that some seem the favorites of circumstance, others the scapegoats. So far as it goes, this is a distinct "election" on the part of God, of some to misery, of others to felicity, irrespective of their personal qualities; accordingly, it may be argued, why should we not expect to find the same in the world of revelation, which is from the hand of the same Creator? But this will scarcely impose on any one. A certain indignation arises within us; conscience uplifts her voice, and we reply, "It may well be that for a short time God may afflict his people without their own fault; but that he should do so forever, that he should make no end of injustice, that he favors one without a reason and condemns another without a fault, — this, come what may, we will not believe; we would sooner cast ourselves at large on the waste of uncertainty. Pass on with your teaching, and ask God, if so be, that he will pardon you for attributing such things to him." We need not further enlarge on this.

Again,—and in the practical conduct of the argument this is a very material consideration,—all revelations impute *intentions* to God. Acts are done, observances enjoined, a Providential plan pursued, for reasons which are explained. The cause of this is evident from our previous reasoning. As we have seen, all revelations profess to vindicate the ways of God to man; and it is impossible to do so effectually without declaring to us at least some of his motives and designs. It is most important to observe that no analogy from nature can justify us in judging of these except by the standard of right or wrong which God has implanted within us. From external observation we learn almost nothing of God's intentions: the scheme is too large, the universe too unbounded. One phenomenon follows another: but except in a few cases, and then very dubiously, we cannot tell which was created for which; which was the design, which the means; which the determining object and which the subservient purpose. Even in the few cases in which we do impute such intentions, we do so because they seem to be in harmony with God's moral character; they are not strictly proved,—they are mere conjectures,—and we should reject at once any that might seem ethically unworthy. But the case is different with a revelation, which from its own nature unfolds ends and instruments in their due measure and their actual subordination, which develops an orderly system and communicates hidden motives and unforeseen designs. A recent writer, for example, thus defends certain apparent cruelties of the Old Testament by stating those of nature:—

"God," he says, "sends his pestilence, and produces horrors on which imagination dares not dwell; horrors not only physical, but indirectly moral, often transforming man into something like the

fiend so many say he can never become. He sends his famine, and
thousands perish—men and women, and 'the child that knows not
its right hand from its left'*—in prolonged and frightful agonies.
He opens the mouth of volcanoes, and bakes, boils, and fries the
population of a whole city in torrents of burning lava,"†

etc., etc., with much else to the same purpose. But
this must not be adduced in extenuation of anything
of which the reasons are narrated; on the contrary,
these last must be judged of by the moral faculties
which are among God's highest gifts. To the inflic-
tion of pain, with an express view to what conscience
tells us to be an unworthy object, outward nature
does and can afford no parallel. She has no avowals;
it is but from conjecture that we conceive her motives.
Her laws pass forward; the crush of her forces is
upon us: like a child in a railway, we know not anything. The incomprehensible has no analogy to the
explained, the mysterious none to that on which the
oracle has intelligibly spoken.

Lastly, for a similar reason it is impossible that
there should be any analogy in nature for a precept
from God opposed to the law of conscience. External
nature gives no precept,—our knowledge of our duty
comes from within; the physical world is subordinate
to our inward teaching, it is silent on points of
morality. On the other hand, a revelation, supposing
satisfactory means of attesting it were found, might
possibly contain such a precept. It is very painful to
put such suppositions before the mind; but the pain
is inherent in the nature of the subject. The topic
of the difficulties and perplexities of man cannot, by
any artifice of rhetoric, be rendered pleasing. In
such a case, supposing there to be no difficulty of

* "Persons that cannot discern between their right hand and their left
hand."—Jonah iv. 11.

† Professor Rogers's "Defense of the 'Eclipse of Faith.'" It is to be
observed, we are not at all speaking of the facts of the Old Testament;
we are but limiting the considerations on which the above writer has rested
its defense. These refined reasonings but weaken the case they are brought
to support. "I did not know," said George III., "that the Bible needed an
apology."—B.

evidence in the case, our duty might be to obey God even against conscience, from that assurance of his essential perfection which is the most certain attestation of conscience. But the existence of such a difficulty is in the highest degree improbable; it is one which ought only to be admitted on the completest proof and after the most rigid straining of evidence; it is, from the nature of the case, without a parallel in the common and unrevealed world.

To all these considerable objections, we believe the argument of the "Analogy" is properly subject. We think in general that according to every reasonable presumption, a revelation would not repeat the same difficulties as are to be found in nature, but would remove and explain some of them; that difficulties which are of small importance in the natural world, on account of the smallness of its sphere and the brevity of its duration, become of insuperable magnitude when extended to infinity and eternity, when alleged to be coextensive with the universe and to be inherent in its scheme and structure; and that — what is of less universal scope, but still of essential importance — nature offers no analogy to the ascription by any professed revelation of an unworthy intention to God, or the inculcation through it of an immoral precept on man.

It is impossible, then, by any such argument as this, to remove from moral criticism the entire contents of any revelation. According to the more natural view, the unimpeachable morality of those contents is a most essential part of the evidence on which our belief must rest: and this seems to remain so, notwithstanding these refinements. On the other hand, we do not contend that the reasoning of the "Analogy" is wholly worthless. If Butler's*

---

* We doubt, however, if Butler would at all have accepted Mr. Rogers's statement of his view, though it is perhaps the most common interpretation of him. Probably he really meant no more than what we contend for, though his language is not always so limited in terms. — B.

argument had only been adduced to this extent, — if it had only been argued that though a revelation might be expected to explain some difficulties, it could not be expected to explain all; that a certain number would, from our ignorance and unworthiness, still remain, and these residuary difficulties would be of the same order, class, and kind, to which we were accustomed; that the style of Providence, if one may so say, would be the same in the newly communicated phenomena as we had observed it to be in those we were familiar with before, — there could be little question of the soundness of the principle. No one would expect that there would be new difficulties introduced by a revelation: what difficulties were found in it we should expect to be identical with those observed before in nature; or at least to be similar to them, and likely to be explained in the same way by a more adequate knowledge of God's purposes. We should particularly expect the difficulties of revelation to be, *like* those of nature, limited in time and range; not extending to the entire scheme of Providence, not diffused through infinity and eternity, not imputing evil intentions to God, not inculcating immoral precepts on man. We can hardly be said to *expect* to find difficulties in revelation at all; the utmost that seems probable, *a priori*, is, that it should leave unnoticed some of those of nature. Nevertheless, there is no violent, no overwhelming improbability in the fact of some perplexing points being contained in a communication from God, — we are so weak that it may be we cannot entirely understand the smallest intimation from the Infinite Being: and if difficulties are found there, they are of course less perplexing when resembling those which we knew before than if they be wholly distinct and new in kind. But this principle is, on the face of it, very different from the admission of an antecedent probability that all the difficulties discoverable in nature would be daguerreotyped in a revelation.

The difference is seen very clearly by looking at the argument which Butler's reasoning is intended to confute. Suppose a professed revelation to be laid before a person who was before unacquainted with it, and that he finds in it several perplexing points. According to Butler's principle, or what is supposed by Mr. Rogers to be Butler's principle, it is enough to reply, "You have those same difficulties in nature before, you cannot consistently object to them now; they have not prevented your ascribing nature to a Divine Author, they should not prevent you from ascribing to him this revelation." Nature is so full of difficulties that almost every doctrine that has ever been attributed to revelation may be provided with a parallel more or less apt: consequently it would be almost needless to criticize the contents of any alleged revelation, when we may be met so easily by such a reply; no careful reasoner would attempt that criticism. According to the doctrine which we have reiterated, we should deem it a difficulty that these perplexing points should be found in a revelation: but that difficulty would not amount to much, would not counterbalance strong evidence, if it could be shown that the system claiming to be revealed, although leaving these points unexplained, threw ample light on others; that what gave cause for perplexity was quite subordinate to what removed perplexity; that no immoral actions were enjoined on man, no unworthy motives imputed to God, no vice attributed to the whole scheme and plan of the Creator. There would therefore remain the largest scope for internal criticism on all systems claiming to be messages from God: on the very face they must seem worthy of him, in their very essence they must seem good.

This is plainly the obvious view. The natural opinion certainly is, that the moral and religious faculties would be those on which we should primarily depend in judging of an alleged communication from heaven, in deciding whether it have a valid claim to that character or no. These faculties are those which, antecedently to revelation, determine our belief in all other moral and religious questions, and it is therefore natural to look to them as the best judges of the authenticity of an alleged revelation. Many divines, however, struggle to deny this. Thus, in the memoir of Butler we are now reviewing, Mr. Rogers observes:—

"The immortal 'Analogy' has probably done more to silence the objections of infidelity than any other ever written from the earliest 'apologies' downwards. It not only most critically met the spirit of unbelief in the author's own day, but is equally adapted to meet that which *chiefly* prevails in all time. In every age, some of the principal—perhaps *the* principal—objections to the Christian revelation have been those which men's *preconceptions* of the Divine character and administration—of what God *must* be and of what God *must* do—have suggested, against certain facts in the sacred history or certain doctrines it reveals. To show the objector, then (supposing him to be a theist, as nine-tenths of all such objectors have been), that the very same or similar difficulties are found in the structure of the universe and the Divine administration of it, is to wrest every *such* weapon completely from his hands, if he be a fair reasoner and remain a theist at all. He is bound, by strict logical obligation, either to show that the parallel difficulties do *not* exist, or to show how he can solve them while he *cannot* solve those of the Bible. In default of doing either of these things, he ought either to renounce all *such* objections to Christianity, or abandon theism altogether. It is true, therefore, that though Butler leaves the alternative of atheism open, he hardly leaves any other alternative to nine-tenths of the theists who have objected to Christianity."

And there is a perpetual reiteration in the "Eclipse of Faith" of the same reasoning; in fact, so far as the latter work has a distinct principle, this argument may be said to be that principle. The answer is, that the proof of all "revelation" itself rests on a "preconception" respecting the Divine character, and that if we assume the truth of that one "preconception" we must not reject any others which may be found to have the same evidence. We refer, of course, to

the assumption of God's veracity ; which can only be
proved by arguments that, if admitted, would likewise
justify our attributing to him all other perfect virtues.
It is evident that a doubt as to this attribute is not
only impious in itself, but quite destructive of all confidence in any communication which may be received
from him ; and yet on what evidence does its acceptance rest ? It cannot be said to be demonstrated by
what scientific men call "natural theology." Competent and careful persons examine the material world,
the structure of animals and plants, the courses of
the planets, the muscles of man, and they find there
a great preponderance of benevolence. They show,
with great labor and great merit, that the Being who
arranged this universe is on the whole a benevolent
Being; but does it follow that he will tell the truth ?
"In crossing a heath," says Paley, "suppose I pitched
my foot against a *stone*, and were asked how the
stone came to be there, I might possibly answer,
that for anything I knew to the contrary it had lain
there forever ; nor would it, perhaps, be very easy
to show the absurdity of this answer. But suppose I
had found a *watch* upon the ground, and it should be
inquired how the watch happened to be in that place,
I should hardly think of the answer which I had
before given,—that for anything I knew, the watch
might have always been there."* And he shows,
with his usual power, that this watch was in all
likelihood made by a watchmaker. There is nothing
cleverer, perhaps, in argumentative writing, than the
way in which that argument is stated and pointed.
But what evidence is there that the watchmaker was
veracious ? The amplest examination of the most
refined designs, the minutest scrutiny of the most
complex contrivances, do not go one hair's-breadth to
establish any such conclusion. Nor can it be shown
that the virtue of veracity is identical with or consequent on the virtue of simple benevolence. We know.

* Opening lines of his " Natural Theology."

well in common life that there are such things as
pleasing falsehoods, and that such things exist as disagreeable truths; a person (what we ordinarily call
a "good-natured" person) whose only motive is simple
benevolence will constantly assert the first and deny
the second. In its application to religion this tendency cannot be illustrated without suppositions which
it is painful even to make; but yet they must be
made for a moment, or the necessary argument must
be left incomplete. Suppose (what is doubtless true)
that the belief in a "future state," even if false, contributes to the temporal happiness of man in this world;
that it does more to enlarge his hopes, stimulate his
imagination, and alleviate his sorrows, than any one
other consideration; that it contributes to the order
of society and the progress of civilization; that it is,
as some one says, "the last restraint of the powerful
and the last hope of the wretched." Indisputably,
a Being whose only motive was benevolence, who
admitted no higher consideration, who looked steadily and solely to our mere happiness, would endeavor
to instill that belief although it were quite untrue,
would not think that *that* had anything to do with
the question, would not hesitate to make a false revelation to confirm men in a belief so pleasant, so advantageous, so consolatory. Perhaps this supposition
drives the argument home. We see that it is necessary for us to admit a "preconception" as to the
character of God before we can even begin to prove
the truth of a revelation; that we *must* reason of
"what God *must* be and God *must* do," before we
show that there is even a presumption in favor of any
facts or any doctrines which are revealed "in the
sacred history."

We have hinted, in an earlier part of this essay,
that this doctrine of God's veracity seems to us to
rest on the general assumption of the existence of a
"perfect" Being, who rules and controls all things.

It is perhaps the Divine attribute of which it is most difficult to find a trace in nature. Of his omnipotence, justice, benevolence, we cannot indeed find absolute proof,—for we believe that those attributes are infinite, and we can only prove them strictly with respect to the finite and very circumscribed world which we see and know,—yet at the same time we discern indications and strong probabilities that the Ruler of the world possesses these attributes. We can hardly be said to be able to do this with his veracity: the speechlessness of nature, if we may again so speak, deprives us of any such evidence. All theism is of the nature of faith : we can never *prove* from experience any being to be infinite, for our experience itself is essentially small and finite ; we can often, however, as in the instance of the attributes of God above enumerated, and of others which might be added, establish by observation that the qualities in question exist in a certain degree, and we have only to rely on the principle of faith for our belief that these qualities exist in a perfect and supreme degree. In the case of the Divine veracity, it should seem that we believe it to exist in a perfect and infinite degree, without, from the peculiarity of our circumstances, being able to fortify it by any test or trial from experience.

Present controversies show that there should be a distinct understanding as to this matter. Such writers as the author of the "Eclipse of Faith" perpetually strive to justify what they think the difficulties of revelation by insinuating—we might say inculcating —a skepticism as to the religious faculties and conscience of man. These faculties are at one time said to be "depraved": once they were trustworthy, but man is fallen from that high estate ; he can only now believe what is announced to him externally. But how can we then rely on those "depraved" faculties for our belief in the truthfulness of the Being who announces these things? At another time all

the horrid superstitions, all the immoral rites, all the
wretched aberrations of savage and licentious nations are enumerated, displayed, inculcated, in order
to convince us that these faculties give no certain
information. We will not quote the passages : we
do not like to read hard attacks even on the worst
side of human nature; we cannot, like some, gloat
upon such details. The argument is plain without
any painful ·accuracy : how can you believe in the
"intuition" of the Divine justice, when the Hindoo
says this? how in that of his holiness, when the
Papuan accepts that impurity ? But this is no defense
for any revelation. The writers who exult in such
errors because they think they can use them in their
logic are really cutting away the substratum of evi-
dentiary argument from under them. The veracity of
God has not been accepted by all nations any more
than his justice : in many times and countries he has
been thought to inspire falsehoods, to put a "lying
spirit" in the mouths of men, to deceive them to their
destruction. Agamemnon's dream is but the type of
a whole class of legends imputing untrue revelations
to the gods; if we liked such work, we might prove,
perhaps, that there is no man on the earth whose
ancestors have not believed the like. And what then ?
Why, we can only answer that, debased, depraved,
imperfect as they may be, these faculties are our all ;
it is on them that we depend for life and breath
and all things. We must believe our heart and conscience, or we shall believe nothing ; we *must* believe
that God cannot lie, or we must renounce all that
our highest and innermost nature most cleaves to.
But if we go so far, we must go further : we cannot believe in God's veracity and deny the intuition
of his justice ; we know that he is pure on the same
ground that we know that he is true. If an alleged
revelation contradict this justice or this purity, we
must at once deny that it can have proceeded ·from
him.

Even admitting, as we think it must be admitted, that Butler did not firmly hold the principle which Mr. Rogers and others ascribe to him, some may find a difficulty in so great a thinker having even a tendency towards that tenet. On examination, however, the very error seems characteristic of him.

A mind such as Butler's was in a previous page described to be, is very apt to be prone to over-refinement. A thinker of what was there called the picturesque order has a vision, a picture of the natural view of the subject. Those certainties and conclusions, those doubts and difficulties which occur on the surface, strike him at once; he sees with his mind's eye some conspicuous instance in which all such certainties are realized and by which all such doubts are suggested. Some great typical fact remains delineated before his mind, and is a perpetual answer to all hypotheses which strive to be over-subtle. But an unimaginative thinker has no such assistance; he has no pictures or instances in his mind: he works by a process like an accountant, and like an accountant he is dependent on the correctness with which he works. He begins with a principle and reasons from it; and if any error have crept into the deduction or into the principle, he has not any means of detecting it. His mind does not yield, as with more fertile fancies, a stock of instances on which to verify his elaborate conclusions; accordingly he is apt to say he has explained a difficulty, when in reality he has but refined it away.

Again, there is likewise a deeper sense in which the argument of the "Analogy" is, even in its least valuable portions, characteristic of Butler. On topics so peculiar, the minds most likely to hold right opinions are exactly those most likely to advance wrong arguments in support of them. The opinions themselves are suggested and supported by deep and strong feelings, which it is painful to analyze and not easy to describe; the real and decisive arguments for those opinions are little save a rational analysis and acute delineation of those feelings. It will necessarily follow that the mind most prone to delineate and analyze that part of itself will be most likely to succeed in the argumentative exposition of these topics; and this is not likely to be the mind which feels those emotions with the greatest intensity. The very keenness of these feelings makes them painful to touch, their depth difficult to find; constancy, too, is liable to disguise them, — the mind which always feels them will, so to speak, be less conscious of them than one which is only visited by them at long and rare intervals. Those who know a place or a person best are not those most likely to describe it best; their knowledge is so familiar that they cannot bring it out in words. A deep, steady under-current of strong feeling is precisely what affects men's highest opinions most, and exactly what prevents men from being able adequately to describe them. In the absence of the delineative faculty, without the power to state their true reasons, minds of this deep and steadfast class are apt to put up with reasons which lie on the surface. They are caught by an appearance of fairness; affect a dry and intellectual tone; endeavor to establish their conclusions without the premises which are necessary, without mention of the grounds on which in their own minds they really rest. The very heartfelt confidence of Butler in Christianity was perhaps the cause of his seeming in part to support it with considerations which appear to be erroneous.

It seems odd to say, and yet it is true, that the power of the "Analogy" is in its rhetoric. The ancient writers on that art made a distinction between the modes of persuasion which lay in the illustrative and argumentative efficacy of what was said, and a yet more subtle kind which seemed to reside in the manner and disposition of the speaker himself. In the first class, as has been before remarked, no writer of equal eminence is so defective as Butler; his thoughts,

if you take each one singly, seem to lose a good deal
from the feeble and hesitating manner in which they
are stated : and yet if you read any considerable portion of his writings, you become sensible of a strong
disinclination to disagree with him. A strong anxiety
first to find the truth and next to impart it, an evident wish not to push arguments too far, a clear
desire not to convince men except by reasonable arguments of true opinions, characterizes every feeble
word and halting sentence. Nothing is laid down
to dazzle or arouse ; it is assumed that the reader
wants to know what is true as much as the writer
does to tell it. Very possibly this may not be the
highest species of religious author : the vehement
temperament, the bold assertion, the ecstatic energy of
men like St. Augustine or St. Paul burn, so to speak,
into the minds and memories of men, and remain
there at once and forever. Such men excel in the
broad statement of great truths, which flash at once
with vivid evidence on the minds which receive them.
The very words seem to glow with life, and even the
skeptical reader is half awakened by them to a kindred and similar warmth. Such are the men who
move the creeds of mankind, and stamp a likeness of
themselves on ages that succeed them. But there is
likewise room for a quieter class, who partially state
arguments, elaborate theories, appreciate difficulties,
solve doubts : who do not expect to gain a hearing
from the many, who do not cry in the streets* or
lift their voice from the hill of Mars† ; who address
quiet and lonely thinkers like themselves, and are
well satisfied if a single sentence in all their writings
remove one doubt from the mind of any man. Of
these was Butler. *Requiescat in pace;* for it was peace
that he loved.

*Isaiah xlii. 2.　　　†Acts xvii. 22.

STERNE AND THACKERAY.*

(1864.)

MR. PERCY FITZGERALD has expressed his surprise that no one before him has narrated the life of Sterne in two volumes: we are much more surprised that he has done so. The life of Sterne was of the very simplest sòrt. He was a Yorkshire clergyman, and lived for the most part a sentimental, questionable, jovial life in the country. He was a queer parson, according to our notions; but in those days there were many queer parsons. Late in life he wrote a book or two, which gave him access to London society; and then he led a still more questionable and unclerical life at the edge of the great world. After that he died in something like distress, and leaving his family in something like misery. A simpler life, as far as facts go, never was known; and simple as it is, the story has been well told by Sir Walter Scott, and has been well commented on by Mr. Thackeray. It should have occurred to Mr. Fitzgerald that a subject may only have been briefly treated because it is a limited and simple subject, which suggests but few remarks and does not require an elaborate and copious description.

There are but few materials, too, for a long life of Sterne. Mr. Fitzgerald has stuffed his volumes with needless facts about Sterne's distant relations, his great-uncles and ninth cousins, in which no one now can take the least interest. Sterne's daughter,

---

*The Life of Laurence Sterne. By Percy Fitzgerald, M. A., M. R. I. A. In two volumes. Chapman & Hall.

Thackeray the Humorist and the Man of Letters. By Theodore Taylor, Esq. London: John Camden Hotten.

who was left ill off, did indeed publish two little volumes of odd letters, which no clergyman's daughter would certainly have published now; but even these are too small in size and thin in matter to be spun into a copious narrative. We should in this *Review* have hardly given even a brief sketch of Sterne's life, if we did not think that his artistic character presented one fundamental resemblance and many superficial contrasts to that of a great man whom we have lately lost. We wish to point these out; and a few interspersed remarks on the life of Sterne will enable us to enliven the tedium of criticism with a little interest from human life.

Sterne's father was a shiftless roving Irish officer in the early part of the last century; he served in Marlborough's wars, and was cast adrift, like many greater people, by the caprice of Queen Anne and the sudden peace of Utrecht. Of him only one anecdote remains. He was, his son tells us, "a little smart man," "in his temper somewhat rapid and hasty;" and during some fighting at Gibraltar he got into a squabble with another young officer, a Captain Phillips. The subject, it seems, was a goose; but that is not now material. It ended in a duel, which was fought with swords in a room. Captain Phillips pinned Ensign Sterne to a plaster wall behind; upon which' he quietly asked, or is said to have asked, "*Do* wipe the plaster off your sword before you pull it out of me,"— which, if true, showed at least presence of mind. Mr. Fitzgerald, in his famine of matter, discusses who this Captain Phillips was; but into this we shall not follow him.

A smart, humorous, shiftless father of this sort is not perhaps a bad father for a novelist. Sterne was dragged here and there, through scenes of life where no correct and thriving parent would ever have taken him; years afterwards, with all their harshness softened and half their pains dissembled, Sterne dashed them upon pages which will live forever. Of money

and respectability Sterne inherited from his father
little or none; but he inherited two main elements of
his intellectual capital,—a great store of odd scenes,
and the sensitive Irish nature which appreciates odd
scenes.

Sterne was born in the year 1713, the year of the
peace of Utrecht, which cast his father adrift upon
the world. Of his mother we know nothing. Years
after, it was said that he behaved ill to her, at least
neglected and left her in misery when he had the
means of placing her in comfort; his enemies neatly
said that he preferred "whining over a dead ass to
relieving a living mother"*: but these accusations
have never been proved. Sterne was not remarkable
for active benevolence, and certainly may have neglected an old and uninteresting woman, even though
that woman was his mother,—he was a bad hand at
dull duties, and did not like elderly females; but we
must not condemn him on simple probabilities, or upon
a neat epigram and loose tradition. "The regiment,"
says Sterne, "in which my father served being broke,
he left Ireland as soon as I was able to be carried,
. . . and came to the family seat at Elvington, near
York, where his mother lived." After this he was
carried about for some years, as his father led the
rambling life of a poor ensign, who was one of very
many engaged during a very great war and discarded
at a hasty peace. Then, perhaps luckily, his father
died, and "my cousin Sterne of Elvington," as he
calls him, took charge of him and sent him to school
and college. At neither of these was he very eminent.
He told one story late in life which may be true,
but seems very unlike the usual school life:—My
schoolmaster, he says, "had the ceiling of the school-
room new whitewashed; the ladder remained there: I
one unlucky day mounted it, and wrote with a brush
in large capital letters LAU. STERNE, for which the

* Byron, Journal, Dec. 1, 1813; but evidently twisted from Horace Walpole ("Walpoliana," cclxv.), who says he had it on "indubitable authority"
that a subscription had to be taken up to keep her from the almshouse. — ED.

usher severely whipped me. My master was very much hurt at this, and said before me that never should that name be effaced, for I was a boy of genius, and he was sure I should come to preferment." But "genius" is rarely popular in places of education; and it is, to say the least, remarkable that so sentimental a man as Sterne should have chanced upon so sentimental an instructor. It is wise to be suspicious of aged reminiscents: they are like persons intrusted with "untold gold,"—there is no check on what they tell us.

Sterne went to Cambridge; and though he did not acquire elaborate learning, he thoroughly learned a gentlemanly stock of elementary knowledge. There is even something scholarlike about his style: it bears. the indefinable traces which an exact study of words will always leave upon the use of words. He was accused of stealing learning, and it is likely enough that a great many needless quotations which were stuck into "Tristram Shandy" were abstracted from second-hand storehouses where such things are to be found; but what he stole was worth very little, and his theft may now at least be pardoned, for it injures the popularity of his works. Our present novel readers do not at all care for an elaborate caricature of the scholastic learning; it is so obsolete that we do not care to have it mimicked. Much of "Tristram Shandy" is a sort of antediluvian fun, in which uncouth saurian jokes play idly in an unintelligible world.

When he left college, Sterne had a piece of good fortune which in fact ruined him: he had an uncle with much influence in the Church, and he was thereby induced to enter the Church. There could not have been a greater error. He had no special vice; he was notorious for no wild dissipation or unpardonable folly; he had done nothing which even in this more discreet age would be considered imprudent; he had even a refinement which must have

saved him from gross vice, and a nicety of nature
which must have saved him from coarse associations:
but for all that, he was as little fit for a Christian
priest as if he had been a drunkard and a profligate,
— perhaps he was less fit.

There are certain persons whom taste guides, much
as morality and conscience guide ordinary persons:
they are "gentlemen"; they revolt from what is
coarse, are sickened by that which is gross, hate what
is ugly. They have no temptation to what we may
call "ordinary vices"; they have no inclination for
such raw food, — on the contrary, they are repelled
by it, and loathe it. The "law in their members" does
not "war against the law of their mind"*; on the
contrary, the *taste* of their bodily nature is mainly
in harmony with what conscience would prescribe or
religion direct. They may not have heard the saying
that "the beautiful is higher than the good, for it
includes the good"†; but when they do hear it, it
comes upon them as a revelation of their instinctive
creed, of the guidance under which they have been
living all their lives. They are pure because it is
ugly to be impure, innocent because it is out of taste
to be otherwise; they live within the hedge-rows of
polished society, they do not wish to go beyond them
into the great deep of human life; they have a horror
of that "impious ocean,"‡ yet not of the impiety, but
of the miscellaneous noise, the disordered confusion
of the whole. These are the men whom it is hardest
to make Christian, — for the simplest reason: paganism is sufficient for them. Their "pride of the eye"
is a good pride; their "love of the flesh"§ is a delicate
and directing love. They keep "within the pathways"‖
because they dislike the gross, the uncultured, and the
untrodden. Thus they reject the primitive precept

* Rom. vii. 23.
† Carlyle in "Hero Worship"; credited to Goethe, from what work I
know not. — ED.
‡ See note to Vol. I., page 43.
§ "Lust of the eyes, . . . lust of the flesh." — 1 John ii. 16.
‖ "In the pathway," Prov. xii. 28.

which comes before Christianity. "Repent! repent!"
says a voice in the wilderness; * but the delicate pagan
feels superior to the voice in the wilderness. Why
should he attend to this uncouth person? He has
nice clothes and well-chosen food, the treasures of
exact knowledge, the delicate results of the highest
civilization. Is he to be directed by a person of savage habits, with a distorted countenance, who lives on
wild honey, who does not wear decent clothes? To
the pure worshiper of beauty, to the naturally refined
pagan, conscience and the religion of conscience are
not merely intruders, but barbarous intruders: at least
so it is in youth, when life is simple, and temptations
if strong are distinct: years afterwards, probably, the
purest pagan will be taught, by a constant accession
of indistinct temptations, and by a gradual declension
of his nature, that taste at the best and sentiment of
the very purest are insufficient guides in the perplexing labyrinth of the world.

Sterne was a pagan. He went into the Church;
but Mr. Thackeray — no bad judge — said most justly
that his sermons "have not a single Christian sentiment." † They are well-expressed, vigorous moral
essays; but they are no more. Much more was not
expected by many congregations in the last age: the
secular feeling of the English people, though always
strong, — though strong in Chaucer's time and though
strong now, — was never so all-powerful as in the last
century. It was in those days that the poet Crabbe
was remonstrated with for introducing heaven and
hell into his sermons: such extravagances, he was
told, were very well for the Methodists, but a *clergyman* should confine himself to sober matters of this
world, and show the prudence and the reasonable-
ness of virtue during this life. There is not much of
heaven and hell in Sterne's sermons; and what there
is, seems a rhetorical emphasis which is not essential
to the argument, and which might perhaps as well be
left out. Auguste Comte might have admitted most

* Matt. iii. 2.
† He says nothing of the sort. In his lecture on *Swift*, he says of the

of these sermons; they are healthy statements of
earthly truths, but they would be just as true if
there was no religion at all. Religion helps the
argument, because foolish people might be perplexed
with this world, and they yield readily to another;
religion enables you — such is the real doctrine of
these divines, when you examine it — to coax and persuade those whom you cannot rationally convince, but
it does not alter the matter in hand, — it does not
affect that of which you wish to persuade men, for
you are but inculcating a course of conduct *in this
life*. Sterne's sermons would be just as true if the
secularists should succeed in their argument, and the
"valuable illusion" of a Deity were omitted from the
belief of mankind.

However, in fact, Sterne took orders, and by the
aid of his uncle, who was a Church politician and
who knew the powers that were, he obtained several
small livings. Being a pluralist was a trifle in those
easy times : nobody then thought that the parishion-
ers of a parson had a right to his daily presence; if
some provision were made for the performance of a
Sunday service, he had done his duty, and he could
spend the surplus income where he liked. He might
perhaps be bound to reside, if health permitted, on
one of his livings ; but the law allowed him to have
many, and he could not be compelled to reside on them
all. Sterne preached well-written sermons on Sundays
and led an easy pagan life on other days, and no one
blamed him.

He fell in love, too ; and after he was dead, his
daughter found two or three of his love-letters to her
mother, which she rashly published. They have been
the unfeeling sport of persons not in love up to the
present time. Years ago, Mr. Thackeray used to make
audiences laugh till they cried by reading one or two
of them, and contrasting them with certain other letters, also about his wife but written many years later.
This is the sort of thing : —

"Yes! I will steal from the world, and not a babbling tongue shall tell where I am, — Echo shall not so much as whisper my hiding-place, — suffer thy imagination to paint it as a little sungilt cottage, on the side of a romantic hill ;—dost thou think I will leave love and friendship behind me? No! they shall be my companions in solitude, for they will sit down and rise up with me in the amiable form of my L. — We will be as merry and as innocent as our first parents in Paradise, before the arch-fiend entered that undescribable scene.

"The kindest affections will have room to shoot and expand in our retirement, and produce such fruit as madness and envy and ambition have always killed in the bud. — Let the human tempest and hurricane rage at a distance, the desolation is beyond the horizon of peace. ——My L. has seen a polyanthus blow in December, — some friendly wall has sheltered it from the biting wind. — No planetary influence shall reach us, but that which presides and cherishes the sweetest flowers. — God preserve us! how delightful this prospect in idea! We will build and we will plant in our own way, — simplicity shall not be tortured by art, — we will learn of Nature how to live, — she shall be our alchymist to mingle all the good of life into one salubrious draught. — The gloomy family of care and distrust shall be banished from our dwelling, guarded by thy kind and tutelary deity ; — we will sing our choral songs of gratitude, and rejoice to the end of our pilgrimage.

"Adieu, my L. Return to one who languishes for thy society.

L. STERNE."*

The beautiful language with which young ladies were wooed a century ago is a characteristic of that extinct age ; at least, we fear that no such beautiful English will be discovered when our secret repositories are ransacked. The age of ridicule has come in, and the age of good words has gone out.

There is no reason to doubt, however, that Sterne was really in love with Mrs. Sterne. People have doubted it because of these beautiful words; but in fact, Sterne was just the sort of man to be subject to this kind of feeling. / He took — and to this he owes his fame — the *sensitive* view of life ; he regarded it not from the point of view of intellect or conscience or religion, but in the plain way in which natural feeling impresses and will always impress a natural

* Letter 1.

person. He is a great author : certainly not because
of great thoughts, for there is scarcely a sentence in
his writings which can be called a thought; nor from
sublime conceptions which enlarge the limits of our
imagination, for he never leaves the sensuous,—but
because of his wonderful sympathy with and wonderful power of representing simple human nature. The
best passages in Sterne are those which every one
knows, like this :—

"Thou hast left this matter short, said my uncle Toby to the
corporal, as he was putting him to bed,—and I will tell thee in
what, Trim. —— In the first place, when thou madest an offer of
my services to Le Fever, — as sickness and traveling are both expensive; and thou knewest he was but a poor lieutenant, with a
son to subsist as well as himself, out of his pay,—that thou didst
not make an offer to him of my purse ; because, had he stood in
need, thou knowest, Trim, he had been as welcome to it as myself.
—— Your Honor knows, said the corporal, I had no orders. ——
True, quoth my uncle Toby, — thou didst very right, Trim, as a
soldier, — but certainly very wrong as a man.

"In the second place, for which, indeed, thou hast the same
excuse, continued my uncle Toby, —— when thou offeredst him whatever was in my house, — thou shouldst have offered him my house
too: — A sick brother officer should have the best quarters, Trim,
and if we had him with us, — we could tend and look to him :—
Thou art an excellent nurse thyself, Trim, — and what with thy care
of him, and the old woman's, and his boy's, and mine together,
we might recruit him again at once, and set him upon his legs. ——
"—— In a fortnight or three weeks, added my uncle Toby,
smiling, — he might march. —— He will never march, an' please
your Honor, in this world, said the corporal. —— He will march,
said my uncle Toby, rising up from the side of the bed, with one
shoe off. —— An' please your Honor, said the corporal, he will
never march, but to his grave. —— He shall march, cried my uncle
Toby, marching the foot which had a shoe on, though without
advancing an inch, — he shall march to his regiment. —— He cannot stand it, said the corporal. —— He shall be supported, said my
uncle Toby. —— He'll drop at last, said the corporal, and what
will become of his boy ?—— He shall not drop, said my uncle
Toby, firmly.—— A-well-o'day, — do what we can for him, said
Trim, maintaining his point, — the poor soul will die. —— He shall
not die, by G—! cried my uncle Toby.

"—The ACCUSING SPIRIT, which flew up to Heaven's chancery with the oath, blushed as he gave it in;—and the RECORDING ANGEL, as he wrote it down, dropped a tear upon the word, and blotted it out forever.

"——My uncle Toby went to his bureau,—put his purse into his breeches pocket, and having ordered the corporal to go early in the morning for a physician,—he went to bed, and fell asleep.

"The sun looked bright the morning after, to every eye in the village but Le Fever's and his afflicted son's; the hand of death pressed heavy upon his eye-lids;——and hardly could the wheel at the cistern turn round its circle,—when my uncle Toby, who had rose up an hour before his wonted time, entered the lieutenant's room, and without preface or apology, sat himself down upon the chair by the bedside, and independently of all modes and customs, opened the curtain in the manner an old friend and brother officer would have done it, and asked him how he did,—how he had rested in the night,—what was his complaint,—where was his pain,—and what he could do to help him:——and without giving him time to answer any one of the inquiries, went on and told him of the little plan which he had been concerting with the corporal the night before for him.——

"——You shall go home directly, Le Fever, said my uncle Toby, to my house,—and we'll send for a doctor to see what's the matter,—and we'll have an apothecary,—and the corporal shall be your nurse;——and I'll be your servant, Le Fever.——

"There was a frankness in my uncle Toby,—not the *effect* of familiarity,—but the *cause* of it,—which let you at once into his soul, and showed you the goodness of his nature; to this there was something in his looks, and voice, and manner, superadded, which eternally beckoned to the unfortunate to come and take shelter under him: so that before my uncle Toby had half finished the kind offers he was making to the father, had the son insensibly pressed up close to his knees, and had taken hold of the breast of his coat, and was pulling it towards him.——The blood and spirits of Le Fever, which were waxing cold and slow within him, and were retreating to their last citadel, the heart,—rallied back, —the film forsook his eyes for a moment;—he looked up wishfully in my uncle Toby's face,—then cast a look upon his boy;——and that *ligament*, fine as it was,—was never broken.————

"Nature instantly ebbed again,—the film returned to its place, ——the pulse fluttered—— stopped—— went on——— throbbed, ——stopped again—— moved——stopped—— shall I go on?—— No."*

<hr>

* "Tristram Shandy," Book vi., Chaps. viii.-x.

In one of the "Roundabout Papers" Mr. Thackeray introduces a literary man complaining of his "sensibility." "Ah," he replies, "my good friend, your sensibility is your livelihood: if you did not feel the events and occurrences of life more acutely than others, you could not describe them better; and it is the excellence of your description by which you live." * This is precisely true of Sterne: he is a great author because he felt acutely; he is the most pathetic of writers because he had — when writing, at least — the most pity. He was, too, we believe, pretty sharply in love with Mrs. Sterne, because he was sensitive to that sort of feeling likewise.

The difficulty of this sort of character is the difficulty of keeping it; it does not last. There is a certain bloom of sensibility and feeling about it which in the course of nature is apt to fade soon, and which when it has faded there is nothing to replace. A character with the binding elements — with a firm will, a masculine understanding, and a persistent conscience — may retain and perhaps improve the early and original freshness; but a loose-set though pure character, the moment it is thrown into temptation, sacrifices its purity, loses its gloss, and gets (so to speak) out of form entirely.

We do not know with great accuracy what Sterne's temptations were; but there was one, which we can trace with some degree of precision, which has left ineffaceable traces on his works, — which probably left some traces upon his character and conduct. There was in that part of Yorkshire a certain John Hall Stevenson, a country gentleman of some fortune, and possessed of a castle which he called "Crazy Castle." Thence he wrote tales, which he named "Crazy Tales," but which certainly are not entitled to any such innocent name. The license of that age was unquestionably wonderful: a man of good property could write any evil; there was no legal check

* "At Dessein's," — dreadfully mangled.

or ecclesiastical check, and hardly any check of public opinion. These "Crazy Tales" have license without humor and vice without amusement: they are the writing of a man with some wit,' but only enough wit for light conversation, which becomes overworked and dull when it is reduced to regular composition and made to write long tales. The author, feeling his wit jaded perpetually, becomes immoral, in the vain hope that he will cease to be dull: he has attained his reward, — he will be remembered for nauseous tiresomeness by all who have read him.

But though the "Crazy Tales" are now tedious, Crazy Castle was a pleasant place, at least to men like Sterne. He was an idle young parson, with much sensibility, much love of life and variety, and not a bit of grave goodness. The dull duties of a country parson, as we now understand them, would never have been to his taste; and the sinecure idleness then permitted to parsons left him open to every temptation. The frail texture of merely natural purity, the soft fiber of the instinctive pagan, yield to the first casualty. Exactly what sort of life they led at Crazy Castle we do not know; but vaguely we do know, and we may be sure *Mrs.* Sterne was against it.

One part of Crazy Castle has had effects which will last as long as English literature. It had a library richly stored in old folio learning, and also in the amatory reading of other days. Every page of "Tristram Shandy" bears traces of both elements. Sterne, when he wrote it, had filled his head and his mind not with the literature of his own age, but with the literature of past ages; he was thinking of Rabelais rather than of Fielding, of forgotten romances rather than of Richardson. He wrote, indeed, of his own times and of men he had seen, because his sensitive vivid nature would only endure to write of present things; but the *mode* in which he wrote was largely colored by literary habits and literary fashions that had long passed away. The oddity of the book was a kind of advertisement to its genius, and that oddity consisted in the use of old manners upon new things. No analysis or account of "Tristram Shandy" could be given which would suit the present generation; being, indeed, a book without plan or order, it is in every generation unfit for analysis. This age would not endure a statement of the most telling points, as the writer thought them; and no age would like an elaborate plan of a book in which there is no plan, in which the detached remarks and separate scenes were really meant to be the whole. The notion that a plot was to hang plums upon* was Sterne's notion exactly.

The real excellence of Sterne is single and simple; the defects are numberless and complicated. He excels, perhaps, all other writers in mere simple description of common sensitive human action. He places before you in their simplest form the elemental facts of human life: he does not view them through the intellect, he scarcely views them through the imagination; he does but reflect the unimpaired impression that the facts of life, which do not change from age to age, make on the deep basis of human feeling, which changes as little though years go on. The example we quoted just now is as good as any other, though not better than any other; our readers should go back to it again, or our praise may seem overcharged. It is the portrait painting of the heart; it is as pure a reflection of mere natural feeling as literature has ever given or will ever give; the delineation is nearly perfect. Sterne's feeling in his higher moments so much overpowered his intellect, and so directed his imagination, that no intrusive thought blemishes, no distorting fancy mars the perfection of the representation. The disenchanting facts which deface, the low circumstances which debase the simpler feelings oftener than any other feelings, his art

* Bayes in "The Rehearsal," Act iii., Scene 1: "What a devil is the plot good for, but to bring in fine things?"

excludes; the feeling which would probably be coarse
in the reality is refined in the picture; the unconscious tact of the nice artist heightens and chastens
reality, but yet it is reality still. His mind was like
a pure lake of delicate water: it reflects the ordinary
landscape, the rugged hills, the loose pebbles, the
knotted and the distorted firs, perfectly and as they
are, yet with a charm and fascination that they have
not in themselves. This is the highest attainment of
art, — to be at the same time nature and something
more than nature.

But here the great excellence of Sterne ends as
well as begins. In "Tristram Shandy" especially
there are several defects which, while we are reading
it, tease and disgust so much that we are scarcely
willing even to admire as we ought to admire the refined pictures of human emotion. The first of these,
and perhaps the worst, is the fantastic disorder of the
form. It is an imperative law of the writing art that
a book should go straight on. A great writer should
be able to tell a great meaning as coherently as a
small writer tells a small meaning. The magnitude
of the thought to be conveyed, the delicacy of the
emotion to be painted, render the introductory touches
of consummate art not of less importance, but of
more importance. A great writer should train the
mind of the reader for his greatest things; that is,
by first strokes and fitting preliminaries he should
form and prepare his mind for the due appreciation
and the perfect enjoyment of high creations. He
should not blunder upon a beauty, nor, after a great
imaginative creation, should he at once fall back to
bare prose; the high-wrought feeling which a poet
excites should not be turned out at once and without
warning into the discomposing world. It is one of
the greatest merits of the greatest living writer of
fiction, — of the authoress of "Adam Bede," — that she
never brings you to anything without preparing you
for it; she has no loose lumps of beauty, she puts in

nothing at random: after her greatest scenes, too, a natural sequence of subordinate realities again tones down the mind to this sublunary world. Her logical style — the most logical, probably, which a woman ever wrote — aids in this matter her natural sense of due proportion; there is not a space of incoherency, — not a gap. It is not natural to begin with the point of a story, and she does not begin with it; when some great marvel has been told, we all wish 'to know what came of it, and she tells us. Her natural way — as it seems to those who do not know its rarity — of telling what happened, produces the consummate effect of gradual enchantment and as gradual disenchantment. But Sterne's style is unnatural: he never begins at the beginning and goes straight through to the end. He shies in a beauty suddenly, and just when you are affected he turns round and grins at it: "Ah," he says, "is it not fine?" and then he makes jokes which at that place and that time are out of place, or passes away into scholastic or other irrelevant matter, which simply disgusts and disheartens those whom he has just delighted. People excuse all this irregularity of form by saying that it was imitated from Rabelais; but this is nonsense. Rabelais, perhaps, could not in his day venture to tell his meaning straight out; at any rate, he did not tell it. Sterne should not have chosen a model so monstrous: incoherency is not less a defect because an imperfect foreign writer once made use of it. "Sir, you may have a reason," said Dr. Johnson, "why two and two should make five; but they will still make but four:"* just so, a writer may have a reason for selecting the defect of incoherency, but it is a defect still. Sterne's best things read best out of his books, — in "Enfield's Speaker" and other places, — and you can say no worse of any one as a continuous artist.

Another most palpable defect — especially palpable nowadays — in "Tristram Shandy" is its indecency.

* Boswell, Chap. xlix.

It is quite true that the customary conventions of writing are much altered during the last century, and much which would formerly have been deemed blameless would now be censured and disliked. The audience has changed, and decency is of course in part dependent on who is within hearing : a divorce case may be talked over across a club table with a plainness of speech and development of expression which would be indecent in a mixed party and scandalous before young ladies. Now, a large part of old novels may very fairly be called "club books": they speak out plainly and simply the·notorious facts of the world, as men speak of them to men. Much excellent and proper masculine conversation is wholly unfit for repetition to young girls ; and just in the same way, books written — as was almost all old literature — for men only, or nearly only, seem coarse enough when contrasted with novels written by young ladies upon the subjects and in·the tone of the drawing-room. The change is inevitable, — as soon as works of fiction are addressed to boys and girls, they must be fit for boys•and girls : they must deal with a life which is real so far as it goes, but which is yet most limited ; which deals with the most passionate part of life, and yet omits the errors of the passions ; which aims at describing men in their relations to women, and yet omits an all-but universal influence which more or less distorts and modifies all these relations.

As we have said, the change cannot be helped : a young-ladies' literature must be a limited and truncated literature ; the indiscriminate study of human life is not desirable for them, either in fiction or in reality. But the habitual formation of a scheme of thought and a code of morality upon incomplete materials is a very serious evil : the readers for whose sake the omissions are made cannot fancy what is left out. Many a girl of the present day reads novels and nothing but novels ; she forms her mind by them, as far as she forms it by reading at all; even if she reads a few dull books, she soon forgets all about them, and remembers the novels only; she is more influenced by them than by sermons. They form her idea of the world, they define her taste and modify her morality; not so much in explicit thought and direct act, as unconsciously and in her floating fancy. How is it possible to convince such a girl, especially if she is clever, that on most points she is all wrong? She has been reading most excellent descriptions of mere "society"; she comprehends those descriptions perfectly, for her own experience elucidates and confirms them: she has a vivid picture of a *patch* of life. Even if she admits in words that there is something beyond, something of which she has no idea, she will not admit it really and in practice: what she has mastered and realized will incurably and inevitably overpower the unknown something of which she knows nothing, can imagine nothing, and can make nothing. "I am not sure," said an old lady, "but I think it's the novels that make my girls so *heady*." It is the novels: a very intelligent acquaintance with limited life makes them think that the world is far simpler than it is, that men are easy to understand, "that mamma is *so* foolish."

The novels of the last age have certainly not this fault,—they do not err on the side of reticence: a girl may learn from them more than it is desirable for her to know. But as we have explained, they were meant for men and not for girls: and if "Tristram Shandy" had simply given a plain exposition of necessary facts,—necessary, that is, to the development of the writer's view of the world, and to the telling of the story in hand,—we should not have complained; we should have regarded it as the natural product of a now extinct society. But there are most unmistakable traces of "Crazy Castle" in "Tristram Shandy": there is indecency for indecency's sake; it is made a sort of recurring and even permeating joke to mention things which are not generally mentioned. Sterne himself made a sort of defense—or rather denial—of this. He once asked a lady if she had read "Tristram." "I have not, Mr. Sterne," was the answer; "and to be plain with you, I am informed it is not proper for female perusal." "My dear good lady," said Sterne, "do not be gulled by such stories; the book is like your young heir there" (pointing to a child of three years old, who was rolling on the carpet in white tunics): "he shows at times a good deal that is usually concealed, but it is all in perfect innocence."* But a perusal of "Tristram" would not make good the plea. The unusual publicity of what is ordinarily imperceptible is not the thoughtless accident of amusing play : it is deliberately sought after as a nice joke; it is treated as a good in itself.

The indecency of "Tristram Shandy"—at least of the early part, which was written before Sterne had been to France — is especially an offense against taste, because of its ugliness. *Moral* indecency is always disgusting. There certainly is a sort of writing which cannot be called decent, and which describes a society to the core immoral, which nevertheless is no offense against art; it violates a higher code than that of taste, but it does not violate the code of taste. The "Mémoires de Grammont"—hundreds of French memoirs about France are of this kind, more or less: they describe the refined, witty, elegant immorality of an idle aristocracy. They describe a life unsuitable to "such a being as man in such a world as the present one"†; in which there are no high aims, no severe duties, where some precepts of morals seem not so much to be sometimes broken as to be generally suspended and forgotten,—such a life, in short, as God has never suffered men to lead on this earth long, which he has always crushed out by calamity and revolution. This life, though an offense in morals,

---

* Scott.   †See note, page 109.

was not an offense in taste : it was an elegant, a
pretty thing while it lasted. Especially in enhancing
description, where the alloy of life may be omitted,
where nothing vulgar need be noticed, where everything elegant may be neatly painted, such a world is
elegant enough. Morals and policy must decide how
far such delineations are permissible or expedient : but
the art of beauty — art criticism — has no objection
to them ; they are pretty paintings of pretty objects,
and that is all it has to say. They may very easily
do harm, — if generally read among the young of the
middle class, they would be sure to do harm : they
would teach not a few to aim at a sort of refinement
denied them by circumstances, and to neglect the duties allotted them ; they would make shopmen "bad
imitations of polished ungodliness," and also bad shopmen. But still, though it would in such places be nox-
ious literature, in itself it would be pretty literature ;
the critic must praise it, though the moralist must
condemn it and perhaps the politician forbid it.

But "Tristram Shandy's" indecency is the very
opposite to this refined sort. It consists in allusions
to certain inseparable accompaniments of actual life
which are not beautiful, which can never be made
interesting, which would *if* they were decent be dull
and uninteresting. There is, it appears, a certain excitement in putting such matters into a book ; there
is a minor exhilaration even in petty crime. At first
such things look so odd in print that you go on reading them to see what they look like ; but you soon
give up, — what is disenchanting or even disgusting
in reality does not become enchanting or endurable
in delineation. You are more angry at it in literature than in life : there is much which is barbarous
and animal in reality that we could wish away, —
we endure it because we cannot help it, because we
did not make it and cannot alter it, because it is an
inseparable part of this inexplicable world ; but why
we should put this coarse alloy, this dross of life, into

the *optional* world of literature, which we can make
as we please, it is impossible to say. The needless introduction of accessory ugliness is always a sin in art,
and is not at all less so when such ugliness is disgusting and improper. "Tristram Shandy" is incurably
tainted with a pervading vice: it dwells at length on,
it seeks after, it returns to, it gloats over the most
unattractive part of the world.

There is another defect in "Tristram Shandy"
which would of itself remove it from the list of first-
rate books, even if those which we have mentioned
did not do so: it contains eccentric characters only.
Some part of this defect may be perhaps explained by
one peculiarity of its origin: Sterne was so sensitive
to the picturesque parts of life that he wished to paint
the picturesque parts of the people he hated. Country towns in those days abounded in odd characters:
they were out of the way of the great opinion of
the world, and shaped themselves to little opinions
of their own; they regarded the customs which the
place had inherited as the customs which were proper
for it, and which it would be foolish if not wicked
to try to change. This gave English country life
a motley picturesqueness then which it wants now,
when London ideas shoot out every morning and
carry on the wings of the railway a uniform creed
to each cranny of the kingdom, north and south, east
and west. These little public opinions of little places
wanted, too, the crushing power of the great public
opinion of our own day; at the worst, a man could
escape from them into some different place which had
customs and doctrines that suited him better. We
now may fly into another "city," but it is all the
same Roman empire; the same uniform justice, the
one code of heavy laws presses us down and makes
us—the sensible part of us at least—as like other
people as we can make ourselves. The public opinion
of county towns yielded soon to individual exceptions;
it had not the confidence in itself which the opinion of

each place now receives from the accordant and simultaneous echo of a hundred places. If a man chose to be queer, he was bullied for a year or two, then it was settled that he was "queer"; that was the fact about him, and must be accepted: in a year or so he became an "institution" of the place, and the local pride would have been grieved if he had amended the oddity which suggested their legends and added a flavor to their life. Of course, if a man was rich and influential he might soon disregard the mere opinion of the petty locality: every place has wonderful traditions of old rich men who did exactly as they pleased, because they could set at naught the opinions of the neighbors, by whom they were feared, and who did not as now dread the unanimous conscience which does not fear even a squire of £2,000 a year or a banker of £8,000, because it is backed by the wealth of London and the magnitude of all the country. There is little oddity in county towns now; they are detached scraps of great places: but in Sterne's time there was much, and he used it unsparingly.

Much of the delineation is of the highest merit. Sterne knew how to describe eccentricity, for he showed its relation to our common human nature; he showed how we were related to it, how in some sort and in some circumstances we might ourselves become it; he reduced the abnormal formation to the normal rules. Except upon this condition, eccentricity is no fit subject for literary art. Every one must have known characters which, if they were put down in books barely and as he sees them, would seem monstrous and disproportioned, which would disgust all readers, which every critic would term unnatural. While characters are monstrous, they should be kept out of books; they are ugly unintelligibilities, foreign to the realm of true art: but as soon as they can be explained to us, as soon as they are shown in their union with, in their outgrowth from, common human nature, they are the best subjects for great art, for

they are new subjects. They teach us not the old lesson which our fathers knew, but a new lesson which
will please us and make us better than they. Hamlet
is an eccentric character,— one of the most eccentric
in literature: but because, by the art of the poet, we
are made to understand that he is a possible, a *vividly*
possible man, he enlarges our conceptions of human
nature; he takes us out of the bounds of commonplace; he "instructs us by means of delight."*
Sterne does this too. Mr. Shandy, Uncle Toby, Corporal Trim, Mrs. Shandy (for in strictness she too
is eccentric from her abnormal commonplaceness)
are beings of which the possibility is brought home
to us, which we feel we could under circumstances
and by influences become; which, though contorted
and twisted, are yet spun out of the same elementary
nature, the same thread as we are. Considering how
odd these characters are, the success of Sterne is
marvelous, and his art in this respect consummate.
But yet on a point most nearly allied it is very faulty:
though each individual character is shaded off into
human nature, the whole is not shaded off into the
world. This society of originals and oddities is left
to stand by itself, as if it were a natural and ordinary
society,— a society easily conceivable and needing no
explanation. Such is not the manner of the great
masters: in their best works a constant atmosphere
of half-commonplace personages surrounds and shades
off, illustrates and explains every central group of
singular persons.

On the whole, therefore, the judgment of criticism
on "Tristram Shandy," is concise and easy. It is immortal because of certain scenes suggested by Sterne's
curious experience, detected by his singular sensibility, and heightened by his delineative and discrimina-
tive imagination. It is defective because its style is
fantastic, its method illogical and provoking; because
its indecency is of the worst sort, as far as in such
matters an artistic judgment can speak of worst and

---

* Sara Coleridge, Introduction to Coleridge's "Biographia Literaria."

best; because its world of characters forms an incongruous group of singular persons, utterly dissimilar to and irreconcilable with the world in which we live. It is a great work of art, but of barbarous art; its mirth is boisterous; it is *provincial.* It is redolent of an inferior society: of those who think crude animal spirits in themselves delightful,—who do not know that without wit to point them or humor to convey them, they are disagreeable to others; who like disturbing transitions, blank pages, and tricks of style; who do not know that a simple and logical form of expression is the most effective, if not the easiest,— the least laborious to readers, if not always the most easily attained by writers.

The oddity of "Tristram Shandy" was, however, a great aid to its immediate popularity. If an author were to stand on his head now and then in Cheapside, his eccentricity would bring him into contact with the police, but it would advertise his writings; they would sell better: people would like to see what was said by a great author who was so odd as to stand so. Sterne put his eccentricity into his writings, and therefore came into collision with the critics; but he attained the same end,—his book sold capitally. As with all popular authors, he went to London; he was fêted. "The *man* Sterne," growled Dr. Johnson, "has had engagements for three months."* The upper world—ever desirous of novelty, ever tired of itself, ever anxious to be amused—was in hopes of a new wit; it naturally hoped that the author of "Tristram Shandy" would talk well, and it sent for him to talk.

He did talk well, it appears, though not always very correctly, and never very clerically. His appearance was curious, but yet refined: eager eyes, a wild look, a long lean frame, and what he called "a bale of cadaverous goods"† for a body, made up an odd exterior, which attracted notice and did not repel liking;

---

* Boswell, Chap. xxvi.   † Letter xcvi., to Stevenson, May, 1767.

he looked like a scarecrow with bright eyes. With a
random manner, but not without a nice calculation,
he discharged witticisms at London parties. His keen
nerves told him which were fit witticisms; *they* took,
and *he* was applauded.

He published some sermons too. That tolerant age
liked, it is instructive as well as amusing to think,
sermons by the author of "Tristram Shandy." People wonder at the rise of Methodism; but ought they
to wonder? If a clergyman publishes his sermons
because he has written an indecent novel, a novel
which is purely pagan, — which is outside the ideas'
of Christianity, whose author can scarcely have been
inside of them, — if a man so made and so circum-
stanced is *as such* to publish Christian sermons, surely
Christianity is a joke and a dream. Wesley was
right in this at least: if Christianity be true, the
upper-class life of the last century was based on rotten falsehood. A world which is really secular, which
professes to be Christian, is the worst of worlds.

The only point in which Sterne resembles a clergyman of our own time is, that he lost his voice. That
peculiar affection of the chest and throat, which is
hardly known among barristers but which inflicts such
suffering upon parsons, attacked him also.* Sterne
too, as might be expected, went abroad for it. He
"spluttered French," he tells us, with success in
Paris:† the accuracy of the grammar some phrases
in his letters would lead us to doubt; but few, very
few Yorkshire parsons could then talk French at all,
and there was doubtless a fine tact and sensibility in
what he said. A literary phenomenon wishing to enjoy society, and able to amuse society, has ever been
welcome in the Parisian world. After Paris, Sterne
went to the South of France, and on to Italy, lounging
easily in pretty places, and living comfortably, as far

---

* Grossly unjust: he burst a blood-vessel in his lungs, and was repeatedly
near death with similar hemorrhages. — ED.

† Letter xxviii., to Lady D——, July 9, 1762.

as one can see, upon the profits of "Tristram Shandy."
Literary success has seldom changed more suddenly
and completely the course of a man's life. For years'
Sterne resided in a country parsonage, and the sources
of his highest excitement were a country town full of
provincial oddities, and a "Crazy Castle" full of the
license and the whims of a country squire; on a sudden London, Paris, and Italy were opened to him,
—from a few familiar things he was suddenly transferred to many unfamiliar things. He was equal to
them, though the change came so suddenly in middle life; though the change from a secluded English
district to the great and interesting scenes was far
greater, far fuller of unexpected sights and unforeseen phenomena, than it can be now, when traveling
is common, when the newspaper is "abroad," when
every one has in his head some feeble image of
Europe and the world. Sterne showed the delicate
docility which belongs to a sensitive and experiencing
nature; he understood and enjoyed very much of this
new and strange life, if not the whole.

The proof of this remains written in the "Sentimental Journey." There is no better painting of first
and easy impressions than that book; after all which
has been written on the *ancien régime*, an Englishman at least will feel a fresh instruction on reading
these simple observations. They are instructive *because* of their simplicity. The old world at heart was
not like that; there were depths and realities, latent
forces and concealed results, which were hidden from
Sterne's eye, which it would have been quite out of
his way to think of or observe: but the old world
seemed like that. This was the spectacle of it as it
was seen by an observing stranger; and we take it
up, not to know what was the truth, but to know
what we should have thought to be the truth if we
had lived in those times. People say "Eōthen" is
not like the real East; very likely it is not, but it is
like what an imaginative young Englishman would

think the East. Just so, the "Sentimental Journey" is not the true France of the old monarchy, but it is exactly what an observant quick-eyed Englishman might fancy that France to be. This has given it popularity; this still makes it a valuable relic of the past. It is not true to the outward nature of real life, but it is true to the reflected image of that life in an imaginative and sensitive man.

Here is the actual description of the old chivalry of France, — "the cheap defense of nations,"* as Mr. Burke called it a little while afterwards : —

"When states and empires have their periods of declension, and feel in their turns what distress and poverty is — I stop not to tell the causes which gradually brought the house d'E—— in Brittany into decay. The Marquis d'E—— had fought up against his condition with great firmness; wishing to preserve, and still show to the world, some little fragments of what his ancestors had been — their indiscretions had put it out of his power. There was enough left for the little exigencies of *obscurity.* But he had two boys who looked up to him for *light* — he thought they deserved it. He had tried his sword — it could not open the way — the *mounting* was too expensive — and simple economy was not a match for it : — there was no resource but commerce.

"In any other province in France, save Brittany, this was smiting the root forever of the little tree his pride and affection wished to see reblossom. But in Brittany, there being a provision for this, he availed himself of it : and taking an occasion when the States were assembled at Rennes, the Marquis, attended with his two boys, entered the court; and having pleaded the right of an ancient law of the duchy, which, though seldom claimed, he said, was no less in force, he took his sword from his side ; — Here, said he, take it ; and be trusty guardians of it, till better times put me in condition to reclaim it.

"The president accepted the Marquis's sword ; — he staid a few minutes to see it deposited in the archives of his house — and departed.

"The Marquis and his whole family' embarked the next day for Martinico, and in about nineteen or twenty years of successful application to business, with some unlooked-for bequests from distant branches of his house, returned home to reclaim his nobility, and to support it.

---

* "Reflections on the Revolution in France," paragraph on Marie Antoinette.

"It was an incident of good fortune which will never happen to any traveler but a sentimental one, that I should be at Rennes at the very time of this solemn requisition. I call it solemn; — it was so to me.

"The Marquis entered the court with his whole family: he supported his lady; — his eldest son supported his sister, and his youngest was at the other extreme of the line next his mother — he put his handkerchief to his face twice. —

"— There was a dead silence. When the Marquis had approached within six paces of the tribunal, he gave the Marchioness to his youngest son, and advancing three steps before his family — he reclaimed his sword.

"His sword was given him; and the moment he got it into his hand, he drew it almost out of the scabbard: — 'twas the shining face of a friend he had once given up; — he looked attentively along it, beginning at the hilt, as if to see whether it was the same — when observing a little rust which it had contracted near the point, he brought it near his eye, and bending his head down over it — I think I saw a tear fall upon the place: I could not be deceived by what followed.

"'I shall find,' said he, 'some *other way* to get it off.'

"When the Marquis had said this, he returned his sword into its scabbard, made a bow to the guardians of it — and with his wife and daughter, and his two sons following him, walked out.

"O how I envied him his feelings!"*

It shows a touching innocence of the imagination to believe, — for probably Sterne did believe, — or to expect his readers to believe, in a *noblesse* at once so honorable and so theatrical.

In two points the "Sentimental Journey," viewed with the critic's eye and as a mere work of art, is a great improvement upon "Tristram Shandy." The style is simpler and better; it is far more connected: it does not jump about, or leave a topic *because* it is interesting; it does not worry the reader with fantastic transitions, with childish contrivances and rhetorical intricacies. Highly elaborate the style certainly is, and in a certain sense artificial; it is full of nice touches which must have come only upon reflection, a careful polish and judicious enhancement in which

* "Sentimental Journey," ii.; "The Sword — Rennes."

the critic sees many a trace of time and toil: but a style delicately adjusted and exquisitely polished belongs to such a subject. Sterne undertook to write *not* of the coarse business of life, — very strong common sort of words are best for that; *not* even of interesting outward realities, which may be best described in a nice and simple style: but of the passing moods of human nature, of the impressions which a sensitive nature receives from the world without, and it is only the nicest art and the most dexterous care which can fit an obtuse language to such fine employment. How language was first invented and made we may not know, but beyond doubt it was shaped and fashioned into its present state by common ordinary men and women using it for common and ordinary purposes; they wanted a carving knife, not a razor or lancet: and those great artists who have to use language for more exquisite purposes, who employ it to describe changing sentiments and momentary fancies and the fluctuating and indefinite inner world, must use curious nicety and hidden but effectual artifice, else they cannot duly punctuate their thoughts and slice the fine edges of their reflections. A hair's breadth is as important to them as a yard's breadth to a common workman. Sterne's style has been criticized as artificial; but it is justly and rightly artificial, because language used in its natural and common mode was not framed to delineate — cannot delineate — the delicate subjects with which he occupies himself.

That contact with the world, and with the French world especially, should teach Sterne to abandon the arbitrary and fantastic structure of "Tristram Shandy" is most natural. French prose may be unreasonable in its meaning, but is ever rational in its structure; it is logic itself: it will not endure that the reader's mind should be jarred by rough transitions or distracted by irrelevant oddities. *Antics* in style are prohibited by its severe code, just as eccentricities in manner are kept down by the critical tone of a fastidious society. In a barbarous country, oddity may be attractive; in the great world it never is except for a moment. It is on trial to see whether it is really oddity, to see if it does not contain elements which may be useful to, which may be naturalized in, society at large. But inherent eccentricity, oddity *pur et simple*, is *immiscible* in the great ocean of universal thought; it is apart from it, even when it floats in and is contained in it; very, very soon it is cast out from the busy waters, and left alone upon the beach. Sterne had the sense to be taught by the sharp touch of the world; he threw aside the "player's garb" which he had been tempted to assume. He discarded, too, as was equally natural, the ugly indecency of "Tristram Shandy." We will not undertake to defend the morality of certain scenes in the "Sentimental Journey,"—there are several which might easily do much harm; but there is nothing displeasing to the natural man in them. They are nice enough; to those whose æsthetic nature has not been laid waste by their moral nature, they are attractive. They have a dangerous prettiness, which may easily incite to practical evil; but in itself, and separated from its censurable consequences, such prettiness is an artistic perfection. It was natural that the aristocratic world should easily teach Sterne that separation between the laws of beauty and the laws of morality which has been familiar to it during many ages,—which makes so much of its essence.

Mrs. Sterne did not prosper all this time. She went abroad and stayed at Montpellier with her husband; but it is not wonderful that a mere "wife," taken out of Yorkshire, should be unfit for the great world. The domestic appendices of men who rise much, hardly ever suit the high places at which they arrive; Mrs. Sterne was no exception. She seems to have been sensible, but it was *domestic* sense: it was of the small world, small; it was fit to regulate the

Yorkshire parsonage, it was suitable to a small *ménage* even at Montpellier, but there was a deficiency in general mind. She did not, we apprehend, comprehend / or appreciate the new thoughts and feelings which a new and great experience had awakened in her husband's mind. His mind moved, but hers could not; she was anchored, but he was at sea.

To fastidious writers, who will only use very dignified words, there is much difficulty in describing Sterne's life in his celebrity; but to humbler persons, who can only describe the things of society in the words of society, the case is simple,—Sterne was "an old flirt." These are short and expressive words, and they tell the whole truth: there is no good reason to suspect his morals, but he dawdled about pretty women. He talked at fifty with the admiring tone of twenty; pretended to "freshness" of feeling; though he had become mature, did not put away immature things. That he had any real influence over women is very unlikely: he was a celebrity and they liked to exhibit him, he was amusing and they liked him to amuse them, but they doubtless felt that he too was himself a joke. Women much respect real virtue; they much admire strong and successful immorality: but they neither admire nor respect the timid age which affects the forms of vice without its substance; which preserves the exterior of youth though the reality is departed; which is insidious but not dangerous, sentimental but not passionate. Of this sort was Sterne; and he had his reward. Women of the world are willing to accept any admiration, but this sort they accept with suppressed and latent sarcasm; they ridiculed his imbecility while they accepted his attentions and enjoyed his society.

Many men have lived this life with but minor penalties, and justly; for though perhaps a feeble and contemptible, it is not a bad or immoral life. But Sterne has suffered a very severe though a delayed and posthumous penalty: he was foolish enough to write letters to some of his friends; and after his death, to get money, his family published them. This is the sort of thing:—

"Eliza will receive my books with this. The sermons came all hot from the heart: I wish that I could give them any title to be offered to yours.—The others came from the head: I am more indifferent about their reception.

"I know not how it comes about, but I am half in love with you—I ought to be wholly so; for I never valued (or saw more good qualities to value) or thought more of one of your sex than of you; so adieu.   "Yours faithfully,

"if not affectionately,

"L. STERNE."*

"I cannot rest, Eliza, though I shall call on you at half-past twelve, till I know how you do.—May thy dear face smile, as thou risest, like the sun of this morning. I was much grieved to hear of your alarming indisposition yesterday; and disappointed too, at not being let in. Remember, my dear, that a friend has the same right as a physician. The etiquettes of this town (you'll say) say otherwise.—No matter! Delicacy and propriety do not always consist in observing their frigid doctrines.

"I am going out to breakfast, but shall be at my lodgings by eleven; when I hope to read a single line under thy own hand, that thou art better, and wilt be glad to see thy Bramin."†

This Eliza was a Mrs. Draper, the wife of a judge in India "much respected in that quarter of the globe."‡ We know little of Eliza, except that there is a stone in Bristol cathedral—

SACRED

TO THE MEMORY

OF

MRS. ELIZABETH DRAPER,

IN WHOM

GENIUS AND BENEVOLENCE

WERE UNITED.

SHE DIED AUGUST 3, 1778, AGED 35.

Let us hope she possessed, in addition to genius and benevolence, the good sense to laugh at Sterne's letters.

---

*Letter lxxx.   †Letter lxxxi.

‡ Thackeray, quoting from editor's note to 1775 edition of Sterne's letters.

In truth, much of the gloss and delicacy of Sterne's pagan instinct had faded away by this time. He still retained his fine sensibility, his exquisite power of entering into and of delineating plain human nature; but the world had produced its inevitable effect on that soft and voluptuous disposition. It is not, as we have said, that he was guilty of grave offenses or misdeeds: he made what he would have called a "splutter of vice,"* but he would seem to have committed very little. Yet, as with most minds which have exempted themselves from rigid principle, there was a diffused texture of general laxity. The fiber had become imperfect; the moral constitution was impaired; the high color of rottenness had come at last out, and replaced the delicate bloom and softness of the early fruit. There is no need to write commonplace sermons on an ancient text: the beauty and charm of natural paganism will not endure the stress and destruction of this rough and complicated world. An instinctive purity will preserve men for a brief time, but hardly through a long and varied life of threescore and ten years.

Sterne, however, did not live so long. In 1768 he came to London for the last time, and enjoyed himself much; he dined with literary friends and supped with fast friends, — he liked both: but the end was at hand. His chest had long been delicate; he got a bad cold which became a pleurisy, and died in a London lodging, — a footman sent by "some gentlemen who were dining," and a hired nurse, being the only persons present. His family were away; and he had devoted himself to intellectual and luxurious enjoyments, which are at least as sure to make a lonely death-bed as a refined and cultivated life. "Self-scanned, self-centered, self-secure," † a man may perhaps live; but even so, by *himself* he will be sure to die. For self-absorbed men the world at large cares

---

* No such words are to be found in his writings. — ED.

† "Self-schooled, self-scanned, self-honored, self-secure." — Matthew Arnold, "Sonnet to Shakespeare."

little; as soon as they cease to amuse or to be useful
it flings them aside, and they die alone. Even Sterne's
grave, they say, was so obscure and neglected that
the corpse-stealers ventured to open it, and his body
was dissected without being recognized. The life of
literary men is often a kind of sermon in itself; for
the pursuit of fame, when it is contrasted with the
grave realities of life, seems more absurd and trifling
than most pursuits, and to leave less behind. Mere
amusers are never respected. It would be harsh to
call Sterne a mere amuser, — he is much more; but so
the contemporary world regarded him. They laughed
at his jests, disregarded his death-bed, and neglected
his grave.

What, it may be asked, is there in such a career
or such a character as this to remind us of the great
writer whom we have just lost? In externals there
seems little resemblance, or rather there seems to be
great contrast: on the one side a respected manhood, a
long industry, an honored memory; on the other hand
a life lax if not dissolute, little labor, and a dishonored grave. Mr. Thackeray, too, has written a most
severe criticism on Sterne's character. Can we, then,
venture to compare the two? We do so venture;
and we allege — and that in spite of many superficial
differences — that there was one fundamental and ineradicable resemblance between the two.

Thackeray, like Sterne, looked at everything — at
nature, at life, at art — from a *sensitive* aspect. His
mind was to some considerable extent like a woman's
mind: it could comprehend abstractions when they
were unrolled and explained before it, but it never
naturally created them; never of itself, and without
external obligation, devoted itself to them. The visible scene of life — the streets, the servants, the clubs,
the gossip, the West End — fastened on his brain.
These were to him reality: they burnt in upon his
brain; they pained his nerves; their influence reached
him through many avenues which ordinary men do

not feel much, or to which they are altogether im-
pervious. He had distinct and rather painful sensations where most men have but confused and blurred
ones. Most men have felt the *instructive* headache,
during which they are more acutely conscious than
usual of all which goes on around them, — during
which everything seems to pain them, and in which
they understand it because it pains them and they
cannot get their imagination away from it. Thackeray had a nerve-ache of this sort always; he acutely
felt every possible passing fact, every trivial interlude
in society. Hazlitt used to say of himself, and used
to say truly, that he could not enjoy the society in a
drawing-room for thinking of the opinion which the
footman formed of his odd appearance as he went
up-stairs.* Thackeray had too healthy and stable a
nature to be thrown so wholly off his balance; but
the footman's view of life was never out of his head.
The obvious facts which suggest it to the footman
poured it in upon him; he could not exempt himself
from them. As most men say that the earth *may* go
round the sun, but in fact, when we look at the sun,
we cannot help believing it goes round the earth, —
just so this most impressible, susceptible genius could
not help half accepting, half believing the common
ordinary sensitive view of life, although he perfectly
knew in his inner mind and deeper nature that this
apparent and superficial view of life was misleading,
inadequate, and deceptive. He could not help seeing
everything, and what he saw made so near and keen
an impression upon him that he could not again exclude it from his understanding; it stayed there, and
disturbed his thoughts.

If, he often says, people could write about that of
which they are really thinking, how interesting books
would be! More than most writers of fiction, he felt
the difficulty of abstracting his thoughts and imagination from near facts which *would* make themselves

---

* No such intimation is to be found in his writings, and it is contrary
to all his utterances about himself. — ED.

felt. The sick wife in the next room, the unpaid baker's bill, the lodging-house keeper who doubts your solvency, — these and such as these, the usual accompaniments of an early literary life, are constantly alluded to in his writings. Perhaps he could never take a grand enough view of literature, or accept the truth of "high art," because of his natural tendency to this stern and humble realism. He knew that he was writing a tale which would appear in a green magazine (with others) on the 1st of March, and would be paid for perhaps on the 11th; by which time, probably, "Mr. Smith" would have to "make up a sum," and would again present his "little account." There are many minds besides his who feel an interest in these realities, though they yawn over "high art" and elaborate judgments.

A painfulness certainly clings like an atmosphere round Mr. Thackeray's writings, in consequence of his inseparable and ever-present realism; we hardly know where it is, yet we are all conscious of it less or more. A free and bold writer, like Sir Walter Scott, throws himself far away into fictitious worlds, and soars there without effort, without pain, and with unceasing enjoyment: you see, as it were, between the lines of Mr. Thackeray's writings, that his thoughts were never long away from the close proximate scene. His writings might be better if it had been otherwise: but they would have been less peculiar, less individual; they would have wanted their character, their flavor, if he had been able while writing them to forget for many moments the ever-attending, the ever-painful sense of himself.

Hence have arisen most of the censures upon him, both as he seemed to be in society and as he was in his writings. He was certainly uneasy in the common and general world, and it was natural that he should be so: the world poured in upon him, and *inflicted* upon his delicate sensibility a number of petty pains and impressions which others do not feel at all, or which they feel but very indistinctly. As he sat, he seemed to read off the passing thoughts — the base, common, ordinary impressions — of every one else. Could such a man be at ease? Could even a quick intellect be asked to set in order with such velocity so many data? Could any temper, however excellent, be asked to bear the contemporaneous influx of innumerable minute annoyances? Men of ordinary nerves, who feel a little of the pains of society, who perceive what really passes, who are not absorbed in the petty pleasures of sociability, could well observe how keen was Thackeray's *sensation* of common events, could easily understand how difficult it must have been for him to keep mind and temper undisturbed by a miscellaneous tide at once so incessant and so forcible.

He could not emancipate himself from such impressions even in a case where most men hardly feel them. Many people have — it is not difficult to have — some vague sensitive perception of what is passing in the minds of the guests, of the ideas of such as sit at meat; but who remembers that there are also nervous apprehensions, also a latent mental life, among those who "stand and wait"* — among the floating figures which pass and carve? But there was no impression to which Mr. Thackeray was more constantly alive, or which he was more apt in his writings to express. He observes: —

"Between me and those fellow-creatures of mine who are sitting in the room below, how strange and wonderful is the partition! We meet at every hour of the daylight, and are indebted to each other for a hundred offices of duty and comfort of life; and we live together for years, and don't know each other. John's voice to me is quite different from John's voice when it addresses his mates below. If I met Hannah in the street with a bonnet on, I doubt whether I should know her. And all these good people, with whom I may live for years and years, have cares, interests, dear friends and relatives, — mayhap schemes, passions, longing hopes, tragedies, — of their own, from which a carpet and a few planks and

* "They also serve who only stand and wait." — Milton, Sonnet xix.

beams utterly separate me. When we were at the seaside, and poor
Ellen used to look so pale, and run after the postman's bell, and
seize a letter in a great scrawling hand, and read it, and cry in a
corner, how should we know that the poor little thing's heart was
breaking? She fetched the water, and she smoothed the ribbons,
and she laid out the dresses, and brought the early cup of tea in
the morning, just as if she had had no cares to keep her awake.
Henry (who lived out of the house) was the servant of a friend of
mine who lived in chambers. There was a dinner one day, and
Henry waited all through the dinner. The champagne was properly
iced, the dinner was excellently served; every guest was attended
to; the dinner disappeared, the dessert was set; the claret was in
perfect order, carefully decanted, and more ready. And then Henry
said, 'If you please, sir, may I go home?' He had received word
that his house was on fire; and having seen through his dinner, he
wished to go and look after his children and little sticks of furniture. Why, such a man's livery is a uniform of honor; the crest
on his button is a badge of bravery." *

Nothing in itself could be more admirable than
this instinctive sympathy with humble persons; not
many things are rarer than this nervous apprehension
of what humble persons think. Nevertheless, it cannot, we think, be effectually denied that it colored Mr.
Thackeray's writings and the more superficial part of
his character — that part which was most obvious in
common and current society — with very considerable
defects. The pervading idea of the "Snob Papers" is
too frequent, too recurring, too often insisted on, even
in his highest writings; there was a slight shade of
similar feeling even in his occasional society, and
though it was certainly unworthy of him, it was
exceedingly natural that it should be so, with such
a mind as his and in a society such as ours.

There are three methods in which a society may
be constituted.

There is the equal system, which with more or less
of variation prevails in France and in the United
States. The social presumption in these countries
always is, that every one is on a level with every

* "Roundabout Papers," "On a Chalk-Mark on the Door."

one else. In America, the porter at the station, the shopman at the counter, the boots at the hotel, when neither a negro nor an Irishman, is your equal. In France, *égalité* is a political first principle; the whole of Louis Napoleon's *régime* depends upon it; remove that feeling, and the whole fabric of the Empire will pass away. We once heard a great French statesman illustrate this. He was giving a dinner to the clergy of his neighborhood, and was observing that he had now no longer the power to help or hurt them; when an eager *curé* said, with simple-minded joy, "Oui, monsieur, maintenant personne ne peut rien,—ni le comte ni le prolétaire."* The democratic priest so rejoiced at the universal leveling which had passed over his nation that he could not help boasting of it when silence would have been much better manners. We are not now able—we have no room and no inclination—to discuss the advantages of democratic society; but we think in England we may venture to assume that it is neither the best nor the highest form which a society can adopt, and that it is certainly fatal to that development of individual originality and greatness by which the past progress of the human race has been achieved, and from which alone, it would seem, all future progress is to be anticipated. If it be said that people are all alike, that the world is a plain with no natural valleys and no natural hills, the picturesqueness of existence is destroyed; and what is worse, the instinctive emulation by which the dweller in the valley is stimulated to climb the hill is annihilated and becomes impossible.

On the other hand, there is the opposite system, which prevails in the East,—the system of irremovable inequalities, of hedged-in castes, which no one can enter but by birth and from which no born member can issue forth. This system likewise, in this

---

* "Yes, sir, nobody has any power now,—neither count nor one of the rabble."

age and country, needs no attack, for it has no defenders. Every one is ready to admit that it cramps originality by defining our work irrespective of our qualities and before we were born; that it retards progress by restraining the wholesome competition between class and class, and the wholesome migration from class to class, which are the best and strongest instruments of social improvement.

And if both these systems be condemned as undesirable and prejudicial, there is no third system except that which we have, — the system of *removable inequalities*, where many people are inferior to and worse off than others, but in which each may *in theory* hope to be on a level with the highest below the throne, and in which each may reasonably and without sanguine impracticability hope to gain one step in social elevation, to be at last on a level with those who at first were just above them. But from the mere description of such a society, it is evident that taking man as he is, with the faults which we know he has and the tendencies which he invariably displays, some poison of "snobbishness" is inevitable. Let us define it as the habit of "pretending to be higher in the social scale than you really are." Everybody will admit that such pretension is a fault and a vice; yet every observant man of the world would also admit that, considering what other misdemeanors men commit, this offense is not inconceivably heinous; and that if people never did anything worse, they might be let off with a far less punitive judgment than in the actual state of human conduct would be just or conceivable. How are we to hope men will pass their lives in putting their best foot foremost, and yet will never boast that their better foot is farther advanced and more perfect than in fact it is? Is boasting to be made a capital crime? Given social ambition as a propensity of human nature; given a state of society like ours, in which there are prizes which every man may seek, degradations

which every one may erase, inequalities which every
one may remove, — it is idle to suppose that there
will not be all sorts of striving to cease to be last
and to begin to be first, and it is equally idle to imagine that all such strivings will be of the highest
kind. This effort will be, like all the efforts of our
mixed and imperfect human nature, partly good and
partly bad; with much that is excellent and beneficial in it, and much also which is debasing and
pernicious. The bad striving after unpossessed distinction is snobbishness; which from the mere definition cannot be defended, but which may be excused
as a natural frailty in an emulous man who is not
distinguished, who hopes to be distinguished, and who
perceives that a valuable means of gaining distinction is a judicious though false pretension that it has
already been obtained.

Mr. Thackeray, as we think, committed two errors
in this matter. He lacerates "snobs" in his books as
if they had committed an unpardonable outrage and
inexpiable crime. "That man," he says, "is anxious
to know lords; and he pretends to know more of
lords than he really does know. What a villain!
what a disgrace to our common nature! what an
irreparable reproach to human reason!" Not at all:
it is a fault which satirists should laugh at and
which moralists condemn and disapprove, but which
yet does not destroy the whole vital excellence of
him who possesses it; which may leave him a good
citizen, a pleasant husband, a warm friend, — "a fellow," as the undergraduate said, "*up* in his *morals.*"
In transient society it is possible, we think, that Mr.
Thackeray thought too much of social inequalities.
They belonged to that common, plain, perceptible
world which filled his mind, and which left him at
times and at casual moments no room for a purely
intellectual and just estimate of men as they really
are in themselves, and apart from social perfection
or defect. He could gauge a man's reality as well as

any observer, and far better than most,—his attainments were great, his perception of men instinctive, his knowledge of casual matters enormous; but he had a greater difficulty than other men in relying only upon his own judgment. What the footman—what Mr. Yellowplush Jeames—would think and say, could not but occur to his mind, and would modify not his settled judgment, but his transient and casual opinion of the poet or philosopher. By the constitution of his mind he thought much of social distinctions; and yet he was in his writings too severe on those who, in cruder and baser ways, showed that they also were thinking much.

Those who perceive that this irritable sensibility was the basis of Thackeray's artistic character,—that it gave him his materials, his implanted knowledge of things and men, and gave him also that keen and precise style which hit in description the nice edges of all objects,—those who trace these great qualities back to their real source in a somewhat painful organization must have been vexed or amused, according to their temperament, at the common criticism which associates him with Fielding. Fielding's essence was the very reverse; it was a bold spirit of bounding happiness. No just observer could talk to Mr. Thackeray, or look at him, without seeing that he had deeply felt many sorrows; perhaps that he was a man *likely* to feel sorrows, that he was of an anxious temperament. Fielding was a reckless enjoyer: he saw the world, wealth and glory, the best dinner and the worst dinner, the gilded *salon* and the low sponging-house, and he saw that they were good; down every line of his characteristic writings there runs this elemental energy of keen delight. There is no trace of such a thing in Thackeray: a musing fancifulness is far more characteristic of him than a joyful energy.

Sterne had all this sensibility also; but—and this is the cardinal discrepancy—it did not make him irritable. He was not hurried away, like Fielding, by buoyant delight: he stayed and mused on painful scenes; but they did not make him angry. He was not irritated at the "foolish fat scullion"*; he did not vex himself because of the vulgar; he did not amass petty details to prove that tenth-rate people were ever striving to be ninth-rate people. He had no tendency to rub the bloom off life; he accepted pretty-looking things, — even the French aristocracy, — and he owes his immortality to his making them prettier than they are. Thackeray was pained by things, and exaggerated their imperfections; Sterne brooded over things with joy or sorrow, and he idealized their sentiment, their pathetic or joyful characteristics. This is why the old lady said "Mr. Thackeray was an uncomfortable writer" — and an uncomfortable writer he is.

· Nor had Sterne a trace of Mr. Thackeray's peculiar and characteristic skepticism. He accepted simply the pains and pleasures, the sorrows and the joys of the world; he was not perplexed by them, nor did he seek to explain them or account for them. There is a tinge — a mitigated but perceptible tinge — of Swift's philosophy in Thackeray. "Why is all this? Surely this is very strange! Am I right in sympathizing with such stupid feelings, such petty sensations? Why are these things? am I not a fool to care about or think of them? The world is dark, and the great curtain hides from us all." This is not a steady or a habitual feeling, but it is never quite absent for many pages. It was inevitable, perhaps, that in a skeptical and inquisitive age like this, some vestiges of puzzle and perplexity should pass into the writings of our great sentimentalist; he would not have fairly represented the moods of his time if he omitted that pervading one.

We had a little more to say of these great men, but our limits are exhausted, and we must pause.

---

* "Tristram Shandy," Book iv., Chap. vii.

Of Thackeray it is too early to speak at length. A certain distance is needful for a just criticism; the present generation have learned too much from him to be able to judge him rightly. We do .not' know the merit of those great pictures which have sunk into our minds and which have colored our thoughts, — which are become habitual memories. In the books we know best, as in the people we know best, small points — sometimes minor merits, sometimes small faults — have an undue prominence. When the young critics of this year have gray hairs, their children will tell them what is the judgment of posterity upon Mr. Thackeray.

THE WAVERLEY NOVELS.*

(1858.)

It is not commonly on the generation which was contemporary with the production of great works of art that they exercise their most magical influence; nor is it on the distant people whom we call "posterity." Contemporaries bring to new books formed minds and stiffened creeds; posterity, if it regard them at all, looks at them as old subjects, worn-out topics, and hears a disputation on their merits with languid impartiality, like aged judges in a court of appeal. Even standard authors exercise but slender influence on the susceptible minds of a rising generation : they are become "papa's books"; the walls of the library are adorned with their regular volumes, but no hand touches them. Their fame is itself half an obstacle to their popularity; a delicate fancy shrinks from employing so great a celebrity as the companion of an idle hour. The generation which is really most influenced by a work of genius is commonly that which is still young when the first controversy respecting its merits arises. With the eagerness of youth they read and reread; their vanity is not unwilling

---

* Library Edition. Illustrated by upwards of Two Hundred Engravings on Steel, after Drawings by Turner, Landseer, Wilkie, Stanfield, Roberts, &c., including Portraits of the Historical Personages described in the Novels. 25 vols. demy 8vo.

Abbotsford Edition. With One Hundred and Twenty Engravings on Steel, and nearly Two Thousand on Wood. 12 vols. super-royal 8vo.

Author's Favorite Edition. 48 vols. post 8vo.

Cabinet Edition. 25 vols. foolscap 8vo.

Railway Edition. Now publishing, and to be completed in 25 portable volumes, large type.

People's Edition. 5 large volumes royal 8vo.

to adjudicate: in the process their imagination is
formed; the creations of the author range themselves
in the memory, they become part of the substance of
the very mind. The works of Sir Walter Scott·can
hardly be said to have gone through this exact process: their immediate popularity was unbounded; no
one — a few most captious critics apart — ever questioned their peculiar power. Still, they are subject to
a transition which is in principle the same. At the
time of their publication, mature contemporaries read
them with delight. Superficial the reading of grown
men in some sort must be; it is only once in a life-
time that we can know the passionate reading of
youth, — men soon lose its eager learning power: but
from peculiarities in their structure which we shall
try to indicate, the novels of Scott suffered less than
almost any book[s] of equal excellence from this inevitable superficiality of perusal. Their plain and (so to
say) cheerful merits suit the occupied man of genial
middle life; their appreciation was to an unusual degree coincident with their popularity. The next generation, hearing the praises of their fathers in their
earliest reading time, seized with avidity on the volumes; and there is much in very many of them which
is admirably fitted for the delight of boyhood. A
third generation has now risen into at least the commencement of literary life, which is quite removed
from the unbounded enthusiasm with which the Scotch
novels were originally received, and does not always
share the still more eager partiality of those who, in
the opening of their minds, first received the tradition
of their excellence. New books have arisen to com-
pete with these; new interests distract us from them.
The time, therefore, is not perhaps unfavorable for a
slight criticism of these celebrated fictions; and their
continual republication without any criticism for many
years seems almost to demand it.

There are two kinds of fiction; which, though in
common literature they may run very much into one

another, are yet in reality distinguishable and separate. One of these, which we may call the *ubiquitous*,
aims at describing the whole of human life in all its
spheres, in all its aspects, with all its varied interests,
aims, and objects. It searches through the whole life
of man, — his practical pursuits, his speculative attempts, his romantic youth and his domestic age : it
gives an entire picture of all these; or if there be any
lineaments which it forbears to depict, they are only
such as the inevitable repression of a regulated society
excludes from the admitted province of literary art.
Of this kind are the novels of Cervantes and Le Sage,
and to a certain extent of Smollett or Fielding. In
our own time, Mr. Dickens is an author whom nature
intended to write to a certain extent with this aim :
he should have given us *not* disjointed novels, with
a vague attempt at a romantic plot, but sketches of
diversified scenes and the obvious life of varied mankind. The literary fates, however, if such beings there
are, allotted otherwise. By a very terrible example of
the way in which in this world great interests are
postponed to little ones, the genius of authors is habitually sacrificed to the tastes of readers. In this age,
the great readers of fiction are young people; the
"addiction" of these is to romance: and accordingly
a kind of novel has become so familiar to us as almost to engross the name, which deals solely with the
passion of love; and if it uses other parts of human
life for the occasions of its art, it does so only cursorily
and occasionally, and with a view of throwing into
a stronger or more delicate light those sentimental
parts of earthly affairs which are the special objects
of delineation. All prolonged delineation of other parts
of human life is considered "dry," stupid, and dis-
tracts the mind of the youthful generation from the
"fantasies" which peculiarly charm it. Mr. Olmsted
has a story of some deputation of the Indians, at
which the American orator harangued the barbarian
audience about the "Great Spirit" and "the land of

their fathers," in the style of Mr. Cooper's novels: during a moment's pause in the great stream, an old Indian asked the deputation, "Why does your chief speak thus to us? We did not wish great instruction or fine words; we desire brandy and tobacco."* No critic in a time of competition will speak uncourteously of any reader of either sex; but it is indisputable that the old kind of novel, full of "great instruction" and varied pictures, does not afford to some young gentlemen and some young ladies either the peculiar stimulus or the peculiar solace which they desire.

The Waverley Novels were published at a time when the causes that thus limit the sphere of fiction were coming into operation, but when they had not yet become so omnipotent as they are now; accordingly, these novels everywhere bear marks of a state of transition. They are not devoted with anything like the present exclusiveness to the sentimental part of human life. They describe great events, singular characters, strange incidents, strange states of society; they dwell with a peculiar interest, and as if for their own sake, on antiquarian details relating to a past society. Singular customs, social practices, even political institutions, which existed once in Scotland and even elsewhere during the Middle Ages, are explained with a careful minuteness. At the same time the sentimental element assumes a great deal of prominence: the book is in fact as well as in theory a narrative of the feelings and fortunes of the hero

---

* A random shot at this delicious passage in "A Journey through Texas," Chap. v., sub-heading "A Capital Scout,"—the scout *loquitur:*—"Why do people who write books always make Indians talk in that hifalutin way they do? Indians don't talk so, and when folks talk that way to them they don't understand it. They don't like it neither. I went up with Lieutenant ——, when he tried to make a treaty with the Northern Apaches. He had been talking up in the clouds, all nonsense, for half an hour, and I was trying to translate it just as foolish as he said it. An old Indian jumped up and stopped me—"What does your chief talk to us in this way for? We a'n't babies, we are fighting men: if he has got anything to tell us we will hear it; but we didn't come here to be amused,—we came to be made drunk and to get some blankets and tobacco."—ED.

and heroine; an attempt—more or less successful—
has been made to insert an interesting love story in
each novel. Sir Walter was quite aware that the best
delineation of the oddest characters or the most quaint
societies or the strangest incidents would not in general satisfy his readers: he has invariably attempted
an account of youthful—sometimes of decidedly juve-
nile—feelings and actions. The difference between
Sir Walter's novels and the specially romantic fictions
of the present day is, that in the former the love
story is always or nearly always connected with some
great event, or the fortunes of some great historical
character, or the peculiar movements and incidents of
some strange state of society; and that the author
did not suppose or expect that his readers would be
so absorbed in the sentimental aspect of human life
as to be unable or unwilling to be interested in, or to
attend to, any other. There is always a *locus in quo*,*
if the expression may be pardoned, in the Waverley
Novels: the hero and heroine walk among the trees
of the forest according to rule, but we are expected to
take an interest in the forest as well as in them.

No novel, therefore, of Sir Walter Scott's can be
considered to come exactly within the class which we
have called the ubiquitous; none of them in any
material degree attempts to deal with human affairs
in all their spheres,—to delineate as a whole the
life of man. The canvas has a large background, in
some cases too large either for artistic effect or the
common reader's interest; but there are always real
boundaries,—Sir Walter had no *thesis* to maintain.
Scarcely any writer will set himself to delineate the
whole of human life unless he has a doctrine concerning human life to put forth and inculcate; the effort
is *doctrinaire*. Scott's imagination was strictly con-
servative. He could understand (with a few exceptions) any considerable movement of human life and
action, and could always describe with easy freshness

---

* "Place in which" [the action takes place].

everything which he did understand; but he was not obliged by stress of fanaticism to maintain a dogma concerning them, or to show their peculiar relation to the general sphere of life. He described vigorously and boldly the peculiar scene and society which in every novel he had selected as the theater of romantic action. Partly from their fidelity to nature, and partly from a consistency in the artist's mode of representation, these pictures group themselves from the several novels in the imagination, and a habitual reader comes to think of and understand what is meant by "Scott's world"; but the writer had no such distinct object before him, — no one novel was designed to be a delineation of the world as Scott viewed it. We have vivid and fragmentary histories; it is for the slow critic of after-times to piece together their teaching.

From this intermediate position of the Waverley Novels, or at any rate in exact accordance with its requirements, is the special characteristic for which they are most remarkable. We may call this in a brief phrase their *romantic sense;* and perhaps we cannot better illustrate it than by a quotation from the novel to which the series owes its most usual name. It occurs in the description of the court ball which Charles Edward is described as giving at Holyrood House the night before his march southward on his strange adventure. The striking interest of the scene before him, and the peculiar position of his own sentimental career, are described as influencing the mind of the hero.

"Under the influence of these mixed sensations, and cheered at times by a smile of intelligence and approbation from the Prince as he passed the group, Waverley exerted his powers of fancy, animation, and eloquence, and attracted the general admiration of the company. The conversation gradually assumed the tone best qualified for the display of his talents and acquisitions. The gayety of the evening was exalted in character, rather than checked, by the approaching dangers of the morrow ; all nerves were strung for the future and prepared to enjoy the present. This mood of mind is highly favorable for the exercise of the powers of imagination, for poetry, and for that eloquence which is allied to poetry."*

Neither "eloquence" nor "poetry" are the exact words with which it would be appropriate to describe the fresh style of the Waverley Novels; but the imagination of their author was stimulated by a fancied mixture of sentiment and fact, very much as he described Waverley's to have been by a real experience of the two at once. The second volume of "Waverley" is one of the most striking illustrations of this peculiarity. The character of Charles Edward, his adventurous undertaking, his ancestral rights; the mixed selfishness and enthusiasm of the Highland chiefs, the fidelity of their hereditary followers, their striking and strange array, the contrast with the Baron of Bradwardine and the Lowland gentry; the collision of the motley and half-appointed host with the formed and finished English society, its passage by the Cumberland mountains and the blue lake of Ullswater, — are unceasingly and without effort present to the mind of the writer, and incite with their historical interest the susceptibility of his imagination. But at the same time the mental struggle, or rather transition, in the mind of Waverley, — for his mind was of a faint order which scarcely struggles, — is never for an instant lost sight of: in the very midst of the inroad and the conflict, the acquiescent placidity with which the hero exchanges the service of the imperious for the appreciation of the "nice" heroine is kept before us, and the imagination of Scott wandered without effort from the great scene of martial affairs to the natural but rather unheroic sentiments of a young gentleman not very difficult to please. There is no trace of effort in the transition, as is so common in the inferior works of later copyists. Many historical novelists, especially those who with care and pains have "read up" their detail, are often evidently in a strait how to pass from their

* Chap. xliii.

history to their sentiment: the fancy of Sir Walter could not help connecting the two. If he had given us the English side of the race•to Derby, he would have described the Bank of England paying in sixpences, and also the loves of the cashier. .

It is not unremarkable, in connection with this the special characteristic of the "Scotch novels," that their author began his literary life by collecting the old ballads of his native country. Ballad poetry is, in comparison at least with many other kinds of poetry, a sensible thing: it describes not only romantic events but historical ones, —incidents in which there is a·form and body and consistence, events which have a result. Such a poem as "Chevy Chase," we need not explain, has its prosaic side. The latest historian of Greece* has nowhere been more successful than in his attempt to derive from Homer, the greatest of ballad poets, a thorough and consistent account of the political working of the Homeric state of society. The early natural imagination of men seizes firmly on all which interests the minds and hearts of natural men: we find in its delineations the council as well as the marriage, the harsh conflict as well as the deep love affair. Scott's own poetry is essentially a modernized edition of the traditional poems which his early youth was occupied in collecting. The "Lady of the Lake" is a sort of *boudoir* ballad, yet it contains its element of common-sense and broad delineation: the exact position of Lowlander and Highlander would not be more aptly described in a set treatise than in the well-known lines—

> "Saxon, from yonder mountain high
> I marked thee send delighted eye
> Far to the south and east, where lay,
> Extended in succession gay,
> Deep waving fields and pastures green,
> With gentle slopes and groves between:
> These fertile plains, that softened vale,
> Were once the birthright of the Gael;

*Grote.

> The stranger came with iron hand,
> And from our fathers reft the land.
> Where dwell we now? See rudely swell
> Crag over crag, and fell o'er fell.
> Ask we this savage hill we tread
> For fattened steer or household bread;
> Ask we for flocks these shingles dry, —
> And well the mountain might reply,
> 'To you, as to your sires of yore,
> Belong the target and claymore!
> I give you shelter in my breast,
> Your own good blades must win the rest.'
> Pent in this fortress of the North,
> Think'st thou we will not sally forth
> To spoil the spoiler as we may,
> And from the robber rend the prey?
> Ay, by my soul! While on yon plain
> The Saxon rears one shock of grain,
> While of ten thousand herds there strays
> But one along yon river's maze, —
> The Gael, of plain and river heir,
> Shall with strong hand redeem his share."

We need not search the same poem for specimens of the romantic element, for the whole poem is full of them. The incident in which Ellen discovers who Fitz-James really is, is perhaps excessively romantic; at any rate, the lines—

> "To him each lady's look was lent;
> On him each courtier's eye was bent:
> Midst furs and silks and jewels sheen,
> He stood in simple Lincoln green,
> The center of the glittering ring,
> And Snowdoun's knight is Scotland's king"—

may be cited as very sufficient example of the sort of sentimental incident which is separable from extreme feeling. When Scott, according to his own half-jesting but half-serious expression, was "beaten out of poetry"* by Byron, he began to express in

---

* I do not find just these words anywhere; their *sense* is stated in the Introduction to "Rokeby," in letter to Countess Purgstall given in Lockhart (Vol. v., Chap. vi.), and elsewhere.— ED.

more pliable prose the same combination which his verse had been used to convey. As might have been expected, the sense became in the novels more free, vigorous, and flowing, because it is less cramped by the vehicle in which it is conveyed. The range of character which can be adequately delineated in narrative verse is much narrower than that which can be described in the combination of narrative with dramatic prose, and perhaps even the sentiment of the novels is manlier and freer: a delicate unreality hovers over the "Lady of the Lake."

The sensible element, if we may so express it, of the Waverley Novels appears in various forms; one of the most striking is in the delineation of great political events and influential political institutions. We are not by any means about to contend that Scott is to be taken as an infallible or an impartial authority for the parts of history which he delineates; on the contrary, we believe all the world now agrees that there are many deductions to be made from, many exceptions to be taken to, the accuracy of his delineations. Still, whatever period or incident we take, we shall always find in the error a great — in one or two cases perhaps an extreme — mixture of the mental element which we term "common-sense." The strongest *un*sensible feeling in Scott was perhaps his Jacobitism, which crept out even in small incidents and recurring prejudice throughout the whole of his active career, and was, so to say, the emotional aspect of his habitual Toryism; yet no one can have given a more sensible delineation — we might say a more statesmanlike analysis — of the various causes which led to the momentary success and to the speedy ruin of the enterprise of Charles Edward.* Mr. Lockhart says that notwithstanding Scott's imaginative readiness to exalt Scotland at the expense of England, no man would have been more willing to join ∙ in emphatic opposition to an anti-English

---

* In "Waverley."   † Concluding chapter.

party, if any such had presented itself with a practical object;* similarly his Jacobitism, though not without moments of real influence, passed away when his mind was directed to broad masses of fact and general conclusions of political reasoning. A similar observation may be made as to Scott's Toryism : although it is certain that there was an enthusiastic and (in the malicious sense) poetical element in Scott's Tóryism, yet quite as indisputably it partook largely of two other elements which are in common repute prosaic. He shared abundantly in the love of administration and organization common to all men of great active powers; he liked to contemplate method at work and order in action. Everybody hates to hear that the Duke of Wellington asked "how the king's Government was to be carried on," †—no amount of warning wisdom will bear so fearful a repetition; still, he *did* say it, and Scott had a sympathizing foresight of the oracle before it was spoken. One element of his Conservatism is his sympathy with the administrative arrangement, which is confused by the objections of a Whiggish Opposition and is liable to be altogether destroyed by uprisings of the populace. His biographer, while pointing out the strong contrast between Scott and the argumentative and parliamentary statesmen of his age, avows his opinion that in other times, and with sufficient opportunities, Scott's ability in managing men would have enabled him to play "either the Cecil or the Gondomar." ‡ We may see how much a suppressed enthusiasm for such abilities breaks out, not only in the description of hereditary monarchs, where the sentiment might be ascribed to a different origin, but also in the delineation of upstart rulers who could have no hereditary sanctity in the eyes of any Tory. Roland Græme, in

---

* Concluding chapter.

† If the Reform Bill of 1832 was carried; said in the House of Lords, repeatedly during the debates. — ED.

‡ Lockhart, Vol. v., Chap. viii., *in re* Scott's management of the Highland pageant on George IV.'s visit to Scotland. — ED.

the " Abbot," is well described as losing in the presence of the Regent. Murray the natural impertinence
of his disposition:—"He might have braved with
indifference the presence of an earl merely distinguished by his belt and coronet; but he felt over-
awed in that of the eminent soldier and statesman,
the wielder of a nation's power and the leader of her
armies."* It is easy to perceive that the author
shares the feeling of his hero, by the evident pleasure
with which he dwells on the Regent's demeanor:—
. "He then turned slowly round towards Roland Græme,
and the marks of gayety, real or assumed, disappeared
from his countenance as completely as the passing
bubbles leave the dark mirror of a still profound lake
into which a traveler has cast a stone; in the course
of a minute his noble features had assumed their
natural expression of a deep and even melancholy
gravity."† In real life, Scott used to say that he
never remembered feeling abashed in any one's presence except the Duke of Wellington's:‡ like that of
the hero of his novel, his imagination was very susceptible to the influence of great achievements and
prolonged success in wide-spreading affairs.

The view which Scott seems to have taken of democracy indicates exactly the same sort of application
of a plain sense to the visible parts of the subject.
His imagination was singularly penetrated with the
strange varieties and motley composition of human
life. The extraordinary multitude and striking contrast of the characters in his novels show this at
once; and even more strikingly is the same habit of
mind indicated "by a tendency never to omit an
opportunity of describing those varied crowds and
assemblages" which concentrate for a moment into a
unity the scattered and unlike varieties of mankind.
Thus, but a page or two before the passage which we
alluded to in the "Abbot," we find the following:—

* Chap. xviii.   † Ibid., two paragraphs previous.
‡ Lockhart, Vol. iii., Chap. xii.

"It was indeed no common sight to Roland, — the vestibule of a palace, traversed by its various groups: some radiant with gayety; some pensive, and apparently weighed down by affairs concerning the state or concerning themselves. Here the hoary statesman, with his cautious yet commanding look, his furred cloak and sable pantoufles; there the soldier in buff and steel, his long sword jarring against the pavement, and his whiskered upper lip and frowning brow looking a habitual defiance óf danger which perhaps was not always made good; there again passed my lord's serving-man, high of heart and bloody of hand, humble to his master and his master's equals, insolent to all others. To these might be added the poor suitor, with his anxious look and depressed mien; the officer, full of his brief authority, elbowing his betters and possibly his benefactors out of the road; the proud priest who sought a better benefice the proud baron who sought a grant of church lands; the robber chief who came to solicit a pardon for the injuries he had inflicted on his neighbors, the plundered franklin who came to seek vengeance for that which he had himself received. Besides, there was the mustering and disposition of guards and soldiers, the dispatching of messengers and the receiving them, the trampling and neighing of horses without the gate, the flashing of arms and rustling of plumes and jingling of spurs within it. In short, it was that gay and splendid confusion in which the eye of youth sees all that is brave and brilliant, and that of experience much that is doubtful, deceitful, false, and hollow, — hopes that will never be gratified, promises which will never be fulfilled, pride in the disguise of humility and insolence in that of frank and generous bounty."*

As in the imagination of Shakespeare, so in that of Scott, the principal form and object were the structure—that is a hard word — the undulation and diversified composition of human society; the picture of this stood in the center, and everything else was accessory and secondary to it. The old "rows of books" † in which Scott so peculiarly delighted were made to contribute their element to this varied imagination of humanity. From old family histories, odd memoirs, old law trials, his fancy elicited new

---

* Chap. xviii., third paragraph.

† Quoted from nowhere in particular; but probably referring to Lockhart, Vol. v., Chap. ii., "extracting the picturesque from old — and generally speaking, dull — books." — ED.

traits to add to the motley assemblage. His objection
to democracy — an objection of which we can only
appreciate the emphatic force when we remember that
his youth was contemporary with the first French
revolution and the controversy as to the uniform and
stereotyped rights of man — was, that it would sweep
away this entire picture, level prince and peasant
in a common *égalité*, substitute a scientific rigidity
for the irregular and picturesque growth of centuries,
replace an abounding and genial life by a symmetrical
but lifeless mechanism. All the descriptions of society
in the novels — whether of feudal society, of modern
Scotch society, or of English society — are largely colored by this feeling: it peeps out everywhere, and
Liberal critics have endeavored to show that it was a
narrow Toryism; but in reality it is a subtle compound of the natural instinct of the artist with the
plain sagacity of the man of the world.

It would be tedious to show how clearly the same
sagacity appears in his delineation of the various great
events and movements in society which are described
in the Scotch novels: there is scarcely one of them
which does not bear it on its surface. Objections
may, as we shall show, be urged to the delineation
which Scott has given of the Puritan resistance and
rebellions, yet scarcely any one will say there is not
a worldly sense in it; on the contrary, the very
objection is, that it is too worldly and far too exclusively sensible.

The same thoroughly well-grounded sagacity and
comprehensive appreciation of human life is shown in
the treatment of what we may call *anomalous* characters. In general, monstrosity is no topic for art.
Every one has known in real life characters which if,
apart from much experience, he had found described
in books, he would have thought unnatural and impossible; Scott, however, abounds in such characters.
Meg Merrilies, Edie Ochiltree, Ratcliffe * are more or

* In "Guy Mannering," "Antiquary," "Heart of Mid-Lothian."

less of that description. That of Meg Merrilies especially is as distorted and eccentric as anything can be; her appearance is described as making Mannering "start," and well it might.

"She was full six feet high, wore a man's greatcoat over the rest of her dress, had in her hand a goodly sloethorn cudgel, and in all points of equipment except her petticoats seemed rather masculine than feminine. Her dark elf-locks shot out like the snakes of the Gorgon between an old-fashioned bonnet called a bongrace, heightening the singular effect of her strong and weather-beaten features, which they partly shadowed, while her eye had a wild roll that indicated something like real or affected insanity." *

Her career in the tale corresponds with the strangeness of her exterior. "Harlot, thief, witch, and gipsy," as she describes herself,† the hero is preserved by her virtues; half-crazed as she is described to be, he owes his safety on more than one occasion to her skill in stratagem, and ability in managing those with whom she is connected and who are most likely to be familiar with her weakness and to detect her craft: yet on hardly any occasion is the natural reader conscious of this strangeness. Something is of course attributable to the skill of the artist; for no other power of mind could produce the effect, unless it were aided by the unconscious tact of detailed expression. But the fundamental explanation of this remarkable success is the distinctness with which Scott saw how such a character as Meg Merrilies arose and was produced out of the peculiar circumstances of gipsy life in the localities in which he has placed his scene. He has exhibited this to his readers not by lengthy or elaborate description, but by chosen incidents, short comments, and touches of which he scarcely foresaw the effect. This is the only way in which the fundamental objection to making eccentricity the subject of artistic treatment can be obviated.

---

* "Guy Mannering," Chap. iii.
† She does not: these words are Dominie Sampson's, same chapter.—ED.

Monstrosity ceases to be such when we discern the laws of nature which evolve it : when a real science explains its phenomena, we find that it is in strict accordance with what we call the "natural type," but that some rare adjunct or uncommon casualty has interfered and distorted a nature which is really the same into a phenomenon which is altogether different. Just so with eccentricity in human character : it becomes a topic of literary art only when its identity with the ordinary principles of human nature is exhibited in the midst of, and as it were by means of, the superficial unlikeness. Such a skill, however, requires an easy careless familiarity with usual human life and common human conduct. A writer must have a sympathy with health before he can show us how and where and to what extent that which is unhealthy deviates from it; and it is this consistent acquaintance with regular life which makes the irregular characters of Scott so happy a contrast to the uneasy distortions of less sagacious novelists.

A good deal of the same criticism may be applied to the delineation which Scott has given us of the *poor*. In truth, poverty is an anomaly to rich people : it is very difficult to make out why people who want dinner do not ring the bell. One half of the world, according to the saying, do not know how the other half lives. Accordingly, nothing is so rare in fiction as a good delineation of the poor ; though perpetually with us in reality, we rarely meet them in our reading. The requirements of the case present an unusual difficulty to artistic delineation : a good deal of the character of the poor is an unfit topic for continuous art, and yet we wish to have in our books a lifelike exhibition of the whole of that character. Mean manners and mean vices are unfit for prolonged delineation ; the every-day pressure of narrow necessities is too petty a pain and too anxious a reality to be dwelt upon. We can bear the mere description of the "Parish Register,"—

> "But this poor farce has neither truth nor art,
> To please the fancy or to touch the heart : . . .
> Dark but not awful, dismal but yet mean,
> With anxious bustle moves the cumbrous scene ;
> Presents no objects tender or profound,
> But spreads its cold unmeaning gloom around ; "*

but who could bear to have a long narrative of fortunes "dismal but yet mean," with characters " dark
but not awful," and no objects "tender or profound"?
Mr. Dickens has in various parts of his writings
been led, by a sort of pre-Raphaelite *cultus* of reality,
into an error of this species : his poor people have
taken to their poverty very thoroughly ; they are poor
talkers and poor livers, and in all ways poor people
to read about. A whole array of writers have fallen
into an opposite mistake : wishing to preserve their
delineations clear from the defects of meanness and
vulgarity, they have attributed to the poor a fancied
happiness and Arcadian simplicity. The conventional
shepherd of ancient times was scarcely displeasing, —
that which is by everything except express avowal
removed from the sphere of reality does not annoy us
by its deviations from reality : but the fictitious poor
of sentimental novelists are brought almost into contact with real life ; half claim to be copies of what
actually exists at our very doors ; are introduced in
close proximity to characters moving in a higher
rank, over whom no such ideal charm is diffused, and
who are painted with as much truth as the writer's
ability enables him to give. Accordingly, the contrast is evident and displeasing : the harsh outlines
of poverty will not bear the artificial rose tint ; they
are seen through it, like high cheek-bones through
the delicate colors of artificial youth. We turn away
with some disgust from the false elegance and unde-
ceiving art ; we prefer the rough poor of nature to
the petted poor of the refining describer. Scott has

---

* Part III., *in re* the burial of the rich absentee " Lady," and utterly irrelevant to Bagehot's subject. — ED.

most felicitously avoided both these errors: his poor people are never coarse and never vulgar. Their lineaments have the rude traits which a life of conflict will inevitably leave on the minds and manners of those who are to lead it; their notions have the narrowness which is inseparable from a contracted experience; their knowledge is not more extended than their restricted means of attaining it would render possible. Almost alone among novelists, Scott has given a thorough, minute, lifelike description of poor persons which is at the same time genial and pleasing. The reason seems to be, that the firm sagacity of his genius comprehended the industrial aspect of poor people's life thoroughly and comprehensively, his experience brought it before him easily and naturally, and his artist's mind and genial disposition enabled him to dwell on those features which would be most pleasing to the world in general. In fact, his own mind, of itself and by its own nature, dwelt on those very peculiarities. He could not remove his firm and instructed genius into the domain of Arcadian unreality; but he was equally unable to dwell principally, peculiarly, or consecutively, on those petty, vulgar, mean details in which such a writer as Crabbe lives and breathes. Hazlitt said that Crabbe described a poor man's cottage like a man who came to distrain for rent,—he catalogued every trivial piece of furniture, defects and cracks and all:* Scott describes it as a cheerful but most sensible landlord would describe a cottage on his property,—he has a pleasure in it. No detail—or few details in the life of the inmates escape his experienced and interested eye; but he dwells on those which do not displease him. He sympathizes with their rough industry and plain joys and sorrows. He does not fatigue himself or excite their wondering smile by theoretical plans of impossible relief; he makes the best of the life which is given, and by a sanguine sympathy makes it still

---

* "Lectures on the English Poets;—on Thomson and Cowper."

better. A hard life many characters in Scott seem to lead; but he appreciates and makes his reader appreciate the full value of natural feelings, plain thoughts, and applied sagacity.

His ideas of political economy are equally characteristic of his strong sense and genial mind. He was always sneering at Adam Smith, and telling many legends of that philosopher's absence of mind and inaptitude for the ordinary conduct of life ;* a contact with the Edinburgh logicians had doubtless not augmented his faith in the formal deductions of abstract economy : nevertheless, with the facts before him, he could give a very plain and satisfactory exposition of the genial consequences of old · abuses, the distinct necessity for stern reform, and the delicate humanity requisite for introducing that reform temperately and with feeling.

"Even so the Laird of Ellangowan ruthlessly commenced his magisterial reform, at the expense of various established and superannuated pickers and stealers who had been his neighbors for half a century. He wrought his miracles like a second Duke Humphrey ; and by the influence of the beadle's rod caused the lame to walk, the blind to see, and the palsied to labor. He detected poachers, black-fishers, orchard-breakers, and pigeon-shooters ; had the applause of the bench for his reward, and the public credit of an active magistrate.

"All this good had its ratable proportion of evil. Even an admitted nuisance, of ancient standing, should not be abated without some caution. The zeal of our worthy friend now involved in great distress sundry personages whose idle and mendicant habits his own *lachesse* had contributed to foster until these habits had become irreclaimable, or whose real incapacity for exertion rendered them fit objects, in their own phrase, for the charity of all well-disposed Christians. 'The long-remembered beggar,' who for twenty years had made his regular rounds within the neighborhood, received rather as a humble friend than as an object of charity, was sent to the neighboring workhouse. The decrepit dame, who traveled round the parish upon a hand-barrow, circulating from house to house like a bad shilling, which every one is in haste to pass to his neighbor, —

---

* I find *nothing* of the sort anywhere. — ED.

she who used to call for her bearers as loud or louder than a traveler demands post-horses, — even she shared the same disastrous fate. The 'daft Jock,' who, half knave, half idiot, had been the sport of each succeeding race of village children for a good part of a century, was remitted to the county bridewell; where, secluded from free air and sunshine, the only advantages he was capable of enjoying, he pined and died in the course of six months. The old sailor, who had so long rejoiced the smoky rafters of every kitchen in the country by singing 'Captain Ward' and 'Bold Admiral Benbow,' was banished from the county, for no better reason than that he was supposed to speak with a strong Irish accent. Even the annual rounds of the peddler were abolished by the Justice, in his hasty zeal for the administration of rural police.

"These things did not pass without notice and censure. We are not made of wood or stone, and the things which connect themselves with our hearts and habits cannot, like bark or lichen, be rent away without our missing them. The farmer's dame lacked her usual share of intelligence; perhaps also the self-applause which she had felt while distributing the *awmous* (alms), in shape of a *gowpen* (handful) of oatmeal, to the mendicant who brought the news. The cottage felt inconvenience from interruption of the petty trade carried on by the itinerant dealers. The children lacked their supply of sugar-plums and toys; the young women wanted pins, ribbons, combs, and ballads, and the old could no longer barter their eggs for salt, snuff, and tobacco. All these circumstances brought the busy Laird of Ellangowan into discredit, which was the more general on account of his former popularity. Even his lineage was brought up in judgment against him. They thought 'naething of what the like of Greenside or Burnville or Viewforth might do, that were strangers in the country; but Ellangowan! that had been a name amang them since the mirk Monanday, and lang before — *him* to be grinding the puir at that rate! — They ca'd his grandfather the Wicked Laird; but though he was whiles fractious aneuch, when he got into roving company and had ta'en the drap drink, he would have scorned to gang on at this gate. Na, na — the muckle chumlay in the Auld Place reeked like a killogie in his time, and there were as mony puir folk riving at the banes in the court and about the door as there were gentles in the ha'. And the leddy, on ilka Christmas night as it came round, gae twelve siller pennies to ilka puir body about, in honor of the twelve apostles like. They were fond to ca' it papistrie; but I think our great folk might take a lesson frae the papists whiles. They gie another sort o' help to puir folk than just dinging down a saxpence

in the brod on the Sabbath, and kilting and scourging and drum-
ming them a' the sax days o' the week besides.'"*

Many other indications of the same healthy and
natural sense which gives so much of their characteristic charm to the Scotch novels might be pointed
out, if it were necessary to weary our readers by
dwelling longer on a point we have already labored
so much. One more, however, demands notice because
of its importance, and perhaps also because, from its
somewhat less obvious character, it might otherwise
escape without notice. There has been frequent
controversy as to the penal code, if we may so call
it, of fiction, — that is, as to the apportionment of reward and punishment respectively to the good and
evil personages therein delineated; and the practice
of authors has been as various as the legislation
of critics. One school abandons all thought on the
matter, and declares that in the real life we see
around us, good people often fail and wicked people
continually prosper; and would deduce the precept
that it is unwise, in an art which should "hold the
mirror up to nature," † not to copy the uncertain and
irregular distribution of its sanctions. Another school,
with an exactness which savors at times of pedantry,
apportions the success and the failure, the pain and
the pleasure of fictitious life to the moral qualities
of those who are living in it; does not think at all,
or but little, of any other quality in those characters, and does not at all care whether the penalty
and reward are evolved in natural sequence from
the circumstances and characters of the tale, or are
owing to some monstrous accident far removed from
all relation of cause or consequence to those facts and
people. Both these classes of writers produce works
which jar on the natural sense of common readers,
and are at issue with the analytic criticism of the

---

* "Guy Mannering," Chap. vi.
† Hamlet, iii. 2.

best critics. One school leaves an impression of an uncared-for world, in which there is no right and no wrong; the other, of a sort of Governesses' Institution of a world, where all praise and all blame, all good and all pain, are made to turn on special graces and petty offenses, pesteringly spoken of and teasingly watched for. The manner of Scott is thoroughly different: you can scarcely lay down any novel of his without a strong feeling that the world in which the fiction has been laid, and in which your imagination has been moving, is one subject to laws of retribution which, though not apparent on a superficial glance, are yet in steady and consistent operation, and will be quite sure to work their due effect if time is only given to them. Sagacious men know that this is in its best aspect the condition of life. Certain of the ungodly may, notwithstanding the Psalmist, flourish even through life like a green bay-tree *; for Providence, in external appearance (far differently from the real truth of things as we may one day see it), works by a scheme of averages. Most people who ought to succeed, do succeed; most people who do fail, ought to fail. But there is no exact adjustment of "mark" to merit; the competitive-examination system appears to have an origin more recent than the creation of the world: "on the whole," † "speaking generally," "looking at life as a whole," are the words in which we must describe the Providential adjustment of visible good and evil to visible goodness and badness. And when we look more closely, we see that these general results are the consequences of certain principles which work half unseen, and which are effectual in the main though thwarted here and there. It is this comprehensive though inexact distribution of good and evil which is suited to the novelist, and it is exactly this which Scott instinctively adopted. ‡ Taking a firm and genial

* Psalms xxxvii. 35.
† Butler's favorite summing up in the "Analogy." — ED.
‡ Of set design as well as instinct: see Introduction to "Ivanhoe." — ED.

view of the common facts of life, — seeing it as an experienced observer and tried man of action, — he could not help giving the representation of it which is insensibly borne in on the minds of such persons. He delineates it as a world moving according to laws which are always producing their effect, never *have* produced it; sometimes fall short a little, are always nearly successful. Good sense produces its effect as well as good intention; ability is valuable as well as virtue. It is this peculiarity which gives to his works, more than anything else, the lifelikeness which distinguishes them: the average of the copy is struck on the same scale as that of reality; an unexplained, uncommented-on adjustment works in the one, just as a hidden, imperceptible principle of apportionment operates in the other.

The romantic susceptibility of Scott's imagination is as obvious in his novels as his matter-of-fact sagacity. We can find mucH of it in the place in which we should naturally look first for it, — his treatment of his heroines. We are no indiscriminate admirers of these young ladies, and shall shortly try to show how much they are inferior as imaginative creations to similar creations of the very highest artists; but the mode in which the writer speaks of them everywhere indicates an imagination continually under the illusion which we term "romance." A gentle tone of manly admiration pervades the whole delineation of their words and actions. If we look carefully at the narratives of some remarkable female novelists, — it would be invidious to give the instances by name, — we shall be struck at once with the absence of this: they do not half like their heroines. It would be satirical to say that they were jealous of them; but it is certain that they analyze the mode in which their charms produce their effects, and the *minutiæ* of their operation, much in the same way in which a slightly jealous lady examines the claims of the heroines of society. The same writers have invented the atrocious species of plain heroines.* Possibly none of the frauds which are now so much the topic of common remark are so irritating as that to which the purchaser of a novel is a victim on finding that he has only to peruse a narrative of the conduct and sentiments of an ugly lady. "Two-and-sixpence to know the heart which has high cheek-bones!" Was there ever such an imposition? Scott would have recoiled from such a conception. Even Jeanie Deans,† though no heroine like Flora MacIvor,‡ is described as "comely," and capable of looking almost pretty when required; and she has a compensating set-off in her sister, who is beautiful as well as unwise. Speaking generally, as is the necessity of criticism, Scott makes his heroines (at least by profession) attractive, and dwells on their attractiveness, — though not with the wild ecstasy of insane youth, yet with the tempered and mellow admiration common to genial men of this world. Perhaps at times we are rather displeased at his explicitness, and disposed to hang back and carp at the admirable qualities displayed to us; but this is only a stronger evidence of the peculiarity which we speak of, — of the unconscious sentiments inseparable from Scott's imagination.

The same romantic tinge undeniably shows itself in Scott's pictures of the past. Many exceptions have been taken to the detail of mediæval life as it is described to us in "Ivanhoe"; but one merit will always remain to it, and will be enough to secure to it immense popularity, — it describes the Middle Ages as we should have wished them to be. We do not mean that the delineation satisfies those accomplished admirers of the old Church system who fancy that they have found among the prelates and barons of the fourteenth century a close approximation to the theocracy which they would recommend for our adoption; on the contrary, the theological merits of the

---

* Incorrect: the species owes its existence to "Jane Eyre," the very reverse of the sort of novel here denounced. — ED.

† In the "Heart of Mid-Lothian."   ‡ In "Waverley."

Middle Ages are not prominent in Scott's delineation. "Dogma" was not in his way : a cheerful man of the world is not anxious for a precise definition of peculiar doctrines. The charm of "Ivanhoe" is addressed to a simpler sort of imagination, — to that kind of boyish fancy which idolizes mediæval society as the "fighting time." Every boy has heard of tournaments, and has a firm persuasion that in an age of tournaments life was thoroughly well understood. A martial society, where men fought hand to hand on good horses with large lances, in peace for pleasure and in war for business, seems the very ideal of perfection to a bold and simply fanciful boy. "Ivanhoe" spreads before him the full landscape of such a realm, with Richard, Cœur-de-Lion, a black horse, and the passage of arms at Ashby : of course he admires it, and thinks there was never such a writer, and will nevermore be such a world. And a mature critic will share his admiration, at least to the extent of admitting that nowhere else have the elements of a martial romance been so gorgeously accumulated without becoming oppressive ; their fanciful charm been so powerfully delineated, and yet so constantly relieved by touches of vigorous sagacity. One single fact shows how great the romantic illusion is : the pressure of painful necessity is scarcely so great in this novel as in novels of the same writer in which the scene is laid in modern times. Much may be said in favor of the mediæval system as contradistinguished from existing society, — much has been said ; but no one can maintain that general comfort was as much diffused as it is now. A certain ease pervades the structure of later society. Our houses may not last so long, are not so picturesque, will leave no such ruins behind them ; but they are warmed with hot water, have no draughts, and contain sofas instead of rushes. A slight daily unconscious luxury is hardly ever wanting to the dwellers in civilization ; like the gentle air of a genial climate, it is a perpetual minute enjoyment.

The absence of this marks a rude barbaric time: we may avail ourselves of rough pleasures, stirring amusements, exciting actions, strange rumors, but life is hard and harsh; the cold air of the keen North may brace and invigorate, but it cannot soothe us. All sensible people know that the Middle Ages must have been very uncomfortable: there was a difficulty about "good food," almost insuperable obstacles to the cultivation of nice detail and small enjoyment. No one knew the abstract facts on which this conclusion rests better than Scott, but his delineation gives no general idea of the result; a thoughtless reader rises with the impression that the Middle Ages had the same elements of happiness which we have at present, and that they had fighting besides. We do not assert that this tenet is explicitly taught; on the contrary, many facts are explained and many customs elucidated from which a discriminating and deducing reader would infer the meanness of poverty and the harshness of barbarism. But these less imposing traits escape the rapid, and still more the boyish reader, — his general impression is one of romance; and though, when roused, Scott was quite able to take a distinct view of the opposing facts, he liked his own mind to rest for the most part in the same pleasing illusion.

The same sort of historical romance is shown likewise in Scott's picture of remarkable historical characters. His Richard I. is the traditional Richard, with traits heightened and ennobled in perfect conformity to the spirit of tradition. Some illustration of the same quality might be drawn from his delineations of the Puritan rebellions and the Cavalier enthusiasm; we might show that he ever dwells on the traits and incidents most attractive to a genial and spirited imagination. But the most remarkable instance of the power which romantic illusion exercised over him is in his delineation of Mary Queen of Scots. He refused at one time of his life to write a biography of that princess, "because his opinion was

contrary to his feeling:"* he evidently considered her
guilt to be clearly established, and thought, with a
distinguished lawyer, that he should "direct a jury to
find her guilty"; but his fancy, like that of most of
his countrymen, took a peculiar and special interest
in the beautiful lady who at any rate had suffered
so much and so fatally at the hands of a queen of
England. He could not bring himself to dwell with
nice accuracy on the evidence which substantiates
her criminality; or on the still clearer indications of
that unsound and over-crafty judgment which was
the fatal inheritance of the Stuart family, and which,
in spite of advantages that scarcely any other family in the world has enjoyed, has made their name a
historical by-word for misfortune. The picture in the
"Abbot"—one of the best historical pictures which
Scott has given us—is principally the picture of the
Queen as the fond tradition of his countrymen exhibited her. Her entire innocence, it is true, is never
alleged: but the enthusiasm of her followers is dwelt
on with approving sympathy; their confidence is set
forth at large; her influence over them is skillfully
delineated; the fascination of charms, chastened by
misfortune is delicately indicated. We see a complete picture of the beautiful queen, of the suffering
and sorrowful but yet not insensible woman. Scott
could not, however, as a close study will show us,
quite conceal the unfavorable nature of his fundamental opinion. In one remarkable passage† the
struggle of the judgment is even conspicuous; and
in others the sagacity of the practiced lawyer—the
"thread of the attorney,"‡ as he used to call it, in

---

* Lockhart, concluding chapter; but his language misled Bagehot. Scott
had no proposition to "refuse": he merely says, in letter to Lockhart of July
14, 1828 (Vol. vii., Chap. iv.):—"I have also had Murray's request to do some
biography for his new undertaking [Family Library]. But I really can't think
of any Life I could easily do, excepting Queen Mary's, and that I decidedly
would not do, because my opinion, in point of fact, is contrary both to the popular feeling and to my own."—ED.

† The description early in Chap. xxi. is doubtless meant.—ED.

‡ Lockhart, concluding chapter.

his nature — qualifies and modifies the sentiment hereditary in his countrymen and congenial to himself.

This romantic imagination is a habit or power (as we may choose to call it) of mind which is almost essential to the highest success in the historical novel. The aim — at any rate the effect — of this class of works seems to be, to deepen and confirm the received view of historical personages. A great and acute writer may, from an accurate study of original documents, discover that those impressions are erroneous, and by a process of elaborate argument substitute others which he deems more accurate; but this can only be effected by writing a regular history, — the essence of the achievement is the proof. If Mr. Froude had put forward his view of Henry VIII.'s character in a professed novel, he would have been laughed at; it is only by a rigid adherence to attested facts and authentic documents that a view so original could obtain even a hearing. We start back with a little anger from a representation which is avowedly imaginative, and which contradicts our impressions. We do not like to have our opinions disturbed by reasoning; but it is impertinent to attempt to disturb them by fancies. A writer of the historical novel is bound by the popular conception of his subject; and commonly it will be found that this popular impression is to some extent a romantic one. An element of exaggeration clings to the popular judgment: great vices are made greater, great virtues greater also; interesting incidents are made more interesting, soft* legends more soft. The novelist who disregards this tendency will do so at the peril of his popularity; his business is to make attraction more attractive, and not to impair the pleasant pictures of ready-made romance by an attempt at grim reality.

We may therefore sum up the indications of this characteristic excellence of Scott's novels by saying that more than any [other] novelist he has given us fresh pictures of practical human society, with its

---

* Text, "softer," an evident slip. — ED.

cares and troubles, its excitements and its pleasures; that he has delineated more distinctly than any one else the framework in which this society inheres, and by the boundaries of which it is shaped and limited; that he has made more clear the way in which strange and eccentric characters grow out of that ordinary and usual system of life; that he has extended his view over several periods of society, and given an animated description of the external appearance of each, and a firm representation of its social institutions; that he has shown very graphically what we may call the worldly laws of moral government; and that over all these he has spread the glow of sentiment natural to a manly mind, and an atmosphere of generosity congenial to a cheerful one. It is from the collective effect of these causes, and from the union of sense and sentiment which is the principle of them all, that Scott derives the peculiar healthiness which distinguishes him. There are no such books as his for the sick-room, or for refreshing the painful intervals of a morbid mind. Mere sense is dull, mere sentiment unsubstantial; a sensation of genial healthiness is only given by what combines the solidity of the one and the brightening charm of the other.

Some guide to Scott's defects (or to the limitations of his genius, if we would employ a less ungenial and perhaps more correct expression) is to be discovered, as usual, from the consideration of his characteristic excellence. As it is his merit to give bold and animated pictures of this world, it is his defect to give but insufficient representations of qualities which this world does not exceedingly prize, of such as do not thrust themselves very forward in it, of such as are in some sense above it. We may illustrate this in several ways.

One of the parts of human nature which are systematically omitted in Scott is the searching and abstract intellect; this did not lie in his way. No man had a stronger sagacity, better adapted for the guidance of common men and the conduct of common

transactions ; few could hope to form a more correct
opinion on things and subjects which were brought
before him in actual life ; no man had a more useful
intellect : but on the other hand, as will be generally
observed to be the case, no one was less inclined to
that probing and seeking and anxious inquiry into
things in general which is the necessity of some
minds, and a sort of intellectual famine in their nature. He had no call to investigate the theory of the
universe, and he would not have been able to comprehend those who did. Such a mind as Shelley's
would have been entirely removed from his comprehension. He had no call to mix "awful talk and
asking looks"* with his love of the visible scene.
He could not have addressed the universe, —

> "I have watched
> Thy shadow, and the darkness of thy steps,
> And my heart ever gazes on the depth
> Of thy deep mysteries. I have made my bed
> In charnels and on coffins, where black Death
> Keep record of the trophies won from thee,
> Hoping to still these obstinate questionings
> Of thee and thine by forcing some lone ghost,
> Thy messenger, to render up the tale
> Of what we are." †

Such thoughts would have been to him "thinking
without an object," "abstracted speculations," "cobwebs of the unintelligible brain." Above all minds, his
had the Baconian propensity to "work upon stuff." ‡
At first sight, it would not seem that this was a
defect likely to be very hurtful to the works of a
novelist. The labors of the searching and introspect-
ive intellect, however needful, absorbing, and in some
degree delicious, to the seeker himself, are not in
general very delightful to those who are not seeking.

---

* Shelley, "Alastor."   † Ibid.
‡ Wild stumbles at this from the "Advancement of Learning," Book i.
—"For the wit and mind of man, if it work upon matter, . . . worketh
according to the stuff ; . . . but if it work upon itself, . . . it . . . brings
forth indeed cobwebs of learning. . . . Fruitless speculation."—ED.

Genial men in middle life are commonly intolerant of that philosophizing which their prototype, in old times, classed side by side with the lisping of youth. The theological novel, which was a few years ago so popular, and which is likely to have a recurring influence in times when men's belief is unsettled, and persons who cannot or will not read large treatises have thoughts in their minds and inquiries in their hearts, suggests to those who are accustomed to it the absence elsewhere of what is necessarily one of its most distinctive and prominent subjects. The desire to attain a belief, which has become one of the most familiar sentiments of heroes and heroines, would have seemed utterly incongruous to the plain sagacity of Scott, and also to his old-fashioned art. Creeds are data in his novels; people have different creeds, but each keeps his own. Some persons will think that this is not altogether amiss; nor do we particularly wish to take up the defense of the dogmatic novel. Nevertheless, it will strike those who are accustomed to the youthful generation of a cultivated time that the passion of intellectual inquiry is one of the strongest impulses in many of them, and one of those which give the predominant coloring to the conversation and exterior mind of many more; and a novelist will not exercise the most potent influence over those subject to that passion, if he entirely omit the delineation of it. Scott's works have only one merit in this relation : they are an excellent rest to those who have felt this passion, and have had something too much of it.

The same indisposition to the abstract exercises of the intellect shows itself in the reflective portions of Scott's novels, and perhaps contributes to their popularity with that immense majority of the world who strongly share in that same indisposition; it prevents, however, their having the most powerful intellectual influence on those who have at any time of their lives voluntarily submitted themselves to this acute

and refining discipline. The reflections of a practiced
thinker have a peculiar charm, like the last touches
of the accomplished artist; the cunning exactitude of
the professional hand leaves a trace in the very language; a nice discrimination of thought makes men
solicitous of the most apt expressions to diffuse their
thoughts; both words and meaning gain a metallic
brilliancy, like the glittering precision of the pure
Attic air. Scott's is a healthy and genial world of
reflection, but it wants the charm of delicate exactitude.

The same limitation of Scott's genius shows itself in
a very different portion of art,—in his delineation of his
heroines. The same blunt sagacity of imagination
which fitted him to excel in the rough description of
obvious life, rather unfitted him for delineating the
less substantial essence of the female character. The
nice *minutiæ* of society, by means of which female
novelists have been so successful in delineating their
own sex, were rather too small for his robust and
powerful mind. Perhaps, too, a certain unworldliness
of *imagination* is necessary to enable men to comprehend or delineate that essence. Unworldliness of *life*
is no doubt not requisite, —rather, perhaps, worldliness
is necessary to the acquisition of a sufficient experience; but an absorption in the practical world does
not seem favorable to a comprehension of anything
which does not precisely belong to it: its interests are
too engrossing, its excitements too keen; it modifies
the fancy, and in the change unfits it for everything
else. Something, too, in Scott's character and history
made it more difficult for him to give a representation of women than of men. Goethe used to say that
his idea of woman was not drawn from his experience, but that it came to him before experience, and
that he explained his experience by a reference to it;*
and though this is a German and not very happy
form of expression, yet it appears to indicate a very

* "Conversations with Eckermann and Soret," Oct. 22, 1828.

important distinction. Some efforts of the imagination are made so early in life, just (as it were) at
the dawn of the conscious faculties, that we are never
able to fancy ourselves as destitute of them; they
are part of the mental constitution with which, so to
speak, we awoke to existence. These are always far
more firm, vivid, and definite than any other images
of our fancy; and we apply them, half unconsciously,
to any facts and sentiments and actions which may
occur to us later in life, whether arising from within
or thrust upon us from the outward world. Goethe
doubtless meant that the idea of the female character
was to him one of these first elements of imagination; not a thing puzzled out, or which he remembered having conceived, but a part of the primitive
conceptions which, being coeval with his memory,
seemed inseparable from his consciousness. The descriptions of women likely to be given by this sort of
imagination will probably be the best descriptions:
a mind which would arrive at this idea of the female character by this process, and so early, would
be one obviously of more than usual susceptibility.
The early imagination does not commonly take this
direction, — it thinks most of horses and lances, tournaments and knights; only a mind with an unusual and
instinctive tendency to this kind of thought would
be borne thither so early or so effectually. And even
independently of this probable peculiarity of the individual, the primitive imagination in general is likely
to be the most accurate which men can form — not,
of course, of the external manifestations and detailed
manners, but — of the inner sentiment and characteristic feeling of women. The early imagination con-
ceives what it does conceive very justly: fresh from
the facts, stirred by the new aspect of things, un-
dimmed by the daily passage of constantly forgotten
images, not misled by the irregular analogies of a dis-
located life, the early mind sees what it does see with
a spirit and an intentness never given to it again.

A mind like Goethe's, of very strong imagination,
aroused at the earliest age, not of course by passions,
but by an unusual strength in that undefined longing
which is the prelude to our passions, will form the
best idea of the inmost female nature which masculine
nature can form. The difference is evident between
the characters of women formed by Goethe's imagination or Shakespeare's, and those formed by such
an imagination as that of Scott, — the latter seem so
external. We have traits, features, manners; we
know the heroine as she appeared in the street; in
some degree we know how she talked : but we never
know how she felt, least of all what she was, — we
always feel there is a world behind, unanalyzed,
unrepresented, which we cannot attain to. Such a
character as Margaret in "Faust" is known to us to
the very soul; so is Imogen; so is Ophelia. Edith
Bellenden, Flora MacIvor, Miss Wardour* are young
ladies who, we are told, were good-looking, and well
dressed (according to the old fashion), and sensible;
but we feel we know but very little of them, and
they do not haunt our imaginations. The failure of
Scott in this line of art is more conspicuous, because
he had not in any remarkable degree the later experience of female detail with which some minds have
endeavored to supply the want of the early essential
imagination, and which Goethe possessed in addition
to it. It was rather late, according to his biographer,
before Scott "set up for a squire of dames"† : he was
a lame young man, very enthusiastic about ballad
poetry; he was deeply in love with a young lady,
supposed to be imaginatively represented by Flora
MacIvor, but he was unsuccessful. It would be over-
ingenious to argue, from his failing in a single love
affair, that he had no peculiar interest in young ladies
in general; but the whole description of his youth
shows that young ladies exercised over him a rather

* In "Old Mortality," "Waverley," "Antiquary."
† William Clerk, in Lockhart, Vol. 1., Chap. vii.

more divided influence than is usual. Other pursuits intervened much more than is common with persons of the imaginative temperament, and he never led the life of flirtation from which Goethe believed that he derived so much instruction. Scott's heroines, therefore, are not unnaturally faulty, since from a want of the very peculiar instinctive imagination he could not give us the essence of women, and from the habits of his life he could not delineate to us their detailed life with the appreciative accuracy of habitual experience. Jeanie Deans is probably the best of his heroines, and she is so because she is the least of a heroine: the plain matter-of-fact element in the peasant-girl's life and circumstances suited a robust imagination. There is little in the part of her character that is very finely described which is characteristically feminine; she is not a masculine, but she is an epicene heroine. Her love-affair with Butler, a single remarkable scene excepted, is rather commonplace than otherwise.

A similar criticism might be applied to Scott's heroes: every one feels how commonplace they are,— Waverley excepted, whose very vacillation gives him a sort of character.* They have little personality. They are all of the same type: excellent young men, rather strong, able to ride and climb and jump. They are always said to be sensible, and bear out the character by being not unwilling sometimes to talk platitudes; but we know nothing of their inner life. They are said to be in love; but we have no special account of their individual sentiments. People show their character in their love more than in anything else: these young gentlemen all love in the same way,— in the vague commonplace way of this world. We have no sketch or dramatic expression of the life within; their souls are quite unknown to us. If there is an exception, it is Edgar Ravenswood†; but if we

---

* Scott said he (Waverley) was "a sneaking piece of imbecility." (Letter to Morritt, July 24, 1814; in Lockhart, Vol. iii., Chap. iv.)— ED.

† In the "Bride of Lammermoor."

look closely, we may observe that the notion which we obtain of his character, unusually broad as it is, is not a notion of him in his capacity of hero, but in his capacity of distressed peer. His proud poverty gives a distinctness which otherwise his lineaments would not have. We think little of his love; we think much of his narrow circumstances and compressed haughtiness.

The same exterior delineation of character shows itself in its treatment of men's religious nature. A novelist is scarcely, in the notion of ordinary readers, bound to deal with this at all; if he does, it will be one of his great difficulties to indicate it graphically, yet without dwelling on it. Men who purchase a novel do not wish a stone or a sermon. All lengthened reflections must be omitted,—the whole armory of pulpit eloquence. But no delineation of human nature can be considered complete which omits to deal with man in relation to the questions which occupy him as man, with his convictions as to the theory of the universe and his own destiny: the human heart throbs on few subjects with a passion so intense, so peculiar, and so typical. From an artistic view, it is a blunder to omit an element which is so characteristic of human life, which contributes so much to its animation, and which is so picturesque; a reader of a more simple mind, little apt to indulge in such criticism, feels "a want of depth," as he would speak, in delineations from which so large an element of his own most passionate and deepest nature is omitted. It can hardly be said that there is an omission of the religious nature in Scott; but at the same time there is no adequate delineation of it. If we refer to the facts of his life, and the view of his character which we collect from them, we shall find that his religion was of a qualified and double sort. He was a genial man of the world, and had the easy faith in the kindly *Dieu des bonnes gens**

---

* "Good people's God." — Béranger, "Le Dieu des Bonnes Gens."

which is natural to such a person; and he had also
a half-poetic principle of superstition in his nature,
inclining him to believe in ghosts, legends, fairies,
and elves, which did not affect his daily life or possibly his superficial belief, but was nevertheless very
constantly present to his fancy, and which affected
(as is the constitution of human nature), through that
frequency, the undefined, half-expressed, inexpressible
feelings which are at the root of that belief. Superstition was a kind of Jacobitism in his religion; as
a sort of absurd reliance on the hereditary principle
modified insensibly his leanings in the practical world,
so a belief in the existence of unevidenced and often
absurd supernatural beings qualified his commonest
speculations on the higher world. Both these elements may be thought to enter into the highest religion: there is a principle of cheerfulness which will
justify in its measure a genial enjoyment, and also
a principle of fear which those who think only of
that enjoyment will deem superstition, and which will
really become superstition in the over-anxious and
credulous accepter of it. But in a true religion these
two elements will be combined: the character of God
images itself very imperfectly in any human soul,
but in the highest it images itself as a whole; it
leaves an abiding impression which will justify anxiety and allow of happiness. The highest aim of the
religious novelist would be to show how this operates in human character; to exhibit in their curious
modification our religious love and also our religious
fear. In the novels of Scott the two elements appear
in a state of separation, as they did in his own
mind. We have the superstition of the peasantry
in the "Antiquary," in "Guy Mannering,"—everywhere, almost; we have likewise a pervading tone
of genial easy reflection, characteristic of the man of
the world who produced, and agreeable to the people
of the world who read, these works: but we have no
picture of the two in combination. We are scarcely

led to think on the subject at all, so much do other
subjects distract our interest; but if we do think, we
are puzzled at the contrast. We do not know which
is true, the uneasy belief of superstition or the easy
satisfaction of the world; we waver between the two,
and have no suggestion even hinted to us of the
possibility of a reconciliation. The character of the
Puritans certainly did not in general embody such
a reconciliation, but it might have been made by a
sympathizing artist the vehicle for a delineation of
a struggle after it. The two elements of love and
fear ranked side by side in their minds with an intensity which is rare even in minds that feel only
one of them. The delineation of Scott is amusing,
but superficial; he caught the ludicrous traits which
tempt the mirthful imagination, but no other side of
the character pleased him. The man of the world
was displeased with their obstinate interfering zeal;
their intensity of faith was an opposition force in the
old Scotch polity, of which he liked to fancy the harmonious working. They were superstitious enough;
but nobody likes other people's superstitions. Scott's
were of a wholly different kind: he made no difficulty as to the observance of Christmas Day, and
would have eaten potatoes without the faintest scruple, although their name does not occur in Scripture.
Doubtless also his residence in the land of Puritanism
did not incline him to give anything except a satirical representation of that belief: you must not expect
from a dissenter a faithful appreciation of the creed
from which he dissents. You cannot be impartial
on the religion of the place in which you live: you
may believe in it, or you may dislike it; it crosses
your path in too many forms for you to be able to
look at it with equanimity. Scott had rather a rigid
form of Puritanism forced upon him in his infancy:
it is asking too much to expect him to be partial to
it. The aspect of religion which Scott delineates best
is that which appears in griefs, especially in the

grief of strong characters: his strong *natural* nature felt the power of death; he has given us many pictures of rude and simple men subdued, if only for a moment, into devotion by its .presence.

On the whole, and speaking roughly, these defects in the delineation which Scott has given us of human life are but two. He omits to give us a delineation ·of the soul: we have mind, manners, animation, but it is the stir of this world. We miss the consecrating power; and we miss it not only in its own peculiar sphere, — which, from the difficulty of introducing the deepest elements into a novel, would have been scarcely matter for a harsh criticism, — but in the place in which a novelist might most be expected to delineate it. There are perhaps such things as the love affairs of immortal beings, but no one would learn it from Scott. His heroes and heroines are well dressed for this world, but not for another; there is nothing even in their love which is suitable for immortality. As has been noticed, Scott also omits any delineation of the abstract side of unworldly intellect. This too might not have been so severe a reproach, considering its undramatic, unanimated nature, if it had stood alone; but taken in connection with the omission which we have just spoken of, it is most important. As the union of sense· and romance makes the world of Scott so characteristically agreeable, — a fascinating picture of this world in the light in which we like best to dwell on it; so the deficiency in the attenuated, striving intellect, as well· as in the supernatural soul, gives to the "world" of Scott the cumbrousness and temporality — in short, the materialism which is characteristic of the world.

We have dwelt so much on what we think are the characteristic features of Scott's imaginative representations that we have left ourselves no room to criticize the two most natural points of criticism in a novelist, — plot and style. This is not, however, so important in Scott's case as it would commonly be.

He used to say "it was of no use having a plot,—you could not keep to it";* he modified and changed his thread of story from day to day, sometimes even from bookselling reasons and on the suggestion of others.† An elaborate work of narrative art could not be produced in this way, every one will concede,—the highest imagination, able to look far over the work, is necessary for that task; but the plots produced, so to say, by the pen of the writer as he passes over the events are likely to have a freshness and a suitableness to those events which is not possessed by the inferior writers who make up a mechanical plot before they commence. The procedure of the highest genius doubtless is scarcely a procedure: the view of the whole story comes at once upon its imagination like the delicate end and the distinct beginning of some long vista. But all minds do not possess the highest mode of conception; and among lower modes, it is doubtless better to possess the vigorous fancy which creates each separate scene in succession as it goes, than the pedantic intellect which designs everything long before it is wanted. There is a play in unconscious creation which no voluntary elaboration and preconceived fitting of distinct ideas can ever hope to produce; if the whole cannot be created by one bounding effort, it is better that each part should be created separately and in detail.

The style of Scott would deserve the highest praise if M. Thiers could establish his theory of narrative language. He maintains that a historian's language

---

* Not found. I can only surmise that Bagehot was thinking of the following passage in a letter of Jan. 31, 1817, to Lady Louisa Stuart (Lockhart, Vol. iv., Chap. ii.):—"Twenty times I have begun a thing on a certain plan, and never in my life adhered to it (in a work of imagination, that is) for half an hour together." See also "Introductory Epistle" to "Fortunes of Nigel."—ED.

† Misleadingly put: the latter changes were made ungraciously and rebelliously enough. His reception of "Blackwood's impudent letter— G— d— his soul," proposing to change the ending of the "Black Dwarf," will be remembered; and he fought hard against Ballantyne's judgment before softening the fate of Clara Mowbray in "St. Ronan's Well."—ED.

approaches perfection in proportion as it aptly communicates what is meant to be narrated without
drawing any attention to itself. Scott's style fulfills
this condition: nobody rises from his works without
a most vivid idea of what is related, and no one is
able to quote a single phrase in which it has been
narrated. We are inclined, however, to differ from
the great French historian, and to oppose to him a
theory derived from a very different writer. Coleridge
used to maintain* that all good poetry was untrans-
latable into words of the same language without injury
to the sense: the meaning was, in his view, to be
so inseparably intertwined even with the shades of
the language, that the change of a single expression
would make a difference in the accompanying feeling, if not in the bare signification; consequently, all
good poetry must be remembered exactly,—to change
a word is to modify the essence. Rigidly this theory
can only be applied to a few kinds of poetry, or special passages in which the imagination is exerting
itself to the utmost, and collecting from the whole
range of associated language the very expressions
which it requires; the highest excitation of feeling
is necessary to this peculiar felicity of choice. In
calmer moments the mind has either a less choice or
less acuteness of selective power; accordingly, in prose
it would be absurd to expect any such nicety. Still,
on great occasions in imaginative fiction, there should
be passages in which the words seem to cleave to the
matter: the excitement is as great as in poetry. The
words should become part of the sense; they should
attract our attention, as this is necessary to impress
them on the memory, but they should not in so doing
distract attention from the meaning conveyed,—on
the contrary; it is their inseparability from their meaning which gives them their charm and their power.
In truth, Scott's language, like his sense, was such as
became a bold, sagacious man of the world. He used

* "Biographia Literaria," Chap. 1.

the first sufficient words which came uppermost, and seems hardly to have been sensible, even in the works of others, of that exquisite accuracy and inexplicable appropriateness of which we have been speaking.

To analyze in detail the faults and merits of even a few of the greatest of the Waverley Novels would be impossible in the space at our command on the present occasion : we have only attempted a general account of a few main characteristics. Every critic must, however, regret to have to leave topics so tempting to remark upon as many of Scott's stories, and a yet greater number of his characters.

CHARLES DICKENS.*

(1858.)

IT must give Mr. Dickens much pleasure to look at the collected series of his writings. He has told us of the beginnings of "Pickwick": —

"I was," he relates in what is now the preface to that work, "a young man of [two or] three and twenty, when the present publishers, attracted by some pieces I was at that time writing in the *Morning Chronicle* newspaper [or had just written in the *Old Monthly Magazine*], (of which one series had lately been collected and published in two volumes, illustrated by my esteemed friend Mr. George Cruikshank,) waited upon me to propose a something that should be published in shilling numbers — then only known to me, or I believe to anybody else, by a dim recollection of certain interminable novels in that form, which used, some five and twenty years ago, to be carried about the country by peddlers, and over some of which I remember to have shed innumerable tears before I had served my apprenticeship to Life.

"When I opened my door in Furnival's Inn to the managing partner who represented the firm, I recognized in him the person from whose hands I had bought, two or three years previously, and whom I had never seen before or since, my first copy of the magazine in which my first effusion [a paper in the "Sketches," called "Mr. Minns and his Cousin"] — dropped stealthily one evening at twilight, with fear and trembling, into a dark letter-box, in a dark office, up a dark court in Fleet Street — appeared in all the glory of print; on which occasion, by the by, — how well I recollect it! — I walked down to Westminster Hall, and turned into it for half an hour, because my eyes were so dimmed with joy and pride that they could not bear the street, and were not fit to be seen there. I told my visitor of the coincidence, which we both hailed as a good omen; and so fell to business." †

---

* Cheap Edition of the Works of Mr. Charles Dickens. The Pickwick Papers, Nicholas Nickleby, etc. London, 1857-8. Chapman & Hall.

† The text of these paragraphs as Dickens finally left it differs a good deal from the one Bagehot copied; I have therefore left the latter untouched and added the new matter in brackets. — ED.

After such a beginning, there must be great enjoyment in looking at the long series of closely printed green volumes; in remembering their marvelous popularity; in knowing that they are a familiar literature wherever the English language is spoken, — that they are read with admiring appreciation by persons of the highest culture at the center of civilization, that they amuse and are fit to amuse the roughest settler in Vancouver's Island.

The penetrating power of this remarkable genius among all classes at home is not inferior to its diffusive energy abroad. The phrase "household book" has, when applied to the works of Mr. Dickens, a peculiar propriety : there is no contemporary English writer whose works are read so generally through the whole house, who can give pleasure to the servants as well as to the mistress, to the children as well as to the master. Mr. Thackeray without doubt exercises a more potent and plastic fascination within his sphere, but that sphere is limited; it is restricted to that part of the middle class which gazes inquisitively at the "Vanity Fair" world. The delicate touches of our great satirist have, for such readers, not only the charm of wit, but likewise the interest of valuable information; he tells them of the topics which they want to know. But below this class there is another and far larger, which is incapable of comprehending the idling world or of appreciating the accuracy of delineations drawn from it, which would not know the difference between a picture of Grosvenor Square by Mr. Thackeray and the picture of it in a Minerva Press novel, which only cares for or knows of its own multifarious, industrial, fig-selling world; and over these also Mr. Dickens has power.

It cannot be amiss to take this opportunity of investigating, even slightly, the causes of so great a popularity : and if, in the course of our article, we may seem to be ready with over-refining criticism, or to be unduly captious with theoretical objections, we hope not to forget that so great and so diffused an influence is a datum for literary investigation; that books which have been thus *tried* upon mankind and have thus succeeded, must be books of immense genius; and that it is our duty as critics to explain as far as we can the nature and the limits of that genius, but never for one moment to deny or question its existence.

Men of genius may be divided into regular and irregular. Certain minds, the moment we think of them, suggest to us the ideas of symmetry and proportion. Plato's name, for example, calls up at once the impression of something ordered, measured, and settled; it is the exact contrary of everything eccentric, immature, or undeveloped. The opinions of such a mind are often erroneous, and some of them may, from change of time, of intellectual data, or from chance, seem not to be quite worthy of it; but the mode in which those opinions are expressed, and (as far as we can make it out) the mode in which they are framed, affect us, as we have said, with a sensation of symmetricalness. It is not very easy to define exactly to what peculiar internal characteristic this external effect is due: the feeling is distinct, but the cause is obscure; it lies hid in the peculiar constitution of great minds, and we should not wonder that it is not very easy either to conceive or to describe. On the whole, however, the effect seems to be produced by a peculiar proportionateness, in each instance, of the mind to the tasks which it undertakes, amid which we see it, and by which we measure it. Thus we feel that the powers and tendencies of Plato's mind and nature were more fit than those of any other philosopher for the due consideration and exposition of the highest problems of philosophy, of the doubts and difficulties which concern man as man. His genius was adapted to its element; any change would mar the delicacy of the thought or the polished accuracy of the expression; the weapon was fitted to its aim. Every instance of proportionateness does not, however, lead us to, attribute this peculiar symmetry to the whole mind we are observing: the powers must not only be suited to the task undertaken, but the task itself must also be suited to a human being, and employ all the marvelous faculties with which he is endowed. The neat perfection of such a mind as Talleyrand's is the antithesis to the symmetry of genius; the niceties neither of diplomacy nor of conversation give scope to the entire powers of a great nature. We may lay down as the condition of a regular or symmetrical genius, that it should have the exact combination of powers suited to graceful and easy success in an exercise of mind great enough to task the whole intellectual nature.

On the other hand, men of irregular or unsymmetrical genius are eminent either for some one or some few peculiarities of mind, have possibly special defects on other sides of their intellectual nature, at any rate want what the scientific men of the present day would call the *definite proportion* of faculties and qualities suited to the exact work they have in hand. The foundation of many criticisms of Shakespeare is, that he is deficient in this peculiar proportion. His overteeming imagination gives at times, and not unfrequently, a great feeling of irregularity; there seems to be confusion. We have the tall trees of the forest, the majestic creations of the highest genius; but we have besides a bushy second growth, an obtrusion of secondary images and fancies which prevent our taking an exact measure of such grandeur. We have not the sensation of intense simplicity which must probably accompany the highest conceivable greatness. Such is also the basis of Mr. Hallam's criticism on Shakespeare's language,* which Mr. Arnold has lately revived:† his expression is often faulty,

---

* "Introduction to the Literature of Europe," Vol. ii., Chap. vi., § iii. 51.
† Preface to Matthew Arnold's Poems.

because his illustrative imagination, somewhat predominating over his other faculties, diffuses about the
main expression a supplement of minor metaphors
which sometimes distract the comprehension, and
almost always deprive his style of the charm that
arises from undeviating directness. Doubtless this is
an instance of the very highest kind of irregular
genius, in which all the powers exist in the mind
in a very high, and almost all of them in the very
highest measure, but in which, from a slight excess
in a single one, the charm of proportion is lessened.
The most ordinary cases of irregular genius are those
in which single faculties are abnormally developed,
and call off the attention from all the rest of the
mind by their prominence and activity. Literature,
as the "fragment of fragments," is so full of the
fragments of such minds that it is needless to specify
instances.

Possibly it may be laid down that one of two
elements is essential to a symmetrical mind: it is
evident that such a mind must either apply itself to
that which is theoretical or that which is practical,
to the world of abstraction or to the world of objects
and realities. In the former case the deductive understanding, which masters first principles and makes
deductions from them,— the thin ether of the intellect,
the "mind itself by itself,"— must evidently assume
a great prominence; to attempt to comprehend principles without it is to try to swim without arms or to
fly without wings. Accordingly, in the mind of Plato,
and in others like him, the abstract and deducing
understanding fills a great place; the imagination
seems a kind of eye to descry its data, the artistic
instinct an arranging impulse which sets in order its
inferences and conclusions. On the other hand, if a
symmetrical mind busy itself with the active side
of human life, with the world of concrete men and
real things, its principal quality will be a practical sagacity which forms with ease a distinct view and just

appreciation of all the mingled objects that the world presents, — which allots to each its own place and its intrinsic and appropriate rank. Possibly no [other] mind gives such an idea of this sort of symmetry as Chaucer's: everything in it seems in its place. A healthy sagacious man of the world has gone through the world: he loves it and knows it; he dwells on it with a fond appreciation; every object of the old life of "merry England" seems to fall into its precise niche in his ordered and symmetrical comprehension. The "Prologue to the Canterbury Tales" is in itself a series of memorial tablets to mediæval society; each class has its tomb, and each its apt inscription. A man without such an apprehensive and broad sagacity must fail in every extensive delineation of various life: he might attempt to describe what he did not penetrate, or if by a rare discretion he avoided that mistake, his works would want the *binding element;* he would be deficient in that distinct sense of relation and combination which is necessary for the depiction of the whole of life, which gives to it unity at first and imparts to it a mass in the memory ever afterwards. And eminence in one or other of these marking faculties — either in the deductive abstract intellect or the practical seeing sagacity — seems essential to the mental constitution of a symmetrical genius, at least in man. There are, after all, but two principal all-important spheres in human life, — thought and action; and we can hardly conceive of a masculine mind symmetrically developed, which did not evince its symmetry by an evident perfection in one or other of those pursuits, which did not leave the trace of its distinct reflection upon the one or of its large insight upon the other of them. Possibly it may be thought that in the sphere of pure art there may be room for a symmetrical development different from these; but it will perhaps be found, on examination of such cases, either that under peculiar and appropriate disguises one of these great qualities is present, or that the apparent symmetry is the narrow perfection of a limited nature, which may be most excellent in itself, as in the stricter form of sacred art, but which, as we explained, is quite opposed to that broad perfection of the thinking being to which we have applied the name of the "symmetry of genius."

ı If this classification of men of genius be admitted, there can be no hesitation in assigning to Mr. Dickens his place in it: his genius is essentially irregular and unsymmetrical, — hardly any English writer perhaps is much more so. His style is an example of it: it is descriptive, racy, and flowing; it is instinct with new imagery and singular illustration: but it does not indicate that due proportion of the faculties to one another which is a beauty in itself, and which cannot help diffusing beauty over every happy word and molded clause. We may choose an illustration at random. The following graphic description will do: —

"If Lord George Gordon had appeared in the eyes of Mr. Willet, overnight, a nobleman of somewhat quaint and odd exterior, the impression was confirmed this morning, and increased a hundred-fold. Sitting bolt upright upon his bony steed, with his long straight hair dangling about his face and fluttering in the wind; his limbs all angular and rigid, his elbows stuck out on either side ungracefully, and his whole frame jogged and shaken at every motion of his horse's feet, — a more grotesque or more ungainly figure can hardly be conceived. In lieu of whip, he carried in his hand a great gold-headed cane, as large as any footman carries in these days; and his various modes of holding this unwieldy weapon — now upright before his face like the saber of a horse-soldier, now over his shoulder like a musket, now between his finger and thumb, but always in some uncouth and awkward fashion — contributed in no small degree to the absurdity of his appearance. Stiff, lank, and solemn, dressed in an unusual manner, and ostentatiously exhibiting — whether by design or accident — all his peculiarities of carriage, gesture, and conduct, all the qualities, natural and artificial, in which he differed from other men, — he might have moved the sternest looker-on to laughter, and fully provoked the smiles and whispered jests which greeted his departure from the Maypole Inn.

"Quite unconscious, however, of the effect he produced, he trotted on beside his secretary, talking to himself nearly all the way, until they came within a mile or two of London, when now and then some passenger went by who knew him by sight, and pointed him out to some one else, and perhaps stood looking after him, or cried, in jest or earnest as it might be, 'Hurrah, Geordie! No Popery!' At which he would gravely pull off his hat, and bow. When they reached the town and rode along the streets, these notices became more frequent; some laughed, some hissed, some turned their heads and smiled, some wondered who he was, some ran along the pavement by his side and cheered. When this happened in a crush of carts and chairs and coaches, he would make a dead stop, and pulling off his hat, cry, 'Gentlemen, No Popery!' to which the gentlemen would respond with lusty voices, and with three times three; and then, on he would go again with a score or so of the raggedest following at his horse's heels, and shouting till their throats were parched.

"The old ladies too — there were a great many old ladies in the streets, and these all knew him. Some of them — not those of the highest rank, but such as sold fruit from baskets and carried burdens — clapped their shriveled hands and raised a weazen, piping, shrill 'Hurrah, my lord.' Others waved their hands or handkerchiefs, or shook their fans or parasols, or threw up windows, and called in haste to those within, to come and see. All these marks of popular esteem he received with profound gravity and respect; bowing very low, and so frequently that his hat was more off his head than on; and looking up at the houses as he passed along, with the air of one who was making a public entry, and yet was not puffed up or proud."*

No one would think of citing such a passage as this as exemplifying the proportioned beauty of finished writing; it is not the writing of an evenly developed or of a highly cultured mind; it abounds in jolts and odd turns; it is full of singular twists and needless complexities, — but on the other hand, no one can deny its great and peculiar merit. It is an odd style, and it is very odd how much you read it. It is the overflow of a copious mind, though not the chastened expression of a harmonious one.

* "Barnaby Rudge," Chap. xxxvii.

The same quality characterizes the matter of his works. His range is very varied: he has attempted to describe every kind of scene in English life, from quite the lowest to almost the highest. | He has not endeavored to secure success by confining himself to a single path, nor wearied the public with repetitions of the subjects by the delineation of which he originally obtained fame. In his earlier works he never writes long without saying something well, something which no other man would have said: but even in them it is the characteristic of his power that it is apt to fail him at once; from masterly strength we pass without interval to almost infantine weakness,— something like disgust succeeds in a moment to an extreme admiration. Such is the natural fate of an unequal mind employing itself on a vast and variegated subject. In writing on the Waverley Novels, we ventured to make a division of novels into the ubiquitous — it would have been perhaps better to say the "miscellaneous" — and the sentimental: the first, as its name implies, busying itself with the whole of human life, the second restricting itself within a peculiar and limited theme. Mr. Dickens's novels are all of the former class: they aim to delineate nearly all that part of our national life which can be delineated, — at least, within the limits which social morality prescribes to social art; but you cannot read his delineation of any part without being struck with its singular incompleteness. An artist once said of the best work of another artist, "Yes, it is a pretty patch:" if we might venture on the phrase, we should say that Mr. Dickens's pictures are graphic scraps, his best books are compilations of them.

The truth is, that Mr. Dickens wholly wants the two elements which we have spoken of as one or other requisite for a symmetrical genius.

He is utterly deficient in the faculty of reasoning. "Mamma, what shall I think about?" said the small girl. "My dear, don't think," was the old-fashioned

reply. We do not allege that in the strict theory of
education this was a correct reply, — modern writers
think otherwise; but we wish some one would say
it to Mr. Dickens. He is often troubled with the idea
that he must reflect, and his reflections are perhaps
the worst reading in the world: there is a sentimental
confusion about them; we never find the consecutive
precision of mature theory or the cold distinctness of
clear thought. Vivid facts stand out in his imagination, and a fresh illustrative style brings them home
to the imagination of his readers; but his continuous
philosophy utterly fails in the attempt to harmonize
them, — to educe a theory or elaborate a precept from
them. Of his social thinking we shall have a few
words to say in detail: his didactic humor is very
unfortunate, — no writer is less fitted for an excursion
to the imperative mood. At present we only say, what
is so obvious as scarcely to need saying, that his
abstract understanding is so far inferior to his picturesque imagination as to give even to his best works
the sense of jar and incompleteness, and to deprive
them altogether of the crystalline finish which is characteristic of the clear and cultured understanding.

Nor has Mr. Dickens the easy and various sagacity
which, as has been said, gives a unity to all which it
touches. He has indeed a quality which is near allied
to it in appearance: his shrewdness in some things,
especially in traits and small things, is wonderful;
his works are full of acute remarks on petty doings,
and well exemplify the telling power of minute cir-
cumstantiality. But the minor species of perceptive
sharpness is so different from diffused sagacity that
the two scarcely ever are to be found in the same
mind; there is nothing less like the great lawyer,
acquainted with broad principles and applying them
with distinct deduction, than the attorney's clerk who
catches at small points like a dog biting at flies.
"Over-sharpness" in the student is the most unprom-
ising symptom of the logical jurist: you must not ask

a horse in blinkers for a large view of a landscape. In the same way, a detective ingenuity in microscopic detail is of all mental qualities most unlike the broad sagacity by which the great painters of human affairs have unintentionally stamped the mark of unity on their productions : they show by their treatment of each case that they understand the whole of life ; the special delineator of fragments and points shows that he understands them only. In one respect the defect is more striking in Mr. Dickens than in any other novelist of the present day. The most remarkable deficiency in modern fiction is its omission of the business of life,—of all those countless occupations, pursuits, and callings in which most men live and move, and by which they have their being : in most novels money *grows ;* you have no idea of the toil, the patience, and the wearing anxiety by which men of action - provide for the day, and lay up for the future, and support those that are given into their care. Mr. Dickens is not chargeable with this omission : he perpetually deals with the pecuniary part of life ; almost all his characters have determined occupations, of which he is apt to talk even at too much length. When he rises from the toiling to the luxurious classes, his genius in most cases deserts him : The delicate refinement and discriminating taste of the idling orders are not in his way ; he knows the dry arches of London Bridge better than Belgravia ; he excels in inventories of poor furniture, and is learned in pawnbrokers' tickets. But although his creative power lives and works among the middle class and industrial section of English society, he has never painted the highest part of their daily intellectual life. He made, indeed, an attempt to paint specimens of the apt and able man of business in "Nicholas Nickleby"; but the Messrs. Cheeryble are among the stupidest of his characters, — he forgot that breadth of platitude is rather different from breadth of sagacity. His delineations of middle-class life have in consequence a harshness and meanness which do not belong to that life in reality : he omits the relieving element; he describes the figs which are sold, but not the talent which sells figs well. And it is the same want of diffused sagacity in his own nature which has made his pictures of life so odd and disjointed, and which has deprived them of symmetry and unity.

The *bizarrerie* of Mr. Dickens's genius is rendered more remarkable by the inordinate measure of his special excellences. The first of these is his power of observation in detail. We have heard — we do not know whether correctly or incorrectly — that he can go down a crowded street and tell you all that is in it, what each shop was, what the grocer's name was, how many scraps of orange-peel there were on the pavement. His works give you exactly the same idea : the amount of detail which there is in them is something amazing, — to an ordinary writer something incredible; there are single pages containing telling *minutiæ* which other people would have thought enough for a volume. Nor is his sensibility to external objects, though omnivorous, insensible to the artistic effect of each : there are scarcely anywhere such pictures of London as he draws; no writer has equally comprehended the artistic material which is given by its extent, its aggregation of different elements, its moldiness, its brilliancy.

Nor does his genius — though from some idiosyncrasy of mind or accident of external situation it is more especially directed to City life — at all stop at the City wall. He is especially at home in the picturesque and obvious parts of country life, particularly in the comfortable and (so to say) moldering portion of it. The following is an instance; if not the best that could be cited, still one of the best : —

"They arranged to proceed upon their journey next evening, as a stage-wagon, which traveled for some distance on the same road as they must take, would stop at the inn to change horses, and the driver for a small gratuity would give Nell a place inside. A bargain was soon struck when the wagon came, and in due time it rolled away; with the child comfortably bestowed among the softer packages, her grandfather and the schoolmaster walking on beside the driver, and the landlady and all the good folks of the inn screaming out their good wishes and farewells.

"What a soothing, luxurious, drowsy way of traveling, to lie inside that slowly moving mountain, listening to the tinkling of the horses' bells, the occasional smacking of the carter's whip, the smooth rolling of the great broad wheels, the rattle of the harness, the cheery good-nights of passing travelers jogging past on little short-stepped horses, — all made pleasantly indistinct by the thick awning, which seemed made for lazy listening under, till one fell asleep! The very going to sleep, still with an indistinct idea, as the head jogged to and fro upon the pillow, of moving onward with no trouble or fatigue, and hearing all these sounds like dreamy music, lulling to the senses; and the slow waking up, and finding one's self staring out through the breezy curtain half-opened in the front, far up into the cold bright sky with its countless stars, and downward at the driver's lantern dancing on like its namesake Jack of the swamps and marshes, and sideways at the dark grim trees, and forward at the long bare road rising up, up, up, until it stopped abruptly at a sharp high ridge as if there were no more road, and all beyond was sky; and the stopping at the inn to bait, and being helped out, and going into a room with fire and candles, and winking very much, and being agreeably reminded that the night was cold, and anxious for very comfort's sake to think it colder than it was! What a delicious journey was that journey in the wagon!

"Then the going on again, — so fresh at first, and shortly afterwards so sleepy. The waking from a sound nap as the mail came dashing past like a highway comet, with gleaming lamps and rattling hoofs, and visions of a guard behind, standing up to keep his feet warm, and of a gentleman in a fur cap opening his eyes and looking wild and stupefied; the stopping at the turnpike, where the man was gone to bed, and knocking at the door until he answered with a smothered shout from under the bed-clothes in the little room above, where the faint light was burning, and presently came down, night-capped and shivering, to throw the gate wide open, and wish all wagons off the road except by day. The cold sharp interval between night and morning; the distant streak of light widening and spreading, and turning from gray to white, and from white to yellow, and from yellow to burning red; the presence of day, with all its cheerfulness and life; men and horses at the plough — birds in the trees and hedges, and boys in solitary fields frightening them away with rattles. The coming to the town: people busy in the market; light carts and chaises round the tavern yard; tradesmen standing at their doors; men running horses up and down the street for sale; pigs plunging and grunting in the dirty distance, getting off with long strings at their legs, running into clean chemists' shops and being dislodged with brooms by 'prentices; the night-coach changing horses, — the passengers cheerless, cold, ugly, and discontented, with three months' growth of hair in one night, the coachman fresh as from a bandbox and exquisitely beautiful by contrast: — so much bustle, so many things in motion, such a variety of incidents — when was there a journey with so many delights as that journey in the wagon!"*

Or, as a relief from a very painful series of accompanying characters, it is pleasant to read and remember the description of the fine morning on which Mr. Jonas Chuzzlewit does not reflect.† Mr. Dickens has, however, no feeling analogous to the nature-worship of some other recent writers. There is nothing Wordsworthian in his bent, — the interpreting inspiration (as that school speak) is not his; nor has he the erudition in difficult names which has filled some pages in late novelists with mineralogy and botany. His descriptions of nature are fresh and superficial, they are not sermonic or scientific.

Nevertheless, it may be said that Mr. Dickens's genius is especially suited to the delineation of City life. London is like a newspaper: everything is there, and everything is disconnected. There is every kind of person in some houses; but there is no more connection between the houses than between the neighbors in the lists of "births, marriages, and deaths." As we change from the broad leader to the squalid police report, we pass a corner and we are in a changed world. This is advantageous to Mr. Dickens's genius: his memory is full of instances of old buildings and curious people, and he does not care to

---

* "Old Curiosity Shop," Chap. xlvi.
† An insoluble puzzle: there is *nothing* of the sort anywhere. — ED.

piece them together; on the contrary, each scene to
his mind is a separate scene, each street a separate
street. He has, too, the peculiar alertness of observation that is observable in those who live by it; he
describes London like a special correspondent for
posterity.

A second most wonderful special faculty which Mr.
Dickens possesses is what we may call his *vivification* of character, or rather of characteristics. His
marvelous power of observation has been exercised
upon men and women even more than upon town or
country; and the store of human detail, so to speak,
in his books is endless and enormous. The boots at
the inn, the pickpockets in the street, the undertaker,
the Mrs. Gamp are all of them at his disposal; he
knows each trait and incident, and he invests them
with a kind of perfection in detail which in reality
they do not possess. He has a very peculiar power
of taking hold of some particular traits and making
a character out of them. He is especially apt to in-
carnate particular professions in this way: many of
his people never speak without some allusion to their
occupation; you cannot separate them from it, nor
does the writer ever separate them. What would Mr.
Mould be if not an undertaker? or Mrs. Gamp if not
a nurse? or Charley Bates* if not a pickpocket? Not
only is human nature in them subdued to what it
works in, but there seems to be no nature to subdue;
the whole character is the idealization of a trade, and
is not in fancy or thought distinguishable from it.
Accordingly, of necessity, such delineations become
caricatures. We do not in general contrast them with
reality; but as soon as we do, we are struck with
the monstrous exaggerations which they present. You
could no more fancy Sam Weller or Mark Tapley or
the Artful Dodger† really existing, walking about

* "Martin Chuzzlewit," do., "Oliver Twist."
† "Pickwick Papers," "Martin Chuzzlewit," "Oliver Twist."

among common ordinary men and women, than you
can fancy a talking duck or a writing bear; they are
utterly beyond the pale of ordinary social intercourse.
We suspect, indeed, that Mr. Dickens does not conceive
his characters to himself as mixing in the society
he mixes in : he sees people in the street, doing certain things, talking in a certain way, and his fancy
petrifies them in the act; he goes on fancying hundreds of reduplications of that act and that speech,
he frames an existence in which there is nothing
else but that aspect which attracted his attention.
Sam Weller is an example : he is a man-servant who
makes a peculiar kind of jokes and is wonderfully
felicitous in certain similes. You see him at his first
introduction : —

"'My friend—' said the thin gentleman.

"'You're one o' the adwice-gratis order,' thought Sam, 'or you
wouldn't be so werry fond o' me all at once.' But he only said,
'Well, sir?'

"'My friend,' said the thin gentleman, with a conciliatory 'hem,'
'have you got many people stopping here now? Pretty busy? eh?'

"Sam stole a look at the inquirer. He was a little high-dried
man, with a dark squeezed-up face, and small restless black eyes,
that kept winking and twinkling on each side of his little inquisitive nose, as if they were playing a perpetual game of peep-bo with
that feature. He was dressed all in black, with boots as shiny as
his eyes, a low white neckcloth, and a clean shirt with a frill to
it. A gold watch-chain, and seals, depended from his fob. He
carried his black kid gloves *in* his hands, not *on* them ; and as he
spoke, thrust his wrists beneath his coat-tails, with the air of a man
who was in the habit of propounding some regular posers.

"'Pretty busy, eh?' said the little man.

"'Oh, werry well, sir,' replied Sam : 'we sha'n't be bankrupts,
and we sha'n't make our fort'ns. We eats our biled mutton without capers, and don't care for horse-radish wen ve can get beef.'

"'Ah,' said the little man, 'you're a wag, ain't you?'

"'My eldest brother was troubled with that complaint,' said
Sam : 'it may be catching, — I used to sleep with him.'

"'This is a curious old house of yours,' said the little man, looking round him.

"'If you'd sent word you was a-coming, we'd ha' had it repaired,' replied the imperturbable Sam.

"The little man seemed rather baffled by these several repulses, and a short consultation took place between him and the two plump gentlemen. At its conclusion, the little man took a pinch of snuff from an oblong silver box, and was apparently on the point of renewing the conversation, when one of the plump gentlemen, who, in addition to a benevolent countenance, possessed a pair of spectacles and a pair of black gaiters, interfered : —

"'The fact of the matter is,' said the benevolent gentleman, 'that my friend here' (pointing to the other plump gentleman) 'will give you half a guinea if you'll answer one or two —'

"'Now, my dear sir — my dear sir,' said the little man, 'pray allow me — my dear sir, the very first principle to be observed in these cases is this : if you place a matter in the hands of a professional man, you must in no way interfere in the progress of the business ; you must repose implicit confidence in him. Really, Mr.' (he turned to the other plump gentleman, and said) — 'I forget your friend's name.'

"'Pickwick,' said Mr. Wardle, for it was no other than that jolly personage.

"'Ah, Pickwick : really, Mr. Pickwick, my dear sir, excuse me — I shall be happy to receive any private suggestions of yours, as *amicus curiæ*, but you must see the impropriety of your interfering with my conduct in this case, with such an *ad captandum* argument as the offer of half a guinea. Really, my dear sir, really' — and the little man took an argumentative pinch of snuff, and looked very profound.

."'My only wish, sir,' said Mr. Pickwick, 'was to bring this very unpleasant matter to as speedy a close as possible.'

"'Quite right — quite right,' said the little man.

"'With which view,' continued Mr. Pickwick, 'I made use of the argument which my experience of men has taught me is the most likely to succeed in any case.'

"'Ay, ay,' said the little man, 'very good, very good indeed ; but you should have suggested it to *me*. My dear sir, I'm quite certain you cannot be ignorant of the extent of confidence which must be placed in professional men. If any authority can be necessary on such a point, my dear sir, let me refer you to the well-known case in Barnwell and —'

"'Never mind George Barnwell,' interrupted Sam, who had remained a wondering listener during this short colloquy : 'everybody knows what sort of a case his was, though it's always been my opinion, mind you, that the young 'oman deserved scragging a precious sight more than he did. Hows'ever, that's neither here nor there. You want me to except of half a guinea. Werry well, I'm agreeable : I can't say no fairer than that, can I, sir ?' (Mr. Pickwick smiled.) 'Then the next question is, What the devil do you want with me ? as the man said wen he see the ghost.'

" 'We want to know—' said Mr. Wardle.   ·

" 'Now, my dear sir—my dear sir,' interposed the busy little man.

"Mr. Wardle shrugged his shoulders, and was silent.

" 'We want to know,' said the little man, solemnly — 'and we ask the question of you, in order that we may not awaken apprehensions inside — we want to know who you've got in this house, at present.'

" 'Who there is in the house !' said Sam, in whose mind the inmates were always represented by that particular article of their costume which came under his immediate superintendence. 'There's a wooden leg in number six ; there's a pair of Hessians in thirteen ; there's two pair of halves in the commercial ; there's these here painted tops in the snuggery inside the bar ; and five more tops in the coffee-room.'

" 'Nothing more ?' said the little man.

" 'Stop a bit,' replied Sam, suddenly recollecting himself. 'Yes : there's a pair of Wellingtons a good deal worn, and a pair o' lady's shoes, in number five.'

" 'What sort of shoes ?' hastily inquired Wardle, who, together with Mr. Pickwick, had been lost in bewilderment at the singular catalogue of visitors.

" 'Country make,' replied Sam.

" 'Any maker's name ?'

" 'Brown.'

" 'Where of ?'

" 'Muggleton.'

" 'It *is* them,' exclaimed Wardle. 'By Heavens, we've found them.'   ∴

" 'Hush !' said Sam.   "The Wellingtons have gone to Doctors' Commons.'

" 'No,' said the little man.

" 'Yes, for a license.'

" 'We're in time,' exclaimed Wardle. 'Show us the room ; not a moment is to be lost.'

" 'Pray, my dear sir—pray,' said the little man, 'caution, caution.' He drew from his pocket a red silk purse, and looked very hard at Sam as he drew out a sovereign.

ong, and every one knows it so well. Some persons may think that this is not a very high species of delineative art: the idea of personifying traits and trades may seem to them poor and meager; anybody, they may fancy, can do that,—but how would they do it? whose fancy would not break down in a page,—in five lines? who could carry on the vivification with zest and energy and humor for volume after volume? Endless fertility in laughter-causing detail is Mr. Dickens's most astonishing\ peculiarity. It requires a continuous and careful reading of his works to be aware of his enormous wealth : writers have attained the greatest reputation for wit and humor, whose whole works do not contain so much of either as are to be found in a very few pages of his.

Mr. Dickens's humor is indeed very much a result of the two peculiarities of which we have been

CHARLES DICKENS.

"Sam grinned expressively.

"'Show us into the room at once, without announcing us,' said the little man, 'and it's yours.'"*

One can fancy Mr. Dickens hearing a dialogue of this sort,—not nearly so good, but something like it,—and immediately setting to work to make it better and put it in a book; then changing a little the situation, putting the boots one step up in the scale of service, engaging him as footman to a stout gentleman (but without for a moment losing sight of the peculiar kind of professional conversation and humor which his first dialogue presents), and astonishing all his readers by the marvelous fertility and magical humor with which he maintains that style. Sam Weller's father is even a stronger and simpler instance. He is simply nothing but an old coachman of the stout and extinct sort,—you cannot separate him from the idea of that occupation ; but how amusing he is! We dare not quote a single word of his talk ; because we should go on quoting so l

*"Pickwick Papers," Chap. ix.

speaking, — his power of detailed observation and his
power of idealizing individual traits of character;
sometimes of one or other of them, sometimes of both
of them together. His similes on matters of external
observation are so admirable that everybody appreciates them, and it would be absurd to quote specimens of them; nor is it the sort of excellence which
best bears to be paraded for the purposes of critical example, — its off-hand air and natural connection with
the adjacent circumstances are inherent parts of its
peculiar merit. Every reader of Mr. Dickens's works
knows well what we mean; and who is not a reader
of them?

But his peculiar humor is even more indebted to
his habit of vivifying external traits than to his
power of external observation. He, as we have explained, expands traits into people; and it is a source
of true humor to place these, when so expanded, in
circumstances in which only people — that is, complete human beings — can appropriately act. The
humor of Mr. Pickwick's character is entirely of this
kind. He is a kind of incarnation of simple-minded-
ness and what we may call obvious-mindedness: the
conclusion which each occurrence or position in life
most immediately presents to the unsophisticated
mind is that which Mr. Pickwick is sure to accept.
The proper accompaniments are given to him: he is
a stout gentleman in easy circumstances, who is irritated into originality by no impulse from within and
by no stimulus from without. He is stated to have
"retired from business," but no one can fancy what
he was in business: such guileless simplicity of heart
and easy impressibility of disposition would soon have
induced a painful failure amid the harsh struggles
and the tempting speculations of pecuniary life. As
he is represented in the narrative, however, nobody
dreams of such antecedents. Mr. Pickwick moves
easily over all the surface of English life, from Gos-
well Street to Dingley Dell, from Dingley Dell to the

Ipswich elections, from drinking milk punch in a wheelbarrow to sleeping in the approximate pound, and no one ever thinks of applying to him the ordinary maxims which we should apply to any common person in life or to any common personage in a fiction. Nobody thinks it is wrong in Mr. Pickwick to drink too much milk punch in a wheelbarrow, to introduce worthless people of whom he knows nothing to the families of people for whom he really cares; nobody holds him responsible for the consequences; nobody thinks there is anything wrong in his taking Mr. Bob Sawyer and Mr. Benjamin Allen to visit Mr. Winkle senior, and thereby almost irretrievably offending him with his son's marriage. We do not reject moral remarks such as these, but they never occur to us: indeed, the indistinct consciousness that such observations are possible, and that they are hovering about our minds, enhances the humor of the narrative; we are in a conventional world, where the mere maxims of common life do not apply, and yet which has all the amusing detail and picturesque elements and singular eccentricities of common life. Mr. Pickwick is a personified ideal; a kind of amateur in life, whose course we watch through all the circumstances of ordinary existence, and at whose follies we are amused just as really skilled people are at the mistakes of an amateur in their art. His being in the pound is not wrong; his being the victim of Messrs. Dodson is not foolish. "Always shout with the mob," said Mr. Pickwick. "But suppose there are two mobs?" said Mr. Snodgrass. "Then shout with the loudest," said Mr. Pickwick.* This is not in him weakness or time-serving or want of principle, as in most even of fictitious people it would be, — it is his way. Mr. Pickwick was expected to say something, so he said "Ah!" in a grave voice: this is

---

* Mangled from Chap. xiii. : — "' It's always best . . . to do what the mob do.' 'But suppose there are two mobs?' suggested Mr. Snodgrass. 'Shout with the largest,' replied Mr. Pickwick."—ED.

not pompous as we might fancy, or clever as it might
be if intentionally devised, — it is simply his way.
Mr. Pickwick gets late at night over the wall behind
the back door of a young-ladies' school, is found in
that sequestered place by the schoolmistress and the
boarders and the cook, and there is a dialogue between them :* there is nothing out of possibility in
this, — it is his way. The humor essentially consists
in treating as a moral agent a being who really is
not a moral agent ; we treat a vivified accident as a
man, and we are surprised at the absurd results ; we
are reading about an acting thing, and we wonder at
its scrapes, and laugh at them as if they were those
of the man. There is something of this humor in
every sort of farce ; everybody knows these are not
real beings acting in real life, though they talk as
if they were and want us to believe that they are.
Here, as in Mr. Dickens's books, we have exaggerations pretending to comport themselves as ordinary
beings, caricatures acting as if they were characters.

At the same time, it is essential to remember that
however great may be and is the charm of such exaggerated personifications, the best specimens of them
are immensely less excellent, belong to an altogether
lower range of intellectual achievements, than the
real depiction of actual living men. It is amusing to
read of beings *out* of the laws of morality ; but it is
more profoundly interesting, as well as more instructive, to read of those whose life in its moral conditions resembles our own. We see this most distinctly
when both representations are given by the genius
of one and the same writer. Falstaff is a sort of
sack-holding paunch, an exaggerated over-development
which no one thinks of holding down to the commonplace rules of the Ten Commandments and the statute law ; we do not think of them in connection with
him, — they belong to a world apart : accordingly, we
are vexed when the king discards him and reproves

* Chap. xvi.

him. Such a fate was a necessary adherence on
Shakespeare's part to the historical tradition; he
never probably thought of departing from it, nor
would his audience have perhaps endured his doing
so. But to those who look at the historical plays as
pure works of imaginative art, it seems certainly an
artistic misconception to have developed so marvelous
an *un*moral impersonation, and then to have subjected
it to an ethical and punitive judgment. Still, notwithstanding this error, which was very likely inevitable,
Falstaff is probably the most remarkable specimen
of caricature representation to be found in literature;
and its very excellence of execution only shows how
inferior is the kind of art which creates only such
representations. Who could compare the genius, marvelous as must be its fertility, which was needful to
create a Falstaff, with that shown in the higher productions of the same mind in Hamlet, Ophelia, and
Lear? We feel instantaneously the difference between the aggregating accident which rakes up from
the externalities of life other accidents analogous to
itself, and the central idea of a real character, which
cannot show itself wholly in any accident but which
exemplifies itself partially in many; which unfolds
itself gradually in wide spheres of action, and yet,
as with those we know best in life, leaves something
hardly to be understood, and after years of familiarity is a problem and a difficulty to the last. In the
same way, the embodied characteristics and grotesque exaggerations of Mr. Dickens, notwithstanding
all their humor and all their marvelous abundance,
can never be for a moment compared with the great
works of the real painters of essential human nature.

There is one class of Mr. Dickens's pictures which
may seem to form an exception to this criticism: it
is the delineation of the outlaw — we might say the
anti-law — world in "Oliver Twist." In one or two
instances Mr. Dickens has been so fortunate as to hit
on characteristics which, by his system of idealization

and continual repetition, might really be brought to look like a character. A man's trade or profession in regular life can only exhaust a very small portion of his nature; no approach is made to the essence of humanity by the exaggeration of the traits which typify a beadle or an undertaker. With the outlaw world it is somewhat different: the bare fact of a man belonging to that world is so important to his nature that if it is artistically developed with coherent accessories, some approximation to a distinctly natural character will be almost inevitably made. In the characters of Bill Sykes and Nancy this is so. The former is the skulking ruffian who may be seen any day at the police courts, and whom any one may fancy he sees by walking through St. Giles's. You cannot attempt to figure to your imagination the existence of such a person without being thrown into the region of the passions, the will, and the conscience; the mere fact of his maintaining, as a condition of life and by settled profession, a struggle with regular society, necessarily brings these deep parts of his nature into prominence; great crime usually proceeds from abnormal impulses or strange effort. Accordingly, Mr. Sykes is the character most approaching to a coherent man who is to be found in Mr. Dickens's works. We do not say that even here there is not some undue heightening admixture of caricature; but this defect is scarcely thought of amid the general coherence of the picture, the painful subject, and the wonderful command of strange accessories. Miss Nancy is a still more delicate artistic effort. She is an idealization of the girl who may also be seen at the police courts and St. Giles's; as bad according to occupation and common character as a woman can be, yet retaining a tinge of womanhood, and a certain compassion for interesting suffering, which under favoring circumstances might be the germ of a regenerating influence. We need not stay to prove how much the imaginative development of

such a personage must concern itself with our deeper
humanity; how strongly, if excellent, it must be
contrasted with everything conventional or casual or
superficial. Mr. Dickens's delineation is in the highest degree excellent. It possesses not only the more
obvious merits belonging to the subject, but also that
of a singular delicacy of expression and idea; nobody
fancies for a moment that they are reading about
anything beyond the pale of ordinary propriety. We
read the account of the life which Miss Nancy leads
with Bill Sykes without such an idea occurring to us;
yet when we reflect upon it, few things in literary
painting are more wonderful than the depiction of a
professional life of sin and sorrow, so as not even to
startle those to whom the deeper forms of either are
but names and shadows. Other writers would have
given as vivid a picture: Defoe would have poured
out even a more copious measure of telling circum-
stantiality, but he would have narrated his story with
an inhuman distinctness which if not impure is *un*-
pure; French writers, whom we need not name, would
have enhanced the interest of their narrative by
trading on the excitement of stimulating scenes. It
would be injustice to Mr. Dickens to say that he has
surmounted these temptations: the unconscious evidence of innumerable details proves that from a certain delicacy of imagination and purity of spirit, he
has not even experienced them. Criticism is the more
bound to dwell at length on the merits of these delineations, because no artistic merit can make "Oliver
Twist" a pleasing work: the squalid detail of crime
and misery oppresses us too much. If it is to be read
at all, it should be read in the first hardness of the
youthful imagination, which no touch can move too
deeply, and which is never stirred with tremulous
suffering at the "still sad music of humanity"*: the
coldest critic in later life may never hope to have
again the apathy of his boyhood.

* Wordsworth, "Tintern Abbey."

It perhaps follows from what has been said of the characteristics of Mr. Dickens's genius, that it would be little skilled in planning plots for his novels; he certainly is not so skilled. He says in his preface to the "Pickwick Papers," "that they were designed for the introduction of diverting characters and incidents; that no ingenuity of plot was attempted, or even at that time considered very feasible by the author in connection with the desultory mode of publication adopted;" and he adds an expression of regret that "these chapters" had not been "strung together on a stronger thread of general interest." It is extremely fortunate that no such attempt was made: in the cases in which Mr. Dickens has attempted to make a long connected story, or to develop into scenes or incidents a plan in any degree elaborate, the result has been a complete failure. A certain consistency of genius seems necessary for the construction of a consecutive plot; an irregular mind naturally shows itself in incoherency of incident and aberration of character. The method in which Mr. Dickens's mind works, if we are correct in our criticism upon it, tends naturally to these blemishes. Caricatures are necessarily isolated: they are produced by the exaggeration of certain conspicuous traits and features; each being is enlarged on its greatest side, and we laugh at the grotesque grouping and the startling contrast. But that connection between human beings on which a plot depends is rather severed than elucidated by the enhancement of their diversities. Interesting stories are founded on the intimate relations of men and women; these intimate relations are based not on their superficial traits or common occupations or most visible externalities, but on the inner life of heart and feeling: you simply divert attention from that secret life by enhancing the perceptible diversities of common human nature and the strange anomalies into which it may be distorted. The original germ of "Pickwick" was a "Club of Oddities": the idea was professedly abandoned, but traces of it are to be found in all Mr. Dickens's books; it illustrates the professed grotesqueness of the characters as well as their slender connection.

The defect of plot is heightened by Mr. Dickens's great — we might say complete — inability to make a love story. A pair of lovers is by custom a necessity of narrative fiction, and writers who possess a great general range of mundane knowledge, and but little knowledge of the special sentimental subject, are often in amusing difficulties; the watchful reader observes the transition from the hearty description of well-known scenes, of prosaic streets or journeys by wood and river, to the pale colors of ill-attempted poetry, to such sights as the novelist evidently wishes that he need not try to see: but few writers exhibit the difficulty in so aggravated a form as Mr. Dickens. Most men by taking thought can make a lay figure to look not so very unlike a young gentleman, and can compose a telling schedule of ladylike charms; Mr. Dickens has no power of doing either. The heroic character — we do not mean the form of character so called in life and action, but that which is hereditary in the heroes of novels — is not suited to his style of art. Hazlitt wrote an essay to inquire "Why the heroes of romances are insipid"; and without going that length, it may safely be said that the character of the agreeable young gentleman, who loves and is loved, should not be of the most marked sort, — flirtation ought not to be an exaggerated pursuit, young ladies and their admirers should not express themselves in the heightened and imaginative phraseology suited to Charley Bates and the Dodger. Humor is of no use, for no one makes love in jokes; a tinge of insidious satire may perhaps be permitted as a rare and occasional relief, but it will not be thought "a pretty book" if so malicious an element be at all habitually perceptible. The broad farce in which Mr. Dickens indulges is thoroughly out of place: if you caricature a pair of lovers ever so little, by the necessity of their calling you make them ridiculous. One of Sheridan's best comedies* is remarkable for having no scene in which the hero and heroine are on the stage together; and Mr. Moore suggests† that the shrewd wit distrusted his skill in the light dropping love talk which would have been necessary. Mr. Dickens would have done well to imitate so astute a policy; but he has none of the managing shrewdness which those who look at Sheridan's career attentively will probably think not the least remarkable feature in his singular character. Mr. Dickens, on the contrary, pours out painful sentiments as if he wished the abundance should make up for the inferior quality. The excruciating writing which is expended on Miss Ruth Pinch‡ passes belief. Mr. Dickens is not only unable to make lovers talk, but to describe heroines in mere narrative. As has been said, most men can make a jumble of blue eyes and fair hair and pearly teeth that does very well for a young lady, at least for a good while: but Mr. Dickens will not — probably cannot — attain even to this humble measure of descriptive art; he vitiates the repose by broad humor, or disenchants the delicacy by an unctuous admiration.

This deficiency is probably nearly connected with one of Mr. Dickens's most remarkable excellences. No one can read Mr. Thackeray's writings without feeling that he is perpetually treading as close as he dare to the border line that separates the world which may be described in books from the world which it is prohibited so to describe. No one knows better than this accomplished artist where that line is, and how curious are its windings and turns. The charge against him is that he knows it but too well; that with an anxious care and a wistful eye he is ever approximating to its edge, and hinting with subtle

* "School for Scandal."   † "Life of Sheridan," Vol. i., Chap. v.
‡ In "Martin Chuzzlewit."

art how thoroughly he is familiar with and how interesting he could make the interdicted region on the
other side. He never violates a single conventional
rule; but at the same time, the shadow of the immorality that is not seen is scarcely ever wanting to
his delineation of the society that is seen, — every
one may perceive what is passing in his fancy. Mr.
Dickens is chargeable with no such defect: he does
not seem to feel the temptation. By what we may
fairly call an instinctive purity of genius, he not only
observes the conventional rules, but makes excursions
into topics which no other novelist could safely han-
dle, and by a felicitous instinct deprives them of all
impropriety: no other writer could have managed the
humor of Mrs. Gamp without becoming unendurable.
At the same time, it is difficult not to believe that
this singular insensibility to the temptations to which
many of the greatest novelists have succumbed, is
in some measure connected with his utter inaptitude
for delineating the portion of life to which their art
is specially inclined: he delineates neither the love
affairs which ought to be nor those which ought not
to be.

Mr. Dickens's indisposition to "make capital" out
of the most commonly tempting part of human sentiment is the more remarkable because he certainly
does not show the same indisposition in other cases.
He has naturally great powers of pathos; his imagination is familiar with the common sort of human
suffering; and his marvelous conversancy with the
detail of existence enables him to describe sick-beds
and death-beds with an excellence very rarely seen
in literature, — a nature far more sympathetic than
that of most authors has familiarized him with such
subjects. In general, a certain apathy is characteristic of book writers, and dulls the efficacy of their
pathos: Mr. Dickens is quite exempt from this defect,
but on the other hand is exceedingly prone to a very
ostentatious exhibition of the opposite excellence: he

dwells on dismal scenes with a kind of fawning fondness; and he seems unwilling to leave them, long
after his readers have had more than enough of them.
He describes Mr. Dennis the hangman* as having a
professional fondness for his occupation : he has the
same sort of fondness apparently for the profession of
death painter. The painful details he accumulates are
a very serious drawback from the agreeableness of his
writings. Dismal "light literature" is the dismalest
of reading; the reality of the police reports is sufficiently bad, but a fictitious police report would be the
most disagreeable of conceivable compositions. Some
portions of Mr. Dickens's books are liable to a good
many of the same objections : they are squalid from
noisome trivialities and horrid with terrifying crime.
In his earlier books this is commonly relieved at frequent intervals by a graphic and original mirth : as
— we will not say age, but — maturity has passed over
his powers, this counteractive element has been lessened; the humor is not so happy as it was, but the
wonderful fertility in painful *minutiæ* still remains.

Mr. Dickens's political opinions have subjected him
to a good deal of criticism and to some ridicule.
He has shown on many occasions the desire — which
we see so frequent among able and influential men —
to start as a political reformer. Mr. Spurgeon said,
with an application to himself, "If you've got the
ear of the public, *of course* you must begin to tell it
its faults:" Mr. Dickens has been quite disposed to
make this use of his popular influence. Even in
"Pickwick" there are many traces of this tendency;
and the way in which it shows itself in that book
and in others is very characteristic of the time at
which they appeared. The most instructive political
characteristic of the years from 1825 to 1845 is the
growth and influence of the scheme of opinion which
we call "Radicalism." There are several species of
creeds which are comprehended under this generic
name, but they all evince a marked reaction against

* In "Barnaby Rudge."

the worship of the English Constitution and the affection for the English *status quo* which were then the established creed and sentiment : all Radicals are anti-Eldonites. This is equally true of the Benthamite or philosophical Radicalism of the early period, and the Manchester or "definite-grievance" Radicalism among the last vestiges of which we are now living. Mr. Dickens represents a species different from either : his is what we may call the "sentimental Radicalism"; and if we recur to the history of the time, we shall find that there would not originally have been any opprobrium attaching to such a name. The whole course of the legislation, and still more of the administration, of the first twenty years of the nineteenth century was marked by a harsh unfeelingness which is of all faults the most contrary to any with which we are chargeable now. The world of the "Six Acts," * of the frequent executions, of the Draconic criminal law, is so far removed from us that we cannot comprehend its having ever existed; it is more easy to understand the recoil which has followed. All the social speculation and much of the social action of the few years succeeding the Reform Bill bear the most marked traces of the reaction ; the spirit which animates Mr. Dickens's political reasonings and observations expresses it exactly. The vice of the then existing social authorities and of the then existing public had been the forgetfulness of the pain which their own acts evidently produced, — an unrealizing habit which adhered to official rules and established maxims, and which would not be shocked by the evident consequences, by proximate human suffering. The sure result of this habit was the excitement of the habit precisely opposed to it. Mr. Carlyle — in his "Chartism," we think — observes of the poor-law reform : —"It was then, above all things, necessary that out-door relief should cease. But how?

---

* Of Nov. 23, Dec. 3, and Dec. 17, 1819; introduced by Eldon, Sidmouth, and Castlereagh, to put down sedition, just after the Manchester massacre and the Cato Street conspiracy. — ED.

What means did great Nature take for accomplishing that most desirable end? She created a race of men who believed the cessation of out-door relief to be the one thing needful."* In the same way, and by the same propensity to exaggerated opposition which is inherent in human nature, the unfeeling obtuseness of the early part of this century was to be corrected by an extreme — perhaps an excessive — sensibility to human suffering in the years which have followed. There was most adequate reason for the sentiment in its origin, and it had a great task to perform in ameliorating harsh customs and repealing dreadful penalties; but it has continued to repine at such evils long after they ceased to exist, and when the only facts that at all resemble them are the necessary painfulness of due punishment and the necessary rigidity of established law.

Mr. Dickens is an example both of the proper use and of the abuse of the sentiment. His earlier works have many excellent descriptions of the abuses which had descended to the present generation from others whose sympathy with pain was less tender. Nothing can be better than the description of the poor debtors jail in " Pickwick," or of the old parochial authorities in " Oliver Twist." No doubt these descriptions are caricatures,— all his delineations are so; but the beneficial use of such art can hardly be better exemplified. Human nature endures the aggravation of vices and foibles in written description better than that of excellences. We cannot bear to hear even the hero of a book forever called "just"; we detest the recurring praise even of beauty, much more of virtue. The moment you begin to exaggerate a character of true excellence, you spoil it, — the traits are too delicate not to be injured by heightening or marred by over-emphasis: but a beadle is made for caricature, — the

* Mangled from this in Chap. iii. of " Chartism ":—" Their Amendment Act . . . was imperatively required to be put in practice, to create men filled with a theory that refusal of out-door relief was the one thing needful. Nature had no readier way of getting out-door relief refused."

slight measure of pomposity that humanizes his unfeelingness introduces the requisite comic element; even
the turnkeys of a debtors' prison may by skillful
hands be similarly used. The contrast between the
destitute condition of Job Trotter and Mr. Jingle and
their former swindling triumph is made comic by a
rarer touch of unconscious art: Mr. Pickwick's warm
heart takes so eager an interest in the misery of
his old enemies that our colder nature is tempted to
smile. We endure the over-intensity — at any rate
the unnecessary aggravation — of the surrounding misery, and we endure it willingly; because it brings out
better than anything else could have done the half-
comic intensity of a sympathetic nature.

It is painful to pass from these happy instances
of well-used power to the glaring abuses of the same
faculty in Mr. Dickens's later books. He began by
describing really removable evils in a style which
would induce all persons, however insensible, to remove them if they could; he has ended by describing
the natural evils and inevitable pains of the present
state of being in such a manner as must tend to
excite discontent and repining. The result is aggravated because Mr. Dickens never ceases to hint that
these evils are removable, though he does not say
by what means. Nothing is easier than to show the
evils of anything: Mr. Dickens has not unfrequently
spoken — and what is worse, he has taught a great
number of parrot-like imitators to speak — in what
really is, if they knew it, a tone of objection to the
necessary constitution of human society. If you will
only write a description of it, any form of government will seem ridiculous. What is more absurd than
a despotism, even at its best? A king of ability or an
able minister sits in an orderly room filled with me-
morials and returns and documents and memoranda.
These are his world; among these he of necessity
lives and moves: yet how little of the real life of the
nation he governs can be represented in an official

form! how much of real suffering is there that sta-
tistics can never tell! how much of obvious good is
there that no memorandum to a minister will ever
mention! how much deception is there in what such
documents contain! how monstrous must be the ignorance of the closet statesman, after all his life of
labor, of much that a ploughman could tell him of!
A free government is almost worse, as it must read
in a written delineation: instead of the real attention of a laborious and anxious statesman, we have
now the shifting caprices of a popular assembly, —
elected for one object, deciding on another; changing
with the turn of debate; shifting in its very composition; one set of men coming down to vote to-day,
to-morrow another and often unlike set, most of them
eager for the dinner hour, actuated by unseen influences, — by a respect for their constituents, by the
dread of an attorney in a far-off borough. What people are these to control a nation's destinies, and wield
the power of an empire, and regulate the happiness of
millions! Either way we are at fault: free government seems an absurdity, and despotism is so too.
Again, every form of law has a distinct expression,
a rigid procedure, customary rules and forms; it is
administered by human beings liable to mistake, confusion, and forgetfulness, and in the long run and on
the average is sure to be tainted with vice and fraud.
Nothing can be easier than to make a case, as we
may say, against any particular system, by pointing
out with emphatic caricature its inevitable miscar-
riages, and by pointing out nothing else. Those who
so address us may assume a tone of philanthropy, and
forever exult that they are not so unfeeling as other
men are; but the real tendency of their exhortations
is to make men dissatisfied with their inevitable condition, and what is worse, to make them fancy that
its irremediable evils can be remedied, and indulge in
a succession of vague strivings and restless changes.
Such, however, — though in a style of expression

somewhat different, — is very much the tone with which Mr. Dickens and his followers have in later years made us familiar. To the second-hand repeaters of a cry so feeble, we can have nothing to say, — if silly people cry because they think the world is silly, let them cry; but the founder of the school cannot, we are persuaded, peruse without mirth the lachrymose eloquence which his disciples have perpetrated. The soft moisture of irrelevant sentiment cannot have entirely entered into his soul : a truthful genius must have forbidden it. Let us hope that his pernicious example may incite some one of equal genius to preach with equal efficiency a sterner and a wiser gospel; but there is no need just now for us to preach it without genius.

There has been much controversy about Mr. Dickens's taste. A great many cultivated people will scarcely concede that he has any taste at all : a still larger number of fervent admirers point, on the other hand, to a hundred felicitous descriptions and delineations, which abound in apt expressions and skillful turns and happy images, — in which it would be impossible to alter a single word without altering for the worse; and naturally inquire whether such excellences in what is written do not indicate good taste in the writer. Ꝩ The truth is, that Mr. Dickens has what we may call "creative taste," — that is to say, the habit or faculty, whichever we may choose to call it, which at the critical instant of artistic production offers to the mind the right word and the right word only; if he is engaged on a good subject for caricature, there will be no defect of taste to preclude the caricature from being excellent. But it is only in moments of imaginative production that he has any taste at all; his works nowhere indicate that he possesses in any degree the passive taste which decides what is good in the writings of other people and what is not, and which performs the same critical duty upon a writer's own efforts when the confusing

mists of productive imagination have passed away.
Nor has Mr. Dickens the gentlemanly instinct which
in many minds supplies the place of purely critical
discernment, and which, by constant association with
those who know what is best, acquires a second-hand
perception of that which is best. He has no tendency
to conventionalism for good or for evil; his merits
are far removed from the ordinary path of writers,
and it was not probably so much effort to him as to
other men to step so far out of that path,—he scarcely
knew how far it was. For the same reason he cannot tell how faulty his writing will often be thought,
for he cannot tell what people will think.

A few pedantic critics have regretted that Mr.
Dickens had not received what they call a "regular
education"; and if we understand their meaning, we
believe they mean to regret that he had not received
a course of discipline which would probably have
impaired his powers. A "regular education" should
mean that ordinary system of regulation and instruction which experience has shown to fit men best for
the ordinary pursuits of life: it applies the requisite
discipline to each faculty in the exact proportion in
which that faculty is wanted in the pursuits of life;
it develops understanding and memory and imagination, each in accordance with the scale prescribed.
To men of ordinary faculties this is nearly essential;
it is the only mode in which they can be fitted for
the inevitable competition of existence. To men of
regular and symmetrical genius also, such a training
will often be beneficial. The world knows pretty well
what are the great tasks of the human mind, and has
learnt in the course of ages with some accuracy what
is the kind of culture likely to promote their exact
performance. A man of abilities extraordinary in degree but harmonious in proportion will be the better
for having submitted to the kind of discipline which
has been ascertained to fit a man for the work to
which powers in that proportion are best fitted: he

will do what he has to do better and more gracefully; culture will add a touch to the finish of nature. But the case is very different with men of irregular and anomalous genius, whose excellences consist in the aggravation of some special faculty, or at the most of one or two. The discipline which will fit such a man for the production of great literary works is that which will most develop the peculiar powers in which he excels; the rest of the mind will be far less important. It will not be likely that the culture which is adapted to, promote this special development will also be that which is most fitted for expanding the powers of common men in common directions: the precise problem is, to develop the powers of a strange man in a strange direction. In the case of Mr. Dickens, it would have been absurd to shut up his observant youth within the walls of a college: they would have taught him nothing about Mrs. Gamp there; Sam Weller took no degree. The kind of early life fitted to develop the power of apprehensive observation is a brooding life in stirring scenes: the idler in the streets of life knows the streets; the bystander knows the picturesque effect of life better than the player; and the meditative idler amid the hum of existence is much more likely to know its sound, and to take in and comprehend its depths and meanings, than the scholastic student intent on books, — which, if they represent any world, represent one which has long passed away, which commonly try rather to develop the reasoning understanding than the seeing observation, which are written in languages that have long been dead. You will not train by such discipline a caricaturist of obvious manners.

Perhaps, too, a regular instruction, and daily experience of the searching ridicule of critical associates, would have detracted from the pluck which Mr. Dickens shows in all his writings. It requires a great deal of courage to be a humorous writer, — you are always afraid that people will laugh at you instead of with you; undoubtedly there is a certain eccentricity about it. You take up the esteemed writers, — Thucydides and the *Saturday Review:* after all, they do not make you laugh. It is not the function of really artistic productions to contribute to the mirth of human beings. All sensible men are afraid of it, and it is only with an extreme effort that a printed joke attains to the perusal of the public : the chances are many to one that the anxious producer loses heart in the correction of the press, and that the world never laughs at all. Mr. Dickens is quite exempt from this weakness : he has what a Frenchman might call "the courage of his faculty." The real daring which is shown in the "Pickwick Papers," in the whole character of Mr. Weller senior as well as in that of his son, is immense, far surpassing any which has been shown by any other contemporary writer. The brooding irregular mind is in its first stage prone to this sort of courage : it perhaps knows that its ideas are "out of the way," but with the infantine simplicity of youth it supposes that originality is an advantage. Persons more familiar with the ridicule of their equals in station (and this is to most men the great instructress of the college time) well know that of all qualities this one most requires to be clipped and pared and measured. Posterity, we doubt not, will be entirely perfect in every conceivable element of judgment; but the existing generation like what they have heard before, — it is much easier. It required great courage in Mr. Dickens to write what his genius has compelled them to appreciate.

We have throughout spoken of Mr. Dickens as he was, rather than as he is; or — to use a less discourteous phrase, and we hope a truer — of his early works rather than of those which are more recent. We could not do otherwise consistently with the true code of criticism. A man of great genius, who has written great and enduring works, must be judged mainly by them; and not by the inferior productions which, from the necessities of personal position, a fatal facility of composition, or other cause, he may pour forth at moments less favorable to his powers. Those who are called on to review these inferior productions themselves must speak of them in the terms they may deserve; but those who have the more pleasant task of estimating as a whole the genius of the writer may confine their attention almost wholly to those happier efforts which illustrate that genius. We should not like to have to speak in detail of Mr. Dickens's later works, and we have not done so. There are, indeed, peculiar reasons why a genius constituted as his is (at least if we are correct in the view which we have taken of it) would not endure without injury during a long life the applause of the many, the temptations of composition, and the general excitement of existence. Even in his earlier works it was impossible not to fancy that there was a weakness of fiber unfavorable to the longevity of excellence; this was the effect of his deficiency in those masculine faculties of which we have said so much, — the reasoning understanding and firm far-seeing sagacity. It is these two component elements which stiffen the mind, and give a consistency to the creed and a coherence to · its effects, — which enable it to protect itself from the rush of circumstances. If to a deficiency in these we add an extreme sensibility to circumstances, — a mobility, as Lord Byron used to call it, of emotions, which is easily impressed, and still more easily carried away by impression, — we have the idea of a character peculiarly unfitted to bear the flux of time and chance. A man of very great determination could hardly bear up against them, with such slight aids from within and with such peculiar sensibility to temptation; a man of merely ordinary determination would succumb to it, and Mr. Dickens has succumbed. His position was certainly unfavorable. He has told us that the works of his later years, inferior as all good critics have

deemed them, have yet been more read than those of
his earlier and healthier years; the most characteristic part of his audience, the lower middle class, were
ready to receive with delight the least favorable productions of his genius.   Human nature cannot endure
this: it is too much to have to endure a coincident
temptation both from within and from without.   Mr.
Dickens was too much inclined by natural disposition
to lachrymose eloquence and exaggerated caricature,
— such was the kind of writing which he wrote most
easily; he found likewise that such was the kind of
writing that was read most readily: and of course he
wrote that kind.   Who would have done otherwise?
No critic is entitled to speak very harshly of such
degeneracy, if he is not sure that he could have
coped with difficulties so peculiar.   If that rule is to
be observed, who is there that will not be silent?   No
other Englishman has attained such a hold on the
vast populace; it is little, therefore, to say that no
other has surmounted its attendant temptations.

HENRY CRABB ROBINSON.*

(1869.)

PERHAPS I should be ashamed to confess it, but I own
I opened the three large volumes of Mr. Robinson's
memoirs with much anxiety. Their bulk, in the first
place, appalled me; but that was by no means my
greatest apprehension. I knew I had a hundred times
heard Mr. Robinson say that he hoped something he
would leave behind would "be published and be worth
publishing." I was aware, too, — for it was no deep
secret, — that for half a century or more he had kept
a diary, and that he had been preserving correspondence besides; and I was dubious what sort of things
these would be, and what — to use Carlyle's words —
any human editor could make of them.   Even when
Mr. Robinson used to talk so, I used to shudder; for
the men who have tried to be memoir-writers and
failed are as numerous, or nearly so, as those who
have tried to be poets and failed, — a specific talent
is as necessary for the one as for the other.   But as
soon as I had read a little of the volumes, all these
doubts passed away.   I saw at once that Mr. Robinson had an excellent power of narrative writing, and
that the editor of his remains had made a most judicious use of excellent materials.

Perhaps more than anything, it was the modesty
of my old friend (I think I may call Mr. Robinson
my old friend, for though he *thought* me a modern
youth, I *did* know him twenty years) — perhaps, I say,

---

* Diary, Reminiscences, and Correspondence of Henry Crabb Robinson,
Barrister-at-Law, F. S. A.   Selected and Edited by Thos. Sadler, Ph. D.   In
Three Volumes.   London, 1869.

it was his modesty which made me nervous about his memoirs more than anything else. I have so often heard him say (and say it with a vigor of emphasis which is rarer in our generation even than in his), "Sir, I have no literary talent. I cannot write. I never *could* write anything and I never *would* write anything," that being so taught, and so vehemently, I came to believe. And there was this to justify my creed : the notes Mr. Robinson used to scatter about him — and he was fond of writing rather elaborate ones — were not always very good; at least they were too long for the busy race of the present generation, and introduced Schiller and Goethe where they need not have appeared. But in these memoirs (especially in the "Reminiscences" and the "Diary"; for the moment he gets to a letter the style is worse) the words flow with such an effectual simplicity that even Southey, the great master of such prose, could hardly have written better. Possibly it was his real interest in his old stories which preserved Mr. Robinson : in his letters he was not so interested, and he fell into words and amplifications; but in those ancient anecdotes which for years were his life and being, the style, as it seems to me, could scarcely be mended even in a word. And though, undoubtedly, the book is much too long in the latter half, I do not blame Dr. Sadler, the editor and biographer, for it, or indeed blame any one. Mr. Robinson had led a very long and very varied life, and some of his old friends had an interest in one part of his reminiscences and some in another. An unhappy editor intrusted with "a deceased's papers" cannot really and in practice omit much that any surviving friends much want to have put in. One man calls with a letter "in which my dear and honored friend gave me advice that was of such inestimable value, I hope — I cannot but think — you will find room for it." And another calls with memoranda of a dinner — a most "superior occasion," as they say in the North — at which, he

reports, "there was conversation to which I never, or
scarcely ever, heard anything equal. There were A B
and C D and E F,—all masters, as you remember,
of the purest conversational eloquence : surely I need
not hesitate to believe that you will say something
of that dinner." And so an oppressed biographer
has to serve up the crumbs of ancient feasts, though
well knowing in his heart that they are crumbs, and
though he feels, too, that the critics will attack him
and cruelly say it is his fault. But remembering this,
and considering that Mr. Robinson wrote a diary
beginning in 1811, going down to 1867, and occupying
thirty-five closely written volumes, and that there
were "Reminiscences" and vast unsorted papers, I
think Dr. Sadler has managed admirably well. His
book is brief to what it might have been, and all his
own part is written with delicacy, feeling, and knowledge. He quotes, too, from Wordsworth, by way of
motto, —

> "A man he seems of cheerful yesterdays
> And confident to-morrows; with a face
> Not worldly minded, for it bears too much
> Of Nature's impress, — gayety and health,
> Freedom and hope, — but keen withal and shrewd :
> His gestures' note, — and hark ! his tones of voice
> Are all vivacious as his mien and looks." *

It was a happy feeling for Mr. Robinson's character
that selected these lines to stand at the beginning of
his memoirs.

And yet in one material respect—in this case perhaps the most material respect—Dr. Sadler has failed,
and not in the least from any fault of his. Sydney
Smith used to complain that "no one had ever made
him his trustee or executor": being really a very
sound and sensible man of business, he felt that it
was a kind of imputation on him, and that he was
not appreciated. But some one more justly replied,

---

* " Excursion," Book vii.

"But how could *you*, Sydney Smith, expect to be made an executor? Is there any one who wants their 'remains' to be made fun of?" Now, every trustee of biographical papers is exactly in this difficulty, that he cannot make fun,—the melancholy friends who left the papers would not at all like it; and besides there grows upon every such biographer an "official" feeling, a confused sense of vague responsibilities, a wish not to impair the gravity of the occasion or to offend any one by levity. But there are some men who cannot be justly described quite gravely; and Crabb Robinson is one of them. A certain grotesqueness was a part of him; and unless you liked it, you lost the very best of him. He is called, and properly called, in these memoirs "Mr. Robinson" but no well-judging person ever called him so in life,— he was always called "Old Crabb," and that is the only name which will ever bring up his curious image to me. He was, in the true old English sense of the word, a "character": one whom a very peculiar life, certainly, and perhaps also a rather peculiar nature to begin with, had formed and molded into something so exceptional and singular that it did not seem to belong to ordinary life, and almost caused a smile when you saw it moving there. "An aberrant form," I believe, the naturalists call the seal and such things in natural history; odd shapes that can only be explained by a long past, and which swim with a certain incongruity in their present *milieu*. Now "Old Crabb" was (to me at least) just like that. You watched with interest and pleasure his singular gestures and his odd way of saying things, and muttered as if to keep up the recollection, "And *this* is the man who was the friend of Goethe and is the friend of Wordsworth!" There was a certain animal oddity about "Old Crabb" which made it a kind of mental joke to couple him with such great names, and yet he was to his heart's core thoroughly coupled with them. If you leave out all his strange ways (I do not say Dr. Sadler has quite left them out, but to some extent he has been obliged, by place and decorum, to omit them), you lose the life of the man; you cut from the Ethiopian his skin, and from the leopard his spots. I well remember how poor Clough, who was then fresh from Oxford, and was much puzzled by the corner of London to which he had drifted, looking at "Old Crabb" in a kind of terror for a whole breakfast time, and muttering in mute wonder, almost to himself, as he came away, "Not at all the regular patriarch;" and certainly no one could accuse Mr. Robinson of an insipid regularity either in face or nature.

Mr. Robinson was one of the original founders of University College, and was for many years both on its senate and council; and as he lived near the college, he was fond of collecting at breakfast all the elder students, especially those who had any sort of interest in literature. Probably he never appeared to so much advantage, or showed all the best of his nature so well, as in those parties. Like most very cheerful old people, he at heart preferred the company of the very young; and a set of young students, even after he was seventy, suited him better as society than a set of grave old men. Sometimes, indeed, he would invite — I do not say some of his contemporaries: few of them even in 1847 were up to breakfast parties; but persons of fifty and sixty, — those whom young students call "old gentlemen": and it was amusing to watch the consternation of some of them at the surprising youth and levity of their host; they shuddered at the freedom with which we treated him. Middle-aged men, of feeble heads and half-made reputations, have a nice dislike to the sharp arguments and the unsparing jests of "boys at college"; they cannot bear the rough society of those who, never having tried their own strength, have not yet

acquired a fellow-feeling for weakness. Many su
persons, I am sure, were half hurt with Mr. Robins
for not keeping "those impertinent boys" more at
just distance; but Mr. Robinson liked fun and mov
ment, and disliked the sort of dignity which shelte
stupidity. There was little to gratify the unintelle
ual part of man at these breakfasts; and what the
was, was not easy to be got at. Your host, just
you were sitting down to breakfast, found he h
forgotten to make the tea, then he could not find h
keys, then he rang the bell to have them search
for; but long before the servant came he had go
off into "Schiller-Goethe," and could not the lea
remember what he had wanted. The more astute
his guests* used to breakfast before they came; a
then there was much interest in seeing a steady l
erary man, who did not understand the region,
agonies at having to hear three stories before he g
his tea, one again between his milk and his suga
another between his butter and his toast, and add
tional zest in making a stealthy inquiry that w
sure to intercept the coming delicacies by bringir
on Schiller and Goethe.

It is said in these memoirs that Mr. Robinson
parents were very good-looking, and that when ma
ried they were called "the handsome couple";† but
his old age very little regular beauty adhered to hir
if he ever had any. His face was pleasing from i
animation, its kindness, and its shrewdness; but tl
nose was one of the most slovenly which nature h
ever turned out, and the chin of excessive lengt
with portentous power of extension. But perhaps, f
the purpose of a social narrator (and in later yea
this was Mr. Robinson's position), this oddity of fe
ture was a gift. It was said, and justly said, th
Lord Brougham used to punctuate his sentences wi
his nose; just at the end of a long parenthesis l

---

* Viz., Bagehot himself. See Mr. Hutton's memoir. — ED.
† Vol. i., Chap. i. (All references are to the American edition.) — ED.

could and did turn up his nose, which served to note
the change of subject as well [as], or better than, a
printed mark. Mr. Robinson was not so skillful as
this; but he made a very able use of the chin at a
conversational crisis, and just at the point of a story
pushed it out, and then very slowly drew it in again,
— so that you always knew when to laugh, and the
oddity of the gesture helped you in laughing.

Mr. Robinson had known nearly every literary
man worth knowing in England and Germany for
fifty years and more. He had studied at Jena in the
"great time," when Goethe and Schiller and Wieland
were all at their zenith; he had lived with Charles
Lamb and his set, and Rogers and his set, besides an
infinite lot of little London people; he had taught
Madame de Staël German philosophy in Germany,
and helped her in business afterwards in England; he
was the real friend of Wordsworth, and had known
Coleridge and Southey almost from their "coming
out" to their death. And he was not a mere literary
man : he had been a *Times* correspondent in the days
of Napoleon's early German battles, now more than
"seventy years since"; he had been off Corunna in
Sir John Moore's time; and last, — but almost first it
should have been, — he was an English barrister, who
had for years a considerable business, and who was
full of picturesque stories about old judges. Such a
varied life and experience belong to very few men;
and his social nature, at once accessible and assailant,
was just the one to take advantage of it. He seemed
to be lucky all through : in childhood he remembered
when "John Gilpin" came out; then he had seen —
he could not hear — John Wesley preach; then he
had heard Erskine, and criticized him intelligently, in
some of the finest of the well-known "state trials":
and so on during all his vigorous period.

I do not know that it would be possible to give a
better idea of Mr. Robinson's best conversations than
by quoting almost at random from the earlier part of
these memoirs : —

"At the spring assizes of 1791, when I had nearly attained my sixteenth year, I had the delight of hearing Erskine. It was a high enjoyment, and I was able to profit by it. The subject of the trial was the validity of a will, — Braham v. Rivett. Erskine came down specially retained for the plaintiff, and Mingay for the defendant. The trial lasted two days. The title of the heir being admitted, the proof of the will was gone into at once. I have a recollection of many of the circumstances after more than fifty-four years; but of nothing do I retain so perfect a recollection as of the figure and voice of Erskine. There was a charm in his voice, a fascination in his eye; and so completely had he won my affection, that I, am sure, had the verdict been given against him, I should have burst out crying. Of the facts and of the evidence, I do not pretend to recollect anything beyond my impressions and sensations. My pocket-book records that Erskine was engaged two and a half hours in opening the case, and Mingay two hours and twenty minutes in his speech in defense; E.'s reply occupied three hours. The testatrix was an old lady in a state of imbecility; the evil spirit of the case was an attorney. Mingay was loud and violent, and gave Erskine an opportunity of turning into ridicule his imagery and illustrations. For instance, M. having compared R. to the Devil going into the Garden of Eden, E. drew a closer parallel than M. intended. Satan's first sight of Eve was related in Milton's words,—

'Grace was in all her steps, heaven in her eye,
    In every gesture dignity and love;'*

and then a picture of idiotcy from Swift was contrasted. But the sentence that weighed on my spirits was a pathetic exclamation,— 'If, gentlemen, you should by your verdict annihilate an instrument so solemnly framed, *I should retire a troubled man from this court;*' and as he uttered the word *court*, he beat his breast, and I had a difficulty in not crying out. When in bed the following night, I awoke several times in a state of excitement approaching fever; the words '*troubled man from this court*' rang in my ears.

"A new trial was granted, and ultimately the will was set aside. I have said I profited by Erskine. I remarked his great artifice, if I may call it so, and in a small way I afterwards practiced it: it lay in his frequent repetitions. He had one or two leading arguments and main facts on which he was constantly dwelling; but then he had marvelous skill in varying his phraseology, so that no one was sensible of tautology in the expressions. Like the doubling

---

* "Paradise Lost," Book viii., concerning *Adam's* first view. — ED.

of a hare, he was perpetually coming to his old place. Other great advocates I have remarked were ambitious of a great variety of arguments.

"About the same time that I thus first heard the most perfect of forensic orators, I was also present at an exhibition equally admirable, and which had a powerful effect on my mind. It was, I believe, in October, 1790, and not long before his death, that I heard John Wesley in the great round Meeting-House at Colchester. He stood in a wide pulpit, and on each side of him stood a minister, and the two held him up, having their hands under his arm-pits. His feeble voice was barely audible; but his reverend countenance, especially his long white locks, formed a picture never to be forgotten. There was a vast crowd of lovers and admirers. It was for the most part pantomime, but the pantomime went to the heart. Of the kind I never saw anything comparable to it in after life." *

And again : —

" It was at the Summer Circuit [1816] that Rolfe made his first appearance. He had been at the preceding Sessions. I have a pleasure in recollecting that I at once foresaw that he would become a distinguished man. In my Diary I wrote :—'Our new junior, Mr. Rolfe, made his appearance. His manners are genteel; his conversation easy and sensible. He is a very acceptable companion, but I fear a dangerous rival.' And my brother asking me who the new man was, I said, 'I will venture to predict that you will live to see that young man attain a higher rank than any one you ever saw upon the circuit.' It is true he is not higher than Leblanc, who was also a puisne judge, but Leblanc was never Solicitor-General; nor probably is Rolfe yet at the end of his career. One day, when some one remarked, 'Christianity is part and parcel of the law of the land,' Rolfe said to me, 'Were you ever employed to draw an indictment against a man for not loving his neighbor as himself?'

" Rolfe is, by universal repute, if not the very best, at least one of the best judges on the Bench. He is one of the few with whom I have kept up an acquaintance." †

FOOT-NOTE BY MR. ROBINSON. — "Since writing the above, Baron Rolfe has verified my prediction more strikingly by being created a peer by the title of Lord Cranworth, and appointed a Vice-Chancellor. Soon after his appointment he called on me, and I dined with him. I related to Lady Cranworth the anecdote given above, of my conversation with my brother, with which she was evidently

* Vol. i., Chap. ii. † Vol. i., Chap. xix.

pleased. Lady Cranworth was the daughter of Mr. Carr, Solicitor to the Excise, whom I formerly used to visit, and ought soon to find some mention of in my journals. Lord Cranworth continues to enjoy universal respect. — H. C. R. 1851."

Of course these stories came over and over again : it is the excellence of a reminiscent to have a few good stories, and his misfortune that people will remember what he says. In Mr. Robinson's case an unskilled person could often see the anecdote somewhere impending, and there was often much interest in trying whether you could ward it off or not. There was one great misfortune which had happened to his guests, though he used to tell it as one of the best things that had ever happened to himself : he had picked up a certain bust of Wieland by Schadow,* which it appears had been lost, and in the finding of which Goethe, even Goethe, rejoiced.† After a very long interval, I still shudder to think how often I have heard that story; it was one which no skill or care could long avert, for the thing stood opposite our host's chair, and the sight of it was sure to recall him. Among the ungrateful students to whom he was so kind, the first question always asked of any one who had breakfasted at his house was, "Did you undergo the *bust?*"

A reader of these memoirs would naturally and justly think that the great interest of Mr. Robinson's conversation was the strength of the past memory; but quite as amusing, or more so, was the present weakness. He never could remember names, and was very ingenious in his devices to elude the defect. There is a story in these memoirs : —

"I was engaged to dine with Mr. Wansey at Walthamstow. When I arrived there I was in the greatest distress, through having forgotten his name; and it was not till after half an hour's worry that I recollected he was a Unitarian, which would answer as well, for I instantly proceeded to Mr. Cogan's. Having been shown into a room, young Mr. Cogan came: 'Your commands, sir?'

* Vol. i., Chap. xxi.   † Vol. ii., Chap. vii.

'Mr. Cogan, I have taken the liberty to call on you in order to know where I am to dine to-day.' He smiled. I went on, 'The truth is, I have accepted an invitation to dine with a gentleman, a recent acquaintance, whose name I have forgotten; but I am sure you can tell me, for he is a Unitarian, and the Unitarians are very few here.'"*

And at his breakfasts it was always the same; he was always in difficulty as to some person's name or other, and he had regular descriptions which recurred like Homeric epithets, and which he expected you to apply to the individual. Thus, poor Clough always appeared — "That admirable and accomplished man. You know whom I mean. The one who never says anything." And of another living poet he used to say, "Probably the most able, and certainly the most consequential, of all the young persons I know. You know which it is. The one with whom I could never *presume* to be intimate. The one whose father I knew so many years." And another particular friend of my own always occurred as — "That great friend of yours that has been in Germany — that most accomplished and interesting person — that most able and excellent young man. Sometimes I like him, and sometimes I *hate* him. You," turning to me, "know whom I mean, you villain!" And certainly I did know; for I had heard the same adjectives and been referred to in the same manner very many times.

Of course a main part of Mr. Robinson's conversation was on literary subjects; but of this, except when it related to persons whom he had known, or sonnets "to the conception of which he was privy," I do not think it would be just to speak very highly. He spoke sensibly and clearly, — he could not on any subject speak otherwise: but the critical faculty is as special and as peculiar almost as the poetical; and Mr. Robinson in serious moments was quite aware of it, and he used to deny that he had the former faculty more than the latter. He used to read much of

* Vol. ii., Chap. vi.

Wordsworth to me: but I doubt—though many of his friends will think I am a great heretic—I doubt if he read the best poems; and even those he did read (and he read very well) rather suffered from coming in the middle of a meal, and at a time when you wanted to laugh and not to meditate. Wordsworth was a solitary man, and it is only in solitude that his best poems, or indeed any of his characteristic poems, can be truly felt or really apprehended. There are some at which I never look, even now, without thinking of the wonderful and dreary faces which Clough used to make while Mr. Robinson was reading them. To Clough certain of Wordsworth's poems were part of his inner being; and he suffered at hearing them obtruded at meal-time, just as a High-Churchman would suffer at hearing the collects of the Church. Indeed, these poems were among the collects of Clough's church.

Still less do I believe that there is any special value in the expositions of German philosophy in these volumes, or that there was any in those which Mr. Robinson used to give on such matters in conversation. They are clear, no doubt, and accurate; but they are not the expositions of a born metaphysician. He speaks in these memoirs of his having a difficulty in concentrating his "attention on works of speculation"*; and such books as Kant can only be really mastered, can perhaps only be usefully studied, by those who have an unusual facility in concentrating their mind on impalpable abstractions, and an uncommon inclination to do so. Mr. Robinson had neither; and I think the critical philosophy had really very little effect on him, and had, during the busy years which had elapsed since he studied it, very nearly run off him. There was something very curious in the sudden way that anything mystical would stop in

---

*I find no such words, or even implication, in the volumes; though he indirectly admits weakness in this line, in a letter to his brother, June 6, 1802 (Vol. i., Chap. vi.), and to Benecke, March 2, 1836 (Vol. ii., Chap. xii.). —ED.

him. At the end of a Sunday breakfast, after inflict-
ing on you much which was transcendental in Wordsworth or Goethe, he would say, as we left him, with
an air of relish, "Now I am going to run down to
Essex Street to hear Madge. I shall not be in time
for the prayers, but I do not so much care about
that: what I do like is the sermon, — it is so clear."
Mr. Madge was a Unitarian of the old school, with
as little mystical and transcendental in his nature
as any one who ever lived: there was a living
piquancy in the friend of Goethe — the man who
would explain to you his writings — being also the
admirer of "Madge"; it was like a proser lengthily
eulogizing Kant to you, and then saying, "Ah! but I
do love Condillac, — he is so clear."

But on the other hand, I used to hold — I was
reading law at the time, and so had some interest in
the matter — that Mr. Robinson much underrated his
legal knowledge and his practical power as a lawyer.
What he used to say was, "I never knew any law,
sir, but I knew the practice. . . . I left the bar because I feared my incompetence might be discovered.
I was a tolerable junior: but I was rising to be a
leader, which I was unfit to be; and so I retired, not
to disgrace myself by some fearful mistake." In these
memoirs he says that he retired when he had made
the sum of money which he thought enough for a
bachelor with few wants and not a single expensive
taste. The simplicity of his tastes is certain, — very
few Englishmen indeed could live with so little show
or pretense; but the idea of his gross incompetence
is absurd, — no one who was incompetent ever said so.
There are, I am sure, plenty of substantial and well-
satisfied men at the English bar who do not know
nearly as much law as Mr. Robinson knew, and who
have not a tithe of his sagacity, but who believe in
themselves and in whom their clients believe. On
the other hand, Mr. Robinson had many great quali-
fications for success at the bar. He was a really

good speaker: when over seventy I have heard him make a speech that good speakers in their full vigor would be glad to make. He had a good deal of the actor in his nature, which is thought — and I fancy justly thought — to be necessary to the success of all great advocates, and perhaps of all great orators. He was well acquainted with the petty technicalities which intellectual men in middle life in general cannot learn, for he had passed some years in an attorney's office. Above all, he was a very thinking man, and had an "idea of business," — that inscrutable something which at once and altogether distinguishes the man who is safe in the affairs of life from those who are unsafe. I do not suppose he knew much black-letter law; but there are plenty of judges on the bench who, unless they are much belied, also know very little, — perhaps none. And a man who can intelligently read Kant, like Mr. Robinson, need not fear the book-work of English law: a very little serious study would have taught him law enough to lead the Norfolk circuit. He really had a sound, moderate, money-making business, and only a little pains was wanted to give him more.

The real reason why he did not take the trouble, I fancy, was that, being a bachelor, he was a kind of amateur in life, and did not really care; he could not spend what he had on himself, and used to give away largely, though in private. And even more, as with most men who have not thoroughly worked when young, daily regular industry was exceedingly trying to him. No man could be less idle; far from it, he was always doing something: but then he was doing what he chose. Sir Walter Scott, one of the best workers of his time, used always to say that he had no temptation to be idle, but the greatest temptation, when one thing was wanted of him, to go and do something else. * Perhaps the only persons who,

---

* "Never a being hated task-work as I hate it. . . . It is not that I am idle in my nature neither. But propose to me to do one thing, and it is inconceivable the desire I have to do something else." — Diary, Dec. 1, 1825; in Lockhart,

not being forced by mere necessity, really conquer this temptation, are those who were early broken to the yoke, and are fixed to the furrow by habit; Mr. Robinson loitered in Germany, so he was not one of these.

I am not regretting this: it would be a base idolatry of practical life to require every man to succeed in it as far as he could, and to devote to it all his mind. The world certainly does not need it: it pays well, and it will never lack good servants. There will always be enough of sound strong men to be working barristers and judges, let who will object to become so. But I own I think a man ought to be able to be a "Philistine" if he chooses,— there is a sickly incompleteness about people too fine for the world, and too nice to work their way in it; and when a man like Mr. Robinson, had a real sagacity for affairs, it is for those who respect his memory to see that his reputation does not suffer from his modesty, and that his habitual self-depreciations — which indeed extended to his powers of writing as well as to those of acting — are not taken to be exactly true.

In fact, Mr. Robinson was usually occupied in University College business and University Hall business, and other such things. But there is no special need to write on them in connection with his name, and it would need a good deal of writing to make them intelligible to those who do not know them now; and the greater part of his life was spent in society, where his influence was always manly and vigorous. I do not mean that he was universally popular; it would be defacing his likeness to say so. "I am a man," he once told me, "to whom a great number of persons entertain the very strongest objection." Indeed, he had some subjects on which he could hardly bear opposition. Twice he nearly quarreled with me: once for writing in favor of Louis Napoleon, which, as he had caught in Germany a thorough antipathy to the first Napoleon, seemed to him quite wicked;

and next for my urging that Hazlitt was a much
greater writer than Charles Lamb, — a harmless opinion which I still hold, but which Mr. Robinson met
with this outburst : — "You, sir, YOU prefer the works
of that scoundrel, that odious, that malignant writer,
to the exquisite essays of that angelic creature!" I
protested that there was no evidence that angels
could write particularly well; but it was in vain, and
it was some time before he forgave me. Some persons who casually encountered peculiarities like these
did not always understand them. In his last years,
too, augmenting infirmities almost disqualified Mr.
Robinson for general society, and quite disabled him
from showing his old abilities in it. Indeed, I think
that these Memoirs will give almost a new idea of
his power to many young men who had only seen
him casually, and at times of feebleness : after ninety
it is not easy to make new friends. And in any case,
this book will always have a great charm for those
who knew Mr. Robinson well when they were themselves young, because it will keep alive for them the
image of his buoyant sagacity and his wise and careless kindness.

RELIGIOUS AND METAPHYSICAL ESSAYS.

THE IGNORANCE OF MAN.*

(1862.)

A BOLD man once said that religion and morality were inconsistent. He argued thus:— The essence of religion — part of the essence, at any rate — is recompense; a belief in another life is only another name for the anticipation of a time when wickedness will be punished and when goodness will be rewarded. If you admit a Providence, you acknowledge the existence of an adjusting agency; of a power which is recompensing by its very definition and of its very nature, which allots happiness to virtue and pain to vice. On the other hand, the essence of morality is disinterestedness: a man who does good for the sake of a future gain to himself is, in a moral point of view, altogether inferior to one who does good for the good's sake, who hopes for nothing again, who is not thinking of himself, who is not calculating his own futurity. Between a man who does good to the world because he takes an intelligent view of his real interest, and another who does harm to the world because he is blind to that interest, there is only an intellectual difference, — the one is mentally long-sighted, the other mentally short-sighted. By the admission of all mankind, a disinterested action is better than a selfish action; a disinterested man is higher than a selfish man. Yet how is it possible

---

* Science in Theology. Sermons preached before the University of Oxford. By the Rev. Adam S. Farrar. Longmans.

that a religious man can be disinterested? Heaven
overarches him, hell yawns before him: how can he
help having his eyes attracted by the one and terrified by the other? He boasts, indeed, that religion
is useful to mankind by producing good actions; he
extols the attractive influence of future reward and
the deterring efficacy of apprehended penalty. But
his boast is absurd and premature: by holding forth
these anticipated bribes, by menacing these pains, he
extracts from virtue *its virtue,*—he makes it selfishness like the rest; he constructs an edifying and
hoping saint, but he spoils the disinterested and un-
calculating man.

These thoughts are not often boldly expressed;
fundamental difficulties rarely are. They constantly
confuse the mind, and they are always floating like
a vague mist in the intellectual air; they distort and
blur the outlines of everything else, but they have
no distinct outline of their own. An obscure difficulty is a pervading evil; the first requisite for removing it is to make it clear,—if you assign a limit,
you notify the frontier at which it may be attacked.

The objection is, in most people's apprehensions
and in its common incomplete expressions, confined
exclusively to the doctrine of a future life; but it
is at least equally applicable to the belief in a God
who rules and governs. We can of course conceive
of supernatural beings who do not interfere with us,
who do not care for us, who do not help us, who
have no connection with our moral life, who do good
to no one, who do evil to no one. Such were the
gods of Lucretius, the most fascinating of pure in-
ventions; but such gods are not the gods of religion.
The ancient Epicurean, in times when obscure difficulties were discussed in plainer words than is now
either possible or advisable, expressly defended them
on that ground. He did not want his gods to interfere with him: he thought it would impair the ideal
languor of their life as well as the inapprehensive

security of his own life. They lived "self-scanned, self-centered, self-secure,"* and he was, in so far as was possible, to do so also; he did not wish the voluptuaries of heaven to become the busybodies of earth; he liked to have a pleasant dream of the upper world, but he did not wish it to descend and rule him. But as soon as we abandon the natural fiction of the voluptuous imagination; as soon as we accept the idea of a God who is a Providence in the universe, and not an idol in heaven; as soon as we allow that he loves good and hates evil; as soon as we are sure that he is our Father, and chastises us as children; as soon as we acknowledge a God such as the human heart and conscience crave for, the God of Christianity,—we at once reach the primitive difficulty. Here is a Being who *we know* will reward the good and punish the evil: how can we do good without reference to that supernatural recompense, or evil without shrinking from that apprehended penalty?

Nor is it for this purpose in the least material (though for many other purposes it is very material) whether we consider God as acting by irrevocable laws fixed once for all, or upon a system which (though foreseen and immutable to him, to whom all the future is as present as all the past) is according to our view of it—to our translation of it, so to speak, into our limited capacities—capable of flexibility at his touch and of modification at his pleasure. If we know that we are rewarded and punished, it matters little, as respects our hope and our apprehension, whether that punishment be inflicted by a machine or by a person: in one case we shall shun the contact with the lacerating wheel, in the other we shall dread a blow from the punitive hand; but in either case the pain will be the determining motive, the deterring thought. We shall act as we do act, not from a disinterested intention to do our duty whatever

* See note to page 185 of this volume.

be the consequences, but from a sincere wish to get off patent and proximate suffering. The difficulty of reconciling a true morality with a true religion is not confined to that part of religion which relates to the anticipated life of man hereafter, but extends to the very idea of a superintending Providence and preadjusting Creator, in whatever mode we conceive that superintendence to be exercised and that adjustment to have been made,

The answer most commonly given to this difficulty is unquestionably fallacious. It is said that the desire of eternal life for ourselves is a motive far greater and far better than the desire of anything else, either for ourselves or for others; it is not conceived as a form of selfishness at all,—at least, not when regarded in this connection and employed to solve this problem. At other times, indeed, divines are ready enough to twist the argument the other way: they will expand at length the notion that there is a "common-sense" in the gospel; that it appeals to "business-like motives"; that there is nothing "high-flown" about it; that it aims to persuade sensible men of this world, on sufficient reasons of sound prudence, to sacrifice the present world in order to gain the invisible one; that whatever sentimentalists may assert, it is reward which incites to achievement and fear that restrains from misdoing. Sermons are written in consecrated paragraphs, each of which is sufficient to itself, and the connection between which is not intended to be precisely adjusted; each has an edifying tendency, and the writer and the hearer wish for no more: otherwise it would not be possible, as it often is, to hear religion commended in the same discourse at one time as self-sacrificing, and at another as prudential; to have a eulogium on disinterestedness in the exordium, and an appeal to selfishness at the conclusion. A mode of composition which less disguised the true ideas of the composer would show that many divines really believe a desire for a long pleasure in heaven to be not only more long-sighted and sensible, but intrinsically higher, nobler, and better than a desire for a short happiness on earth; yet when stated in short sentences and plain English, the idea is palpably absurd, — the "wish to come into a good thing" is of the same ethical order whether the good thing be celestial or be terrestrial, be distantly future or be close at hand.

A second mode of solving the difficulty, though more ingenious and in every way far better, is erroneous also. It is said, "Men generally act from mixed motives, and they do so in this case. They are partly disinterested and partly not disinterested. They are desirous of doing good because it is good, and they are desirous also of having the reward of goodness hereafter. They wish at the very same time to benefit their neighbor in this world and also to benefit themselves in the world to come." The reply is ingenious, but it overlooks the point of the difficulty; it mistakes the nature of mixed motives. The constitution of man is such that if you strengthen one of two co-operating motives, you weaken, other things being equal, the force of the other: the lesser impulse tends always to be absorbed in the stronger, and it may pass entirely out of thought if the stronger is strengthened, if the greater become more prominent. We see this in common life. It is undoubtedly possible for a statesman to act at the same moment both from the love of office and from the love of his country, from a wish to prolong his power and a wish to benefit his nation: but strengthen one of these motives, and *cœteris paribus* you weaken the other; make the statesman love office more, you thereby make him love his country less, — he will be readier to sacrifice what he will call "a vague theory and an impracticable purpose" for the sake of the power which he loves, he will cease to care to do what he ought from a wish to retain the capacity of doing something. Or suppose a further case. There have been many times and countries where the loss of office was equivalent to the loss of liberty, perhaps to that of life. In one age of English history, one great historian says, "There was but a single step from the throne to the scaffold;"* in another age, another great historian says, "It was . . . as safe to be a highway-man as to be a distinguished leader of Opposition." † The possessors of power in those times, upon principle, destroyed or endeavored to destroy their predecessors. Such a prospect would induce a statesman to love office for its own sake; it would absorb the whole of his attention; he could hardly be asked to think of his country. Extraordinary men would do so, but ordinary men would be overwhelmed by the "violent motive" of personal fear; they would only be think-ing of themselves even when they were doing what in truth and fact was beneficial to their country. The case is similar to the "violent motive," as Paley calls it,‡ of religion, when presented in the same manner in which Paley presents it. If you could extend before men the awful vision of everlasting perdition; if they could see it as they see the things of earth, — as they see Fleet Street and St. Paul's; if you could show men likewise the inciting vision of an everlasting heaven, if they could see that too with undeniable certainty and invincible distinctness, — who could say that they would have a thought for any other mo-tive? The personal incentive to good action and the personal dissuasion from bad action would absorb all other considerations, whether deterrent or persuasive; we could no more break a divine law than we could commit a murder in the open street. The fact that men act from mixed motives is no explanation of the great difficulty with which we started; for the precise peculiarity of that difficulty is to raise one of those mixed motives to an intensity which seems likely to absorb, extinguish, and annihilate the other.

* Undiscoverable.
† Macaulay, Essay on Mackintosh's History.
‡ "Moral Philosophy," Book ii., Chaps. ii., iii.

The true explanation is precisely the reverse. The moral part of religion — the belief in a moral state hereafter, dependent for its nature on our goodness or our wickedness, the belief in a moral Providence who apportions good to good and evil to evil — does not annihilate the sense of the inherent nature of good and evil, because it is itself the result of that sense. Our only ground for accepting an ethical and retributive religion is the inward consciousness that virtue being virtue must prosper, that vice being vice must fail. From these axioms we infer, not logically but practically, that there is a continuous eternity in which what we expect will be seen, that there is a Providence who will apportion what is good and punish what is evil. Of the mode in which we do so we will speak presently more at length; but granting that this description of our religion is true, it undeniably solves our difficulty : our religion cannot by possibility swallow up morality, because it is dependent for its origin, for its continuance, on that morality.

Suppose a person, say in a prison, to have no knowledge by the senses that there was such a thing as human law; suppose that he never saw either the judicial or the executive authorities, and that no one ever told him of their existence; suppose that by a consciousness of the inherent nature of good and evil, the fact that such an institution *must* exist should dawn upon his mind, — of course it would not, but imagine that it should, — it is absurd to suppose that he would feel his power of doing what is right *because* it is right diminished. When he goes out into the world, when he hears his judge, when he sees the policeman, when he surveys the intrusive, the incessant, the pervading moral apparatus of human society, — *then* he would be unable* to disregard and to forget what is due to intrinsic goodness and what is to be feared from intrinsic evil. No one will or can say that he now abstains from stealing oranges under a

---

* An evident misprint for "able." — ED.

policeman's eyes from any motive, good or bad, save
fear of the policeman,—that motive is so evident, so
pressing, so irresistible, that it becomes the only motive;—but if he only thought the policeman *must* exist
because he believed stealing oranges to be wrong, he
would feel it quite possible to abstain from stealing
oranges out of pure and unselfish considerations. Assume that a person only knows a particular fact from
a certain informant, and suppose that on a sudden he
doubts that informant,—of course his confidence in
the communicated fact ceases or is diminished; so,
if all our knowledge of the religious part of morality
be derived from the intrinsic impression of morality,
as soon as we question the accuracy of the informant,
that instant we must be dubious of the information.
The derivative cannot be stronger than the original;
cannot overpower it; must grow when it grows, and
wane when it wanes.

But is our knowledge of the moral part of religion thus derivative and dependent? Two classes of
disputants will deny it entirely: one class will say
they derived* their knowledge from natural theology,
another will say they derive it from revelation; and
until the arguments of both classes are examined, the
subject must remain in partial darkness. Natural
theology is the simplest of theologies; it contains only
a single argument, and establishes but one conclusion.
Observing persons have gone to and fro through the
earth, and they have accumulated a million illustrations of a single analogy; they have accumulated
indications of design from all parts of the universe.
They have not, indeed, shown that *matter* was created:
the substance of matter, if there be a substance, shows
no structure, no evidence of design; according to all
common belief, according to the admission of such
scientific men as admit its existence, that matter is
unorganized. By its nature it is a raw material; it
is that to which manufacture, manipulation, design—

---

* The final "d" is an improper addition in the reprint. — ED.

call it what you like — is to be applied: necessarily therefore it shows no indication of design itself. The reasoners from the workmanship of man to that of God must always fail in this: man only adapts what he finds, God creates what he uses. But within its legitimate limits the argument from design has been most effectual for two thousand years. On a certain class of purely intellectual minds, who think more than they live, who reason more than they imagine, it has produced the strongest and most vivid conception of God which, with their experience and their mental limitation, they are capable of receiving. It has shown that *out of the causes we know*, none is so likely to have worked up the substance of matter into its present form as a designing and powerful mind; *subject to this assumption*, it shows that this mind intended to erect that mixed, composite, involved human society which we see. These theologians prove, for example, that man has a structure of body which enables him to be what he is, which prevents his being in appearance and in most real particularities different from what he is. They show that the physical world is constructed so as to enable man to be what he is and to show what he is; so as to limit his power of being greatly different or of seeming so. They show in fact that — if the expression be allowed — we live, as far as *they* can tell us, in a factory, the builder of which projected certain results, contrived certain large plans, devised certain particular machines, foresaw certain functions, which he meant for us, which he made our interest, which he gave us wages to perform. They show — not indeed that an omnipotent Being created the universe, but — that an able Being has been (so to say) about it. They do not demonstrate that an infinite Being created all things; but they *do* show, and show so that the mass of ordinary men will comprehend and believe it, that a large mind has been concerned in manufacturing most things.

But these results do not constitute the interior essence — scarcely indeed begin the exterior outwork — of a substantial religion; they touch neither that part of it which moves men's hearts nor that part which occasions our primary difficulty. They do not show us an eternal state of man hereafter, in which the anomalies of this world may be rectified and recompensed; they do not show us an infinite Perfection, distributing just reward with an omniscient accuracy according to a perfect law. It is not indeed to be expected that natural philosophy should prove the immortality of man, since it does not prove the immortality of God. It shows that an artful and able Designer has been concerned in the construction of the strange existing world; but may it not have been the last work of the great artist? There is nothing in contriving skill to evince immortality; nothing to prove that the "great Artificer" has always been or is always going to be. Of his moral views we collect from natural theology as much as this: there are certain laws of the physical universe which cannot be broken without pain, which avenge themselves on those who overlook, neglect, or violate them. These were presumedly designed (according to the moral assumption of natural theology) for the end which they effect; they were doubtless meant to accomplish that which they conspicuously do. On a disregard of such laws, natural theology shows that the Providence of which it speaks has imposed a penalty: the *contriving* God (so to speak, for it is necessary to speak plainly) is opposed to recklessness; he does not wish his devices to be impaired or his plans neglected. Every animal has in natural theology, if not a mission, at least a function. There are certain results which a polyp must produce or die; certain others which a horse must effect, or it will be first in pain and then die too; certain other and more complex results which man must produce, or he also will suffer and perish. But recklessness is only a single form of vice; a

watchful, heedful selfishness is another form. For
the latter, there is no indication in natural theology
of any Divine disapprobation or of any impending
penalty. A heedful being contriving for himself, living in the framework of, adjusting himself with nice
discernment and careful discretion to, the laws of the
visible world, incurs no censure from the theology of
design; on the contrary, he could justly say he had
done what was required of him. He had studiously
observed, he could say, the rules of the factory in
which he lived; he had finished his own work, he
had not hindered any others from accomplishing
theirs; he had complied with the arrangements of the
establishment: natural theology seems to require no
more. Self-absorbed foresight and contriving discretion may not be great virtues according to a high
morality or according to a true religion, but they are
profitable in the visible world; they are the virtues
of men skillful in what they see. Accordingly, they
suit a theology which is exclusively based upon an
analysis of the visible world, which computes physical
profits and sensible results, which aims to show that
Providence is prudent, that God is wise in his generation.

Natural theology, therefore, contains nothing to disturb the explanation we have given of our original
difficulty; the most cursory examination of it would
show as much. We have only to open the well-known
volumes in which the munificence of a former generation has embalmed the most striking arguments of
a theology which that generation valued at more than
it is worth. We find there pictures of a bat's wing,
of the human hand, of a calf's eye; and we are told
how ingenious, how clever — so to say, for it is the
true word — these contrivances are. But no one could
learn or expect to learn from a calf's eye that the
Creator is pure, just, merciful; that he is eternal or
omnipotent; that he rewards good and punishes evil.
Throughout all the physical world he sends rain upon

the just and the unjust, and no refined analysis of
that world will detect in it a preference of the former
to the latter. As it is with the moral holiness of God,
so it is with the immortality of man : no one could
expect to discover by a minute inspection of the perishable body what was the fate of the imperceptible
soul. Physical science may examine the structure of
the brain, but it cannot foresee the fortunes of the
mind.

What, then, of revelation ? does this informant
disturb the solution of our problem? The change
from the world of natural theology to that of any
revelation is most striking. The most impressive
characteristic of natural theology is its bareness : it
accumulates facts and proves little; it has voluminous evidences and a short creed. Accordingly, the
reason why it does not disturb our philosophy is that
its communications are insufficient. It does not impart to us *such* a knowledge of a Divine rewarder and
punisher, of future human punishment and future
human reward, as would render it impossible to be
disinterested and hardly possible not to be foreseeing
and selfish, because it communicates *no* knowledge on
the subject. It does not teach the Divine characteristic which involves the difficulty; it does not tell,
either, that part of man's future fate which involves
it likewise. With revelation it is far otherwise : that
informant is precise, full, and clear. It tells us plainly
what God is; it warns us what may happen and
easily happen to ourselves. We learn from it that
God is the divine ruler; we learn from it that we
are punishable creatures, whose fate depends on ourselves. The observations which have been justly
made on natural theology are here entirely inapplicable : we have passed from a *vacuum* into a *plenum*.

The real reason why revealed religion does not
invalidate our pre-existing moral nature is because it
is itself dependent on that nature. When we examine the evidence for revelation, we alight at once on

a great and fundamental postulate: we assume that God is veracious. We are so familiar with this great truth that we hardly think of it save as an axiom; both the readers of the treatises on the evidences and the writers of them pass rapidly and easily over it. But putting aside for a moment the evidence of our inner consciousness, and regarding the subject with the pure intellect and bare eyes, the assumption is an audacious one: how do we know that it is true? We have proved by natural theology that a designing Being, of great power, considerable age, ingenious habits, and benevolent motives, somewhere exists; but how do we know that Being to be "veracious"? We see that among human beings — the class of intellectual beings of whom we know most and whom we can observe best — veracity is a rare virtue; we know that some nations seem wholly destitute of it, and that one sex in all countries is deficient in it. We know that a human being may have great power, and not tell the truth; ingenious habits, and not tell the truth; kind intentions, and not tell the truth: why may not a superhuman Being be constituted in the same way, possess a character similarly mixed, be remarkable not only for morals similar to man's but also for defects analogous to his? Our inner nature revolts at the supposition; but we are not now concerned with our inner nature, — we have, for the sake of distinctness, abstracted and left it on one side. We are dealing now not with the evidence of the heart, but with the evidence of the eyes; we are discussing not what really is, but what would seem to be — what is all we could know to be — if we had only five senses and a reasoning understanding. From these informants, how could we know enough of the ingenious unknown Being, who is so useful in the world, as to be confident he would tell us the truth in every case? How could we presume to guess his unexperienced speech, his latent motives, his imperceptible character? Our knowledge of the moral part of the Divine character—

of his veracity as well as of his justice — comes from
our own moral nature. We feel that God is holy,
just as we feel that holiness *is* holiness; just as we
know by internal consciousness that goodness is good
in itself and by itself; just as we know that God
in himself is pure and holy. We feel that God is
true, for veracity is a part of holiness and a condition of purity; but if we did not think holiness to
be excellent in itself, if we did not feel it to be a
motive unaffected by consequences and independent
of calculation, our belief in the Divine holiness would
fade away, and with it would fade our belief in the
Divine veracity also.

Revelation, therefore, cannot undermine the very
principle upon which it is itself dependent. Our
notion of the character of God, being revealed to us
by our moral nature, cannot impair or weaken the
conclusion of that nature. This is the meaning of
the profound saying of Coleridge, that *all* religion
is revealed;* he meant that all knowledge of God's
character which is worth naming or regarding, which
excites any portion of the religious sentiment, which
excites our love, our awe, or our fear, is communicated to us by our internal nature, by that spirit
within us which is open to a higher world, by that
spirit which is in some sense God's Spirit. True religion of this sort does not impair the moral spirit
which revealed it; it does not dare do so, for it knows
that spirit to be its only evidence.

But all religion is not true. A superstitious mind
permits a certain aspect of God's character, say its
justice, to obtain an exclusive hold on it, to tyrannize
over it, to absorb it; the soul becomes bound down
by the weight of its own revelation; conscience is
overshadowed, weakened, and almost destroyed by the
very idea which it originally suggested, and of which
it is really the only reliable informant. Such minds
are incapable of true virtue: the essential opposition

* "Aids to Reflection," sub-head "Aphorisms on that which is indeed
Spiritual Religion," comment on Aphorism vii.

which is alleged to exist between morality and *all* religion does exist between morality and *their* religion; they have a selfish fear of the future, which destroys their disinterestedness and almost destroys their manhood.

The same effect is undeniably produced on many minds — not necessarily produced, but in fact produced — by a belief in revelation: they are fearful of future punishment, because some Being in the air has threatened it. They have not the true belief in the Divine holiness which arises from a love of holiness; they have not the true conception of God which was suggested by conscience and is kept alive by the activity of conscience: but they have a vague persuasion that a great Personage has asserted this, and why they should believe that Personage they do not ask or know. While revelation remains connected in the mind with the spirituality on which it is based, it is as consistent with true morality as religion of any other sort; but if disconnected from that spirituality, if it has become an isolated terrific tenet like any other superstition, it is inconsistent.

The original difficulty with which we started, and the true answer to that difficulty, may be summed up thus: — The objection is, that the extrinsic motive to goodness (which religion reveals) must absorb the intrinsic motives to goodness (which morality reveals): the answer is, that the second revelation is contingent upon the first; that those only have a substantial ground for believing the extrinsic motive who retain a lively confidence in the intrinsic. Perhaps some may think this principle too plain; perhaps others may think it too unimportant to justify so long an exposition and such a strenuous inculcation. But if we dwell upon it, and trace it to its attendant results and consequences, we shall find that it will account for more of the world than almost any other single principle; at any rate, will explain much which puzzles us and much which is important to us.

First, this principle will explain to us the use and
the necessity of what we may call the *screen* of the
physical world. Every one who has religious ideas
must have been puzzled by what we may call the
irrelevancy of creation to his religion. We find ourselves lodged in a vast theater, in which a ceaseless
action, a perpetual shifting of scenes, an unresting
life, is going forward; and that life seems physical,
unmoral, having no relation to what our souls tell
us to be great and good, to what religion says is the
design of all things. Especially when we see any
new objects or scenes or countries, we feel this.
Look at a great tropical plant, with large leaves
stretching everywhere, and great stalks branching
out on all sides; with a big beetle on a leaf, and a
humming-bird on a branch, and an ugly lizard just
below : what has such an object to do with *us*,—with
anything we can conceive or hope or imagine? what
could it be created for, if creation has a moral end
and object? Or go into a gravel pit or stone quarry :
you see there a vast accumulation of dull matter,
yellow or gray, and you ask, involuntarily and of
necessity, Why is all this waste and irrelevant production, as it would seem, of material? can anything
seem more stupid than a big stone *as* a big stone,
than gravel for gravel's sake? what is the use of
such cumbrous, inexpressive objects, in a world where
there are minds to be filled and imaginations to be
aroused and souls to be saved? A clever skeptic once
said on reading Paley that *he* thought the universe
was a furniture warehouse for unknown beings; he
assented to the indications of design visible in many
places, but what the end of most objects was, why
such things were, what was the ultimate object contemplated by the whole, he could not understand; he
thought, "Divines are right in saying that much of
the universe has an expression, but surely skeptics
are right in saying that as much or more has no
expression." Some of the world seems designed to

show a little of God; but much more seems also designed to hide him and keep him off. The reply is, that if morality is to be disinterested, some such irrelevant universe is essential. Life, moral life, the life of tempted beings capable of virtue and liable to vice, of necessity involves a theater of some sort : it could not be carried on in a vast vacuum; *some* means of communication between mind and mind, *some* external motive to question inward impulses, *some* outward events as the result of past action and the stimulus to new action, seem essential to the life of a voluntary moral being, to a being tempted as a man is, living as a man lives. The only admissible question is the nature of that theater : is it to be in all its parts and objects expressive of God's character and communicative of man's fate? or is it, as many say, in most parts to express nothing and tell nothing? The reply is, that *if* the universe were to be incessantly expressive and incessantly communicative, morality would be impossible : we should live under the unceasing pressure of a supernatural interference, which would give us selfish motives for doing everything, which would menace us with supernatural punishment if we left anything undone; we should be living in a *chastising* machine, of which the secret would be patent and the penalties apparent. We are startled to find a universe we did not expect : but if we lived in the universe we did expect, the life which we lead and were meant to lead would be impossible; we should expect a punitive world sanctioning moral laws, and the perpetual punishment of those laws would be so glaringly apparent that true virtue would become impossible. An "unfeeling nature,"* an unmoral universe, a sun that shines and a rain which falls equally on the evil and on the good, are essential to morality in a being free like man and created as man was. A miscellaneous world is a suitable theater for a single-minded life, and so far as we can see, the only one.

---

* Goethe, "The Godlike" (short poem).

The same sort of reasoning partly elucidates, even
if it does not explain, the brevity of our apparent
life. If visible life were eternal, future punishments
must be visible; we should meet in our streets with
old, old men enduring the consequences of offenses
which happened before we were born. We should
not see, perhaps, old age as we now see it; decrepi-
tude would be unknown to us. If there was immortal
life on earth, there would probably also be immortal
youth, at any rate immortal activity; the perpetuity
of existence would not be divided from the perpetuity
of what makes life desirable, of what makes effective
life possible. But if children saw their fathers, and
their fathers' fathers, and their fathers' ancestors, in
an unending chain, suffering penalties for certain
acts and obtaining rewards for certain deeds, how is
it possible that they could act otherwise than according to those visible and evident examples? The consecutive tradition of self-interest would be so strong. •
among a perpetual race of immortal men that disinterested virtue would be not so much impracticable
as unthought-of and unknown; the exact line of real
self-benefit would be chalked out so plainly, so conspicuously, so glaringly, that no other action would
be conceivable or possible; the evidence of *all* consequences would be like the evidences of legal consequences now, only infinitely more effective and
infinitely more perceptible. In human law, the *detec-
tion* of the offense by man is a prerequisite of all
punishment by man; an offense not proved to the
"satisfaction of the court" escapes the judgment of
the court: but in a visible immortal life, this prerequisite would not be needful. *If* there be a future
punishment, and *if* man lived for all futurity upon
earth, that future punishment would be on earth, and
it would be inflicted by God; undetected crime, that
general bad character without specific proved offense
which now mocks all law and laughs at visible punishment, would then under our very eyes receive that

punishment. Job's friends kindly argued with him, "You are suffering, therefore you are guilty"; and the argument was bad, because they only saw an exceptional accident in the life of a good man, not his entire life through a subsequent eternity: but if that eternal life had been passed in continuous residence on this globe, if notorious bad fortune had pursued him through eternity, in the nineteenth generation his descendants might well have said, "O Job, there is something wrong in you, for you never come out right." A great historian has observed:—

"That honesty is the best policy is a maxim which we firmly believe to be generally correct, even with respect to the temporal interest of individuals; but with respect to societies the rule is subject to still fewer exceptions, and that for this reason, that the life of societies is longer than the life of individuals. It is possible to mention men who have owed great worldly prosperity to breaches of private faith; but we doubt whether it be possible to mention a state which has, on the whole, been a gainer by a breach of public faith."*

If the visible life of individuals were yet longer than the life of societies, the rule would be subject to still fewer exceptions; if that visible life were eternal, the rule would be subject to no exceptions,—the staring evidence of conspicuous results would purge temptation out of the world.

The physical world now rewards what we may call the physical virtues, and punishes what we may call the physical vices. There is a certain state of the body which is a condition of physical well-being, and (as life is constituted) very much of all well-being; if by gross excess any man should impair that condition, physical law will punish him. The body is our schoolmaster to bring us to the soul; it enforces on us the preparatory merits, it scourges out of us the preparatory defects. The law of human government is similar: it enforces on us that adherence to obvious virtue, and that avoidance of obvious vice, which are

---

* Macaulay, Essay on Lord Clive.

316 THE TRAVELERS INS. CO.'S BAGEHOT.

the essential preliminaries of real virtue. There is no true virtue or vice, so long as physical law and human law are what they are in any such matters: the dread of the penalties is too powerful not to extinguish (speaking generally, and peculiar cases excepted) all other motives. But these teachers strengthen the mental instruments of real virtue; they strengthen our will, they hurt our vanity, they confirm our manhood. Physical law and human law train and build up, if the expression may be permitted, that good pagan, that sound-bodied, moderate, careful creature, out of which a good Christian may, if he will and by God's help, in the end be constructed. If visible life were eternal instead of temporary, the same intense discipline which so usefully creates the preparatory prerequisites would likewise efface the possibility of disinterested virtue.

Again, the great scene of human life may be explained, or at least illustrated, in like manner: *we are souls in the disguise of animals.* We lead a life in great part neither good nor evil, neither wicked nor excellent. The larger number of men seem to an outside observer to walk through life in a torpid sort of sleep. They are decent in their morals, respectable in their manners, stupid in their conversation; the incentives of their life are outward, its penalties are outward too. The life of such people seems to some men always — to many men at times — inexplicable; but if such beings were not permitted in the world, perhaps a higher life might be impossible for any beings. They act like a living screen, just as we say matter acts like a dead screen. It is not desirable that the results of goodness should be distinctly apparent; and if all human life were intensely and exclusively moral, if all men were with all their strength pursuing good or pursuing evil, the isolated consequences of that isolated principle must be apparent, — at least, could scarcely fail to be so. If one set of men were cooped up in the exclusive pursuit of virtue and were very ardent and warm about it, and another set of men were eager in the pursuit of evil and cared for nothing but evil, the world would fall asunder into two dissimilar halves. If goodness in the visible world had *any*—the least—tendency to produce visible happiness, then incessant goodness would be very happy; the accumulations of the slight tendency by perpetual renewal would amount of necessity to a vast sum-total; incessant badness would produce awful misery. Those absorbed in vice would be warnings dangerous to disinterestedness; those absorbed in virtue, attractions and examples almost more dangerous. The mischief is prevented by those *unabsorbed*, purposeless, divided characters which seem to puzzle us; they complicate human life, and they do so the more effectually that they typify and represent so much of what every man feels and must feel within himself. In each man there is so much which is unmoral; so much which comes from an unknown origin and passes forward to an unknown destination, which is "of the earth, earthy," which has nothing to do with hell or heaven, which occupies a middle place not recognized in any theology, which is hateful both to the impetuous "friends of God" and his most eager enemies! This pervading and potent element involves life, as it were, in confusion and hurry; we do not see distinctly whither we are going: disinterestedness is possible, for calculation is confused. Doubtless, even on earth, virtue of all kinds eventually must have, on a large average of cases, some slight tendency to produce happiness: this earth is an extract from the moral universe,— partakes its nature. But that tendency is too slight to be a considerable motive to high action; it would not be discovered but for the inward principle which sets us to look for it: and even when we find it, it is transient and small and dubious,—it is lost in the vast results of the unmoral universe, in the vague shows, the multiform spectacle of human life.

Again, we may understand why the convictions
of what duty is, and what religion is, vary so much
and so often among men. If all our convictions on
these points, on these infinitely important points,
were identical and alike, an accumulated public opinion would oppress us, would destroy the freedom of
our action and the purity of our virtue. If every one
said that certain penalties would be the consequence
of certain actions, we should believe that the consequences would be so and so, not because we felt
those actions to be intrinsically bad, but because we
were told that such would be the consequences; we
should believe upon report, and a vague impression
would haunt us, not produced by our own conscience
or our own sense of right and wrong, and would impair both our manhood and our virtue. The extraordinary discrepancies of believed religion and believed
morality have weighed on many and will weigh on
many; but they have this use, — they enable men to
be disinterested. As there is no sanctioned invincible
firm custom, there are no customary penalties, there
is nothing men must shun; as the world has not
made up its mind, there is no executioner of the
world ready to enforce that mind upon every one.

Lastly, the same essential argument may be applied to a problem yet more delicate and difficult, to
one which it is difficult to treat in reviewer's phraseology. Why is God so far from us? is the agonizing
question which has depressed so many hearts as long
as we knew there were hearts, has puzzled so many
intellects since intellects began to puzzle themselves.
But the moral part of God's character could not be
shown to us with sensible conspicuous evidence — it
could not be shown to us as Fleet Street is shown to
us — without impairing the first prerequisite of disinterestedness and the primary condition of man's
virtue; and if the moral aspect of God's character
must of necessity be somewhat hidden from us, other
aspects of it must be equally hidden. An infinite

Being may be viewed under innumerable aspects; God has many qualities in his essence which the word "moral" does not exhaust, which it does not even hint at. Perhaps this essay has seemed to read too sternly; as if the moral side of the Divine character, which is and must be to imperfect beings in some sense a terrible side, as' if the moral side of human life, which must be to mankind not always a pleasant side, had been forced into an exclusive prominence which of right did not belong to it. But the *attractive* aspects of God's character must not be made more apparent to such a being as man than his chastening· and severer aspects; we must not be invited to approach the Holy of Holies without being made aware, painfully aware, what holiness is; we must know our own unworthiness ere we are fit to approach or imagine an infinite Perfection. The most nauseous of false religions is that which affects a fulsome fondness for a Being not to be thought of without awe or spoken of without reluctance.

On the whole, therefore, the necessary ignorance of man explains to us much: it shows us that we could not be what we ought to be if we lived in the sort of universe we should expect; it shows us that a latent Providence, a confused life, an odd material world, an existence broken short in the midst and on a sudden, are not real difficulties, but real helps,— that they or something like them are essential conditions of a moral life to a subordinate being. If we steadily remember that we only know the ultimate fate — the extrinsic consequences — of vice and virtue because we know of their inherent nature and intrinsic qualities, and that any other evidence of the first would destroy the possibility of the second, *then* much which used to puzzle us may become clear to us.

But it may be said, What sort of evidence is this on which you base the future moral life of man and the present existence of a moral Providence? is it not impalpable? It is so, and necessarily so. If a consecutive logical deduction, such as has often been sought between an immutable morality and a true religion, could in fact be found, we should be again met with our fundamental difficulty, though in a disguised and secondary form: morality might fall out of sight because religion was obtruded upon us. Morality would be the axiom, religion the deduction; and as a geometer does not keep Euclid's axioms in his head when he is employed upon conic sections, as a student of the differential calculus may half forget the commencement of algebra, — so the great truths of religion, if rigorously and mathematically deduced from the beginnings of morality, might overshadow and destroy those "beggarly elements." No one who has proved important doctrines by rigorous reasoning always retains in his mind the primitive principles from which he set out; as the concrete deductions advance, the primary abstractions recede. Happily, the connection between morality and religion is of a very different kind: religion (in its moral part) is a secondary impression, produced and kept alive by the first impression of morality; the intensity of the second feeling depends on the continued intensity of the first feeling.

The highest part of human belief is based upon certain developable instincts; not the most important but the most obvious of these is the instinct of beauty. Since the commencement of speculation, ingenious thinkers, who delight in difficulties, have rejoiced to draw out at length the difficulties of the subject. It is said, How can you be certain that there is such an attribute as beauty, when no one is sure what it is or to what it should be applied? A barbarian thinks one thing charming, the Greek another. Modern nations have a standard different most materially from the ancient standard; founded upon it in several important respects, no doubt, but differing from it in others as important and almost

equally striking. Even within the limits of modern
nations this standard differs: the taste of the vulgar
is one thing, the taste of the refined and cultivated
is altogether at variance with it. The mass of mankind prefer a gaudy modern daub to a faded picture
by Sir Joshua, or to the cartoons of Raphael. What
certainty, the skeptic triumphantly asks, can there be
in matters on which people differ so much, on which
it seems so impossible to argue; which seem to depend on causes and relations simply personal; which
are susceptible of no positive test or ascertained criterion? You talk of impalpability, he adds: here it
is in perfection. But these recondite doubts impose
on no one. Not a single educated person would sleep
less soundly if he were told that his life depended
on the correctness of his notion that the cartoons of
Raphael are more sublime and beautiful than a common daub. He cannot prove it, and he cannot prove
that Charles I. was beheaded; but he is quite as certain of one as of the other. This is an instance of an
obvious, unmistakable instinct, which does produce
effectual belief, though skeptics explain to us that it
should not.

The nature of this instinct differs altogether from
that of those intuitive and universal axioms which
are borne in infallibly upon all the human race, in
every age and every place. It is not like the assertion that "two straight lines cannot inclose a space,"
or the truth that two and two make four: these are
believed by every one, and no one can dream of not
believing them; but half of mankind would reject the
idea that the cartoons were in any sense admirable, —
they would prefer the overgrown enormities of West,
which are side by side with them. The characteristic
peculiarity of this instinct is, not that it is irresistible, but that it is *developable*. The higher students
of the subject, the more cultivated, meditate upon it,
acquire a new sense, which conveys truth to them,
though others are ignorant of it and though they

themselves cannot impart it to those others. The appeal is not to the many, as with axioms of Euclid, but to those few — the exceptional few — at whom the many scoff.

The case is similar with the yet higher instincts of morality and of religion. It is idle to pretend that much of them can be found among bloody savages, or simple and remote islanders, or a degraded populace; it is still idler to fancy that because they cannot be discovered there full-grown and complete and paramount, there is no evidence for them and no basis for relying upon them. They resemble the instinct of beauty precisely: the evidence of the few — of the small, high-minded minority, who are the exception of ages and the salt of the earth — outweighs the evidence of countless myriads who live as their fathers lived, think as they thought, die as they died; who would have lived and died in the very contrary impressions, if by chance they had inherited these instead of the others. The criterion of true beauty is with those (and they are not many) who have a sense of true beauty; the criterion of true morality is with those who have a sense of true morality; the criterion of true religion is with those who have a sense of true religion.

Nor can this defect of an absolute criterion throw the world into confusion; we see it does not, and there was no reason to expect it would. We all of us feel an analogous fluctuation and variation in ourselves: we all of us feel that there are times in which first principles seem borne in upon us by evidence as bright as noonday, and that there are also times in which that evidence is much less, in which it seems to fade away, in which we reckon up the number of persons who differ from us, who reject our principles; times at which we ask, Who are *we*, that we should be right and other men wrong? The unbelieving moods of each mind are as certain as the unbelieving state of much of the world; but no sound mind permits itself to be permanently disturbed, though it may be transiently distracted, by these variations in its own state. We have a *criterion* faculty within us, which tells us which are lower moods and which are higher. This faculty is a phase of conscience; and if at its bidding we struggle *with* the good moods and *against* the bad moods, we shall find that great beliefs remain and that mean beliefs pass away.

There is an analogous phenomenon in the history of the world. Beliefs altogether differ at the base of society, but they agree or tend to agree at its summit. As society goes on, the standard of beauty, and of morality, and of religion also, tends to become fixed. The creeds of the higher classes throughout the world, though far from identical in these respects, are not entirely unlike, approach to similarity, approach to it more and more as cultivation augments, goodness improves, and disturbing agencies fall aside.

> "The Ethiop gods have Ethiop lips,
>   Bronze cheeks, and wooly hair;
> The Grecian gods are like the Greeks,
>   As keen-eyed, cold, and fair."*

Such is the various and miscellaneous religion of barbarism; but the religion and the morality of all the best among all nations tend more and more to be the same with "the progress of the suns," and as society itself improves.

The instincts of morality and religion, though we have called them two for facility of speech, run into one another, and in practical human nature are not easily separated. The distinction, like so many others in mental philosophy, is not drawn where accurate science would have directed, but where the first notions of mankind, and the necessity of easy speaking in a language shaped according to those notions, have suggested. In a refined analysis, the instinct of

---

* Undiscoverable; I suspect Bagehot's own. — ED.

religion, as we have called it, is a complex aggregate
of various instincts, not a single and homogeneous
one; but to analyze these, or even to name them,
would be far from our purpose now, — our business is
with the relation between the instinct of morality and
that of religion, and with no other perplexities or
difficulties. The instinct of morality is the basis, and
the instinct of moral religion is based upon it and
arises out of it. We feel first the intrinsic qualities
of good actions and bad actions; then, as the Greek
proverb expressed it, "Where there is shame there is
fear,"— we expect consequences apportioned to our
actions, good and evil; lastly, — for within the limits
of purely moral ideas there is no higher stage, — we
rise to the conception of Him who in his wisdom ad-
justs and allots those far-off consequences to those
conspicuous actions. The higher instinct is based on
the lower, would fade in the mind should the lower
fade. The coalescence of instinct effects what no
other contrivance known to us could effect, — it enables us to be disinterested although we know the
consequences of evil actions; because conscience is
the revealing sensation, and we only know those
consequences so long as we are disinterested.

These fundamental difficulties of life and morals
are little discussed. Few think of them clearly, and
still fewer speak of them much; but they cloud the
brain and confuse the hopes of many who never
stated them explicitly to themselves and never heard
them stated explicitly by others. Meanwhile, superficial difficulties are in every one's mouth; we are
deafened with controversies on remote matters which
do not concern us; we are confused with "Aids to
Faith" which neither harm nor help us. A tumult
of irrelevant theology is in the air, which oppresses
men's heads and darkens their future and scatters
their hopes. For such a calamity there is no thorough cure: it belongs to the confused epoch of an
age of transition, and is inseparable from it. But the

best palliative is a steady attention to primary difficulties : if possible, a clear mastery over them; if
not, a distinct knowledge how we stand respecting
them. The shrewdest man of the world who ever
lived tells us that "If we begin with certainties we
shall end in doubts; but if we begin with doubts
. . . we shall end in certainties :"* and the maxim
is even more applicable to matters which are not of
this world than to those which are.

---

* Bacon, "Advancement of Learning," Book i. (page 52, Bohn).

ON THE EMOTION OF CONVICTION.

(1871.)

WHAT we commonly term "belief" includes, I apprehend, both an intellectual and an emotional element; the first we more properly call "assent," and the second "conviction." The laws of the intellectual element in belief are "the laws of evidence," and have been elaborately discussed; but those of the emotional part have hardly been discussed at all, — indeed, its existence has been scarcely perceived.

In the mind of a rigorously trained inquirer, the process of believing is, I apprehend, this : — First comes the investigation, — a set of facts are sifted and a set of arguments weighed; then the intellect perceives the result of those arguments, and we say assents to it; then an emotion more or less strong sets in, which completes the whole. In calm and quiet minds, the intellectual part of this process is so much the strongest that they are hardly conscious of anything else; and as these quiet, careful people have written our treatises, we do not find it explained in them how important the emotional part is.

But take the case of the Caliph Omar, according to Gibbon's description of him : he burnt the Alexandrine Library, saying, "All books which contain what is not in the Koran are dangerous; all those which contain what is in the Koran are useless."* Probably no one ever had an intenser belief in anything than Omar had in this; yet it is impossible to

---

* "Decline and Fall," Chap. li. It is scarcely necessary to remind readers that this is *not* "according to Gibbon's description," as he discredits the story; and that Omar pretty certainly did nothing of the sort. A Christian bishop did burn the library from theological rancor two hundred and fifty years before, and Julius Cæsar by accident four centuries earlier still. — ED.

(326)

imagine it preceded by an argument. His belief in Mahomet, in the Koran, and in the sufficiency of the Koran, came to him probably in spontaneous rushes of emotion; there may have been little vestiges of argument floating here and there, but they did not justify the strength of the emotion, still less did they create it, and they hardly even excused it.

There is so commonly some considerable argument for our modern beliefs that it is difficult nowadays to isolate the emotional element; and therefore, on the principle that in metaphysics "egotism is the truest modesty," I may give myself as an example of utterly irrational conviction. Some years ago I stood for a borough in the West of England, and after a keen contest was defeated by seven. Almost directly afterwards there was accidentally another election; and as I would not stand, another candidate of my own side was elected, and I of course ceased to have any hold upon the place or chance of being elected there. But for years I had the deepest conviction that I should be "Member for Bridgewater"; and no amount of reasoning would get it out of my head. The borough is now disfranchised; but even still, if I allow my mind to dwell on the contest, — if I think of the hours I was ahead in the morning, and the rush of votes at two o'clock by which I was defeated, and even more if I call up the image of the nomination day, with all the people's hands outstretched,. and all their excited faces looking the more different on account of their identity in posture, — the old feeling almost comes back upon me, and for a moment I believe that I shall be "Member for Bridgewater."

I should not mention such nonsense, except on an occasion when I may serve as an intellectual "specimen";* but I know I wish that I could feel the same hearty, vivid faith in many conclusions of which my understanding says it is satisfied, that I

---

* It should be stated that this essay was originally read as a paper before a society which discusses subjects of a metaphysical nature. — B.

did in this absurdity. And if it should be replied that such folly could be no real belief, for it could not influence any man's action, I am afraid I must say that it did influence my actions: for a long time the ineradicable fatalistic feeling that I should some time have this constituency, of which I had no chance, hung about my mind, and diminished my interest in other constituencies, where my chances of election would have been rational at any rate.

This case probably exhibits the maximum of conviction with the minimum of argument; but there are many approximations to it. Persons of untrained minds cannot long live without some belief in any topic which comes much before them. It has been said that if you can only get a middle-class Englishman to think whether there are "snails in Sirius," he will soon have an opinion on it; it will be difficult to make him think, but if he does think he cannot rest in a negative, — he will come to some decision. And on any ordinary topic, of course it is so: a grocer has a full creed as to foreign policy, a young lady a complete theory of the sacraments, as to which neither has any doubt whatever. But in talking to such persons, I cannot but remember my Bridgewater experience, and ask whether causes like those which begat my folly may not be at the bottom of their "invincible knowledge."

Most persons who observe their own thoughts must have been conscious of the exactly opposite state: there are cases where our intellect has gone through the arguments, and we give a clear assent to the conclusions, but our minds seem dry and unsatisfied. In that case we have the intellectual part of belief, but want the emotional part.

That belief is not a purely intellectual matter is evident from dreams, where we are always believing but scarcely ever arguing; and from certain forms of insanity, where fixed delusions seize upon the mind and generate a firmer belief than any sane person is capable of. These are of course "unorthodox" states of mind ; but a good psychology must explain them, nevertheless, and perhaps it would have progressed faster if it had been more ready to compare them with the waking states of sane people.

Probably, when the subject is thoroughly examined, "conviction" will be proved to be one of the intensest of human emotions, and one most closely connected with the bodily state. In cases like the Caliph Omar's, it governs all other desires, absorbs the whole nature, and rules the whole life. And in such cases it is accompanied or preceded by the sensation that Scott makes his seer describe as the prelude to a prophecy : —

> " 'At length the fatal answer came,
> In characters of living flame, —
> Not spoke in word nor blazed in scroll,
> But borne and branded on my soul.' "*

A hot flash seems to burn across the brain. Men in these intense states of mind have altered all history, changed for better or worse the creed of myriads, and desolated or redeemed provinces and ages. Nor is this intensity a sign of truth, for it is precisely strongest in those points in which men differ most from each other. John Knox felt it in his anti-Catholicism, Ignatius Loyola in his anti-Protestantism ; and both, I suppose, felt it as much as it is possible to feel it.

Once acutely felt, I believe it is indelible; at least it does something to the mind which it is hard for anything else to undo. It has been often said that a man who has once really loved a woman never can be without feeling towards that woman again : he may go on loving her, or he may change and hate her. In the same way, I think, experience proves that no one who has had real passionate conviction of a creed, the sort of emotion that burns hot upon the brain, can ever be indifferent to that creed again.

---

* " Lady of the Lake," Canto iv.

He may continue to believe it and to love it ; or he
may change to the opposite, vehemently argue against
it and persecute it : but he cannot forget it. Years
afterwards, perhaps, when life changes, when external
interests cease to excite, when the apathy to surround-
ings which belongs to the old begins, — all at once,
to the wonder of later friends, who cannot imagine
what is come to him, the gray-headed man returns
to the creed of his youth.

The explanation of these facts in metaphysical
books is very imperfect ; indeed, I only know one
school which professes to explain the emotion[al] as
distinguished from the intellectual element in belief.
Mr. Mill (after Mr. Bain)* speaks very instructively
of the animal nature of belief ; but when he comes
to trace its cause, his analysis seems, to me at least,
utterly unsatisfactory. He says that "the state of
belief is identical with the activity or active disposition of the system at the moment with reference to
the thing believed ;" but in many cases there is firm
belief where there is no possibility of action or tendency to it. A girl in a country parsonage will be sure
that "Paris never can be taken," or that "Bismarck
is a wretch," without being able to act on these ideas
or wanting to act on them. Many beliefs, in Coleridge's happy phrase, slumber in the "dormitory of
the mind"† ; they are present to the consciousness, but
they incite to no action. And perhaps Coleridge is
an example of misformed mind, in which not only
may "faith" not produce "works," but in which it
had a tendency to prevent works : strong convictions
gave him a kind of cramp in the will, and he could
not act on them. And in very many persons, much-
indulged conviction exhausts the mind with the attached ideas ; teases it, and so, when the time of
action comes, makes it apt to turn to different (perhaps
opposite) ideas, and to act on them in preference.

---

* The two names should be transposed : the quotation is from Bain's
Note 107 on Chap. xi. of James Mill's "Analysis of the Human Mind."— ED.

† "Dormitory of the soul:" Aphorism 1 of "Aids to Reflection."

As far as I can perceive, the power of an idea to cause conviction, independently of any intellectual process, depends on four properties : —

1. *Clearness.* · The more unmistakable an idea is to a particular mind, the more is that mind predisposed to believe it. In common life we may constantly see this : if you once make a thing quite clear to a person, the chances are that you will almost have persuaded him of it. Half the world only understand what they believe, and always believe what they understand.

2. *Intensity.* This is the main cause why the ideas that flash on the minds of seers, as in Scott's description, are believed : they come mostly when the nerves are exhausted by fasting, watching, and longing ; they have a peculiar brilliancy, and therefore they are believed. To this cause I trace too my fixed folly as to Bridgewater : the idea of being member for the town had been so intensely brought home to me by the excitement of a contest that I could not eradicate it, and that as soon as I recalled any circumstances of the contest it always came back in all its vividness.

3. *Constancy.* As a rule, almost every one does accept the creed of the place in which he lives, and every one without exception has a tendency to do so. There are, it is true, some minds which a mathematician might describe as minds of "contrary flexure," whose particular bent it is to contradict what those around them say ; and the reason is, that in their minds the opposite aspect of every subject is always vividly presented. But even such minds usually accept the *axioms* of their district, the tenets which everybody always believes ; they only object to the variable elements, to the inferences and deductions drawn by some but not by all.

4. On the *Interestingness* of the idea ; by which I mean the power of the idea to gratify some wish or want of the mind. The most obvious is curiosity

about something which is important to me.* Rumors
that gratify this excite a sort of half-conviction without the least evidence, and with a very little evidence
a full, eager, not to say a bigoted one. If a person
go into a mixed company, and say authoritatively
that "the Cabinet is nearly divided on the Russian
question," and that "it was only decided by one vote
to send Lord Granville's dispatch," most of the company will attach some weight, more or less, to the
story, without asking how the secret was known; and
if the narrator casually add that he has just seen a
subordinate member of the Government, most of the
hearers will go away and repeat the anecdote with
grave attention, though it does not in the least appear
that the lesser functionary told the anecdote about
the Cabinet, or that he knew what passed at it.

And the interest is greater when the news falls
in with the bent of the hearer: a sanguine man will
believe with scarcely any evidence that good luck is
coming, and a dismal man that bad luck is coming.
As far as I can make out, the professional "bulls"
and "bears" of the City *do* believe a great deal of
what they say; though of course there are exceptions,
and though neither the most sanguine "bull" nor the
most dismal "bear" can believe *all* he says.

Of course I need not say that this "quality" peculiarly attaches to the greatest problems of human
life. The firmest convictions of the most inconsistent
answers to the everlasting questions "Whence?" and
"Whither?" have been generated by this "interestingness," without evidence on which one would invest a
penny.

In one case, these causes of irrational conviction
seem contradictory. Clearness, as we have seen, is one
of them; but obscurity, when obscure things are interesting, is a cause too. But there is no real difficulty
here: human nature at different times exhibits contrasted impulses. There is a passion for sensualism,—

---

* Doubtless a misprint for " one." — ED.

that is, to eat and drink; and a passion for asceticism, — that is, not to eat and drink: so it is quite likely that the clearness of an idea may sometimes cause a movement of conviction, and that the obscurity of another idea may at other times cause one too.

These laws, however, are complex: can they be reduced to any simpler law of human nature? I confess I think that they can, but at the same time I do not presume to speak with the same confidence about it that I have upon other points. Hitherto I have been dealing with the common facts of the adult human mind, as we may see it in others and feel it in ourselves; but I am now going to deal with the "prehistoric" period of the mind in early childhood, as to which there is necessarily much obscurity.

My theory is, that in the first instance a child believes everything. Some of its states of consciousness are perceptive or presentative, — that is, they tell it of some heat or cold, some resistance or non-resistance, then and there present; other states of consciousness are representative, — that is, they say that certain sensations could be felt or certain facts perceived, in time past or in time to come, or at some place, no matter at what time, then and there out of the reach of perception and sensation. In mature life, too, we have these presentative and representative states in every sort of mixture, but we make a distinction between them: without remark and without doubt we believe the "evidence of our senses," — that is, the facts of present sensation and perception; but we do not believe at once and instantaneously the representative states as to what is non-present, whether in time or space. But I apprehend that this is an acquired distinction, and that in early childhood every state of consciousness is believed, whether it be presentative or representative.

Certainly at the beginning of the "historic" period we catch the mind at a period of extreme credulity. When memory begins, and when speech and signs

suffice to make a child intelligible, belief is almost
omnipresent and doubt almost never to be found:
"childlike credulity" is a phrase of the highest antiquity and of the greatest present aptness.

So striking, indeed, on certain points, is this impulse to believe, that philosophers have invented various theories to explain in detail some of its marked
instances. Thus, it has been said that children have
an intuitive disposition to believe in "testimony,"—
that is, in the correctness of statements orally made
to them; and that they do so is certain. Every child
believes what the footman tells it, what its nurse tells
it, and what its mother tells it; and probably every
one's memory will carry him back to the horrid mass
of miscellaneous confusion which he acquired by believing all he heard. But though it is certain that
a child believes all assertions made to it, it is not
certain that the child so believes in consequence of
a special intuitive predisposition restricted to such
assertions; it may be that this indiscriminate belief
in all sayings is but a relic of an omnivorous acquiescence in all states of consciousness, which is only
just extinct when childhood is plain enough to be
understood or old enough to be remembered. Again,
it has been said much more plausibly that we want
an intuitive tendency to account for our belief in
memory; but I question whether it can be shown
that a little child *does* believe in its memories more
confidently than in its imaginations. A child of my
acquaintance corrected its mother, who said that
they should never see two of its dead brothers again,
and maintained, "Oh, yes, mamma, we shall: we
shall see them in heaven, and they will be so glad
to see us;" and then the child cried with disappoint-
ment because its mother, though a most religious lady,
did not seem exactly to feel that seeing her children
in that manner was as good as seeing them on earth.
Now, I doubt if that child did not believe this expectation quite as confidently as it believed any past

fact, or as it could believe anything at all; and though the conclusion may be true, plainly the child believed not from the efficacy of the external evidence, but from a strong rush of inward confidence. Why then should we want a special intuition to make children believe past facts, when in truth they go farther, and believe with no kind of difficulty future facts as well as past?

If on so abstruse a matter I might be allowed a graphic illustration, I should define doubt as "a hesitation produced by collision." A child possessed with the notion that all its fancies are true, finds that acting on one of them brings its head against the table; this gives it pain, and makes it hesitate as to the expediency of doing it again. Early childhood is an incessant education in skepticism, and early youth is so too; all boys are always knocking their heads against the physical world, and all young men are constantly knocking their heads against the social world: and both of them from the same cause, — that they are subject to an eruption of emotion which engenders a strong belief, but which is as likely to cause a belief in falsehood as in truth. Gradually, under the tuition of a painful experience, we come to learn that our strongest convictions may be quite false, that many of our most cherished ones are and have been false; and this causes us to seek a "criterion" as to which beliefs are to be trusted and which are not: and so we are beaten back to the laws of evidence for our guide, though, as Bishop Butler said in a similar case, we object to be bound by anything so "poor."*

That it is really this contention with the world which destroys conviction and which causes doubt, is shown by examining the cases where the mind is secluded from the world. In dreams, where we are out of collision with fact, we accept everything as it comes, believe everything and doubt nothing; and in

---

* "Analogy," Part ii., Chap. viii., fourth paragraph.

violent cases of mania, where the mind is shut up
within itself, and cannot from impotence perceive
what is without, it is as sure of the most chance
fancy as in health it would be of the best proved
truths.

And upon this theory we perceive why the four
tendencies to irrational conviction which I have set
down survive, and remain in our adult hesitating
state as vestiges of our primitive all-believing state.
They are all from various causes "adhesive" states:
states which it is very difficult to get rid of, and
which in consequence have retained their power of
creating belief in the mind, when other states which
once possessed it too have quite lost it. *Clear* ideas
are certainly more difficult to get rid of than obscure
ones; indeed, some obscure ones we cannot recover
if we once lose them. Everybody, perhaps, has felt
all manner of doubts and difficulties in mastering
a mathematical problem: at the time, the difficulties
seemed as real as the problem; but a day or two
after a man has mastered it, he will be wholly unable to imagine or remember where the difficulties
were. The demonstration will be perfectly clear to
him, and he will be unable to comprehend how any
one should fail to perceive it. For life he will recall
the clear ideas; but the obscure ones he will never recall, though for some hours, perhaps, they were painful,
confused, and oppressive obstructions. *Intense* ideas
are, as every one will admit, recalled more easily than
slight and weak ideas. *Constantly* impressed ideas
are brought back by the world around us; and if
they are so often, get so tied to our other ideas that
we can hardly wrench them away. *Interesting* ideas
stick in the mind by the associations which give them
interest. All the minor laws of conviction resolve
themselves into this great one: that at first we believe all which occurs to us; that afterwards we have
a tendency to believe that which we cannot help often
occurring to us, and that this tendency is stronger or

weaker in some sort of proportion to our inability to prevent their recurrence. When the inability to prevent the recurrence of the idea is very great, so that the reason is powerless on the mind, the consequent "conviction" is an eager, irritable, and ungovernable passion.

If these principles are true, they suggest some lessons which are not now accepted. They prove —

1. That we should be very careful how we let ourselves believe that which may turn out to be error. Milton says that "error is but opinion" (meaning true opinion) "in the making."* But when the conviction of any error is a strong passion, it leaves, like all other passions, a permanent mark on the mind; we can never be as if we had never felt it. "Once a heretic, always a heretic" is thus far true, — that a mind once given over to a passionate conviction is never as fit as it would otherwise have been to receive the truth on the same subject. Years after, the passion may return upon him; and inevitably, small recurrences of it will irritate his intelligence and disturb its calm. We cannot at once expel a familiar idea; and so long as the idea remains, its effect will remain too.

2. That we must always keep an account in our minds of the degree of evidence on which we hold our convictions, and be most careful that we do not permanently permit ourselves to feel a stronger conviction than the evidence justifies; if we do, since evidence is the only criterion of truth, we may easily get a taint of error that may be hard to clear away. This may seem obvious; yet if I do not mistake, Father Newman's "Grammar of Assent" is little else than a systematic treatise designed to deny and confute it.

3. That if we do, as in life we must sometimes, indulge a "provisional enthusiasm," as it may be

---

* Incorrect: "Opinion is but knowledge in the making," in the "Areopagitica." — ED.

called, for an idea, — for example, if an actor* in the
excitement of speaking does not keep his phrases to
probability, and if in the hurry of emotion he quite
believes all he says, his plain duty is on other occasions to watch himself carefully, and to be sure that
he does not as a permanent creed believe what in a
peculiar and temporary state he was led to say he
felt and to feel.

Similarly, we are all, in our various departments of
life, in the habit of assuming various probabilities as
if they were certainties. In Lombard Street the dealers assume that "Messrs. Baring's acceptance at three
months' date is sure to be paid," and that "Peel's Act
will always be suspended in a panic"; and the familiarity of such ideas makes it nearly impossible for
any one who spends his day in Lombard Street to
doubt of them. But nevertheless, a person who takes
care of his mind will keep up the perception that they
are not certainties.

Lastly, we should utilize this intense emotion of
conviction as far as we can. Dry minds, which give
an intellectual "assent" to conclusions, which feel no
strong glow of faith in them, often do not know what
their opinions are; they have every day to go over
the arguments again, or to refer to a note-book to
know what they believe : but intense convictions make
a memory for themselves, and if they can be kept to
the truths of which there is good evidence, they give
a readiness of intellect, a confidence in action, a consistency in character, which are not to be had without
them. For a time, indeed, they give these benefits
when the propositions believed are false: but then
they spoil the mind for seeing the truth; and they
are very dangerous, because the believer may discover
his error, and a perplexity of intellect, a hesitation in
action, and an inconsistency in character are the sure
consequences of an entire collapse in pervading and
passionate conviction.

---

*An evident misprint for "orator." — ED.

THE METAPHYSICAL BASIS OF TOLERATION.

(1874.)

ONE of the most marked peculiarities of recent times in England is the increased liberty in the expression of opinion. Things are now said constantly and without remark, which even ten years ago would have caused a hubbub, and have drawn upon those who said them much obloquy. But already I think there are signs of a reaction; in many quarters of orthodox opinion I observe a disposition to say, "Surely this is going too far; really we cannot allow such things to be said." And what is more curious, some writers whose pens are just set at liberty, and who would, not at all long ago, have been turned out of society for the things that they say, are setting themselves to explain the "weakness" of liberty and to extol the advantages of persecution. As it appears to me that the new practice of this country is a great improvement on its old one, and as I conceive that the doctrine of "toleration" rests on what may be called a "metaphysical" basis, I wish shortly to describe what that basis is.

I should say that except where it is explained to the contrary, I use the word "toleration" to mean toleration by law. Toleration by society of matters not subject to legal penalty is a kindred subject, on which if I have room I will add a few words; but in the main I propose to deal with the simpler subject, toleration by law. And by toleration, too, I mean, when it is not otherwise said, toleration in the public expression of opinions; toleration of acts and practices is another allied subject, on which I can, in a paper like this, but barely hope to indicate what seems to me to be the truth. And I should add that I deal only with the discussion of impersonal doctrines: the law of libel, which deals with accusations of living persons, is a topic requiring consideration by itself.

Meaning this by "toleration," I do not think we ought to be surprised at a reaction against it. What was said long ago of slavery seems to be equally true of persecution: it "exists by the law of nature." It is so congenial to human nature that it has arisen everywhere in past times, as history shows; that the cessation of it is a matter of recent times in England; that even now, taking the world as a whole, the practice and the theory of it are in a triumphant majority. Most men have always much preferred persecution, and do so still; and it is therefore only natural that it should continually reappear in discussion and argument.

One mode in which it tempts human nature is very obvious. Persons of strong opinions wish above all things to propagate those opinions. They find close at hand what seems an immense engine for that propagation, — they find the *state*, which has often in history interfered for and against opinions, which has had a great and undeniable influence in helping some and hindering others: and in their eagerness they can hardly understand why they should not make use of this great engine to crush the errors which they hate and to replace them with the tenets they approve. So long as there are earnest believers in the world, they will always wish to punish opinions, even if their judgment tells them it is unwise and their conscience that it is wrong; they may not gratify their inclination, but the inclination will not be the less real.

Since the time of Carlyle, "earnestness" has been a favorite virtue in literature, and it is customary to treat this wish to twist other people's belief into ours as if it were a part of the love of truth,—and in the highest minds so it may be; but the mass of mankind have, as I hold, no such fine motive. Independently of truth or falsehood, the spectacle of a different belief from ours is disagreeable to us, in the same way that the spectacle of a different form of dress and manners is disagreeable. A set of schoolboys will persecute a new boy with a new sort of jacket; they will hardly let him have a new-shaped penknife. Grown-up people are just as bad, except when culture has softened them: a mob will hoot a foreigner who looks very unlike themselves. Much of the feeling of "earnest believers" is, I believe, altogether the same: they wish others to think as they do, not only because they wish to diffuse doctrinal truth, but also and much more because they cannot bear to hear the words of a creed different from their own. At any rate, without further analyzing the origin of the persecuting impulse, its deep root in human nature and its great power over most men are evident.

But this natural impulse was not the only motive —perhaps was not the principal one—of historical persecutions: the main one, or a main one, was a most ancient political idea which once ruled the world, and of which deep vestiges are still to be traced on many sides. The most ancient conception of a state is that of a "religious partnership," in which any member may by his acts bring down the wrath of the gods on the other members, and so to speak on the whole company. This danger was, in the conception of the time, at once unlimited and inherited: in any generation, partners A, C, D, etc., might suffer loss of life or health or goods, the whole association even might perish, because in a past generation the ancestors of Z had somehow offended the gods. Thus, the historian of Athens tells us that after a particular act of sacrilege,—a breach of the local privileges of sanctuary,—the perpetrators were compelled to "retire into banishment"; and that those who had died

before the date he is speaking of "were disinterred
and cast beyond the borders." "Yet," he adds, "their
exile, continuing as it did only for a time, was not
held sufficient to expiate the impiety for which they
had been condemned. The Alkmæonids, one of the
most powerful families in Attica, long continued to
be looked upon as a tainted race, and in cases of
public calamity were liable to be singled out as having by their sacrilege drawn down the judgment of
the gods upon their countrymen."*   And as false
opinions about the gods have almost always been
thought to be peculiarly odious to them, the misbe-
liever, the "miscreant," has been almost always
thought to be likely not only to impair hereafter the
salvation of himself and others in a future world, but
also to bring on his neighbors and his nation grievous
calamities immediately in this; he has been persecuted to stop political danger more than to arrest intellectual error.

But it will be said, Put history aside, and come to
things now. Why should not those who are convinced that certain doctrines are errors, that they are
most dangerous, that they may ruin man's welfare
here and his salvation hereafter, use the power of the
state to extirpate those errors? Experience seems to
show that the power of the state can be put forth in
that way effectually: why then should it not be put
forth? If I had room, I should like for a moment to
criticize the word "effectually." I should say that
the state, in the cases where it is most wanted, is not
of the use which is thought. I admit that it extirpates error, but I doubt if it creates belief,—at least
if it does so in cases where the persecuted error is
suitable to the place and time: in such cases, I think
the effect has often been to eradicate a heresy among
the few, at the cost of creating a skepticism among
the many,—to kill the error, no doubt, but also to
ruin the general belief. And this is the cardinal

* Grote's "History of Greece," Part ii., Chap. x.

point; for the propagation of the "truth" is the end
of persecution, all else is only a means.   But I have
not space to discuss this, and will come to the main
point.

I say that the state power should not be used to
arrest discussion, because the state power may be used
equally for truth or error, for Mohammedanism or
Christianity, for belief or no-belief; but in discussion,
truth has an advantage.   Arguments always tell for
truth as such, and against error as such: if you let
the human mind alone, it has a preference for good
argument over bad; it oftener takes truth than not.
But if you do not let it alone, you give truth no advantage at all; you substitute a game of force where
all doctrines are equal, for a game of logic where the
truer have the better chance.

The process by which truth wins in discussion is
this.   Certain strong and eager minds embrace original
opinions, seldom all wrong, never quite true, but of a
mixed sort, part truth, part error; these they inculcate
on all occasions and on every side, and gradually
bring the cooler sort of men to a hearing of them.
These cooler people serve as quasi-judges, while the
more eager ones are a sort of advocates; a "court
of inquisition" is sitting perpetually, investigating —
informally and silently, but not ineffectually — what,
on all great subjects of human interest, are truth and
error.   There is no sort of infallibility about the court;
often it makes great mistakes, most of its decisions
are incomplete in thought and imperfect in expression: still, on the whole the force of evidence keeps
it right, — the truth has the best of the proof, and
therefore wins most of the judgments.   The process is
slow, far more tedious than the worst Chancery suit;
time in it is reckoned not by days, but by years, or
rather by centuries: yet on the whole it creeps along,
if you do not stop it.   But all is arrested if persecution begins, — if you have a *coup d'état*, and let loose
soldiers on the court; for it is perfect chance which

litigant turns them in, or what creed they are used to compel men to believe.

This argument, however, assumes two things. In the first place, it presupposes that we are speaking of a state of society in which discussion is possible; and such societies are not very common. Uncivilized man is not capable of discussion. Savages have been justly described as having "the character of children with the passions and strength of men"*; before anything like speculative argument can be used with them, their intellect must be strengthened and their passions restrained. There was, as it seems to me, a long preliminary period, before human nature as we now see it existed, and while it was being formed: during that preliminary period, persecution, like slavery, played a most considerable part. Nations mostly became nations by having a common religion; it was a necessary condition of the passage from a loose aggregate of savages to a united polity, that they should believe in the same gods and worship these gods in the same way. What was necessary was, that they should for a long period — for centuries, perhaps — lead the same life and conform to the same usages; they believed that the "gods of their fathers" had commanded these usages. Early law is hardly to be separated from religious ritual; it is more like the tradition of a church than the enactments of a statute book: it is a thing essentially immemorial and sacred; it is not conceived of as capable either of addition or diminution; it is a body of holy customs which no one is allowed either to break or to impugn. The use of these is to aid in creating a common national character, which in after times may be tame enough to bear discussion, and which may suggest common axioms upon which discussion can be founded. Till that common character has been formed, discussion is impossible; it cannot be used to find out truth, for it cannot exist: it is not that we have to forego its efficacy on purpose, — we have not the choice of

* Lubbock's "Prehistoric Times," page 465.

it, for its prerequisites cannot be found. The case of civil liberty is, as I conceive, much the same: early ages need a coercive despotism more than they need anything else; the age of debate comes later. An omnipotent power to enforce the sacred law is that which is then most required: a constitutional opposition would be born before its time; it would be dragging the wheel before the horses were harnessed. The strongest advocates both of liberty and toleration may consistently hold that there were unhappy ages before either became possible, and when attempts at either would have been pernicious.

The case is analogous to that of education. Every parent wisely teaches his child his own creed, and till the child has attained a certain age it is better that he should not hear too much of any other. His mind will in the end be better able to weigh arguments because it does not begin to weigh them so early; he will hardly comprehend any creed unless he has been taught some creed: but the restrictions of childhood must be relaxed in youth and abandoned in manhood. One object of education is to train us for discussion; and as that training gradually approaches to completeness, we should gradually begin to enter into and to take part in discussion. The restrictions that are useful at nine years old are pernicious at nineteen.

This analogy would have seemed to me obvious, but there are many most able persons who turn the matter just the other way: they regard the discipline of education as a precedent for persecution. They say, "I would no sooner let the nation at large read that bad book than I would let my children read it:" they refuse to admit that the age of the children makes any difference; at heart they think that they are wiser than the mass of mankind, just as they are wiser than their children, and would regulate the studies of both unhesitatingly. But experience shows that no man is on all points so wise as the mass of men are after a good discussion, and that if the ideas of the very wisest were by miracle to be fixed on the race, the certain result would be to stereotype monstrous error. If we fixed the belief of Bacon, we should believe that the earth went round the sun; if we fixed that of Newton, we should believe "that the Argonautic expedition was a real event, and occurred B. C. 937; that Hercules was a real person, and delivered Theseus, another real person, B. C. 936; that in the year 1036 Ceres, a woman of Sicily, in seeking her daughter who was stolen, came into Attica, and thére taught the Greeks to sow corn."* And the best † is, that the minds of most would-be persecutors are themselves unfixed; their opinions are in a perpetual flux; they would persecute all others for tenets which yesterday they had not heard of and which they will not believe to-morrow.

But it will be said, The theory of toleration is not so easy as that of education. We know by a certain fact when a young man is grown up and can bear discussion; we judge by his age, as to which every one is agreed: but we cannot tell by any similar patent fact when a state is mature enough to bear discussion, — there may be two opinions about it. And I quite agree that the matter of fact is more difficult to discover in one case than in the other; still, it is a matter of fact which the rulers of the state must decide upon their responsibility, and as best they can. And the highest sort of rulers will decide it like the English in India, — with no reference to their own belief. For years the English prohibited the preaching of Christianity in India, though it was their own religion, because they thought that it could not be tranquilly listened to; they now permit it, because they find that the population can bear the discussion. Of course, most governments are wholly unequal to so high a morality and so severe a self-command: the governments of most countries

---

* A *mélange* from "Chronology of the Ancient Kingdoms," pp. 15, 26, 27.
† An evident slip for "worst." — ED.

are composed of persons who wish everybody to believe as they do, merely because they do. Some here
and there, from a higher motive, so eagerly wish to
propagate their opinions that they are unequal to consider[ing] the problem of toleration impartially; they
persecute till the persecuted become strong enough
to make them desist. But the delicacy of a rule
and the unwillingness of governments to adopt it do
not prove that it is not the best and the right one.
There are already in inevitable jurisprudence many
lines of vital importance just as difficult to draw:
the line between sanity and insanity has necessarily
to be drawn, and it is as nice as anything can be.
The competency of people to bear discussion is not
intrinsically more difficult than their competency to
manage their own affairs, though perhaps a government is less likely to be impartial and more likely to
be biased in questions of discussion than in pecuniary
ones.

Secondly, the doctrine that rulers are to permit
discussion assumes not only, as we have seen, that
discussion is possible, but also that discussion will not
destroy the government. No government is bound to
permit a controversy which will annihilate itself: it
is a trustee for many duties, and if possible it must
retain the power to perform those duties. The controversies which may ruin it are very different in
different countries: the government of the day must
determine in each case what those questions are.
If the Roman emperors who persecuted Christianity
really did so because they imagined that Christianity
would destroy the Roman empire, I think they are
to be blamed not for their misconception of duty, but
for their mistake of fact. The existence of Christianity was not really more inconsistent with the existence of the empire in the time of Diocletian than in
that of Constantine; but if Diocletian thought that it
was inconsistent, it was his duty to preserve the
empire.

It will be asked, "What do you mean by preserving a society? All societies are in a state of incipient change; the best of them are often the most changing: what is meant, then, by saying you will 'preserve' any? You admit that you cannot keep them unaltered: what then do you propose to do?" I answer that in this respect the life of societies is like the life of the individuals composing them. You cannot interfere so as to keep a man's body unaltered; you can interfere so as to keep him alive. What changes in such cases will be fatal is a question of fact: the government must determine what will, so to say, "break up the whole thing," and what will not. No doubt it may decide wrong. In France, the country of experiments, General Cavaignac said, "A government which allows its principle to be discussed is a lost government;" and therefore he persecuted on behalf of the Republic, thinking it was essential to society. Louis Napoleon similarly persecuted on behalf of the Second Empire; M. Thiers on behalf of the Republic again; the Duc de Broglie now persecutes on behalf of the existing nondescript. All these may be mistakes, or some of them, or none. Here, as before, the practical difficulties in the application of a rule do not disprove its being the true and the only one.

It will be objected that this principle is applicable only to truths which are gained by discussion. "We admit," such objectors say, "that where discussion is the best or the only means of proving truth, it is unadvisable to prohibit that discussion: but there are other means besides discussion of arriving at truth, which are sometimes better than discussion even where discussion is applicable, and sometimes go beyond it and attain regions in which it is inapplicable; and where those more efficient means are applicable it may be wise to prohibit discussion, for in these instances discussion may confuse the human mind and impede it in the use of those higher means. The case is analogous to that of the eyes. For the most part, it is a sound rule to tell persons who want to see things that they must necessarily use *both* their eyes, and rely on them; but there are cases in which that rule is wrong: if a man wants to see things too distant for the eyes, as the satellites of Jupiter and the ring of Saturn, you must tell him, on the contrary, to shut one eye and look through a telescope with the other. The ordinary mode of using the common instruments may, in exceptional cases, interfere with the right use of the supplementary instruments." And I quite admit that there are such exceptional cases and such additional means; but I say that their existence introduces no new difficulty into the subject, and that it is no reason for prohibiting discussion except in the cases in which we have seen already that it was advisable to prohibit it.

Putting the matter in the most favorable way for these objectors, and making all possible concessions to them, I believe the exceptions which they contend for must come at last to three :—

First, there are certain necessary propositions which the human mind *will* think, must think, and cannot help thinking. For example, we must believe that things which are equal to the same thing are equal to each other, that a thing cannot *both* be and not be, that it must *either* be or not be. These truths are not gained by discussion; on the contrary, discussion presupposes at least some of them, for you cannot argue without first principles any more than you can use a lever without a fulcrum. The prerequisites of reasoning must somehow be recognized by the human mind before we begin to reason. So much is obvious; but then it is obvious also that in such cases, attempts at discussion cannot do any harm. If the human mind has in it certain first principles which it cannot help seeing, and which it accepts of itself, there is no harm in arguing against those first principles. You may contend as long as you like that things which are equal to the same thing are *not* equal to each other, or that a thing *can* both exist and not exist at the same time, but you will not convince any one; if you could convince any one .you would do him irreparable harm, for you would hurt the basis of his mind and destroy the use of his reason, but happily you cannot convince him. That which the human mind cannot help thinking it cannot help thinking, and discussion can no more remove the primary perceptions than it can produce them. The multiplication table will remain the multiplication table, neither more nor less, however much we may argue either for it or against it.

But though the denial of the real necessary perceptions of the human mind cannot possibly do any harm, the denial of alleged necessary perceptions is often essential to the discovery of truth. The human mind, as experience shows, is apt to manufacture sham self-evidences. The most obvious case is, that men perpetually "do sums" wrong. If we dwell long enough and intently enough on the truths of arithmetic, they are in each case self-evident; but if we are too quick, or let our minds get dull, we may make any number of mistakes. A certain deliberation and a certain intensity are both essential to correctness in the matter. Fictitious necessities of thought will be imposed on us without end unless we are careful. The greatest minds are not exempt from the risk of such mistakes even in matters most familiar to them; on the contrary, the history of science is full of cases in which the ablest men and the most experienced assumed that it was impossible to think things which are in matter of fact true, and which it has since been found possible to think quite easily. The mode in which these sham self-evidences are distinguished from the real ones is by setting as many minds as possible to try as often as possible whether they can help thinking the thing or not; but such trials will never exist without discussion. So far, therefore, the existence of self-evidences in the human mind is not a reason for discouraging discussion, but a reason for encouraging it.

Next, it· is certainly true that many conclusions which are by no means self-evident, and which are gradually obtained nevertheless, are not the result of discussion. For example, the opinion of a man as to the characters of his friends and acquaintances is not the result of distinct argument, but the aggregate of distinct* impressions; it is not the result of an investigation consciously pursued, but the effect of a multiplicity of facts involuntarily presented: it is a definite thing and has a most definite influence on the mind, but its origin is indefinite and not to be traced; it is like a great fund raised in very small subscriptions and of which the subscribers' names are lost. But here again, though these opinions too were not gained by discussion, their existence is a reason for promoting discussion, not for preventing it. Every-day experience shows that these opinions as to character are often mistaken in the last degree: human character is a most complex thing, and the impressions which different people form of it are as various as the impressions which the inhabitants of an impassable mountain have of its shape and size. Each observer has an aggregate idea derived from certain actions and certain sayings, but the real man has always or almost always said a thousand sayings of a kind quite different and in a connection quite different; he has done a vast variety of actions among "other men" and "other minds"; a mobile person will often seem hardly the same if you meet him in very different societies : and how, except by discussion, is the true character of such a person to be decided? Each observer must bring his contingent to the list of data; those data must be arranged and made use of. The certain and positive facts as to which every one is agreed must have their due weight; they must be combined and compared with

---

* *Review*, "*indistinct*," with obvious accuracy. — ED.

the various impressions as to which no two people exactly coincide: a rough summary must be made of the whole. In no other way is it possible to arrive at the truth of the matter: without discussion each mind is dependent on its own partial observation. A great man is one image — one thing, so to speak — to his valet, another to his son, another to his wife, another to his greatest friend. None of these must be stereotyped; all must be compared. To prohibit discussion is to prohibit the corrective process.

Lastly, I hold that there are first principles or first perceptions which are neither the result of constant though forgotten trials like those last spoken of, nor common to all the race like the first. The most obvious seem to me to be the principles of taste. The primary perceptions of beauty vary much in different persons, and in different persons at the same time,* but no one can say that they are not most real and most influential parts of human nature. There is hardly a thing made by human hands which is not affected more or less by the conception of beauty felt by the maker; and there is hardly a human life which would not have been different if the idea of beauty in the mind of the man who lived it had been different. But certainly it would not answer to exclude subjects of taste from discussion, and to allow one school of taste-teachers to reign alone, and to prohibit the teaching of all rival schools. The effect would be to fix on all ages the particular ideas of one age, on a matter which is beyond most others obscure and difficult to reduce to a satisfactory theory. The human mind evidently differs at various times immensely in its conclusions upon it; and there is nothing to show that the era of the persecutor is wiser than any other era, or that his opinion is better than any one else's.

The case of these variable first principles is much like that of the "personal equation," as it is called in the theory of observations. Some observers, it is

---

* An obvious slip of pen for "the same person at different times."—ED.

found, habitually see a given phenomenon — say the star coming to the meridian — a little sooner than most others, some later; no two persons exactly coincide. The first thing done when a new man comes into an observatory for practical work is to determine whether he sees quick or slow; and this is called the "personal equation." But according to the theory of persecution, the national astronomer in each country would set up his own mind as the standard: in one country he would be a quick man, and would not let the slow people contest what he said; in another he would be a slow man, and would not tolerate the quick people or let men speak their minds: and so the astronomical observations — the astronomical *creeds*, if I may say so — of different countries would radically differ. But as toleration and discussion are allowed, no such absurd result follows: the observations of different minds are compared with those of others, and truth is assumed to lie in the mean between the errors of the quick people and the errors of the slow ones.

No such accurate result can be expected in more complex matters. The phenomena of astronomical observation relate only to very simple events, and to a very simple fact about these events; but perceptions of beauty have an infinite complexity, — they are all subtle aggregates of countless details, and about each of these details probably every mind in some degree differs from every other one. But in a rough way the same sort of agreement is possible: discussion is only an organized mode by which various minds compare their conclusions with those of various others. Bold and strong minds describe graphic and definite impressions; at first sight these impressions seem wholly different. Writers of the last century thought classical architecture altogether inferior* to Gothic; many writers now put it just the other way, and maintain a mediæval cathedral to be a thing altogether superior in kind and nature to anything classical. For years the world thought Claude's landscapes

---

* An obvious misprint for " superior." — ED.

perfect; then came Mr. Ruskin, and by his ability
and eloquence he has made a whole generation depreciate them, and think Turner's altogether superior.
The extrication of truth by such discussions is very
slow; it is often retarded; it is often thrown back; it
often seems to pause for ages: but upon the whole it
makes progress, and the principle of that progress is
this:—Each mind which is true to itself, and which
draws its own impressions carefully, and which com-
pares those impressions with the impressions of others,
arrives at certain conclusions, which as far as that
mind is concerned are ultimate, and are its highest
conclusions. These it sets down as expressively as
it can on paper, or communicates by word of mouth,
and these again form data which other minds can
contrast with their own. In this incessant comparison, eccentric minds fall off on every side: some like
Milton, some Wordsworth; some can see nothing in
Dryden, some find Racine intolerably dull, some think
Shakespeare barbarous, others consider the contents
of the "Iliad" "battles and schoolboy stuff." With
history it is the same: some despise one great epoch,
some another. Each epoch has its violent partisans,
who will listen to nothing else, and who think every
other epoch in comparison mean and wretched. These
violent minds are always faulty and sometimes absurd, but they are almost always useful to mankind:
they compel men to hear neglected truth. They uniformly exaggerate their gospel; but it generally *is*
a gospel. Carlyle said many years since of the old
Poor Law in England:—"It being admitted, then,
that outdoor relief should at once cease, what means
did great Nature take to make it cease? She created
various men who thought the cessation of outdoor
relief the one thing needful."* In the same way, it
being desirable that the taste of men should be improved on some point, Nature's instrument on that

---

* Quoted, *more Bagehoti*, from "Chartism," Chap. iii. See page 270 of
this volume for the correct form.— ED.

point is some man of genius, of attractive voice and limited mind, who declaims and insists, not only that the special improvement is a good thing in itself, but the best of all things and the root of all other good things. Most useful, too, are others less apparent: shrinking, sensitive, testing minds, of whom often the world knows nothing, but each of whom is in the circle just near him an authority on taste, and communicates by personal influence the opinions he has formed. The human mind of a certain maturity, if left alone, prefers real beauty to sham beauty, and prefers it the sooner if original men suggest new charms and quiet men criticize and judge of them.

But an æsthetical persecution would derange all this, for generally the compulsive power would be in the hands of the believers in some tradition. The state represents "the rough force of society," and is little likely to be amenable to new charms or new ideas; and therefore the first victim of the persecution would be the original man who was proposing that which in the end would most improve mankind, and the next would be the testing and discerning critic who was examining these ideas and separating the chaff from the wheat in them. Neither would conform to the old tradition,—the inventor would be too eager, the critic too scrupulous; and so a heavy code of ancient errors would be chained upon mankind. Nor would the case be at all the better if by some freak of events the propounder of the new doctrine were to gain full control, and to prohibit all he did not like: he would try, and try in vain, to make the inert mass of men accept or care for his new theory, and his particular enemy would be the careful critic who went with him a little way and then refused to go any further. If you allow persecution, the partisans of the new sort of beauty will, if they can, attack those of the old sort, and the partisans of the old sort will attack those of the new sort, while both will turn on the quiet and discriminating person who is trying to select what is good from each. Some chance taste will be fixed for ages.

But it will be said, "Who ever heard of such nonsense as an æsthetical persecution? Everybody knows such matters of taste must be left to take care of themselves: as far as they are concerned, nobody wants to persecute or prohibit."* But I have spoken of matters of taste because it is sometimes best to speak in parables. The case of morals and religion, in which people have always persecuted and still wish to persecute, is the very same: if there are (as I myself think there are) ultimate truths of morals and religion which more or less vary for each mind, some sort of standard and some kind of agreement can only be arrived about it in the very same way. The same comparison of one mind with another is necessary; the same discussion; the same use of criticizing minds, the same use of original ones. The mode of arriving at truth is the same, and also the mode of stopping it.

We now see the reason why, as I said before, religious persecution often extirpates new doctrines, but commonly fails to maintain the belief in old tenets: you can prevent whole classes of men from hearing of the religion which is congenial to them, but you cannot make men believe a religion which is uncongenial. You can prevent the natural admirers of Gothic architecture from hearing anything of it, or from seeing it; but you cannot make them admire classical architecture. You may prevent the admirers of Claude from seeing his pictures, or from praising them; but you cannot make them admirers of Turner. Just so, you may by persecution prevent minds prone to be Protestant from being Protestant, but you will not make men real Catholics; you may prevent naturally Catholic minds from being Catholic, but you will not make them genuine Protestants. You will not make those believe your religion who are pre-

---

* The persecution of the French " Romantics " by the " Classics," 1820 +, in which even government intervention was sought, refutes this.—ED.

disposed by nature in favor of a different kind of religion; you will make of them, instead, more or less conscious skeptics. Being denied the sort of religion of which the roots are in their minds and which they could believe, they will forever be conscious of an indefinite want. They will constantly feel after something which they are never able to attain; they will never be able to settle upon anything, they will feel an instinctive repulsion from everything; they will be skeptics at heart, because they were denied the creed for which their heart craves; they will live as indifferentists, because they were withheld by force from the only creed to which they would not be indifferent. Persecution in intellectual countries produces a superficial conformity, but also underneath an intense, incessant, implacable doubt.

Upon examination, therefore, the admission that certain truths are not gained by discussion introduces a* new element into the subject: the discussion of such truths is as necessary as of all other truths. The only limitations are that men's minds shall in the particular society be mature enough to bear the discussion, and that the discussion shall not destroy the society.

I acknowledge these two limitations to the doctrine that discussion should be free, but I do not admit another which is often urged: it is said that those who write against toleration should not be tolerated, that discussion should not aid the enemies of discussion. But why not? if there is a strong government and a people fit for discussion, why should not the cause be heard? We must not assume that the liberty of discussion has no case of exception: we have just seen that there are in fact several such. In each instance, let the people decide whether the particular discussion shall go on or not. Very likely, in some cases, they may decide wrong; but it is better that they should so decide than that we

---

* An obvious misprint for "no."—ED.

should venture to anticipate all experience, and to make sure that they cannot possibly be right.

It is plain, too, that the argument here applied to the toleration of opinion has no application to that of actions. The human mind, in the cases supposed, learns by freely hearing all arguments; but in no case does it learn by trying freely all practices. Society, as we now have it, cannot exist at all unless certain acts are prohibited; it goes on much better because many other acts are prohibited also. The government must take the responsibility of saying what actions it will allow; that is its first business, and the allowance of all would be the end of civilization: but it must, under the conditions specified, hear all opinions, for the tranquil discussion .of all more than anything else promotes the progressive knowledge of truth, which is the mainspring of civilization.

Nor does the argument that the law should not impose a penalty on the expression of any opinion, equally prove that society should not in many cases apply a penalty to that expression. Society can deal much more severely than the law with many kinds of acts, because it need be far less strict in the evidence it requires. It can take cognizance of matters of common repute, and of things of which every one is sure but which nobody can prove. Particularly, it can fairly well compare the character of' the doctrine with the character of the agent, which law can do but imperfectly if at all. And it is certain that opinions are evidence of the character of those who hold them,—not conclusive evidence, but still presumptive. Experience shows that every opinion is compatible with what every one would admit to be a life fairly approvable, a life far higher than that of the mass of men. Great skepticism and great belief have both been found in characters whom both skeptics and believers must admire. Still, on the whole, there is a certain kinship between belief and character: those who disagree with a man's fundamental creed will generally disapprove of his habitual character.   If therefore society sees a man maintaining opinions which by experience it has been led to connect with actions such as it discountenances, it is justified in provisionally discountenancing the man who holds those opinions.   Such a man should be put to the proof to show by his life that the opinions which he holds are not connected with really pernicious actions, as society thinks they are.   If he is visibly leading a high life, society should discountenance him no longer: it is then clear that he did not lead a bad life, and the idea that he did or might lead such a life was the only reason for so doing; a doubt was suggested, but it also has been removed.   This habit of suspicion does not, on the whole, impair free discussion,—perhaps even it improves it: it keeps out the worst disputants, — men of really bad character, whose opinions are the results of that character, and who refrain from publishing them because they fear what society may say.   If the law could similarly distinguish between good disputants and bad, it might usefully impose penalties on the bad; but of course this is impossible.   Law cannot distinguish between the niceties of character; it must punish the publication of an opinion, if it punishes at all, no matter whether the publisher is a good man or whether he is a bad one.   In such a matter, society is a discriminating agent; the law is but a blind one.

To most people I may seem to be slaying the slain and proving what no one doubts: people, it will be said, no longer wish to persecute.   But I say they *do* wish to persecute; in fact, from their writings, and still better from their conversation, it is easy to see that very many believers would persecute skeptics and that very many skeptics would persecute believers. Society may be wiser; but most earnest believers and most earnest unbelievers are not at all wiser.

THE PUBLIC WORSHIP REGULATION BILL.*

(1874.)

IF the "Public Worship Regulation Bill" dealt only
with subjects theological or religious, we should not
interfere in the discussion; but it deals also with
political questions, on which we do not think it right
to be silent, — especially as many whom we much
respect have, we think, selected a policy of which
the effect will be the reverse of what they expect,
and the success of which they may hereafter much
regret.

All changes in England should be made slowly
and after long discussion; public opinion should be
permitted to ripen upon them. And the reason is,
that all the important English institutions are the
relics of a long past; that they have undergone
many transformations; that like old houses which
have been altered many times, they are full both of
conveniences and inconveniences which at first sight
would not be imagined. Very often a rash alterer
would pull down the very part which makes them
habitable, to cure a minor evil or improve a defective
outline.

The English Church is one of those among our
institutions which, if it is to be preserved at all,
should be touched most anxiously : it is one of our
oldest institutions; every part of it has a history,
which few of us thoroughly understand, but which
we all know to be long and important. In its political

---

*Namely, that introduced by Mr. Russell Gurney, and adopted by the
Government of the day. — Ed. Reprint.

relations it has been altered many times, and each time under circumstances of considerable complexity. The last settlement was made more than two hundred years ago, when men's minds were in a very different state from what they are now; when Newton had not written, when Locke had not thought, when physical science as we now have it did not exist, when modern philosophy (for England at least) had not begun. The railways, the telegraphs, the very common-sense of these times would have been unintelligible in the year 1660; they would have been still more unintelligible in the reign of Queen Elizabeth. To attempt to enforce on us now a settlement made in times so different is a grave undertaking; it ought only to be made after the most ample discussion, and when every competent person has had time to consider the effect.

We have as yet felt little inconvenience from our old law, because we have dealt with it in a truly English manner: always refusing to change it explicitly, always saying that we would never so change it, we were changing it silently all the while; year by year this practice was omitted or this habit insensibly changed. Each generation differed from its fathers; and though they might in part utter the same words, they did not mean the same things,— their intellectual life was different. Incessant changes in science, in literature, in art, and in politics — in all that forms thinking minds — have made it impossible that really and in fact we should think the same things in 1874 as our ancestors in 1674 or 1774. Just as in legal theory Queen Victoria has pretty much the same prerogative as Queen Elizabeth, so too in legal theory the English Church may be identical with that of two hundred years ago: but the Church is not a legal theory, it is "a congregation of faithful men"*; and no one of these is in a state of mind identical,

---

* No. 19 of the "Articles."

or nearly identical, with those of two hundred years ago.

Many Continental statesmen would be much puzzled at this insensible alteration; they would have a difficulty in imagining a law which was a law in theory but not a law in practice, which no one would alter in word and no one enforce in reality : but the English are very practiced in this sort of arrangement, — they have a kind of genius for the compensation of errors. For many years we had probably the worst and most bloody penal law in Europe; it is awful to read the old statutes which fix death as the penalty for minor acts altogether undeserving of it: but these statutes did not work nearly so much evil as might have been expected. There was besides a complex system of indictments which let off very many culprits upon trifling flaws, and there was also an absurd system of incessant remissions and pardons; the worst evils of an excessively bad law were exceedingly mitigated by a very bad mode of applying it. Speaking roughly, and subject to minor criticism, the history has been the same in the Church: in it, too, an imperfect law has been remedied by an imperfect mode of procedure. The Church has been allowed to change in this and that because it has been exceedingly difficult to interfere with it. The legal penalty against change has been distant, costly, and uncertain, and therefore it has not been applied; change has been possible because the punishment of change was difficult. But the essence of the "Public Worship Regulation Bill" is to make that punishment easy: "If the Rubric says so," say its supporters, "the Rubric ought to be enforced." This is as if Sir Samuel Romilly had attacked, not our bad penal code, but our bad penal procedure. If, by the historical growth of approximate equivalents, A mitigates B, you will deteriorate, not improve, the world if you change A without changing B, though both may be evils.

The analogy, indeed, very imperfectly expresses the truth. In the recent history of the Church, the English have conspicuously shown another of their predominant peculiarities, — indifference to abstract truth. When, a quarter of a century ago, English lawyers in the Court of Privy Council were first required to decide theological questions, they did so in a way which astonished theologians : they declined to supply any abstract proposition. If the enacted formularies contained such and such words, no clergyman of the Church could, according to them, contradict those words; but they allowed the clergy to say anything else. We cannot use theological terms here; but suppose, by an economical analogy, the formulary had said that "free trade was beneficial to mankind": the lawyers would have decided that no clergyman could say that free trade was not beneficial; but they would have allowed him to say that "commercial liberty was inexpressibly disastrous to mankind," because as lawyers they would not undertake to say that "free trade" and "commercial liberty" meant the same thing, or that in an abstract subject the two phrases might not in some way and to some minds seem consistent. In mere description this kind of decision may not seem very sensible, and it is utterly contrary to any which a theologian would ever have adopted; but in practice it preserved the Church Establishment. It was first applied in the Gorham case, and retained the Evangelical clergy in the Church; then, in the "Essays and Reviews" case, it retained the Broad Church; and lastly, in Mr. Bennett's case, it retained the High Church.* If the Establishment was to be maintained, it was necessary that all these parties should be kept side by side within it; and by this system of interpretation they were thus kept.

Unfortunately, the courts of law have not been able to apply the same sort of judicial decision to the practical directions for the public worship of the

* See note, page 368.

Church which they applied to her theoretical teachings: there is inevitably something more distinct and clear about acts which are required to be done at a given time and place than in statements of abstract doctrine. When the courts have been appealed to, it has not been possible to apply to ritual the same comprehensiveness which has had such excellent political effects in the case of doctrine; but nevertheless, there is exactly the same necessity for it. Almost every party in the Church is harassed by some of her rules, just as it is hampered by some of her words. The Broad Church dislikes the Athanasian creed, and avoids the use of it; the Low Church and the High Church are in vital and necessary opposition as to the mode of conducting the sacramental services: in every characteristic church, every party thinks probably something is done which the strict Rubric would forbid, or something omitted which it would prescribe. Until now this difficulty has not been very acutely felt: as we have explained, the imperfection of the law was cured by the imperfection of the procedure. No doubt the Rubrics were framed in other days; no doubt they took no notice of the wants of the present day; no doubt a strict adherence to them would expel from the Church very many whose doctrines had been decided to be consistent with hers: but then, to enforce the observance of the Rubric was difficult, costly, and dubious, and so the natural evil did not happen. The wants of various minds were variously met by various deviations from the law, which in theory were liable to penalties but which in practice were unpunished.

The scope of the "Public Worship Regulation Bill" is to destroy this variety. It is a new Act of Uniformity as far as public worship is concerned. A short and simple process — which has been so often stated that we need not here describe it — is prescribed, which will enable objectors to enforce any rubric, and which no doubt will cause them to be so

enforced. The proposers of the bill have not enough
considered the applicability of this primary assumption: No church can have only a single form of
public worship unless it has also a single creed. An
apparent uniformity may be maintained in specified
details; but in spirit, in feeling, in its deepest consequences on those who habitually hear and see, the
effect will be different. A service conducted by a
Broad Churchman, explained in his sermon and commented upon in his manner, will be very unlike what
it would be if that service is conducted by a *bona fide*
dogmatic believer. No mere Act of Uniformity can
prevent this; still less can it efface the inevitable
difference between a sacramental service in the hands
of a High Church clergyman and in those of a Low
Church. The two belong to separate and unlike
species: the one believes that the service contains a
supernatural act, the other that it is an edifying rite;
the one regards it as an invisible miracle, the other
as a conspicuous exhortation. Make what laws you
like, how can the two perform these services with the
same tone of mind, the same kind of thought, the
same effect on the congregation? You may dress two
men up in the same clothes, but they will be two
men for all that. If once you permit two or more
faiths in a church, you in truth permit two or more
rituals. The various feelings and the various creeds
will somehow find a means of bringing themselves
into contact with the minds with which they wish to
be in contact; you have "swallowed the camel" when
you permitted the creed, and it is useless to "strain
at the gnat"* and forbid the expression of it.

This is to be especially borne in mind by those
who think that there is a party in the Church that
desires to introduce Romanism, and who approve of
this bill because they think it will counteract that
party. The essence of Romanism is not in its ceremonies, but in its doctrines. As was explained to the

---

* Matt. xxiii., 24.

House of Commons on Wednesday, nothing could be simpler than the mode in which Mr. Newman used to conduct his services at Oxford; and yet he then held "Roman" doctrine, and penetrated half the young men about him with a deep faith in the highest sacramental principle. Unless you reverse the decision in the Bennett case, a doctrine which no common person will distinguish from Romanism will continue to be and must be taught in the Church of England. We do not believe it will lose in strength by being denied this or that form of ritual: it will attract in any case the minds to whom it is congenial, and it will rather gain than lose in *éclat* by seeming to be persecuted.

We shall be told that this argument proves too much, for that it proves that this bill will do nothing at all, and that therefore at least it will do no harm; but it will, we think, do great harm, — at least if it be good to keep the Establishment, and if it does harm to weaken it. The real danger of the Establishment is from within, not from without. The manner in which its sections have been retained within its limits has in part developed, and as time goes on is still developing more largely, a great evil. Specially the Low Church, specially the Broad Church, and specially the High Church, have all been kept in her communion because the judges refused to draw certain logical inferences from her formularies; as lawyers they declined to draw them: but intellectual young men who are thinking of becoming clergymen do not like this reasoning. They say, "The courts of law may not like to draw these inferences, but I must. I have spent my youth in a mental training which has prepared me to draw them and which compels me to do so. Educated as I have been, I cannot take half an argument and leave it; I must work it out to the end. That end seems to me inconsistent with this or that of the formularies of the Church. Others say it is not, but I am not sure that it is not; at any rate, I do not like to risk the happiness of my life upon its being consistent. If in after years my investigation should run counter to a vast collection of assertions framed by various men, in various ages, of various minds, what will be my fate? I must either sacrifice the profession by which I live or the creed in which I believe. The lawyers probably might not turn me out, indeed; but my conscience was not made by lawyers, — I shall have to turn myself out." This is the sort of thought which more and more prevents intellectual young men from taking orders, and we are beginning to see the effect. The moral excellence and the practical piety of the clergy are as good as ever, but they want individuality of thought and originality of mind; they have too universal a conformity to commonplace opinion. They are not only conscientious, but indecisive; more and more they belong to the most puzzling class to argue with, for more and more they "candidly confess" that they must admit your premises, but "on account of the obscurity of the subject" must decline to draw the inevitable inference. Already this intellectual poorness is beginning to be felt, and if it should augment it will destroy the Establishment: she will not have in her ranks arguers who can maintain her position either against those who believe more or against those who believe less. Skepticism sends trained and logical minds to the intellectual conflict; Romanism does so also: but the Established Church refuses them, — refuses them silently and indirectly, but still effectually. The "Public Worship Bill" will, we conceive, augment this difficulty almost *at the very point at which its being augmented will be most calamitous. Many young men who are acutely conscious of the restraints of the Establishment in speculation are attracted by its freedom in practice: "I may be cramped in metaphysics," they think at heart, "but I shall be free in action." But

---

*Some word like "fatally" is evidently omitted here. — Ed.

this bill will be a measure—for aught young men can tell, the first of a series—which will limit the freedom of their lives, and cramp them on the side of practice as they already are on the side of thought. The most malevolent enemy of the Established Church could deal her no acuter wound.

Upon the whole, we can conceive nothing clearer than that this bill should not pass this year. We are certain that members of Parliament have not considered the necessary arguments, and that the nation has not done so either.*

---

* It did pass, however.—ED.

NOTE TO PAGE 363. — *Gorham Case.* Rev. G. C. Gorham, an ex-fellow of Cambridge, was presented to the vicarage of Brampford Speke in 1847 by the Lord Chancellor; the Bishop of Exeter refused to institute him because (with the Evangelicals in general) he denied that baptism confers spiritual regeneration, and that infants are made "members of Christ and children of God" by it; the Arches Court of Canterbury sustained the bishop; the Privy Council annulled the decision. — *"Essays and Reviews"* Case. A volume with this title was published in 1860, composed of articles by Rev. Drs. Frederick Temple and Rowland Williams, Profs. Baden-Powell and Jowett, Revs. H. B. Wilson and Mark Pattison, and C. W. Goodwin (layman); it met a storm of denunciation from the general Orthodox body (being answered in various books and articles, and in 1864, after the decision hereafter noted, formally condemned by Convocation), and Revs. Williams and Wilson were prosecuted for heresy respectively by the Bishop of Salisbury and a clergyman in the diocese of Ely, and sentenced by the Arches Court to suspension for one year with costs; the Privy Council annulled the decision. — *Bennett Case.* Rev. William J. E. Bennett, B. A. of Christ Church, Oxford, and later a prolific theological writer and editor, resigned his living of St. Paul's, Knightsbridge, in 1851, on account of outcry against his "Tractarianism"; was shortly presented to the vicarage of Frome Selwood, and in 1867 published a book entitled "The Church and the World" and a pamphlet-letter to Dr. Pusey entitled "A Plea for Toleration in the Church of England," maintaining the *visible* presence of Christ among the sacraments; a revised edition of the pamphlet in 1868 retracted the term "visible," but a suit for heresy was instituted. The Bishop of London passed the case along to the Bishop of Bath and Wells, who sent the case in 1869 to the Arches Court, which declined to act on the ground that the Bishop was shirking his own duties on them; but later in the year, on formal articles, decided against the prosecutor, and on appeal the Privy Council sustained the court. Amusingly enough, the High Church party were the instigators and furious backers of the previous suits and most other cases of church discipline, and Mr. Bennett had preached and written vehemently against permitting dissidents from the formularies of the Church to remain in it. — ED.

LETTERS ON THE
FRENCH COUP D'ÉTAT
OF 1851.

ADDRESSED TO THE EDITOR OF *The Inquirer.**

LETTER I.

THE DICTATORSHIP.

PARIS, Jan. 8, 1852.

SIR,—You have asked me to tell you what I think of French affairs. I shall be pleased to do so; but I ought perhaps to begin by cautioning you against believing, or too much heeding, what I say. However, I do not imagine that I need do so; for with your experience of the public journals, you will be quite aware that it is not difficult to be an "occasional correspondent." Have your boots polished in a blacking-shop, and call the interesting officiator an "intelligent *ouvrier*"; be shaved, and cite the *coiffeur* as "a person in rather a superior station"; call your best acquaintance "a well-informed person," and all others "persons whom I have found to be occasionally not in error": and—abroad, at least—you will soon have matter for a newspaper letter. I should quite deceive you if I professed to have made these profound researches; nor, like Sir Francis Head, do I "no longer know where I am" because the French President has asked me to accompany him in his ride,— my perception of personal locality has not as yet been so tried: I only know what a person who is in a foreign country during

---

an important political catastrophe cannot avoid knowing, what he runs against, what is beaten into him, what he can hardly help hearing, seeing, and reflecting.

That Louis Napoleon has gone to Notre Dame to return thanks to God for the seven millions and odd suffrages of the French people; that he has taken up his abode at the Tuileries, and that he has had new napoleons coined in his name; that he has broken up the "trees of liberty" for firewood; that he has erased (or is erasing, for they are many) *Liberté*, *Egalité*, and *Fraternité* from the national buildings, — all these things are so easy and so un-English that I am pretty sure with you they will be thought signs of pompous impotence, and I suppose many people will be inclined to believe the best comment to be the one which I heard: — "Mon Dieu, il a sauvé la France: la rue du Coq s'appelle maintenant la rue de l'Aigle!"*

I am inclined, however, to imagine that this idea would be utterly erroneous; that on the contrary, the President is just now, at least, really strong and really popular; that the act of Dec. 2 did succeed and is succeeding; that many, that most of the inferior people do really and sincerely pray, *Domine, salvum fac Napoleonem.*

In what I have seen of the comments of the English press upon recent events here, two things are not quite enough kept apart: I mean the temporary dictatorship of Louis Napoleon to meet and cope with the expected crisis of '52, and the continuance of that dictatorship hereafter, — the new, or as it is called, the *Bas* Empire; in a word, the coming Constitution and questionable political machinery with which "the nephew of my uncle" is now proposing to endow

---

*["He has saved France: Cock Street is now called Eagle Street!"] The general reader may not before have read that the Rue du Coq l'Honoré is an old and well-known street in Paris, and that notwithstanding the substitution of the eagle for [the] cock as a military emblem, there is no thought of changing its name. — B.

France. Of course, in reality these two things *are* separate. It is one thing to hold that a military rule is required to meet an urgent and temporary difficulty; another, to advocate the continuance of such a system when so critical a necessity no longer exists.

It seems to me—or would seem, if I did not know that I was contradicted both by much English writing and opinion, and also by many most competent judges here—that the first point, the temporary dictatorship, is a tolerably clear case; that it is not to be complicated with the perplexing inquiry what form of government will permanently suit the French people; that the President was, under the actual facts of the case, quite justified in assuming the responsibility, though of course I allow that responsibility to be tremendous. My reasons for so believing I shall in this letter endeavor to explain,—except that I shall not, I fancy, have room to say much on the moral defensibility or indefensibility of the *coup d'état;* nor do I imagine that you want from me any ethical speculation,—that is manufactured in Printing-house Square: but I shall give the best account I can of the matter-of-fact consequences and antecedents of the new revolution, of which in some sense a resident in France may feel without presumption that he knows something hardly so well known to those at home.

The political justification of Louis Napoleon is, as I apprehend, to be found in the state of the public mind which immediately preceded the *coup d'état.* It is very rarely that a country expects a revolution at a given time; indeed, it is perhaps not common for ordinary persons in any country to anticipate a revolution at all,—though profound people may speculate, the mass will ever expect to-morrow to be as this day at least, if not more abundant. But once name the day, and all this is quite altered: as a general rule, the very people who would be most likely to neglect general anticipation are exactly those most likely to exaggerate the proximate consequences of

a certain impending event. At any rate, in France
five weeks ago, the tradespeople talked of May, '52,
as if it were the end of the world. Civilization and
Socialism might probably endure, but buying and
selling would surely come to an end; in fact, they
anticipated a worse era than February, '48, when
trade was at a stand-still so long that it has hardly
yet recovered, and when the government stocks fell
forty per cent. It is hardly to be imagined upon
what petty details the dread of political dissolution
at a fixed and not distant time will condescend to
intrude itself. I was present when a huge *Flamande*,
in appearance so intrepid that I respectfully pitied
her husband, came to ask the character of a *bonne;*
I was amazed to hear her say, "I hope the girl is
strong, for when the revolution comes next May and
I have to turn off my helper, she will have enough
to do." It seemed to me that a political apprehension must be pretty general when it affected that
most non-speculative of speculations, the *reckoning* of
a housewife. With this feeling, everybody saved
their money : who would spend in luxuries that which
might so soon be necessary and invaluable! This
economy made commerce — especially the peculiarly
Parisian trade, which is almost wholly in articles
that *can* be spared — worse and worse ; the more depressed trade became the more the traders feared,
and the more they feared the worse all trade inevitably grew.

I apprehend that this feeling extended very generally among all the classes who do not find or make
a livelihood by literature or by politics. Among the
clever people who understood the subject, very likely
the expectation was extremely different; but among
the stupid ones who mind their business and have a
business to mind, there was a universal and excessive
tremor. The only notion of '52 was "on se battra dans
la rue." * Their dread was especially of Socialism :

* "There will be fighting in the streets."

they expected that the followers of M. Proudhon,
who advisedly and expressly maintains "anarchy"
to be the best form of government, would attempt to
carry out their theories in action, and that the division
between the legislative and executive power would
so cripple the party of order as to make their means
of resistance for the moment feeble and difficult to
use. The more sensible did not, I own, expect the
annihilation of mankind,—civilization dies hard, the
organized sense in all countries is strong; but they
expected vaguely and crudely that the party which
in '93 ruled for many months, and which in June
'48 fought so fanatically against the infant republic,
would certainly make a desperate attack,—*might* for
some time obtain the upper hand. Of course it is
now matter of mere argument whether the danger
was real or unreal, and it is in some quarters rather
the fashion to quiz the past fear and to deny that
any Socialists anywhere exist; in spite of the literary
exertions of Proudhon and Louis Blanc, in spite of
the prison quarrels of Blanqui and Barbés, there are
certainly found people who question whether anybody
buys the books of the two former or cares for the
incarcerated dissensions of the two latter. But however this may be, it is certain that two days after the
coup d'état a mass of persons thought it worth while
to erect some dozen barricades: and among these, and
superintending and directing their every movement,
there certainly were (for I saw them myself) men
whose physiognomy and accoutrements exactly resembled the traditional Montagnard,—sallow, stern, compressed, with much-marked features which expressed
but resisted suffering and brooding one-ideaed thought;
men who from their youth upward had forever imagined, like Jonah, that they did well—immensely well
—to be angry; men armed to the teeth, and ready,
like the soldiers of the first Republic, to use their
arms savagely and well in defense of theories broached
by a Robespierre, a Blanqui, or a Barbés; gloomy

fanatics, *over*-principled ruffians. I may perhaps be mistaken in reading in their features the characters of such men; but I know that when one of them disturbed my superintendence of barricade-making with a stern *allez-vous en*, it was not too slowly that I departed, for I *felt* that he would rather shoot me than not. Having seen these people, I conceive that they exist: but supposing that they were all simply fabulous, it would not less be certain that they were *believed* to be, and to be active; nor would it impair the fact that the quiet classes awaited their onslaught in morbid apprehension, with miserable and craven — and I fear we ought to say *commercial*—disquietude.

You will not be misled by any high-flown speculations about liberty or equality. You will, I imagine, concede to me that the first duty of a government is to insure the security of that industry which is the condition of social life and civilized cultivation; that — especially in so excitable a country as France — it is necessary that the dangerous classes should be saved from the strong temptation of long idleness; and that no danger could be more formidable than six months' beggary among the revolutionary *ouvriers*, immediately preceding the exact period fixed by European as well as French opinion for an apprehended convulsion. It is from this state of things, whether by fair means or foul, that Louis Napoleon has delivered France. The effect was magical: like people who have nearly died because it was prophesied they would die at a specified time, and instantly recovered when they found or thought that the time was gone and past, so France, timorously anticipating the fated revolution, in a moment revived when she found or fancied that it was come and over. Commerce instantly improved; New-Year's Day, when all the boulevards are one continued fair, has not (as I am told) been for some years so gay and splendid; people began to buy, and consequently to sell: for though it is quite possible, or even probable, that new misfortunes

and convulsions may be in store for the French people, yet no one can say when they will be, and to
wait till revolutions be exhausted is but the best
Parisian for our old acquaintance *Rusticus expectat.**
Clever people may now prove that the dreaded peril
was a simple chimera; but they can't deny that the
fear of it was very real and painful, nor can they
dispute that in a week after the *coup d'état* it had at
once and apparently forever passed away.

I fear it must be said that no legal or constitutional act could have given an equal confidence.
What was wanted was the assurance of an audacious
government, which would stop at nothing, scruple at
nothing, to secure its own power and the tranquillity
of the country. That assurance all now have : a man
who will in this manner dare to dissolve an assembly
constitutionally his superiors, then prevent their meeting by armed force; so well and so sternly repress
the first beginning of an outbreak; with so little mis-
giving assume and exercise sole power, — may have
enormous other defects, but is certainly a bold ruler,
most probably an unscrupulous one, little likely to
flinch from any inferior trial.

Of Louis Napoleon, whose personal qualities are for
the moment so important, I cannot now speak at
length. But I may say that with whatever other deficiencies he may have, he has one excellent advantage
over other French statesmen, — he has never been a
professor, nor a journalist, nor a promising barrister,
nor by taste a *littérateur*. He has not confused
himself with history; he does not think in leading
articles, in long speeches, or in agreeable essays : but
he is capable of observing facts rightly, of reflecting
on them simply, and [of] acting on them discreetly.
And his motto is Danton's, "De l'audace et toujours
de l'audace;"† and this you know, according to
Bacon,‡ in time of revolution will carry a man far, —
perhaps even to ultimate victory, and that ever-future
millennium "la consolidation de la France."

---

* "The countryman waits" (for the stream to run dry, so he can cross).

But on these distant questions I must not touch. I have endeavored to show you what was the crisis, how strong the remedy, and what the need of a dictatorship. I hope to have convinced you that the first was imminent, the second effectual, and the last expedient.

I remain yours,   AMICUS.

LETTER II.

THE MORALITY OF THE COUP D'ÉTAT.

PARIS, Jan. 15, 1852.

SIR, — I know quite well what will be said about or in answer to my last letter. It will be alleged that I think everything in France is to be postponed to the Parisian commerce; that a constitution, equality, liberty, a representative government, are all to be set aside if they interfere even for a moment with the sale of *étrennes* * or the manufacture of gimcracks.

I, as you know, hold no such opinions; it would not be necessary for me to undeceive you, who would, I rather hope, never suspect me of *that* sort of folly: but as St. Athanasius aptly observes, "for the sake of the women who may be led astray, I will this very instant explain my sentiments."

Contrary to Sheridan's rule, I commence by a concession. I certainly admit — indeed, I would upon occasion maintain — *bonbons* and bracelets to be things less important than common law and constitutional action. A *coup d'état* would, I may allow, be mischievously supererogatory if it only promoted the enjoyment of what a lady in the highest circles is said to call "bigotry and virtue." But the real question is not to be so disposed of: the Parisian trade, the jewelry, the baubles, the silks, the luxuries, which the Exhibition showed us to be the characteristic industry of France, are very dust in the balance if weighed against the hands and arms which their

* New-Year gifts.

manufacture employs, the industrial habits which their regular sale rewards, the hunger and idle weariness which the certain demand for them prevents. For this is the odd peculiarity of commercial civilization: the life, the welfare, the existence of thousands depend on their being paid for doing what seems nothing when done. That gorgeous dandies should wear gorgeous studs, that pretty girls should be prettily dressed, that pleasant drawing-rooms should be pleasantly attired, may seem to people of our age sad trifling; but grave as we are, we must become graver still when we reflect on the horrid suffering which the sudden cessation of large luxurious consumption would certainly create, if we imagine such a city as Lyons to be without warning turned out of work, and the population feelingly told "to cry in the streets when no man regardeth."

The first duty of society is the preservation of society. By the sound work of old-fashioned generations, by the singular painstaking of the slumberers in churchyards, by dull care, by stupid industry, a certain social fabric somehow exists; people contrive to go out to their work, and to find work to employ them actually until the evening; body and soul are kept together, — and this is what mankind have to show for their six thousand years of toil and trouble.

To keep up this system we must sacrifice everything. Parliaments, liberty, leading articles, essays, eloquence, all are good, but they are secondary; at all hazards, and if we can, mankind must be kept alive. And observe, as time goes on, this fabric becomes a tenderer and a tenderer thing. Civilization can't bivouac; dangers, hardships, sufferings, lightly borne by the coarse muscle of earlier times, are soon fatal to noble and cultivated organization. Women in early ages are masculine; and as a return match, the men of late years are becoming women. The strong apprehension of a Napoleonic invasion has perhaps just now caused more substantial misery in England than once the wars of the Roses.

To apply this "screed of doctrine" to the condition of France:—I do not at all say that but for the
late *coup d'état*, French civilization would certainly
have soon come to a final end. *Some* people might
have continued to take their meals; even Socialism
would hardly abolish *eau sucrée:* but I do assert that
according to the common belief of the common
people, their common comforts were in considerable
danger. The debasing torture of acute apprehension
was eating into the crude pleasure of stupid lives.
No man liked to take a long bill; no one could imagine to himself what was coming. Fear was para-
lyzing life and labor; and as I said at length in my
last, fear so intense, whether at first reasonable
or unreasonable, will ere long invincibly justify itself.
May, 1852, would in all likelihood have been an
evil and bloody time if it had been preceded by six
months' famine among the starvable classes.

At present all is changed. Six weeks ago society was living from hand to mouth; now she feels
sure of her next meal. And this, in a dozen words,
is the real case, the political excuse for Prince Louis
Napoleon. You ask me, or I should not do so, to
say a word or two on the moral question and the
oath. You are aware how limited my means of
doing so are; I have forgotten Paley, and have never
read the Casuists: but it certainly does not seem
to me proved or clear that a man who has sworn,
even in the most solemn manner, to see another
drown, is therefore quite bound or even at liberty
to stand placidly on the bank. What ethical philosopher has demonstrated this? Coleridge said it was
difficult to advance a new error in morals, yet this,
I think, would be one; and the keeping of oaths is
peculiarly a point of mere science, for Christianity—
in terms at least—only forbids them all. And supposing I am right, such certainly was the exact position of Louis Napoleon: he saw society—I will not
say dying or perishing, for I hate unnecessarily to
overstate my point—in danger of incurring extreme

and perhaps lasting calamities, likely not only to impair the happiness but moreover to debase the character of the French nation; and these calamities he could prevent. Now, who has shown that ethics require of him to have held his hand?

The severity with which the riot was put down on the first Thursday in December has, I observe, produced an extreme effect in England; and with our happy exemption from martial bloodshed, it must of course do so. But better one *émeute* now than many in May, be it ever remembered: there are things more demoralizing than death, and among these is the sickly-apprehensive suffering for long months of an entire people.

Of course you understand that I am not holding up Louis Napoleon as a complete standard either of ethical scrupulosity or disinterested devotedness: veracity has never been the family failing, for the great Emperor was a still greater liar; and Prince Louis has been long playing what, morality apart, is the greatest political misfortune to any statesman,—a visibly selfish game. Very likely, too, the very high heroes of history—a Washington, an Aristides, by Carlyle profanely called "favorites of Dryasdust"—would have extricated the country more easily and perhaps more completely from its scrape: their ennobling rectitude would have kept M. de Girardin consistent, and induced M. Thiers to vote for the revision of the Constitution; and even though, as of old, the Mountain were deafer than the uncharmed adder, a sufficient number of self-seeking Conservatives might have been induced, by perfect confidence in a perfect President, to mend a crotchety performance that was visibly ruining what the poet calls "the ever-ought-to-be-conserved thing," their country.

I remember reading, several years ago, an article in the *Westminster Review* on the lamented Armand Carrel, in which the author* (well known to be one of our most distinguished philosophers) took occasion to observe that what the French most wanted was

---

* John Stuart Mill, October, 1837; reprinted in Mill's works.

"un homme de caractère." Everybody is aware—for
all except myself know French quite perfectly—that
this expression is not by any means equivalent to our
common phrase a "man of character," or "respectable individual"; it does not at all refer to mere goodness: it is more like what we sometimes say of an
eccentric country gentleman, "He is a character;" for
it denotes a singular preponderance of peculiar qualities, an accomplished obstinacy, and inveterate fixedness of resolution and idea that enables him to get
done what he undertakes. The Duke of Wellington is
par excellence homme de caractère; Lord Palmerston
rather so; Mr. Cobden a little; Lord John Russell
not at all. Now, exactly this, beyond the immense
majority of educated men, Louis Napoleon is, as a
pointed writer describes him:—"The President is a
superior man, but his superiority is of the sort that is
hidden under a dubious exterior: his life is entirely
internal,—his speech does not betray his inspiration,
his gesture does not copy his audacity, his look does
not reflect his ardor, his step does not reveal his
resolution; his whole mental nature is in some sort
repressed by his physical; he thinks and does not
discuss, he decides and does not deliberate, he acts
without agitation, he speaks and assigns no reason;
his best friends are unacquainted with him,—he ob-
tains their confidence but never asks it."* Also, his
whole nature is and has been absorbed in the task
which he has undertaken. For many months, his
habitual expression has been exactly that of a gambler who is playing for his highest and last stake;
in society it is said to be the same,—a general and
diffusive politeness, but an ever-ready reflection and
a constant reserve. His great qualities are rather peculiar. He is not, like his uncle, a creative genius who
will leave behind him social institutions such as those
which nearly alone, in this changeful country, seem
to be always exempt from every change; he will

---

* M. de la Guerronnière in the Paris *Pays;* translated (differently) in London *Morning Chronicle;* that translation reprinted in *Littell's,* Nov. 1, 1851.

suggest little; he has hardly an organizing mind: but he will coolly estimate his own position and that of France; he will observe all dangers and compute all chances. He can act, he can be idle; he may work what is, he may administer the country. Anyhow, *il fera son possible,** and you know in the nineteenth century how much and how rare that is.

I see many people are advancing beautiful but untrue ethics about his private character. Thus I may quote as follows from a very estimable writer:— "On the 14th October he requested his passports, and left Arenenberg for London. In this capital he remained from the end of 1838 to the month of August, 1840. In these twenty months, instead of learning to command armies and to govern empires, his days and nights, when not given to frivolous pleasures, were passed on the turf, in the betting-room, or in clubs where high play and desperate stakes roused the jaded energy of the *blasé* gambler."— (A. V. Kirwan, Esq., Barrister-at-Law, in *Fraser's Magazine.*†) The notion of this gentleman clearly is, that a betting man can't in nature be a good statesman; that horse-racing is providentially opposed to political excellence; that "by an interesting illustration of the argument from design, we notice an antithesis alike marvelous and inevitable" between turf and tariffs. But setting Paley for a moment apart, how is a man by circumstances excluded from military and political life, and by birth from commercial pursuits, really and effectually to learn administration? Mr. Kirwan imagines that he should read all through Burke, commonplace Tacitus, collate Cicero, and annotate Montesquieu. Yet take an analogous case,— suppose a man shut out from trading life is to qualify himself for the practical management of a counting-house: do you fancy he will do it by "a judicious study of the principles of political economy," and by elaborately

---

* "He will do his utmost."   † Of January, 1852.

rereading Adam Smith and John Mill? He had better be at Newmarket, and devote his *heures perdues* to the Oaks and the St. Leger. He may learn there what he will never acquire from literary study,— the instinctive habit of applied calculation, which is essential to a merchant and extremely useful to a statesman. Where, too, did Sir Robert Walpole learn business, or Charles Fox, or anybody in the eighteenth century? And after all, M. Michel de Bourges gave the real solution of the matter:—"Louis Napoleon," said the best orator of the Mountain, "may have had rather a stormy youth [laughter]. But don't suppose that any one in all France imagines you, you *Messieurs* of the immaculate majority, to be the least better [sensation]. I am not speaking to saints [uproar]." If compared with contemporary French statesmen, and the practical choice is between him and them, the President will not seem what he appears when measured by the notions of a people who exact at least from inferior functionaries *a rigid decorum in the pettiest details of their private morals.*

I have but one last point to make about this *coup d'état*, and then I will release you from my writing. I do not know whether you in England rightly realize the French Socialism. Take, for instance, M. Proudhon, who is perhaps their ideal and perfect type; he was *représentant de la Seine* in the late Assembly, elected (which is not unimportant) after the publication of his books and on account of his opinions: in his "Confessions d'un Révolutionnaire," a very curious book (for he writes extremely well), after maintaining that our well-known but (as we imagine) advanced friends, Ledru Rollin and Louis Blanc and Barbès and Blanqui, are all *réactionnaires*, and clearly showing, to the grief of mankind, that once the legislator of the Luxembourg wished to preserve "equilibrium" and the author of the provincial circulars to maintain "tranquillity," he gives the following *bona fide* and amusing account of his own investigations:—

"I commenced my task of solitary conspiracy by the study of the socialisms of antiquity necessary in my judgment to determine the law, whether practical or theoretical, of progress; these socialisms I found in the Bible. A memoir on the institution of the Sabbath — considered with regard to morals, to health, and in its relation to the family and the city — procured for me a bronze medal from my academy. From the faith in which I had been reared, I had precipitated myself headlong, head-foremost, into pure reason; and already, what was wonderful and a good omen, when I made Moses a philosopher and a socialist I was greeted with applause. If I am now in error, the fault is not merely mine: was there ever a similar seduction?

"But I studied, above all, with a view to action: I cared little for academical laurels; I had no leisure to become a *savant*, still less a *littérateur* or an archæologist. I began immediately upon political economy.

"I had assumed, as the rule of my investigations, that every principle which pushed to its consequences should end in a contradiction must be considered false and null; and that if this principle had been developed into an institution, the institution itself must be considered as factitious, as utopian.

"Furnished with this criterion, I chose for the subject of investigation what I found in society the most ancient, the most respectable, the most universal, the least controverted, — property. Everybody knows what happened: after a long, a minute, and above all an impartial analysis, I arrived, as an algebraist guided by his equations, at this surprising conclusion, — Property, consider it as you will, refer it to what principle you may, is a contradictory idea; and as the denial of property carries with it of necessity that of authority, I deduced immediately from my first axiom also this corollary, not less paradoxical, — the true form of government is *anarchy*. Lastly, finding by a mathematical demonstration that no amelioration in the economy of society could be arrived at by its natural constitution, or without the concurrence and reflective adhesion of its members; observing also that there is a definite epoch in the life of societies, in which their progress, at first unreflecting, requires the intervention of the free reason of man, — I concluded that this spontaneous and impulsive force [*cette force d'impulsion spontanée*], which we call Providence, is not everything in the affairs of this world: from that moment, without being an Atheist, I ceased to worship God. 'He'll get on without your so doing,' said to me one day the *Constitutionnel.* Well, perhaps he may."*

These theories have been expanded into many and weary volumes, and condensed into the famous phrase,

* A *very* free translation. — ED.

"La propriété c'est le vol;"* and have procured their author, in his own sect, reputation and authority.

The *Constitutionnel* had another hit against M. Proudhon a day or two ago: they presented their readers with two decrees in due official form (the walls were at the moment covered with those of the 2d of December), as the last ideal of what the straitest sect of the Socialists particularly desire. It was as follows:—"Nothing any longer exists. Nobody is charged with the execution of the aforesaid decree. Signed, VACUUM."

Such is the speculation of the new reformers; what their practices would be I can hardly tell you. My feeble income does not allow me to travel to the Basses Alpes and really investigate the subject; but if one quarter of the stories in circulation are in the least to be believed (we are quite dependent on oral information, for the government papers deal in asterisks and "details unfit for publication," and the rest are devoted to the state of the navy and say nothing), the atrocities rival the nauseous corruption of what our Liberal essayist† calls "Jacobin carrion," the old days of Carrier and Barère. This is what people here are afraid of; and that is why I write such things, and not to horrify you or amuse you or bore you— anything rather than that; and they think themselves happy in finding a man who, with or without whatever other qualities or defects, will keep them from the vaunted Millennium and much-expected *Jacquerie.* I hope you think so too; and that I am not, as they say in my native Tipperary, "whistling jigs to a milestone."

I am, sir, yours truly,   AMICUS.

P. S.—You will perhaps wish me to say something on the great event of this week,—the exile of the more dangerous members of the late Assembly, and the transportation of the Socialists to Cayenne. Both

---

* "Property is robbery."   † Macaulay, close of Essay on Barère.

measures were here expected, though I think that both lists are more numerous than was anticipated; but no one really knew what would be done by this silent government. You will laugh at me when I tell you that both measures have been well received; but properly limited and understood, I am persuaded that the fact is so.

Of course, among the friends of exiled *représentants*, among the *littérateurs* throughout whose ranks these measures are intended to "strike terror and inspire respect,"* you would hear that there never was such tyranny since the beginning of mankind; but among the mass of the industrious classes, between whom and the politicians there is internecine war, I fancy that on turning the conversation to either of the most recent events, you would hear something of this sort : — "Ça ne m'occupe pas."† "What is that to me?" "Je suis pour la tranquillité, moi."‡ "I sold four brooches yesterday." The Socialists who have been removed from prison to the colony, it is agreed were "pestilent fellows, perverting the nation" and forbidding to pay tribute to M. Bonaparte. Indeed, they can hardly expect commercial sympathy : "Our national honor rose, our stocks fell," is Louis Blanc's perpetual comment on his favorite events; and it is difficult to say which of its two clauses he dwells upon with the intenser relish. It is generally thought, by those who think about the matter, that both the transportation and — in all cases, certainly — the exile will only be a temporary measure, and that the great mass of the people in both lists will be allowed to return to their homes when the present season of extreme excitement has passed over. Still, I am not prepared to defend the *number* of the transportations. That strong measures of the sort were necessary, I make no doubt : if Socialism exist and the fear of it exist, something must be done to reassure the people.

---

* Kinglake, "Eöthen."   † "That doesn't concern me."
‡ "For my part, I am for peace."

You will understand that it is not a judicial proceeding either in essence or in form; it is not to be considered as a punishment for what men have done, but as a perfect precaution against what they may do. Certainly it is to be regretted that the cause of order is so weak as to need such measures; but if it *is* so weak, the government must no doubt take them. Of course, however, "our brethren," who are retained in such numbers to write down Prince Louis, are quite right to use without stint or stopping this most un-English proceeding: it is their case, and you and I from old misdeeds know pretty well how it is to be managed. There will be no imputation of reasonable or humane motives to the government, and no examination of the existing state of France, — let both these come from the other side; but elegiac eloquence is inexhaustibly exuded, the cruel corners of history are ransacked for petrifying precedents, and I observe much excellent weeping on the Cromwellian deportations and the ten-years' exile of Madame de Staël. But after all they have missed the tempting parallel, — I mean the "rather long" proscription list which Octavius, "l'ancien neveu de l'ancien oncle," concocted with Mark Antony in the marshes of Bononia, and whereby they thoroughly purged old Rome of its turbulent and revolutionary elements. I suspect our estimable contemporaries regret to remember of how much good order, long tranquillity, "*beata pleno copia cornu*," and other many "little comforts" to the civilized world, that very "strong" proceeding, whether in ethics justifiable or not, certainly was in fact the beginning and foundation.

The fate of the African generals is much to be regretted, and the government will incur much odium if the exile of General Changarnier is prolonged any length of time. He is doubtless "dangerous" for the moment, for his popularity with the army is considerable and he divides the party of order; he is also a practical man and an unpleasant enemy: but he is much respected, and little likely (I fancy) to attempt anything against any settled government.

As for M. Thiers and M. Emile de Girardin, the ablest of the exiles, I have heard no one pity them; they have played a selfish game, they have encountered a better player, they have been beaten — and this is the whole matter. You will remember that it was the adhesion of these two men that procured for M. Bonaparte a large part of his *first* six millions [of votes] : M. de Girardin, whom General Cavaignac had discreetly imprisoned and indiscreetly set free, wrote up the "opposition candidate" daily in the *Presse* (he has since often and often tried to write him down), and M. Thiers was his Privy Councillor. "*Mon cher Prince*," they say, said the latter, "your address to the people won't do at all : I'll get one of the *rédacteurs* of the *Constitutionnel* to draw you up something tolerable." You remember the easy patronage with which Cicero speaks in his letter of the "boy" that was outwitting him all the while. But, however, observe I do not at all, notwithstanding my Latin, insinuate or assert that Louis Napoleon, though a considerable man, is exactly equal to keep the footsteps of Augustus : a feeble parody may suffice for an inferior stage and not too gigantic generation.

Now I really *have* done.

LETTER III.

ON THE NEW CONSTITUTION OF FRANCE, AND THE APTITUDE OF THE FRENCH CHARACTER FOR NATIONAL FREEDOM.

PARIS, Jan. 20, 1852.

SIR, — We have now got our Constitution. The Napoleonic era has commenced : the term of the dictatorship is fixed, and the consolidation of France is begun. You will perhaps anticipate, from the conclusion of the last letter, that apropos of this great event I

should gratify you with bright anticipations of an
Augustan age and a quick revival of Catonic virtue,
with an assurance that the night is surely passed and
the day altogether come, with a solemn invocation to
the rising luminary and an original panegyric on the
"golden-throned morning."

I must always regret to disappoint any one; but I
feel obliged to entertain you instead with torpid philosophy, constitutional details, and a dull disquisition
on national character.

The details of the new institutions you will have
long ago learnt from the daily papers; I believe they
may be fairly and nearly accurately described as the
Constitution of the Consulate, *minus* the ideas of the
man who made it. You will remember that besides
the First Magistrate, the Senate, the House of Representatives, the Council of State (which we may call
in legal language the "common form" of Continental
constitution), the ingenious Abbé Sièyes had devised
some four principal peculiarities, which were to be
remembered to all time as masterpieces of political
invention: these were the utter inaction of the First
Magistrate (copied, as I believe, from the English
Constitution); the subordination to him of two Con-
suls, one to administer peace and the other war, who
were intended to be the real hands and arms of the
government; the silence of the Senate; the double
and very peculiar election of the House of Representatives. Napoleon the Great, as we are now to speak,
struck out the first of these, being at the moment
working some fifteen hours a day at the reorganiza-
tion of France; he said plainly and rather sternly that
he had no intention of doing nothing. The *idéologue*
went to the wall; the "excellent idea," put forth in
happy forgetfulness of real facts and real people, was
instantly abandoned; for the Grand Elector was sub-
stituted a First Consul, who, so far from being nothing,
was very soon the whole government. Napoleon the
Little, as I fear the Parisian multitude may learn

to call him, has effaced the other three "strokes of statesmanship": the new constitution of France is exactly the "common form" of political conveyancing, *plus* the *idée Napoléonienne* of an all-suggesting and all-administering mind.

I have extremely little to tell you about its reception : it has made no "sensation," not so much as even the "fortified camps" which his Grace is said to be devising for the defense of our own London. Indeed, "Il a peur"* is a very common remark (conceivable to everybody who knows "the Duke"), and it would seem even a refreshing alleviation of their domestic sorrows. In fact, home politics are now *the* topic : geography and the state of foreign institutions are not indeed the true Parisian line, but it has in fine been distinctly discovered that there are no *salons* in Cayenne, — which once certain, the logical genius of the nation with incredible swiftness deduced the clear conclusion that it was better not to go there. Seriously, I fancy — for I have no data on which to found real knowledge of so delicate a point — the new Constitution is regarded merely as what Father Newman would call a "preservative addition" or a "necessary development," essential to the "chronic continuance" of the Napoleonic system : for the moment the mass of the people wish the President to govern them, but they don't seem to me to care how. The political people, I suppose, hate it because for some time it will enable him, if not shot, to govern effectually. I say if not shot ; for people are habitually recounting under their breath some new story of an attempt at assassination which the papers suppress. I am inclined to think that these rumors are pure lies ; but they show the feeling. You know, according to the Constitution of 1848, the President would now be a mere outlaw, and whoever finds him may slay him if he can. It is true that the elaborate masterpiece of M. Marrast is already fallen into utter oblivion (it is no more remembered

* "He is afraid."

than yesterday's *Times,* or the political institutions of
Saxon Mercia); but nevertheless such, according to
the antediluvian *régime,* would be the law, and it
is possible that a mindful Montagnard may upon
occasion recall even so insignificant a circumstance.

I have a word to say on the Prologue of the
President. When I first began to talk politics with
French people, I was much impressed by the fact to
which he has there drawn attention. You know that
all such conversation, when one of the interlocutors is
a foreigner, speaking slowly and but imperfectly the
language of the country in which he is residing, is
pretty much in the style of that excellent work which
was the terror of our childhood, Joyce's "Scientific
Dialogues"; wherein, as you may remember, an accomplished tutor, with a singular gift of scholastic
improvisation, instructs a youthful pupil exceedingly
given to feeble questions and auscultatory repose.
Now, when I began in Parisian society thus to enact
the *rôle* of "George" or "Caroline," I was, I repeat,
much struck with the fact that the Emperor had done
everything : to whatever subject my diminutive inquiry related, the answer was nearly universally the
same, — an elegy on Napoleon. Nor is this exactly
absurd ; for whether or not "the nephew" is right in
calling the uncle the greatest of modern statesmen,
he is indisputably the modern statesman who has
founded the greatest number of existing institutions.
In the pride of philosophy and in the madness of
an hour, the Constituent Assembly and the Conven-
tion swept away not only the monstrous abuses of
the old *régime,* but that *régime* itself, its essence and
its mechanism, utterly and entirely; they destroyed
whatever they could lay their hands on : the consequence was certain, — when they tried to construct
they found they had no materials ; they left a vacuum.
No greater benefit could have been conferred on politicians gifted with the creative genius of Napoleon :
it was like the fire of London to Sir Christopher

Wren. With a fertility of invention and an obstinacy in execution equaling if not surpassing those of Cæsar and Charlemagne, he had before him an open stage more clear and more vast than in historical times fortune has ever offered to any statesman. He was nearly in the position of the imagined legislator of the Greek legends and the Greek philosophers, — he could enact any law and rescind any law. Accordingly, the educational system, the banking system, the financial system, the municipal system, the administrative system, the civil legislation, the penal legislation, the commercial legislation, besides all manner of secondary creations, public buildings and public institutions without number, all date from the time, and are more or less deeply inscribed with the genius, the firm will, and [the] unresting energies of Napoleon. And this, which is the great strength of the present President, is the great difficulty — I fear the insurmountable difficulty — in the way of Henry V. The first Revolution is to the French what the Deluge is to the rest of mankind : the whole system then underwent an entire change. A French politician will no more cite as authority the domestic policy of Colbert or Louvois than we should think of going for ethics and æsthetics to the bigamy of Lamech or the musical accomplishments of Tubal Cain. If the Comte de Chambord be (as it is quite on the cards that he may be) within a few years restored, he must govern by the instrumentality of laws and systems devised by the politicians whom he execrates and denounces, and devised, moreover, often enough, especially to keep out him and his. It is difficult to imagine that a strong government can be composed of materials so inharmonious. Meanwhile, to the popular imagination, "the Emperor" is the past : the house of Bourbon is as historical as the house of Valois ; a peasant is little oftener reminded of the "third dynasty" than of the long-haired kings.

In discussing any constitution, there are two ideas

to be first got rid of. The first is the idea of our barbarous ancestors, — now happily banished from all civilized society, but still prevailing in old manor-houses, in rural parsonages, and other curious repositories of moldering ignorance, and which in such arid solitudes is thus expressed : — "Why can't they have Kings, Lords, and Commons, *like we have?* What fools foreigners are!" The second pernicious mistake is, like the former, seldom now held upon system, but so many hold it in bits and fragments and without system that it is still rather formidable: I allude to the old idea — which still here [and there] creeps out in conversation, and sometimes in writing — that politics are simply a subdivision of immutable ethics; that there are certain rights of men in all places and all times, which are the sole and sufficient foundation of all government; and that accordingly a single stereotype government is to make the tour of the world, — that you have no more right to deprive a Dyak of his vote in a "possible" Polynesian Parliament than you have to steal his mat.

Burke first taught the world at large, in opposition to both and especially to the latter of these notions, that politics are made of time and place; that institutions are shifting things, to be tried by and adjusted to the shifting conditions of a mutable world; that in fact, politics are but a piece of business, to be determined in every case by the exact exigencies of that case, — in plain English, by sense and circumstances.

This was a great step in political philosophy, though it *now* seems the events of 1848 have taught thinking persons (I fancy) further : they have enabled us to say that of all these circumstances so affecting political problems, by far and out of all question the most important is *national character.* In that year the same experiment — the experiment, as its friends say of liberal and constitutional government, as its enemies say of anarchy and revolution — was tried in every nation of Europe ; with what varying futures and differing results! The effect has been to teach men not only speculatively to know, but practically to feel, that no absurdity is so great as to imagine the same species of institutions suitable or possible for Scotchmen and Sicilians, for Germans and Frenchmen, for the English and the Neapolitans. With a well-balanced national character (we now know), liberty is a stable thing; a really practical people will work in political business, as in private business, almost the absurdest, the feeblest, the most inconsistent set of imaginable regulations. Similarly, or rather reversely, the best institutions will not keep right a nation that *will* go wrong: paper is but paper, and no virtue is to be discovered in it to retain within due boundaries the undisciplined passions of those who have never set themselves seriously to restrain them. In a word, as people of "large roundabout common-sense"* will as a rule somehow get on in life, no matter what their circumstances or their fortune, so a nation which applies good judgment, forbearance, a rational and compromising habit, to the management of free institutions will certainly succeed; while the more eminently gifted national character will but be a source and germ of endless and disastrous failure if, with whatever other eminent qualities, it be deficient in these plain, solid, and essential requisites.

The formation of *this* character is one of the most secret of marvelous mysteries. Why nations have the character we see them to have is, speaking generally, as little explicable to our shallow perspicacity as why individuals, our friends or our enemies, for good or for evil, have the character which they have: why one man is stupid and another clever, why another volatile and a fourth consistent, this man by instinct generous, that man by instinct niggardly. I am not speaking of actions, you observe, but of tendencies and temptations. These and other similar problems daily crowd on our observation in millions

* See note to page 103.

and millions, and only do not puzzle us because we are too familiar with their difficulty to dream of attempting their solution. Only this much is most certain: all men and all nations have a character, and that character when once taken is—I do not say unchangeable: religion modifies it, catastrophe annihilates it, but—the least changeable thing in this ever-varying and changeful world. Take the soft mind of the boy, and (strong and exceptional aptitudes and tendencies excepted) you may make him merchant, barrister, butcher, baker, surgeon, or apothecary: but once make him an apothecary, and he will never afterwards bake wholesome bread; make him a butcher, and he will kill too extensively even for a surgeon; make him a barrister, and he will be dim on double-entry and crass on bills of lading. Once conclusively form him to one thing, and no art and no science will ever twist him to another. Nature, says the philosopher, has no Delphic daggers, no men or maids of all work: she keeps one being to one pursuit; to each is a single choice afforded, but no more again thereafter forever. And it is the same with nations: the Jews of to-day are the Jews in face and form of the Egyptian sculptures, in character they are the Jews of Moses; the negro is the negro of a thousand years, the Chinese by his own account is the mummy of a million. "Races and their varieties," says the historian, "seem to have been created with an inward *nisus* diminishing with the age of the world." The people of the South are yet the people of the South, fierce and angry as their summer sun; the people of the North are still cold and stubborn like their own north-wind; the people of the East "mark not, but are still"; the people of the West are "going to and fro in the earth, and walking up and down in it." The fact is certain, the cause beyond us; the subtle system of obscure causes, whereby sons and daughters resemble not only their fathers and mothers, but even their great-great-grandfathers and their great-great-grandmothers, may very likely be destined to be very inscrutable: but as the fact is so, so moreover in history nations have one character, one set of talents, one list of temptations, and one duty,—to use the one and get the better of the other. There are breeds in the animal man just as in the animal dog: when you hunt with greyhounds and course with beagles, then and not till then may you expect the inbred habits of a thousand years to pass away, that Hindoos can be free or that Englishmen will be slaves.

I need not prove to you that the French *have* a national character, nor need I try your patience with a likeness of it: I have only to examine whether it be a fit basis for national freedom. I fear you will laugh when I tell you what I conceive to be about the most essential mental quality for a free people whose liberty is to be progressive, permanent, and on a large scale; it is much *stupidity*. I see you are surprised; you are going to say to me, as Socrates did to Polus, "My young friend, *of course* you are right; but will you explain what you mean? as yet you are not intelligible."* I will do so as well as I can, or† endeavor to make good what I say, not by an *a priori* demonstration of my own, but from the details of the present and the facts of history. Not to begin by wounding any present susceptibilities, let me take the Roman character; for with one great exception,—I need not say to whom I allude,—they are the great political people of history. Now, is not a certain dullness their most visible characteristic? What is the history of their speculative mind? a blank; what their literature? a copy. They have left not a single discovery in any abstract science, not a single perfect or well-formed work of high imagination. The Greeks, the perfection of narrow and accomplished genius, bequeathed to mankind the ideal forms of self-idolizing art, the Romans imitated and admired;

---

* Presumptively in Plato's "Gorgias"; but there is nothing of the sort in it.—ED.　† An evident misprint for "and."—ED.

the Greeks explained the laws of nature, the Romans wondered and despised; the Greeks invented a system of numerals second only to that now in use, the Romans counted to the end of their days with the clumsy apparatus which we still call by their name; the Greeks made a capital and scientific calendar, the Romans began their month when the Pontifex Maximus happened to spy out the new moon. Throughout Latin literature, this is the perpetual puzzle:—Why are we free and they slaves, we prætors and they barbers? why do the stupid people always win and the clever people always lose? I need not say that in real sound stupidity, the English are unrivaled: you'll hear more wit and better wit in an Irish street row than would keep Westminster Hall in humor for five weeks. Or take Sir Robert Peel, our last great statesman, the greatest member of Parliament that ever lived, an absolutely perfect transacter of public business,—the type of the nineteenth-century Englishman, as Sir R. Walpole was of the eighteenth: was there ever such a dull man? Can any one without horror foresee the reading of his memoirs? A *clairvoyante*, with the book shut, may get on; but who now in the flesh will ever endure the open *vision* of endless recapitulation of interminable Hansard? Or take Mr. Tennyson's inimitable description:—

> "No little lily-handed baronet he:
> A great broad-shouldered genial Englishman,
> A lord of fat prize oxen and of sheep,
> A raiser of huge melons and of pine,
> A patron of some thirty charities,
> A pamphleteer on guano and on grain,
> A quarter-sessions chairman, abler none."*

Whose company so soporific? His talk is of truisms and bullocks; his head replete with rustic visions of mutton and turnips and a cerebral edition of Burn's "Justice"! Notwithstanding, he is the salt of the earth, the best of the English breed: who is like him for sound sense? But I must restrain my enthusiasm.

---

* "The Princess," near the close.

You don't want me to tell you that a Frenchman — a real Frenchman — can't be stupid: *esprit* is his essence, wit is to him as water, *bons-mots* as *bonbons*. He reads and he learns by reading; levity and literature are essentially his line. Observe the consequence: the outbreak of 1848 was accepted in every province in France; the decrees of the Parisian mob were received and registered in all the municipalities of a hundred cities; the Revolution ran like the fluid of the telegraph down the *Chemin de fer du Nord*,* it stopped at the Belgian frontier; once brought into contact with the dull phlegm of the stupid Fleming, the poison was powerless. You remember what the Norman butler said to Wilkin Flammock of the fulling mills, at the castle of the Garde Douloureuse: — "That which will but warm your Flemish hearts will put wildfire into Norman brains; and what may only encourage your countrymen to man the walls will make ours fly over the battlements."† *Les braves Belges*, I make no doubt, were quite pleased to observe what folly was being exhibited by those very clever French, whose tongue they want to speak and whose literature they try to imitate. In fact, what we opprobriously call "stupidity," though not an enlivening quality in common society, is nature's favorite resource for preserving steadiness of conduct and consistency of opinion: it enforces concentration; people who learn slowly, learn only what they must. The best security for people's doing their duty is, that they should not know anything else to do; the best security for fixedness of opinion is, that people should be incapable of comprehending what is to be said on the other side. These valuable truths are no discoveries of mine: they are familiar enough to people whose business it is to know them. Hear what a dense and aged attorney says of your peculiarly promising barrister: — "Sharp? Oh yes, yes! he's too

* Northern Railroad.
† "The Betrothed" (Waverleys), Chap. iii.

sharp by half. He is not *safe*, not a minute, isn't that young man." — "What style, sir," asked of an East India Director some youthful aspirant for literary renown, "is most to be preferred in the composition of official dispatches?" "My good fellow," responded the ruler of Hindostan, "the style *as we like* is the Humdrum." I extend this, and advisedly maintain that nations, just as individuals, may be too clever to be practical and not dull enough to be free.

How far this is true of the French, and how far the gross deficiency I have indicated is modified by their many excellent qualities, I hope at a future time to inquire.

I am, sir, yours truly,

AMICUS.

LETTER IV.

ON THE APTITUDE OF THE FRENCH CHARACTER FOR
NATIONAL SELF-GOVERNMENT.

PARIS, Jan. 29, 1852.

SIR, — There is a simple view of the subject on which I wrote to you last week, that I wish to bring under your notice. The experiment (as it is called) of establishing political freedom in France is now sixty years old; and the best that we can say of it is, that it is an experiment still. There have been perhaps half a dozen new beginnings, half a dozen complete failures. I am aware that each of these failures can be excellently explained, each beginning shown to be quite necessary: but there are certain reasonings which, though outwardly irrefragable, the crude human mind is always most unwilling to accept; among these are different and subtle explications of several apparently similar facts. Thus, to choose an example suited to the dignity of my subject, if a gentleman from town takes a day's shooting in the country, and should chance (as has happened) at first going off to

miss some six times running, how luminously soever
he may "explain" each failure as it occurs, however
"expanded a view" he may take of the whole series,
whatever popular illustrations of projectile philosophy
he may propound to the bird-slaying agriculturist,—
the impression on the crass intelligence of the game-
keeper will quite clearly be, "He beint noo shot hom-
soever, aint thickeer." Similarly, to compare small
things with great, when I myself read, in Thiers and
the many other philosophic historians of this literary
country, various and excellent explanations of their
many mischances,—of the failure of the Constitution
of 1791, of the Constitution of the year 3, of the Constitution of the year 5, of the *Charte*, of the system of
1830, and now we may add of the second republic,
the annotated Constitution of M. Dupin,—I can't help
feeling a suspicion lingering in my crude and uncultivated intellect that some common principle is at
work in all and each of these several cases ; that over
and above all odd mischances, so many bankruptcies
a little suggest an unfitness for the trade ; that besides
the ingenious reasons of ingenious gentlemen, there
is some lurking quality or want of a quality in the
national character of the French nation which renders
them but poorly adapted for the form of freedom and
constitution which they have so often, with such zeal
and so vainly, attempted to establish.

In my last letter I suggested that this might be
what I ventured to call a want of stupidity. I will
now try to describe what I mean in more accurate
though not perhaps more intelligible words.

I believe that I am but speaking what is agreed
on by competent observers, when I say that the essence of the French character is a certain mobility :
that is, as it has been defined, a certain "excessive
sensibility to *present* impressions," which is sometimes
"levity," for it issues in a postponement of seemingly
fixed principles to a momentary temptation or a transient whim ; sometimes "impatience," as leading to

an exaggerated sense of existing evils; often "excitement," a total absorption in existing emotion; oftener
"inconsistency," the sacrifice of old habits to present
emergencies; and yet other unfavorable qualities.
But it has also its favorable side: the same man who
is drawn aside from old principles by small pleasures,
who can't bear pain, who forgets his old friends when
he ceases to see them, who is liable in time of excitement to be a one-idea being with no conception of
anything but the one exciting object, yet who nevertheless is apt to have one idea to-day and quite another to-morrow, — and this, and more than this, may
I fancy be said of the ideal Frenchman, — may and
will have the subtlest perception of existing niceties,
the finest susceptibility to social pleasure, the keenest
tact in social politeness, the most consummate skill-
fulness in the details of action and administration;
may, in short, be the best companion, the neatest man
of business, the lightest *homme de salon*, the acutest
diplomat of the existing world.

It is curious to observe how this reflects itself in
their literature. "I will believe," remarks Montaigne,
"in anything rather than in any man's consistency."*
What observer of English habits, what person in-
wardly conscious of our dull and unsusceptible English nature, would ever say so? Rather, in our country, obstinacy is the commonest of the vices and
perseverance the cheapest of the virtues. Again,
when they attempt history, the principal peculiarity
(a few exceptions being allowed for) is an utter incapacity to describe graphically a long-passed state of
society. Take for instance — assuredly no unfavorable example — M. Guizot. His books, I need not say,
are nearly unrivaled for eloquence, for philosophy
and knowledge. You read there, how in the middle
age there were many "principles," — the principle of
Legitimacy, the principle of Feudalism, the principle
of Democracy, — and you come to know how one grew
and another declined and a third crept slowly on;

* " Of the Inconsistency of our Actions," — in substance.

and the mind is immensely edified, when perhaps at the 315th page a proper name occurs, and you mutter, "Dear me, — why, if there were not *people* in the time of Charlemagne! who would have thought that?" But in return for this utter incapacity to describe the people of past times, a Frenchman has the gift of perfectly describing the people of his own: no one knows so well, no one can tell so well, the facts of his own life; the French memoirs, the French letters, are and have been the admiration of Europe: is not now Jules Janin unrivaled at pageants and *prima donnas?*

It is the same in poetry. As a recent writer excellently remarks, "A French Dante or Michel-Angelo or Cervantes or Murillo or Goethe or Shakespeare or Milton we at once perceive to be a mere anomaly; a supposition which may indeed be proposed in terms, but which in reality is inconceivable and impossible." Yet, in requital as it were of this great deficiency, they have a wonderful capacity for expressing and delineating the poetical and voluptuous element of every-day life. We know the biography of De Béranger: the young ladies whom he has admired, the wine that he has preferred, the fly that buzzed on the ceiling and interrupted his delicious and dreaming solitude, are as well known to us as the recollections of our own lives. As in their common furniture, so in their best poetry: the materials are nothing, — reckon up what you have been reading, and it seems a *congeries* of stupid trifles; begin to read, — the skill of the workmanship is so consummate, the art so high and so latent, that while time flows silently on, our fancies are enchanted and our memories indelibly impressed. How often, asks Mr. Thackeray, have we read De Béranger, how often Milton?* Certainly, since Horace there has been no such manual of the philosophy of this world.

I will not say that the quality which I have been trying to delineate is exactly the same thing as

---

* "Paris Sketch Book, — The French School of Painting."

"cleverness"; but I do allege that it is sufficiently near it for the rough purposes of popular writing. For this *quickness* in taking in—so to speak—the present gives a corresponding celerity of intellectual apprehension; an amazing readiness in catching new ideas and maintaining new theories; a versatility of mind which enters into and comprehends everything as it passes; a concentration in what occurs, so as to use it for every purpose of illustration, and consequently (if it happen to be combined with the least fancy) quick repartee on the subject of the moment and *bons-mots* also without stint and without end,— and these qualities are rather like what we style cleverness. And what I call a proper stupidity keeps a man from all the defects of this character: it chains the gifted possessor mainly to his old ideas, it takes him seven weeks to comprehend an atom of a new one; it keeps him from being led away by new theories, for there is nothing which bores him so much; it restrains him within his old pursuits, his well-known habits, his tried expedients, his verified conclusions, his traditional beliefs. He is not tempted to "levity" or "impatience," for he does not see the joke and is thick-skinned to present evils. Inconsistency puts him out: "What I says is this here, as I was a-saying yesterday," is his notion of historical eloquence and habitual discretion. He is very slow indeed to be "excited,"—his passions, his feelings, and his affections are dull and tardy strong things, falling in a certain known direction, fixing on certain known objects, and for the most part acting in a moderate degree and at a sluggish pace. You always know where to find his mind.

Now, this is exactly what (in politics at least) you do not know about a Frenchman. "I like," I have heard a good judge say, "to hear a Frenchman talk: he strikes a light, but what light he will strike it is impossible to predict; I think he doesn't know himself." Now, I know you see at once how this would operate on a parliamentary government, but I give you a gentle illustration. All England knows Mr. Disraeli, the witty orator, the exceedingly clever *littérateur*, the versatile politician; and all England has made up its mind that the stupidest country gentleman would be a better Home Secretary than the accomplished descendant of the "Caucasian race." Now suppose, if you only can, a House of Commons all Disraelis, and do you imagine that Parliament would work? It would be what M. Proudhon said of some French Assemblies, "a box of matches."

The same quality acts in another way, and produces to English ideas a most marvelous puzzle both in the philosophical literature and the political discussion of the French; I mean their passion for logical deduction. The[ir] habitual mode of argument is to get hold of some large principle, to begin to deduce immediately, and to reason down from it to the most trivial details of common action. "Il faut être conséquent avec soi-même"* is their fundamental maxim; and in a world the essence of which is compromise, they could not well have a worse. I hold — metaphysically, perhaps — that this is a consequence of that same impatience of disposition to which I have before alluded: nothing is such a bore as looking for your principles, nothing so pleasant as working them out. People who have thought, know that inquiry is suffering: a child stumbling timidly in the dark is not more different from the same child playing on a sunny lawn than is the philosopher groping, hesitating, doubting, and blundering about his primitive postulates, from the same philosopher proudly deducing and commenting on the certain consequences of his established convictions. On this account, mathematics have been called the paradise of the mind: in Euclid at least you have your principles, and all that is required is acuteness in working them out.

* "It must be consistent with itself."

The long annals of science are one continued commentary on this text. Read in Bacon, the beginner of intellectual philosophy in England, and every page of the "Advancement of Learning" is but a continued warning against the tendency of the human mind to start at once to the last generalities from a few and imperfectly observed particulars; read in the "Meditations" of Descartes, the beginner of intellectual philosophy in France, and in every page (once I read five) you will find nothing but the strictest, the best, the most lucid, the most logical deduction of all things actual and possible, from a few principles obtained without evidence and retained in defiance of probability. Deduction is a game and induction a grievance. Besides, clever impatient people want not only to learn but to teach, and instruction expresses at least the alleged possession of knowledge: the obvious way is to shorten the painful, the slow, the tedious, the wearisome process of preliminary inquiry; to assume something pretty, to establish its consequences, discuss their beauty, exemplify their importance, extenuate their absurdities. A little vanity helps all this. Life is short, art is long, truth lies deep: take some side, found your school, open your lecture-rooms; tuition is dignified, learning is low.

I do not know that I can exhibit the way these qualities of the French character operate on their opinions better than by telling you how the Roman Catholic Church deals with them. I have rather attended to it since I came here: it gives sermons almost an interest, their being in French, and to those curious in intellectual matters it is worth observing. In other times—and even now in out-of-the-way Spain I suppose it may be so—the Catholic Church was opposed to inquiry and reasoning; but it is not so now and here: loudly, from the pens of a hundred writers, from the tongues of a thousand pulpits, in every note of thrilling scorn and exulting derision, she proclaims the contrary. Be she Christ's workman or Anti-Christ's, she knows her work too well. "Reason, reason, reason!" exclaims she to the philosophers of this world; "put in practice what you teach, if you would have others believe it; be consistent; do not prate to us of private judgment when you are but yourselves repeating what you heard in the nursery,—ill-mumbled remnants of a Catholic tradition. No! exemplify what you command,—inquire and make search; seek, though we warn you that ye will never find—yet do as ye will. Shut yourself up in a room, make your mind a blank, go down (as ye speak) into the 'depths of your consciousness,' scrutinize the mental structure, inquire for the elements of belief, spend years, your best years, in the occupation; and at length, when your eyes are dim and your brain hot and your hand unsteady, then reckon what you have gained: see if you cannot count on your fingers the certainties you have reached; reflect which of them you doubted yesterday, which you may disbelieve to-morrow: or rather, make haste, assume at random some essential *credenda*, write down your inevitable postulates, enumerate your necessary axioms; toil on, toil on, spin your spider's-web, adore your own souls; or if you prefer it, choose some German nostrum,—try the 'intellectual intuition' or the 'pure reason' or the 'intelligible' ideas or the mesmeric *clairvoyance*, —and when so or somehow you have attained your results, try them on mankind. Don't go out into the highways and hedges,—it's unnecessary: ring the bell, call in the servants, give them a course of lectures; cite Aristotle, review Descartes, panegyrize Plato, and see if the *bonne* will understand you. It is you that say 'Vox populi, vox Dei'; but you see the people reject you. Or suppose you succeed,—what you call succeeding: your books are read; for three weeks or even a season you are the idol of the *salons;* your hard words are on the lips of women,— then a change comes: a new actress appears at the

Théâtre Français or the Opéra, — her charms eclipse
your theories; or a great catastrophe occurs, political
liberty (it is said) is annihilated, — 'Il faut se faire
mouchard' * is the observation of scoffers: anyhow,
you are forgotten; fifty years may be the gestation
of a philosophy, not three its life; before long, before
you go to your grave, your six disciples leave you
for some newer master or to set up for themselves.
The poorest priest in the remote region of the *Basses
Alpes* has more power over men's souls than human
cultivation: his ill-mouthed masses move women's
souls, — can you? Ye scoff at Jupiter: yet he at
least was believed in, you never have been; idol
for idol, the *de*throned is better than the *un*throned.
No: if you would reason, if you would teach, if you
would speculate, come to us. We have our *premises*
ready: years upon years before you were born, intellects whom the best of you delight to magnify, toiled
to systematize the creed of ages; years upon years
after you are dead, better heads than yours will find
new matter there to define, to divide, to arrange. Consider the hundred volumes of Aquinas: which of you
desire a higher life than that, — to deduce, to subtilize,
discriminate, systematize, and decide the highest truth,
and to be believed? yet such was his luck, his enjoyment; he was what you would be. No, no: *credite,
credite.* Ours is the life of speculation; the cloister
is the home for the student. Philosophy is stationary,
Catholicism progressive. You call, we are heard — "
etc., etc., etc. So speaks each preacher according to
his ability. And when the dust and noise of present
controversies have passed away, and in the silence of
the night some grave historian writes out the tale
of half-forgotten times, let him not forget to observe
that skillfully as the mediæval Church subdued the
superstitious cravings of a painful and barbarous age,
in after years she dealt more discerningly still with

---

* "He will have to turn police-spy."

the feverish excitement, the feeble vanities, and the dogmatic impatience of an over-intellectual generation. And as in religion, so in politics, we find the same desire to teach rather than to learn, the same morbid appetite for exhaustive and original theories. It is as necessary for a public writer to have a system as it is for him to have a pen. His course is obvious: he assumes some grand principle,— the principle of Legitimacy or the principle of Equality or the principle of Fraternity,— and thence he reasons down without fear or favor to the details of every-day politics. Events are judged of, not by their relation to simple causes, but by their bearing on a remote axiom. Nor are these speculations mere exercises of philosophic ingenuity: four months ago, hundreds of able writers were debating with the keenest ability and the most ample array of generalities whether the country should be governed by a legitimate monarchy or an illegitimate, by a social or an old-fashioned republic, by a two-chambered constitution or a one-chambered constitution; on "revision" or non-revision, on the claims of Louis Napoleon or the divine right of the national representation. Can any intellectual food be conceived more dangerous or more stimulating for an over-excitable population? It is the same in Parliament. The description of the Church of Corinth may stand for a description of the late Assembly: every one had a psalm, had a doctrine, had a tongue, had a revelation, had an interpretation. Each member of the Mountain had his scheme for the regeneration of mankind; each member of the vaunted majority had his scheme for newly consolidating the government; Orleanist hated Legitimist, Legitimist Orleanist, moderate Republican detested undiluted Republican; scheme was set against scheme, and theory against theory. No two Conservatives would agree what to conserve; no Socialist could practically associate with any other. No deliberative assembly can exist with every member wishing to lead and no one wishing to follow;

not the meanest act of Parliament could be carried without more compromise than even the best French statesmen were willing to use on the most important and critical affairs of their country. Rigorous reasoning would not manage a parish vestry, much less a great nation. In England, to carry half your own crotchets you must be always and everywhere willing to carry half another man's; practical men must submit as well as rule, concede as well as assume. Popular government has many forms, a thousand good modes of procedure; but no one of those modes can be worked, no one of those forms will endure, unless by the continual application of sensible heads and pliable judgments to the systematic criticism of stiff axioms, rigid principles, and incarnated propositions.

I am, etc., AMICUS.

P. S.—I was in hopes that I should have been able to tell you of the withdrawal of the decree relative to the property of the Orleans family. The withdrawal was announced in the *Constitutionnel* of yesterday; but I regret to add was contradicted in the *Patrie* last evening. I need not observe to you that it is an act for which there is no defense, moral or political; it has immensely weakened the government.

The change of ministry is also a great misfortune to Louis Napoleon. M. de Morny, said to be a son of Queen Hortense (if you believe the people in the *salons*, the President is not the son of his father, and everybody else is the son of his mother), was a statesman of the class best exemplified in England by the late Lord Melbourne,—an acute, witty, fashionable man, acquainted with Parisian persons and things, and a consummate judge of public opinion. M. Persigny was in exile with the President, is said to be much attached to him, to repeat his sentiments and exaggerate his prejudices. I need not point out which of the two is just now the sounder counselor.

LETTER V.

ON THE CONSTITUTION OF THE PRINCE-PRESIDENT.

[Undated.]

SIR, — The many failures of the French in the attempt to establish a predominantly parliamentary government have a strong family likeness. Speaking a little roughly, I shall be right in saying that the constitutions of France have perished, both lately and formerly, either in a street row, or under the violence of a military power aided and abetted by a diffused dread of impending street rows and a painful experience of the effects of past ones. Thus the Constitution of 1791 (the first of the old series) perished on Aug. 10, amid the exultation of the brewer Santerre; the last of the old series fell on the 18th Brumaire, under the hands of Napoleon, when the five per cents. were at 12, the whole country in disorder, and all ruinable persons ruined; the monarchy of 1830 began in the riot of the three days, and ended in the riot of Feb. 24; the republic of February perished but yesterday, mainly from terror that Paris might again see such days as the "days of June."

I think all sensible Englishmen who review this history (the history of more than sixty years) will not be slow to divine a conclusion peculiarly agreeable to our orderly national habits: viz., that the first want of the French is somebody or something able and willing to keep down street rows, to repress the frightful elements of revolution and disorder which every now and then astonish Europe; capable of maintaining and desirous to maintain the order and tranquillity which are (all agree) the essential and primary prerequisites of industry and civilization. If any one seriously and calmly doubts this, I am afraid nothing that I can further say will go far in convincing him: but let him read the account of any scene in any French revolution, old or new; or better, let him come here and learn how people look back to the time I have mentioned (to June, 1848), when the Socialists — not under speculative philosophers like Proudhon or Louis Blanc, but under practical rascals and energetic murderers like Sobrier and Caussidière — made their last and final stand, and against them on the other side the National Guard (mostly solid shopkeepers, three parts ruined by the events of February) fought, I will not say bravely or valiantly, but furiously, frantically, savagely, as one reads in old books that half-starved burgesses in beleaguered towns have sometimes fought for the food of their children. Let any skeptic hear of the atrocities of the friends of order and the atrocities of the advocates of disorder, and he will, I imagine, no longer be skeptical on two points: he will hope that if he ever have to fight, it will not be with a fanatic Socialist, nor against a demi-bankrupt fighting for "his shop"; and he will admit that in a country subject to collisions between two such excited and excitable combatants, no earthly blessing is in any degree comparable to a power which will stave off, long delay, or permanently prevent the actual advent and ever-ready apprehension of such bloodshed. I therefore assume that the first condition of good government in this country is a really strong. a reputedly strong, a continually strong executive power.

Now, on the face of matters, it is certainly true that such a power is perfectly consistent with the most perfect, the most ideal type of parliamentary government; rather, I should say, such and so strong an executive is a certain consequence of the existence of that ideal and rarely found type. If there is among the people and among their representatives a strong, a decided, an unflinching preference for particular ministers or a particular course of policy, that course of policy can be carried out and will be carried out as certainly as by the Czar Nicholas, whose ministers can do exactly what they will. There was something very like this in the old days of King George III., of

Mr. Pitt, and [of] Mr. Perceval: in those times, I have been told, the great Treasury official of the day, Mr. George Rose (still known to the readers of Sydney Smith), had a habit of observing, upon occasion of anything utterly devoid of decent defense, "Well, well, this *is* a little too bad: we must apply our *majority* to this difficulty." The effect is very plain: while Mr. George Rose and his betters respected certain prejudices and opinions then all but universal in Parliament, they in all other matters might do precisely what they would; and in all out-of-the-way matters, in anything that Sir John could not understand, on a point of cotton-spinning or Dissent, be as absolute as the Emperor Napoleon. But the case is. (as we know by experience of what passes under our daily observation) immensely altered when there is no longer this strong, compact, irrefragable "following," — no distinctly divided definite faction, no regular Opposition to be daily beaten, no regular official party to be always victorious, — but instead a mere aggregate of "independent members," each thinking for himself, propounding as the case may be his own sense or his own nonsense: one, profound ideas applicable to all time; another, something meritorious from the Eton Latin Grammar, and a mangled republication of the morning's newspaper: some exceedingly philosophical, others only crotchety, but (what is my point) each acting on his own head, assuming not Mr. Pitt's infallibility but his own. Again, divide a political assembly into three parties any two of which are greater than the third, and it will be always possible for an adroit and dexterous intriguer (M. Thiers has his type in most assemblies) to combine, three or four times a fortnight, the two opposition parties into a majority on some interesting question, on some matter of importance. The best government possible under the existing circumstances will be continually — and in a hazardous state of society, even desperately and fatally — weakened. We have had in our own

sensible House of Commons, — aye, and among the
most stupid and sensible portion of it, the country
gentlemen, — within these few years, a striking example of how far party zeal, the heat of disputation,
and a strong desire for a deep revenge will carry the
best intentioned politicians in destroying the executive
efficiency of an obnoxious Government : I mean the
division of the House of Commons on the Irish
Army Bill, which ended in the resignation of Sir
Robert Peel.* You remember [that] on that occasion
the Country Party, under the guidance of Lord G.
Bentinck, in the teeth of the Irish policy which they
had been advocating and supporting all their lives
and which they would advocate and support again
now, in the teeth of their previous votes and (I am
not exaggerating the history) almost of their avowed
present convictions, defeated a Government not on
a question of speculative policy or recondite importance, but upon the precautionary measures necessary
(according to every idea that a Tory esquire is capable of entertaining) for preventing a rebellion the
occurrence of which they were told (and as the event
proved, told truly) might be speedy, hourly, and
immediate. Of course I am not giving any opinion
of my own about the merits of the question. The
Whigs may be right; it may be good to have shown
the world how little terrible is the bluster of Irish
agitation : but I cite the event as a striking example of an essential evil in a three-sided parliamentary
system; as practically showing that a generally well-
meaning Opposition will, in defiance of their own
habitual principles, cripple an odious executive even
in a matter of street rows and rebellions. I won't
weary you with tediously pointing the moral : if such
things are done in the green tree, what may be done
in the dry ? if party zeal and disputation excitement
so hurry men away in our own grave, business-like,
experienced country, what may we expect from a
vain, a volatile, an ever-changing race ?   ·

* See Peel's speech of April 27, 1846.

Nor am I drawing a French Assembly from mere history, or from my own imagination. In the late Chamber, the great subject of the very last *Annual Register*, there were not only three parties but four : there was a perpetually shifting element of two hundred members, calling itself "The Mountain," which had in its hands the real casting vote between the President's Government and the constitutional Opposition. In the very last days of the Constitution they voted against, and thereby negatived, the proposition of the questors for arming the assembly : partly because they disliked General Changarnier and detested General Cavaignac ; partly because, being extreme Socialists, they would not arm anybody who was likely to use his arms against their friends on the barricades. The same party was preparing to vote for the Bill on the Responsibility of the President — actually, and according to the design of its promoters, in the nature of a bill of indictment against him — because they feared his rigor and efficiency in repressing the anticipated convulsion. The question, the critical question, *Who* shall prevent a new revolution ? was thus actually, and owing to the lamentable divisions of the friends of order, in the hands of the parliamentary representatives of the very men who wished to effect that revolution ; was determined, I may say, ultimately and in the last resort by the party of disorder.

Nor on lesser questions was there any steady majority, any distinctive deciding faction, any administering phalanx, anybody regularly voting with anybody else often enough or in number enough to make the legislative decision regular, consistent, or respectable. Their very debates were unseemly : on anything not pleasing to them, the Mountain — as I said, a yellow and fanatical generation — had, I am told, an engaging knack of rising *en masse* and screaming until they were tired. It will be the same — I do not say in degree, for the Mountain would certainly lose several votes now, and the numbers of the late Chamber

were unreasonably and injudiciously large; but in
a measure you will be always subject to the same
disorder, — a fluctuating majority, and a minority
(often a ruling minority) favorable to rebellion. The
cause, as I believe, is to be sought in the peculiarities of the French character, on which I dwelt —
prolixly, I fear, and *ad nauseam* — in my last two letters. If you have to deal with a mobile, a clever, a
versatile, an intellectual, a dogmatic nation, inevitably and by necessary consequence you will have con-
flicting systems ; every man speaking his own words,
and always giving his own suffrage to what seems
good in his own eyes ; many holding to-day what
they will regret to-morrow ; a crowd of crotchety theories and a heavy percentage of philosophical nonsense ; a great opportunity for subtle stratagem and
intriguing selfishness ; a miserable division among
the friends of tranquillity, and a great power thrown
into the hands of those who, though often with the
very best intentions, are practically and in matter of
fact opposed both to society and civilization. And
moreover, beside minor inconveniences and lesser
hardships, you will indisputably have periodically —
say three or four times in fifty years — a great crisis :
the public mind much excited ; the people in the
streets swaying to and fro with the breath of every
breeze ; the discontented *ouvriers* meeting in a hundred knots, discussing their real sufferings and their
imagined grievances with lean features and angry
gesticulations ; the parliament all the while in perma-
nence very ably and eloquently expounding the whole
subject, one man proposing this scheme and another
that ; the Opposition expecting to oust the ministers
and ride in on the popular commotion, the ministers
fearing to take the odium of severe or adéquate
repressive measures lest they should lose their salary,
their places, and their majority ; finally a great crash,
a disgusted people overwhelmed by revolutionary violence or seeking a precarious, a pernicious, but after

all a precious protection from the bayonets of military despotism.

Louis Philippe met these dangers and difficulties in a thoroughly characteristic manner : he bought his majority ; being a practical and not over-sentimental public functionary, he went into the market and purchased a sufficient number of constituencies and members. Of course the *convenances* were carefully preserved, — grossness of any kind is too jarring for French susceptibility : the purchase money was not mere coin (which indeed the buyers had not to offer), but a more gentlemanly commodity, — the patronage of the government. The electoral colleges were extremely small, the number of public functionaries is enormous ; so that a very respectable body of electors could always be expected to have, like a four-year-old barrister since the county courts, an immense prejudice for the existing government. One man hoped to be *maire*, another wanted his son got into St. Cyr or the Polytechnic School ; and this could be got and was daily got (I am writing what is hardly denied) by voting for the government candidate. In a word, a sufficient proportion of the returns of the electoral colleges resembled the returns from Harwich or Devonport, only that the government was the only bidder ; for there are not, I fancy, in any country but England, people able and willing to spend, election after election, great sums of money for procuring the honor of a seat in a representative assembly. In fact, to copy the well-known phrase, just as in the time of Burke certain gentlemen had the expressive nickname of "the King's friends," so these constituencies may aptly be called "the King's constituencies." Of course, on the face of it this system worked, as far as business went, excellently well : for eighteen years the tranquillity was maintained ; France, it may be, has never enjoyed so much calm civilization, so much private happiness : and yet, after all such and so long blessings, it fell in a mere riot, it fell unregretted..

It is a system which no wise man can wish to see restored: it was a system of regulated corruption. But it does not at all follow, nor I am sure will you be apt so to deduce, that because I imagine that France is unfit for a government in which a House of Commons is, as with us, the sovereign power in the state, I therefore believe that it is fit for no freedom at all. Our own constitutional history is the completest answer to any such idea. For centuries the House of Commons was habitually, we know, but a third-rate power in the state. First the Crown, then the House of Lords, enjoyed the ordinary and supreme dominion; and down almost to our own times the Crown and House of Lords, taken together, were much more than a sufficient match for the people's House: but yet we do not cease to proclaim, daily and hourly, in season and out of season, that the English people never have been slaves. It may therefore well be that, our own country having been free under a Constitution in which the representative element was but third-rate in power and dignity, France and other nations may contrive to enjoy the advantage from institutions in which it is only second-rate.

Now, of this sort is the Constitution of Louis Napoleon. I am not going now, after prefacing so much, to discuss its details; indeed, I do not feel competent to do so. What should we say to a Frenchman's notion of a £5 householder or the fourth and fifth clauses of the new Reform Bill? and I quite admit that a paper building of this sort can hardly be safely criticized till it is carried out on *terra firma*, till we see not only the theoretic ground-plan but the actual inhabited structure. The life of a constitution is in the spirit and disposition of those who work it, and we can't yet say in the least what that in this case will be; but so far as the Constitution shows its meaning on the face of it, it clearly belongs to the class which I have named. The Corps Législatif is not the administering body; it is not even what perhaps it might with advantage have been, a petitioning and remonstrating body : but it possesses the legislative veto and the power of stopping *en masse* the supplies. It is not a working, a ruling, or an initiative or supremely decisive, but an immense checking power. It will be unable to change ministers or aggravate the course of revolutions ; but it could arrest an unpopular war, it could reject an unpopular law, it is (at least in theory) a powerful and important drag-chain. Out of the mouths of its · adversaries this system possesses what I have proved or conjectured or assumed to be the prime want of the French nation, a strong executive ; the objection to it is, that the objectors find nothing else in it. We confess there is no doubt now of a power adequate to repress street rows and revolutions.

At the same time, I guard myself against intimating any opinion on the particular minutiæ of this last effort of institutional invention. I do not know enough to form a judgment ; I sedulously at present confine myself to this one remark : that the new government of France belongs, in theory at least, to the right class of constitutions, — the class that is most exactly suited to French habits, French nature, French social advantages, French social dangers ; the class, I mean, in which the representative body has a consultative, a deliberative, a checking, and a minatory — not as with us a supreme, nearly an omnipotent, and exclusively initiatory — function.

I am yours, etc.,   AMICUS.

P. S. — You may like five words on a French in-vasion. I can't myself imagine — and what is more to the point, I do not observe that anybody here has any notion of — any such inroad into England as was contemplated and proposed by General Changarnier. No one in the actual conduct of affairs, with actual responsibility for affairs, — not, as the event proved, even Ledru Rollin, — could according to me encounter

the risk and odium of such a hateful and horribly
dangerous attempt. But I regret to add, there is a
contingency which sensible people here (so far as I
have had the means of judging) do not seem to regard as at all beyond the limits of rational probability, by which a war between England and France
would most likely be superinduced ; that is, a French
invasion of Belgium. I do not mean to assure you
that this week or next the Prince-President will make
a *razzia* in Brussels ; but I do mean that it is thought
not improbable that somehow or other, on some wolf-
and-the-lamb pretext, he may pick a quarrel with
King Leopold and endeavor to restore to the French
the "natural limit" of the Rhine. Now, I have never
seen the terms of the guaranty which the shrewd
and cautious Leopold exacted from England before
he would take the throne of Belgium : but as the
only real risk was a French aggression upon this
tempting territory, I do not make any doubt but that
the expressions of that instrument bind us to go to
war in defense of the country whose limits and independence we have guaranteed ; and in this case an
invasion of England would be as admissible a military movement as an invasion of France. I hope,
therefore, you will use your best rhetoric to induce
people to put our pleasant country in a state of adequate and tolerable defense.

I see by the invaluable *Galignani* that some excellent people at Manchester are indulging in a little
arithmetic. "Suppose," say they, "all the French
got safe, and each took away £50 : now, how much
do you fancy it would come to (40,000 men by £50,
naught's naught is naught, naught and carry two)
compared to the *existing* burden of the National
Debt ?" Was there ever such amiable infatuation !
It is not what the French could carry off, but what
they would leave behind them, which is in the reasonable apprehension of reasonable persons : the funds
at 50, broken banks, the *Gazette* telling you who had

not failed, Downing Street *vide* Wales, destitute families, dishonored daughters, one-legged fathèrs, the mourning shops utterly sacked, the customers in tears, a pale widow in a green bonnet, the Exchange in ruins, five notches on St. Paul's, and a big hole in the Bank of England, — these, though but a few of the certain consequences of a French visit to London, are quite enough to terrify even an adamantine editor and a rather reckless correspondent.

LETTER VI.

THE FRENCH NEWSPAPER PRESS.

PARIS, Feb. 10, [1852.]

SIR, — We learn from an Oriental narrative in considerable circulation that the ancient Athenians were fond of news. Of course they were : it is the nature of a mass of clever and intellectual people living together to want something to talk about. Old ideas, common ascertained truths, are good things enough to live by, but are very rare and soon sufficiently discussed ; something else — true or false, rational or nonsensical — is quite essential : and therefore in the old literary world men gathered round the traveling sophist, to learn from him some thought, crotchet, or speculation. And what the vagabond speculators were once, that pretty exactly is the newspaper now : to it the people of this intellectual capital look for that daily mental bread which is as essential to them as the less ethereal sustenance of ordinary mortals. With the spread of education this habit travels downward : not the literary man only, but the *ouvrier* and the *bourgeois* live on the same food ; this day's *Siècle* is discussed not only in gorgeous drawing-rooms, but in humble reading-rooms and still humbler workshops. According to the printed notions of us journalists, this is a matter of pure rejoicing : the influence of the Press, if you believe writers and printers, is the one sufficient condition of social well-being. Yet there are many considerations which make very much against this idea : I can't go into several of them now, but those that I shall mention are suggested at once by matters before me. First, newspaper people are the only traders that thrive upon convulsion. In quiet times, who cares for the paper? in times of tumult, who does not? Commonly, the *Patrie* (the *Globe* of this country) sells, I think, for three sous : on the evening of the *coup d'état*, itinerant ladies were crying under my window, "Demandez la *Patrie* — journal du soir — trente sous — journal du soir ;"* and I remember witnessing even in our sober London, in February, 1848, how bald fathers of families paid large sums, and encountered bare-headed the unknown inclemencies of the night air, that they might learn the last news of Louis Philippe, and if possible be in at the death of the revolutionary Parisian. "Happy," says the sage, "are the people whose annals are vacant;" but "Woe! woe! woe!" he might add, "to the wretched journalists that have to compose and sell leading articles therein."

I am constrained to say that even in England this is not without its unfavorable influence on literary morals. Take in the *Times,* and you will see it assumed that every year ought to be an era : "The Government does nothing," is the indignant cry, and simple people in the country don't know that this is merely a civilized *façon de parler* for "I have nothing to say." Lord John Russell must alter the suffrage, that we may have something pleasant in our columns.

I am afraid matters are worse here. The leading French journalist is, as you know, the celebrated Émile de Girardin ; and so far as I can learn anything about him, he is one of the most fickle politicians in existence. Since I have read the *Presse*

---

* "Ask for the *Patrie* — evening paper — thirty sous — evening paper."

regularly, it has veered˙ from every point of the
compass well-nigh to every other: now for, now
against the revision of the Constitution ; now lauding
Louis Napoleon to the skies, now calling him plain
"M. Bonaparte" and insinuating that he had not
two ideas and was incapable of moral self-government ; now connected with the Red party, now praising the majority : but all and each of these veerings
and shiftings determined by one most simple and
certain principle, — to keep up the popular excitement,
to maintain the gifted M. de Girardin at the head of
it. Now, a man who spends his life in stimulating
excitement and convulsion is really a political incendi-
ary ; and however innocent and laudable his brother
exiles may be, the old editor and founder of the *Presse*
is, as I believe, now only paying the legitimate penalty of systematic political *arson*.

When a foreigner — at least an Englishman — begins to read the French papers, his first idea is,
"How well these fellows write ! Why, every one
of them has a style, and a good style too. Really,
how clear, how acute, how clever, how perspicuous !
I wish our journalists would learn to write like this."
But a little experience will modify this idea ; at least
I have found it so. I read for a considerable time
these witty periodicals with pleasure and admiration ;
after a little while I felt somehow that I took them
up with an effort, but I fancied (knowing my disposition) that this was laziness : when on a sudden, in
the waste of *Galignani*, I came across an article of
the *Morning Herald*. Now, you'll laugh at me if I
tell you it was a real enjoyment : there was no toil,
no sharp theory, no pointed expression, no fatiguing
brilliancy, — in fact, what the man in Lord Byron
desired, " no nothing,"*— but a dull, creeping, satisfactory sensation that now at least there was nothing
to admire. As long walking in picture galleries
makes you appreciate a mere wall, so I felt that I

* Letter to Murray, June 4, 1817.

understood for the first time that really dullness had
its interest; I found a pure refreshment in coming
across what possibly might be latent sense, but was
certainly superficial stupidity.

I think there is nothing we English hate like a
clever but prolonged controversy : now, this is the
life and soul of the Parisian press, — everybody writes
against everybody. It is not mere sly hate or solemn
invective, nothing like what we occasionally indulge
in about the misdemeanors of a morning contemporary ; but they take the other side's article piece by
piece, and comment on him, and (as they say in libel
cases) *innuendo* him, and satisfactorily show that according to his arithmetic two and two make five.
Useful knowledge that, — it is really good for us to
know that some fellow (you never heard of him) it
rather seems can't add up : but it interests people
here, — " C'est logique," they tell you ; and if you are
trustful enough to answer, " Mon Dieu, c'est ennuy-
eux, je n'en sais rien," * they look as if you sneered
at the Parthenon.

It is out of these controversies that M. de Girardin
has attained his power and his fame. His articles
(according to me, at least) have no facts and no
sense ; he gives one all pure reasoning, little scrappy
syllogisms, — as some one said most unjustly of old
Hazlitt, he " writes pimples." † But let an unfortunate writer in the *Assemblée Nationale,* or anywhere
else, make a little refreshing blunder in his logic,
and next morning small punning sentences (one to
each paragraph, like an equation) come rattling down
on him : it is clear as noonday that somebody said
" something followed," and it does *not* follow, and it
is so agreed in all the million *cabinets de lecture* after
due gesticulation ; and moreover, that M. de Girardin
is the man to expose it, and what clever fellows they
are to appreciate him ! but what the truth is, who
cares ? the subject is forgotten.

* " It's a bore, I don't know anything about it."
† " Talks pimples." — Byron, Journal in Italy, Jan. 28, 1821.

Now, all this to my notion does great harm. Nothing destroys commonplace like the habit of arguing for arguing's sake; nothing is so bad for public matters as that they should be treated not as the data for the careful formation of a sound judgment, but as a topic or background for displaying the shining qualities of public writers. It is no light thing this. M. de Girardin for many years has gained more power, more reputation, more money than any of his rivals, not because he shows more knowledge, — he shows much less; not because he has a wiser judgment, — he has no fixed judgment at all: but because he has a more pointed, sharp way of exposing blunders intrinsically paltry, obvious to all educated men, and does not care enough for any subject to be diverted from this logical trifling by a serious desire to convince anybody of anything.

Don't think I wish to be hard on this accomplished gentleman. I am not going to require of hack writers to write only on what they understand: if that were the law, what a life for the sub-editor! I should not be writing these letters, and how seldom and how timidly would the morning journals creep into the world! Nor do I expect (though I may still, in sentimental moods, desire) middle-aged journalists to be buoyed up by chimerical visions of improving mankind. You know what our eminent *chef* (by Thackeray profanely called "Jupiter Jeames") has been heard to say over his gin and water, in an easy and voluptuous moment : — "Enlightenment be —— : I want the fat fool of a thick-headed reader to say, 'Just *my own* views,' else he ain't pleased, and maybe he stops the paper." I am not going to require supernatural excellence from writers. Yet there are limits : if I were a chemist I should not mind, I suppose, selling now and then a deleterious drug, on a due affidavit of rats then and there filed before me ; yet I don't feel as if I could live comfortably on the sale of mere arsenic, — I fancy I should like to sell something

wholesome occasionally. So, though one might upon
occasion egg on a riot or excite to a breach of the
peace, I should not like to be every day feeding on
revolutionary excitement; nor should I like to be exclusively selling diminutive, acute, quibbling leaders
(what they call in the Temple "special demurrers"),
certain to occupy people with small fallacies and lead
away their minds from the great questions actually
at issue. Sometimes I might like to feel as if I understood what I wrote on; but of course with me this indulgence must be very rare. You know in France
journalism is not only an occupation, it is a career:
as in far-off Newcastle a coal-fitter's son looks wist-
fully to the bar, in the notion that he too may emu-
late the fame and fortune of Lord Eldon or Lord
Stowell, so in fair Provence a pale young aspirant
packs up his little bundle in the hope of rivaling the
luck and fame of M. Thiers; he comes to Paris; he
begins, like the great historian, by dining for thirty
sous in the Palais Royal, in the hope that after long
years of labor and jealousy he too may end by sleeping amid curtains of white muslin lined with pink
damask. Just consider for a moment what a difference this one fact shows between France and England: here, a man who begins life by writing in the
newspapers has an appreciable chance of arriving to
be Minister of Foreign Affairs; the class of public
writers is the class from which the equivalent of
Lord Aberdeen, Lord Palmerston, or Lord Granville
will most likely be chosen. Well, well, under that
régime you and I might have been important people;
we might have handled a red box, we might have
known what it was to have a reception, to dine with
the Queen, to be respectfully mystified by the *corps
diplomatique.* But angry Jove forbade: of course we
can hardly deny that he was wrong, — and yet if the
revolutions of 1848 have clearly brought out any fact,
it is the utter failure of newspaper statesmen. Everywhere they have been tried: everywhere they have

shown great talents for intrigue, eloquence, and agitation: how rarely have they shown even fair aptitude for ordinary administration! how frequently have they gained a disreputable renown by a laxity of principle surpassing the laxity of their aristocratic and courtly adversaries! Such being my imperfect account of my imperfect notions of the French press, I can't altogether sympathize in the extreme despondency of many excellent persons at its temporary silence since the *coup d'état;* I might even rejoice at it, if I thought that the Parisian public could in any manner be broken of their dependence on the morning's article. But I have no such hope: the taste has got down too deep into the habits of the people; some new thing will still be necessary; and every government will find some of its most formidable difficulties in their taste for political disputation and controversial excitement. The ban must sooner or later be taken off; the President sooner or later must submit to censure and ridicule: and whatever laws he may propose about the press, there is none which scores of ingenious men, now animated by the keenest hatred, will not try every hazard to evade. What he may do to avoid this is as yet unknown. One thing, however, I suppose is pretty sure, and I fancy quite wise, — the press will be restrained from discussing the principles of the government: Socialists will not be allowed to advocate a democratic republic; Legitimists will not be allowed to advocate the cause of Henri Cinq, nor Orleanists the cause of the Comte de Paris. Such indulgence might be tolerable in more temperate countries, but experience shows that it is not safe now and here.

A really sensible press, arguing temperately after a clear and satisfactory exposition of the facts, is a great blessing in any country. It would be still more a blessing in a country where, as I tried to explain formerly, the representative element must play (if the public security is to be maintained) a rather secondary part: it would then be a real stimulus to deliberate inquiry and rational judgment upon public affairs; to the formation of common-sense views upon the great outlines of public business; to the cultivation of sound moral opinions and convictions on the internal and international duties of the state. Even the actual press which we may expect to see here may not be pernicious. It will doubtless stimulate to many factious proceedings and many interruptions of the public prosperity; it may very likely conduce to drive the President (contrary, if not to his inclination, at least to his personal interest) into foreign hostilities and international aggression: but it may be, notwithstanding, useful in preventing private tyranny, in exposing wanton oppression, in checking long-suffering revenge; it may prevent acts of spoliation like what they call here "le premier vol de l'aigle,"* the seizure of the Orleans property, — in a word, being certain to oppose the executive, where the latter is unjust its enemy will be just.

I had hopes that this letter would be the last with which I should tease you; but I find I must ask you to be so kind as to find room for one and only for one more.

I am yours, etc.,   AMICUS.

LETTER VII.

CONCLUDING LETTER.

PARIS, Feb. 19, 1852.

SIR, — There is a story† of some Swedish abbé, in the last century, who wrote an elaborate work to prove the then Constitution of his country to be immortal and indestructible. While he was correcting the proof-sheets, a friend brought him word that — behold! the King had already destroyed the said polity.

---

* "The eagle's first flight " or "theft "—a pun on "vol."
† Byron, Letter to Moore, March 27, 1815.

"Sir," replied the gratified author, "our sovereign, the illustrious Gustavus, may certainly overthrow the Constitution, but never *my book.*" I beg to parody this sensible remark; for I wish to observe to you that even though Louis Napoleon should turn out a bad and mischievous ruler, he won't in the least refute these letters.

What I mean is as follows:—Above all things, I have designed to prove to you that the French are by character unfit for a solely and predominantly parliamentary government; that so many and so great elements of convulsion exist here that it will be clearly necessary that a strong, vigorous, anti-barricade executive should, at whatever risk and cost, be established and maintained; that such an Assembly as the last is irreconcilable with this,— in a word, that riots and revolutions must if possible come to an end, and only such a degree of liberty and democracy be granted to the French nation as is consistent with the consolidated existence of the order and tranquillity which are equally essential to rational freedom and civilized society.

In order to combine the maintenance of order and tranquillity with the maximum of possible liberty, I hope that it may in the end be found possible to admit into a political system a representative and sufficiently democratic assembly, without that assembly assuming and arrogating to itself those nearly omnipotent powers which in our country it properly and rightfully possesses, but which in the history of the last sixty years we have, as it seems to me, so many and so cogent illustrations that a French Chamber is, by genius and constitution, radically incapable to hold and exercise. I hope that some checking, consultative, petitioning assembly,— some $\beta ov\lambda\acute\eta$, in the real sense of the term,— some *council*, some provision by which all grave and deliberate public opinion (I do not speak more definitely, because an elaborate constitution from a foreigner must be an absurdity) may organize and express itself, yet at the same time without utterly hampering and directing — and directing amiss — those more simple elements of national polity on which we must after all rely for the prompt and steady repression of barricade-making and bloodshed.

I earnestly desire to believe that some such system as this may be found in practice possible : for otherwise, — unless I quite misread history and altogether mistake what is under my eyes, — after many more calamities, many more changes, many more great Assemblies abounding in Vergniauds and Berryers, the essential deficiencies of debating Girondin statesmen will become manifest ; the uncompact, unpractical, over-volatile, over-logical, indecisive, ineffectual rule of Gallican Parliaments will be unequivocally manifest (it is *now* plain, I imagine, but a truth so humiliating must be written large in letters of blood before those that run will read it) : and no medium being held or conceived to be possible, the nation will sink back, not contented but discontented, not trustfully but distrustfully, under the rule of a military despot. And if they yield to this, it will be from no faith, no loyalty, no credulity ; it will be from a sense — a hated sense — of unqualified failure, a miserable skepticism in the probable success and the possible advantages of long-tried and ill-tried rebellion.

Now, whether the Constitution of Louis Napoleon is calculated to realize this ideal and intermediate system is, till we see it at work, doubtful and disputable. It is not the question so much of what it may be at this moment as of 'what it may become in a brief period, when things have begun to assume a more normal state and the public mind shall be relaxed from its present and painful tension. However, I should be deceiving you if I did not inform you that the state of men's minds towards the Prince-President is not, so far as 1 can make it out, what it was the day after the *coup d'état.* The measures taken against the Socialists are felt to have been several degrees too severe, the list of exiles too numerous; the confiscation of the Orleans property could not but be attended with the worst effect; the law announced by the government organs respecting or rather against the press is justly (though you know from my last letter I have no partiality for French newspapers) considered to be absurdly severe, and likely to countenance much tyranny and gross injustice : above all, instead of maintaining mere calm and order, the excessive rigor and sometimes the injustice of the President's measures have produced a breathless pause (if I may so speak) in public opinion; political conversation is a whispered question, What will he do next? Firstly, the government is dull, and the French want to be amused; secondly, it is going to spoil the journals (depreciate newspapers to a Frenchman, disparage nuts to a monkey); thirdly, it is producing (I do not say it has yet produced, but it has made a beginning in producing) a habit of apprehension. In fact, I believe the French opinion of the Prince-President is near about that of the interesting damsel in George Sand's comedy, concerning her uninteresting *prétendu:* — "Vous l'aimez, n'est-ce pas?" — "Oui, oui, oui, certainement je l'aime. Oui, oui, mille fois oui, je dis que oui. Je vous assure. *Au moins* je fais mon possible à l'aimer :"* the first attachment is not extinct, but people have begun — awful symptom — to add the withering and final saving clause. Yet it is, I imagine, a great mistake to suppose that the present Constitution, if it work at all, will permanently work as a despotism, or that the Corps Législatif will be without a measure of popular influence : the much more helpless Tribunal was not so in the much more troublesome times of the Consulate. And the source of such influence and

* "You love him, don't you?"—"Yes, yes, yes, certainly I love him. Yes, yes, a thousand times yes, I tell you yes. I assure you. *At least* I am doing my best to love him."

the manner of its operation may be, I imagine, well enough traced in the nature of the forces whereby Louis Napoleon holds his power.

A truly estimable writer says, I know, that "the legislative body cannot have, by possibility, any analogy with the consultative and petitioning senate of the Plantagenets"; nor can any one deny that the likeness is extremely faint (no illustration ever yet ran on all fours), the practical differences clear and convincing. But yet, according to the light which is given me now, I affirm that for one vital purpose, — the resisting and criticizing any highly unpopular acts of a highly unpopular government, — the Corps Législatif of Louis Napoleon must and will inevitably possess a power compared with which the forty-day followers of the feudal *noblesse* seem as impotent as a congregation of Quakers; a force the peculiarity of which is, that you can't imprison, can't dissolve, can't annihilate it: I mean, of course, the moral power of civilized opinion. You may put down newspapers, dissolve parliaments, imprison agitators, almost stop conversation, but you can't stop thought; you can't prevent the silent, slow, creeping, stealthy progress of hatred and scorn and shame; you can't attenuate easily the stern justice of a retarded retaliation. These influences affect the great reservoir of physical force, — they act on the army. A body of men enlisted daily from the people take to the barracks the notions of the people: in spite of new associations, the first impressions are apt to be retained; you overlay them, but they remain, — what is believed elsewhere and out of doors gives them weight. Each soldier has relations, friends, a family; he knows what they think. Much more with the officers: these are men moving in Parisian society, accessible to its influences, responsible to its opinion, apt to imbibe its sentiments. Certainly *esprit de corps*, the habit of obedience, the instinct of discipline, are strong and will carry men far, but certainly also they have natural limits: men won't stand being cut, being ridiculed, being detested, being despised, daily and forever, and that for measures which their own understandings disapprove of. Remember, there is not here any question of barbarous bands overawing a civilized and imperial city; no question of ugly Croats keeping down cultivated Italians: it is but a question of French gentlemen and French peasantry in uniform acting in opposition to other French gentlemen and other French peasants without uniform. Already there has been talk (I do not say well-founded, but still the matter was named) of breaking two or three hundred officers for speaking against the Orleans decrees: do you fancy that can be done every day? do you imagine that a Parliament, whatever its nominal functions may be (remember those of the old *régime*), speaking the sense of the people about the question of the day, in a time of convulsion and in a critical hour, would not be attended to, 'or at any rate thought of and considered, by an army taken from the people, — commanded by men selected from and every day mixing with common society and very ordinary mankind? The 2d of December showed how readily such troops will support a decided and popular President against an intriguing, divided, impotent Chamber; but such hard blows won't bear repetition. Soldiers — French soldiers, I take it, especially, from their quickness and intelligence — are neither deaf nor blind. If there be truth in history or speculation, national forces can't long be used against the nation. They are unmerciful and often cruel to feeble minorities; they are ready now for a terrible onslaught on mere Socialists, just as of old they turned out cheerfully for awful *dragonnades* on the ill-starred Protestants: but once let them know and feel that everybody is against them, — that they are alone, that their acts are contemned and their persons despised, — and gradually or all at once discipline and habit surely fail, men murmur or desert, officers hesitate or disobey, one regiment is

dismissed to the Cabyles, another relegated to rural
solitudes; at last, most likely in the decisive moment
of the whole history, the rulers, who relied only on
their troops, are afraid to call them out, — they hesitate, send spies and commissioners to inquire. "Vive
le Gouvernement Provisoire!" — the black and roar-
ing multitude rises and comes on; but two seconds,
and the obnoxious institutions are lost in the flood;
nothing is heard but the cry of the hour, sounding
shrill and angry over the waste of Revolution, —
"Vive le Diable!" With such a force behind them, a
French parliament, of whatever nature, with whatever written duties, is, if at the head of the movement, in the critical hour apt to be stronger than the
strongest of the barons.

Nor do I concur with those who censure the President for "recommending" avowedly the candidates
he approves. It is a part of the great question, How
is universal suffrage to be worked successfully in such
a country as France? The peasant proprietors have
but one political idea, — that they wish the Prince
to govern them: they wish to vote for the candidate
most acceptable to him, and they wish nothing else.
Why is he wrong in telling them which candidate
that is?

Still, no doubt the reins are now strained a great
deal too tight. It is possible, quite possible, that
a majority in this Parliament may be packed; but
what I would impress on you is, that it can't always
be packed. Sooner or later, constituencies who wish
to oppose the government will, in spite of *maires* and
préfets, elect the opposition candidate: it is in the
nature of any, even the least vigorous system of popular election, to struggle forwards and progressively
attain to some fair and reasonable correspondence
with the substantial views and opinions of the constituent people.

I therefore fall back on what I told you before,
— my essential view or crotchet about the mental

aptitudes and deficiencies of the French people. The French, said Napoleon, are *des machines nerveuses.* The point is, Can their excitable, volatile, superficial, over-logical, uncompromising character be [so] managed and manipulated as to fit them for entering on a practically uncontrolled system of parliamentary government ? will not any large and omnipotent Assembly resemble the stormy Constituent and the late Chamber, rather than the business-like, formal, ennui-diffusing Parliament to which in our free and dull country we are felicitously accustomed? can one be so improved as to keep down a riot? I foresee a single and but a single objection. I fancy, indeed I know, that there is a school of political thinkers— not yet in possession of any great influence, but perhaps a little on the way thereto—which has improved or invented a capital panacea whereby all nations are, within very moderate limits of time, to be surely and certainly fitted for political freedom, and that no matter how formed, how seemingly stable, how long ago cast and constructed, be the type of popular character to which the said remedy is sought to be applied : this panacea is the foundation or restoration of provincial municipalities. Now, I am myself prepared to go a considerable length with the school in question ; I do myself think that a due and regular consideration of the knotty points of paving and lighting, and the deciding in the last resort upon them, is a valuable discipline of national character, — it exercises people's minds on points they know, in things of which there is a test. Very few people are good judges of a good constitution ; but everybody's eyes are excellent judges of good light, every man's feet are profound in the theory of agreeable stones. Yet I can't altogether admit, nevertheless, that municipalities are the sufficient and sole—though they may be very likely an essential—prerequisite of political freedom. There is the great instance of Hindostan to the contrary. The whole old and national system of

that remarkable country—a system in all probability
as ancient as the era of Alexander—is a village system; and one so curious, elaborate, I fancy I might
say so profound, that the best European observers—
Sir Thomas Munro and that sort of people—are most
strenuous for its being retained unimpaired. According to them, the village hardly heard of the imperial
government, except for the purpose of imperial tax-
ation; the business of life through that whole vast
territory has always been practically determined by
potails and parish vestries: and yet nevertheless and
in spite of this capital and immemorial municipal
system, our subjects the Hindoos are still slaves, and
still likely to be slaves; still essentially slavish, and
likely, I much fear, very long indeed to remain so.
It is therefore quite certain that rural and provincial
institutions won't so alter and adapt all national
characters as to fit all nations for a parliamentary
constitution; consequently the *onus probandi* is on
those who assert that it will so alter and mold the
French. Again, I assure you that the French do
think of paving and lighting; not enough, perhaps,
but still they have begun. The country is, as you
know, divided into departments, arrondissements, and
communes; in each of these there is a council—variously elected, but in all cases popularly and from the
district—which has the sole control over the expend-
iture of the particular locality for every special and
local purpose, and which, if I am rightly informed,
has (in theory at least) the sole initiative in every
local improvement. The defect, I fancy, is, that in
the exercise of these, considerable bodies are hampered and controlled by the veto and supervision of
the central authority. The rural councils discuss and
decide what in their judgment should then be done,
and what money should be so spent; the better sort
of the agricultural population have much more voice
in the latter than have the corresponding class in
England in the determination and imposition of our

own county rate: but it is the central authority
which decides whether such proposals and recom-
mendations shall in fact be carried out, — in a word,
the provinces have to *ask leave* of the Parisian
Ministry of the Interior. Now, I admit this is an
abuse; I should maintain that elderly gentlemen with
bald heads and local influence ought to feel that they,
in the final resort, settle and determine all truly local
matters; human nature likes its own road, its own
bridge, its own lapidary obstacles, its own deceptive
luminosity: but I ask again, Can you fancy that
these luxuries, to whatever degree indulged in, [would]
alter and modify in any essential particular the levity
and volatility of the French character?—how much
light to how much logic? how many paving-stones
to how much mobility? I can't foresee any such
change; and even if so, what in the mean time?

We are left, then, I think, to deal with the
French character pretty much as we find it. What
stealthy, secret, unknown, excellent forces may, in
the wisdom of Providence, be even now modifying
this most curious intellectual fabric, neither you nor
I can know or tell. Let us hope they may be many;
but if we indulge — and from the immense records of
revolutionary history, I think with due distrust we
may legitimately and even beneficially indulge — in
system-building and speculation, we must take the
data which we have, and not those which we desire
or imagine. Louis Napoleon has proposed a system;
English writers by the thousand (if I was in harness instead of holiday-making, I should be most
likely among them) proclaim his system an evil one:
what then? Do you know what Father Newman says
to the religious reformers, — rather sharply, but still
well? "Find out first of all where you stand; [take
your position;] write down your creed; draw up
your catechism."* So I answer to the English eloquence, "State first of all what you would have; draw

* "Difficulties felt by Anglicans in Catholic Teaching," Lecture vii., § 7.

up your novel system for the French government;
write down your political constitution." Don't criticize, but produce; do not find fault, but propose:
and when you have proposed upon theory and have
created upon paper, let us see whether the system
be such a one as will work in fact and be accepted
by a willful nation in reality, — otherwise your work
is naught.

And mind, too, that the system to be sketched
out must be fit to protect the hearths and homes of
men. It is easy to compose politics * if you do but
neglect this one essential condition. Four years ago,
Europe was in a ferment with the newest ideas,
the best theories, the most elaborate — the most artistic — constitutions; there was the labor and toil
and trouble of a million intellects, — as good taken on
the whole, perhaps, as the. world is likely to see, —
of old statesmen and literary gentlemen and youthful
enthusiasts all over Europe, from the Baltic Sea to the
Mediterranean, from the frontiers of Russia to the
Atlantic Ocean : well, what have we gained ? A Parliament in Sardinia! Surely this is a lesson against
proposing politics † which won't work; convening assemblies that can't legislate; constructing executives
that aren't able to keep the peace; founding constitutions inaugurated with tears and eloquence, soon
abandoned with tears and shame; beginning a course
of fair auguries and liberal hopes, but one from
whose real dangers and actual sufferings a frightened
and terrified people in the end flee for a temporary
(or maybe a permanent) refuge under a military and
absolute ruler.

Mazzini sneers at the selfishness of shopkeepers :
I am for the shopkeepers against him. There are
people who think because they are republican "there
shall be no more cakes and ale" ‡ : aye, verily, but
there will though, or else stiffish ginger will be hot
in the mouth. Legislative assemblies, leading articles,

---

* † Obvious misprints for "politics." — ED.   ‡ "Twelfth Night," ii. 3.

essay eloquence, — such are good, very good; useful, very useful: yet they can be done without; we can want them. Not so with all things: the selling of figs, the cobbling of shoes, the manufacturing of nails, — these are the essence of life; and let whoso frameth a constitution of his country think on these things.

I conclude, as I ought, with my best thanks for the insertion of these letters; otherwise I was so full of the subject that I might have committed what Disraeli calls "the extreme act of human fatuity," — I might have published a pamphlet: from this your kindness has preserved me, and I am proportionally grateful.

I am yours,   AMICUS.

A LATER JUDGMENT.

CÆSARISM AFTER THIRTEEN YEARS.

[Maturer years, and the development of the germinal tendencies of Louis Napoleon's *régime*, greatly modified Mr. Bagehot's youthful estimate of its character and utility. He never formally abandoned his position on the justifiableness of accepting a constitutional office for the purpose of seizing the government as soon as one's fellow-administrators should become unpopular, — for the executive weakness of the administration and the vacillating selfishness of its members were of course only an eagerly desired pretext, and not in any sense a reason *pro bono publico*, of the usurpation ; but he probably wished that these letters should not be regarded as his final and matured conclusion on the political merits of the Imperial system, and shortly after a visit to France in 1865, and the publication of the "Life of Julius Cæsar" nominally written by one of the most unliterary of sovereigns, he published the following article in the *Economist.* — ED.]

THAT the French Emperor should have spare leisure and unoccupied reflection to write a biography is astonishing ; but if he wished to write a biography, his choice of a subject is very natural. Julius Cæsar was the first who tried on an imperial scale the characteristic principles of the French Empire as the first Napoleon revived them, as the third Napoleon has consolidated them. The notion of a demagogue ruler, both of a fighting demagogue and a talking demagogue, was indeed familiar to the Greek republics, but their size was small and their history unemphatic : on the big page of universal history, Julius Cæsar is the first instance of a democratic despot. He overthrew an aristocracy—a corrupt and perhaps effete aristocracy, it is true, but still an aristocracy— by the help of the people, of the unorganized people ;

he said to the numerical majority of Roman citizens, "I am your advocate and your leader: make me supreme, and I will govern for your good and in your name." This is exactly the principle of the French Empire. No one will ever make an approach to understanding it who does not separate it altogether and on principle from the despotisms of feudal origin and legitimate pretensions. The old monarchies claim the obedience of the people upon grounds of duty; they say they have consecrated claims to the loyalty of mankind; they appeal to conscience, even to religion: but Louis Napoleon is a Benthamite despot; he is for the "greatest happiness of the greatest number"; he says, "I am where I am because I know better than any one else what is good for the French people, and they know that I know better." He is not the Lord's anointed, he is the people's agent.

We cannot here discuss what the effect of this system was in ancient times, — these columns are not the best place for a historical dissertation; but we may set down very briefly the results of some close and recent observation of the system as it now exists, as it is at work, in France. Part of its effects are well understood in England; but a part of them are, we think, but mistily seen and imperfectly apprehended.

In the first place, the French Empire is really the *best finished* democracy which the world has ever seen. What the many at the moment desire, is embodied with a readiness and efficiency and a completeness which have no parallel either in past history or present experience: an absolute government with a popular instinct has the unimpeded command of a people renowned for orderly dexterity. A Frenchman will have arranged an administrative organization really and effectually while an Englishman is still bungling and a German still reflecting. An American is certainly as rapid, and in some measure as

efficient ; but his speed is a little headlong and his
execution is very rough, — he tumbles through much,
but he only tumbles. A Frenchman will not hurry :
he has a deliberate perfection in detail which may
always be relied on, for it is never delayed. The
French Emperor knows well how to use these powers :
his bureaucracy is not only endurable but pleasant ;
an idle man who wants his politics done for him has
them done for him. The welfare of the masses —
the present good of the present multitude — is felt
to be the object of the government and the law of
the polity. The Empire gives to the French the full
gratification of their main wishes and the almost
artistic culture of an admirable workmanship, of an
administration finished as only Frenchmen can finish
it and as it never was finished before.

It belongs to such a government to care much for
material prosperity, and it does care : it makes the
people as comfortable as they will permit. If they
are not more comfortable, it is their own fault : the
government would give them Free Trade and consequent diffused comfort if it could, — no former French
government has done as much for Free Trade as this
government ; no government has striven to promote
railways and roads and industry like this government. France is much changed in twelve years, —
not exactly by the mere merit of the Empire, for it
entered into a great inheritance ; it succeeded to the
silent work of the free monarchy, which revolution
had destroyed and impeded. There were fruitful and
vigorous germs of improvement ready to be elicited,
ready to start forth, but under an unintelligent government they would not have started forth, they
would have lain idle and dead ; but under the adroit
culture of the present government they have grown
so as to amaze Europe and France itself.

If indeed, as is often laid down, the *present happiness* of the greatest number was the characteristic
object of* government, it would be difficult to make

* I have canceled the word "the" here. See line 12, next page. — ED.

out that any probable French government would be better [than], or indeed nearly so good as, the present. The intelligence of the Emperor on economical subjects — on the bread and meat of the people — is really better than that of the classes opposed to him : he gives the present race of Frenchmen more that is good than any one else would give them, and he gives it them in their own name ; they have as much as they like of all that is good for them. But if not the present happiness of the greatest number, but *their future elevation*, be — as it is — the true aim and end of government, our estimate of the Empire will be strangely altered; it is an admirable government for present and coarse purposes, but a detestable government for future and refined purposes.

In the first place, it stops the *teaching apparatus;* it stops the effectual inculcation of important thought upon the mass of mankind. All other mental effort but this, the Empire not only permits but encourages ; the high intellect of Paris is as active, as well represented, as that of London, and it is even more keen. Intellect still gives there, and has always given, a distinctive position, — to be a *Membre de l'Institut* is a recognized place in France ; but in London it is an ambiguous distinction to be a "clever fellow." The higher kinds of thought are better discussed in Parisian society than in London society, and better argued in the *Revue des Deux Mondes* than in any English periodical. The speculative thought of France has not been killed by the Empire, — it is as quick, as rigorous, as keen as ever ; but though still alive, it is no longer powerful, — it cannot teach the mass. The *Revue* is permitted, but newspapers — effectual newspapers — are forbidden. A real course of free lectures on popular subjects would be impossible in Paris. *Agitation* is forbidden, and it is agitation *and agitation alone* which teaches. The crude mass of men bear easily philosophical treatises, refined articles, elegant literature : there are but two instruments penetrative enough to reach their opaque minds, — the newspaper article and the popular speech; and both of these are forbidden.

In London the reverse is true : we may say that only the loudest sort of expression is permitted to attain its due effect. The popular organs of literature so fill men's minds with incomplete thoughts that deliberate treatment, that careful inquiry, that quiet thought have no hearing. People are so deafened with the loud reiteration of many half-truths that they have neither curiosity nor energy for elaborate investigations. The very word "elaborate" is become a reproach : it produces* something which the mass of men do not like because it is above them, which is tiresome because it needs industry, difficult because it wants attention, complicated because it is true. On the whole, perhaps, English thought has rarely been so unfinished, so piecemeal, so *ragged* as it is now. We have so many little discussions that we get no full discussion; we eat so many sandwiches that we spoil our dinner. And on the Continent, accordingly, the speculative thought of England is despised : it is believed to be meager, uncultivated, and immature. We have only a single compensation : our thought may be poor and rough and fragment-ary, but it is effectual. With our newspapers and our speeches, with our clamorous multitudes of indiffer-ent tongues, we beat the ideas of the few into the minds of the many. The head of France is a better head than ours, but it does not move her limbs ; the head of England is in comparison a coarse and crude thing, but rules her various frame and regulates her whole life.

France *as it is* may be happier because of the Empire, but France *in the future* will be more igno-rant because of the Empire : the daily play of the higher mind upon the lower mind is arrested. The present government has given an installment of Free Trade, but it could not endure an agitation for Free

* An evident misprint for something like "implies." — ED.

Trade. A democratic despotism is like a theocracy: it assumes its own correctness. It says, "I am the representative of the people; I am here because I know what they wish, because I know what they should have." As Cavaignac once said, "A government which permits its principles to be questioned is a lost government." All popular discussion whatever which aspires to *teach* the government is radically at issue with the hypothesis of the Empire: it says that the Cæsar, the omniscient representative, is a mistaken representative, that he is not fit to be Cæsar.

The deterioration of the future is one inseparable defect of the imperial organization, but it is not the only one; for the moment, it is not the greatest: the greatest is the corruption of the present. A greater burden is imposed by it upon human nature than human nature will bear. Everything requires the support, aid, countenance of the central government, and yet that government is expected to keep itself pure. Concessions of railways, concessions of the privilege of limited liability, — on a hundred subjects, legal permission, administrative help are necessary to money-making; you concentrate upon a small body of leading official men the power of making men's fortunes, and it is simple to believe they will not make their own fortunes. The very principle of the system is to concentrate power, and power is money. Sir Robert Walpole used to say no honest man could be a minister, and in France the temptations would conquer all men's honesty; the system requires angels to work it, and perhaps it has not been so fortunate as to find angels, — the nod of a minister on the Bourse is a fortune, and somehow or other ministers make fortunes. The Bourse of Paris is still so small that a leading capitalist may produce a great impression on it, and a leading capitalist working with a great minister a vast impression. Accordingly, all that goes with sudden wealth, all that follows from the misuse of the two temptations of civilization, money and women, is concentrated round the imperial court. The Emperor would cure much of it if he could, but what can he do? They say he has said that he will not change his men; he will not substitute fleas that are hungry for fleas which at least are partially satisfied. He is right: the defect belongs to the system, [not] to these men,—an enormous concentration of power in an industrial system insures an accumulation of pecuniary temptation.

These are the two main disadvantages which France suffers from ·her present government, the greater part of the price which she has to pay for her present happiness: she endures the daily presence of an efficient immorality, she sacrifices the educating apparatus which would elevate Frenchmen yet to be born. But these two disadvantages are not the only ones.

France gains the material present, but she does not gain the material future. All that secures present industry her government confers; in whatever needs confidence in the future she is powerless. *Credit* in France, to an Englishman's eye, has almost to be created. The *country* deposits in the Bank of France are only £1,000,000 sterling: that bank has fifty-nine branches, is immeasurably the greatest country bank in France. All discussions on the currency come back to the *cours forcé,* to the inevitable necessity of making inconvertible notes an irrefusable tender during a revolution. If you propose the simplest operations of credit to a French banker, he says, "You do not remember 1848:. I do." And what is the answer? The present government avowedly depends on, is ostentatiously concentrated in, the existing Cæsar; its existence depends on the permanent occupation of the Tuileries by an extraordinary man. The democratic despot, the representative despot, must have the sagacity to divine the people's will and the sagacity to execute it: what is the likelihood that these will be hereditary? can they be expected in the next heirs,—

a child for Emperor and a woman for Regent? The present happiness of France is happiness on a short life-lease; it may end with the life of a man who is not young, who has not spared himself, who has always thought, who has always *lived*.

Such are the characteristics of the Empire as it is; such is the nature of Cæsar's government as we know it at the present. We scarcely expect that even the singular ability of Napoleon III. will be able to modify by a historical retrospect the painful impressions left by actual contact with a living reality.*

* As a curious illustration of Mr. Bagehot's estimate of the character of the third Empire, I may mention that all the earlier part of this paper, all that which dwelt on the good side of the imperial *régime* in relation to matters of material prosperity, was reproduced in the French official journals, while all the equally true and even more useful criticism on its moral deficiencies was carefully omitted. — *Note by Mr. Hutton.*